MW00564850

Florida's Freedom Struggle:

The Black Experience from Colonial Time to the New Millennium

Irvin D.S. Winsboro

Florida's Freedom Struggle: The Black Experience from Colonial Time to the New Millennium

Author: Irvin D.S. Winsboro

ISBN 10: 1-886104-43-3
ISBN 13: 978-1-886104-43-3

The Florida Historical Society Press
435 Brevard Avenue
Cocoa, FL 32922
www.myfloridahistory.org/fhspress

In memory of the "everyday" people who struggled through the centuries to make Florida a land of dignity and opportunity for all.

Publisher's Note

The Florida Historical Society was established in 1856, making it the oldest existing cultural organization in the state. An important part of our mission is to preserve Florida's past through the publication of scholarly research. Our primary method of accomplishing that goal is through our academic journal, the *Florida Historical Quarterly*, which was first published in April 1908. While the Florida Historical Society has occasionally published books since its inception, the FHS Press has consistently been publishing both history-based fiction and non-fiction books since 2001.

Both the articles in the *Florida Historical Quarterly* and the books of the Florida Historical Society Press represent some of the most outstanding research ever done on Florida history and culture. With very few exceptions, the most noteworthy Florida historians of the past century have had their work published by the Florida Historical Society.

The "Gold Seal Series" brings together both publishing arms of the Florida Historical Society. This series of books published by the Florida Historical Society Press assembles articles on specific issues or topics that originally appeared in the *Florida Historical Quarterly*. These articles are given context and analysis by guest editors who specialize in the subject matter being explored.

The first book in our "Gold Seal Series" was *Florida's Civil War: Explorations into Conflict, Interpretations and Memory* edited by Irvin D. S. Winsboro, a tenured Professor of History at Florida Gulf Coast University. The author of numerous articles and award-winning books, Dr. Winsboro also serves on the Board of Editors for the *Florida Historical Quarterly*. This book continues to be a valuable resource in classrooms throughout the state, as well as a favorite among historians and general interest readers.

Irvin D. S. Winsboro returns as editor for the second book in our "Gold Seal Series," *Florida's Freedom Struggle: The Black Experience from Colonial Time to the New Millennium*. Again, Dr. Winsboro brings together a diverse group of historians writing on separate but related topics, and synthesizes their work into a cohesive and enlightening study through his insightful commentary. *Florida's Freedom Struggle* now joins *Florida's Civil War* as a favorite among teachers, students, and history enthusiasts alike.

We anticipate that future titles in our "Gold Seal Series" will include examinations of Spanish colonial Florida, economics, politics, the environment, tourism, women's issues, and a variety of other topics central to Florida history. Knowledgeable historians will offer analysis and insight as they provide context for articles carefully selected from the *Florida Historical Quarterly*. We welcome input from teachers, historians, and readers regarding subjects for future books in this series that would be particularly useful.

Dr. Ben Brotemarkle
Executive Director
Florida Historical Society
December 2010

TABLE OF CONTENTS

Preface

The purpose of this book is to provide a broad readership with a collection of cutting-edge articles from the *Florida Historical Quarterly* that capture transformational events, themes, and ideologies from Florida's historical and ongoing freedom struggle by black men and women. While the articles provide original interpretations of Florida's unfolding eras of resistance, they are best understood thematically and historically in conjunction with my own additions and analyses to this work. In that fashion, readers can better understand the circumstances of black activism in Florida and obtain a greater appreciation for its deep and complex story.

Each article is written by a specialist in the area of inquiry and speaks cogently to what I see as the major themes and eras of the state's freedom struggle, beginning with the first European contact with *La Florida* and progressing through time periods and evolving concerns up to the 21st century. Wherever possible, I have chosen articles that framed the critical issues of this freedom struggle from "the bottom up," in the "voices" of the African-American participants themselves, and around topics little known and discussed in the conventional literature—for example, the long and convoluted colonial and territorial periods, free blacks in the antebellum era, black religion, blacks in the military, and black resistance through the eyes of black women and "everyday people." Each article, in conjunction with my own Introductions and Further Readings (chosen with care to guide both students and researchers) will provide readers with a succinct perspective of the major themes and interpretations of the freedom struggle as well as its broader historical contextualization.

No single anthology on Florida can be comprehensive. Therefore, this work is designed to present studies and analyses most reflective of critical aspects of the centuries-old freedom struggle in Florida. Reviewing over 110 articles for this volume, I was forced to exclude numerous articles and topics of importance and, of necessity, leave noticeable gaps in the coverage. For example, I excluded extensive coverage of the Civil War, since *Florida's Civil War: Explorations into Conflict, Interpretations and Memory* (the first book in the Florida Historical Society Press's Gold Seal Series) covers it so thoroughly. Why be redundant? In sum, readers should view Florida's *Freedom Struggle* as representative discussions of black Floridians' long road to freedom and dignity and of Florida's often troubling racial heritage. It is my hope that this work will result in a teaching and learning tool, generate new research, and cause all readers to reflect on the Sunshine State's diverse and complex racial and ethnic mosaic, past and present.

ACKNOWLEDGMENTS

Whatever merits this book may have are the result of many scholars', educators', graduate students', and general readers' contributions to the thematic progression and substantive development of the work. I owe, therefore, profound thanks to all those who assisted me in various ways with the completion of this new book for the Florida Historical Society Press.

At the Press itself, Executive Director Benjamin D. Brotemarkle warmly received my proposal for this subject and offered significant advice and guidance toward my focusing on many of the lesser-known/ discussed periods and aspects of the black struggle in Florida. I owe him particular thanks for his time and concerns. I would also like to express my deep gratitude to the many readers of my numerous drafts; their editorial comments, facts checking, and recurring advice certainly improved this volume. Florida scholar Joe Knetsch helped immensely with editorial advice and facts "revision" on my manuscript. Leonard R. Lempel of Daytona State College, Jean McNary, Florida educator, Abel A. Bartley, Director of Pan-African Studies at Clemson University, and Paul Ortiz, Director of the Samuel Proctor Oral History Program at the University of Florida, provided key advice and assistance to me in the writing and revising processes. Bartley, Ortiz, and Ronald L. Lewis, former Stuart and Joyce Robbins Chair of History at West Virginia University, proved instrumental, as well, in the conceptual design of *Florida's Freedom Struggle*. Connie L. Lester, editor of the *Florida Historical Quarterly*, David B. Mock, professor at Tallahassee Community College, and Donald K. Routh, journal editor and professor at the University of Miami (emeritus), made useful suggestions on the qualitative aspects of the book in response to my many email correspondences with them.

Jake Aaronson offered valuable advice on legal aspects of the subject matter herein, and Jim Occhiogrosso cast a keen eye on the grammatical and syntactical aspects of the text. Graduate students Jack Bovee, Marty Roland, and Andy Coy contributed meaningful insight into what a book of this nature should address during our discussion in my graduate seminar on Florida historiography at Florida Gulf Coast University. I remain especially indebted to my two graduate assistants, William B. Mack and Alexander Jordan, who contributed heavily to the research and textual themes of *Florida's Freedom Struggle.* I certainly see two budding scholars in them.

Finally, I reserve my deepest gratitude to Betsy L. Winsboro for her admirable intellectual and editorial skills lent to this book and to her making my life a joy for the last thirty-one years. To my wife, I dedicate this book, as I have my previous seven books.

INTRODUCTION

Since the explosion of social history in the past several decades, the understanding of the African-American experience in the land Europeans first called *La Florida* has undergone profound changes. This new outpouring in African-American history has greatly expanded our understanding of not only the black struggle for freedom but also of the very nature of life and transformation in the Sunshine State. By concentrating on the black freedom struggle—a struggle that dates back virtually to the earliest days of *La Florida* itself—this work offers both conventional and alternative perspectives of the racial experiences of the Sunshine State.

Brought to the New World involuntarily, African-Americans can yet claim roots in North America as early as Europeans. Although it is possible that people of African descent reached Florida via undocumented slaver and treasure-seeking voyages prior to the incursion of Juan Ponce de León in 1513, the record does reflect that his expeditions, as well as that of Panfilio de Narváez in 1528, included black explorers. Soon after Pedro Menéndez de Avilés founded *San Augustín* (St. Augustine) in 1565, black people inhabited that town. Within a few decades, Spanish officials tallied 625 persons in the colony, including 56 African slaves. In ensuing years, people of African heritage would inhabit the first free, all-black community in North America, Fort Mose, two miles north of St. Augustine. To put this into perspective, people of African background were among the first "foreigners" to the shores of *La Florida* and North

America, and they achieved this over one-hundred years prior to the settlement of the Pilgrims and Puritans in New England.

Unlike the white European immigrants of New England, black explorers and settlers in Spanish Florida did not appropriate land from the Native Americans in attempts to create autonomous and self-perpetuating communities. Rather, blacks under Spanish rule, and later under British rule, faced political and social restrictions from the earliest contact that sought to reduce them to servitude. From the advent of the Spanish notions of inferiority and race-based oppression, blacks originated and sustained a freedom struggle that would last in Florida under different regimes, political entities, and social conditions for almost five centuries.

That personal and cultural struggle over time is the centerpiece of this book. As witnessed through an examination of scholarship from the files of the *Florida Historical Quarterly*, persons of African descent, be it during Spanish, British, or American rule, have always challenged the tenets of white supremacy and the practice of racial degradation. Indeed, they have continually struggled to overcome it right into the new millennium. That is the premise that informs this book.

In that light, this work is designed to illuminate the black freedom struggle in Florida by focusing the historical lens not only on the better-known instances of resistance but also on the collective traditions, vision, and memories of black Floridians. The black perspective on their struggle is a compelling story of one of Florida's earliest, largest, and most significant non-indigenous groups of people. It is the chronicle of a caste system based solely on racial protocols. Of all the groups that have interacted to weave the human tapestry of this land, it is arguably blacks (who often combated systems of oppression with Native Americans) who have best exemplified the fiction between promise and reality in this "State of Dreams," as noted historian Gary R. Mormino has termed it.[1] For all students of history, this story will serve as a window on the Sunshine State's diverse and troubling past.

It should be noted, as well, that blacks played significant roles in pop-

1 Gary R. Mormino, *Land of Sunshine, State of Dreams: A Social History of Modern Florida* (Gainesville: University Press of Florida, 2005).

ulating and developing Florida in all its decisive periods. Even though demographic data are scarce for the first Spanish colonial era (1565-1763), the British colonial interregnum (1763-1783/84), and the second Spanish colonial period (1783-1819/21), the record clearly reflects a large African-American population in Florida during those eras. For much of those years, blacks suffered persecution under the Spanish but still managed to secure certain rights as "free blacks" as long as they purported to adopt Catholic beliefs. After 1670, the nature of life for both enslaved and free blacks in Florida was complicated by the British-Spanish rivalry for sovereignty over the "debatable lands," and when the British assumed control of their East and West Florida colonies from 1763-1783, the racial codes and practices of the new governing nation became much harsher than those of the Spanish. Further complicating the racial policies of both British and Spanish overlords was the propensity for large numbers of blacks to escape bondage in neighboring Georgia and the Carolinas and to seek refuge either among the Native Americans or in "maroon" colonies in Florida. A British official lamented to his superiors in 1763, "You know it is very difficult to prevent Negroes from running away."[2] As the British prepared to return Florida to Spain following the American Revolution, the number of blacks approximated almost 10,000, which represented a ratio of two blacks for every white in the colony. Whether enslaved or free, under Spanish control or British rule, rooted in Florida or escaped from neighboring environs, African-Americans toiled, sacrificed, and populated Florida in significant ways.[3]

This trend continued during territorial and statehood days (1821-1845 and afterwards). Throughout the epoch of slavery, blacks fled to frontier Florida, often joining in alliances with the Seminoles, themselves Creek and Miccosukee refugees from white oppression in lands north of the Florida-Georgia boundary. Literally thousands of black Americans, mostly escaped slaves, intermingled with the Native Americans produc-

---

2 Quoted in Patrick Riordan, "Finding Freedom in Florida: Native Peoples, African Americans, and Colonists, 1670-1816," *Florida Historical Quarterly* Vol. 75, No. 1 (1996), 33.

3 J. Leitch Wright, Jr., "Blacks in British East Florida," *Historical Quarterly* Vol. 54, No. 4 (1976), 427.

ing yet another in a long line of racial and ethnic groups in Florida, the Black Seminoles (a term not necessarily based on blood relations). So vexing did this prove to white masters that this was certainly one of the factors motivating Southern planter and U.S. military officer Andrew Jackson to destroy the so-called Negro Fort on the Apalachicola River, home to roughly 300 blacks and Indians. Jackson's military actions in 1816 proved prologue to the ensuing era of black enslavement in Florida until Union troops raised the U. S. flag in 1865. From the sacking of the Negro Fort until the eve of the Civil War, blacks continued to populate Florida and intermingle with the Native Americans in ways disturbing to land-hungry whites, both privileged planters and hardscrabble farmers. Partly as a result, Florida witnessed three bloody, destructive, and costly wars. In all three phases of the conflicts, white fear of black autonomy played a major role in the instigation of military action. As Florida historian Joe Knetsch has noted in his study of these events, U.S. General Thomas Jesup characterized his efforts to recapture escaped slaves in the Second Seminole War as his "Negro War."[4]

As Jesup uttered these words in the 1830s, blacks comprised a large percentage of Florida's population and would continue to do so well into future eras. In 1830, blacks accounted for roughly 47 percent of Florida's population, a number that held fairly steady through the Civil War, although that percentage in 1860 included 61,746 slaves and 932 free blacks.[5] Florida contained a proportionately large black population until the "Yankee" in-migration boom years of the 1920s, at which time blacks declined to 21.8 percent of the population. The proportional decline continued until blacks accounted for 13.8 percent of the population by the 1980s, a figure that has held somewhat firm through the turn of the century.

Not only have students of Florida often neglected the ancient roots of its significant black population, but they just as frequently have under-recognized the periodization of Florida's civil rights movement (in actu-

---

4 Joe Knetsch, *Florida's Seminole War, 1817-1858* (Charleston, SC: Arcadia, 2003), 8.

5 See Irvin D.S. Winsboro, "Give Them Their Due: A Reassessment of African Americans and Union Military Service in Florida During the Civil War," *Journal of African American History* Vol. 92 (2007), 327-46.

ality from first contact to the new millennium) and the illustrious blacks born and raised in the state. Contrary to many traditional accounts, scholars now know that Florida's freedom struggle started as resistance to the first instances of racial oppression in colonial times and persisted as a continuum through the election of America's first self-identified African-American president, Barack Obama. Most narratives of the Sunshine State overlook, as well, the richly nuanced factors of the black experience. While subjects such as Fort Mose, the slave experience, Civil War and Reconstruction, Jim Crow, the Rosewood massacre, and the modern civil rights years have received probing treatment in the literature, far less is known about such transformational factors as those of free blacks in the antebellum era, religion and the sense of black community and struggle, agrarian events, labor in the cities, turpentine camps, railroad inequality in the years of Jim Crow, and blacks in the military affairs of Florida.

Similarly, much more scholarship is needed to create a heightened awareness of the individual and collective struggles of black women, who so consistently undertook protest fitted to their particular circumstances within the family, church, and community. While even beginning students of Florida's history might recognize the names Mary McLeod Bethune and Zora Neale Hurston, how many scholars could provide details of the countless black women in the state's long history who, through their own power and creativeness, challenged the contradictions of negative stereotypes and gender injustices? While the historical studies of Florida's freedom struggle are rich with details on the lives of a Harry T. Moore and Virgil D. Hawkins, how many works provide insight into the lives of notable black women such as Blanche Armwood, a pioneering educator and the first black woman in Florida to receive a law degree from an accredited law school, and C. Bette Wimbish, St. Petersburg lunch counter protester in 1960 and tireless crusader for black dignity and equal rights in the Tampa Bay area?[6] While offering only a glimpse into Florida's incomplete history of struggle, the res-

---

6 See Maxine D. Jones and Kevin M. McCarthy, *African Americans in Florida* (Sarasota: Pineapple Press, 1993), 87-89; Jack E. Davis, ed., *The Civil Rights Movement* (Malden, Mass.: Blackwell, 2001), 1-2.

urrection of lives like Armwood's and Wimbish's serve to remind us just how incoherent the past is without historians recreating it with all the richness of the full human experience. To do so will not only change the history books but also the way Floridians think about themselves.

Although too numerous to note in this publication, from first contact to the new millennium, as rightly noted in the Florida Department of State's *Florida: Black Heritage Trail,* "Florida's African-Americans have made significant contributions to the development of the state and continue to play a key role in creating modern Florida."[7] This statement could go on to note the centuries of black contributions to the economy, religion, music and literature, military, and, especially significant for this book, the struggles for freedom, dignity, and opportunity for all residents of the Sunshine State.

It is, therefore, the intent of this book to reflect through the pages of the *Florida Historical Quarterly* and accompanying explication the various and historical ways black men and women have struggled for freedom and in the process have played such a "key role" in Florida's rich and diverse past. The centrality of their struggle as a people and community underscored the Spanish and British colonial periods and all ensuing eras through the present day. For debatable reasons, this experience has often been ignored or little noted in the traditional histories of the Sunshine State. Fortunately, this gap in the literature has narrowed recently as scholars of many disciplines and backgrounds have reconceptualized the black freedom struggle in Florida. Yet, their contributions and this present volume can only serve to remind scholars and students alike how much more of this intriguing record needs to be illuminated in order to produce truly encompassing histories of the ancient and present land called Florida.

---

7 Florida Department of State, Division of Historical Resources, *Florida: Black Heritage Trail* (Tallahassee: Florida Department of State, 2007), 1.

1

THE ROOTS OF A PEOPLE

In this article, Vanderbilt University professor Jane L. Landers provides an original examination of the Spanish "lenient" policy for fugitive slaves from the British colonies to the north of *La Florida* and analyzes that policy within the framework of international affairs. Landers finds that Florida in the sixteenth and seventeenth centuries offered little of substance to Spain, which, nevertheless, sought to retain the colony for strategic purposes and as a buffer against the English colonies of North America. As an evolving aspect of the Spanish/British rivalry for control of the "debatable lands," Spain adopted a practice of offering Florida as a haven for escaped slaves from British colonies such as Georgia and South Carolina until it no longer served its purpose.

The author argues that the policies which granted this freedom emerged from a sense of competition in the international arena: Spain felt that allowing slaves to gain asylum and freedom from their British masters would weaken British colonies while at the same time benefit Spain's empire in the New World. While Spanish rhetoric often presented these practices as humane and evidence of the religious superiority of Catholicism over Protestantism, the actual reasons for them were more practical and political. The author then points out that the propensity for slaves to escape to Florida affected the British in ways both immediate and gradual—while those slaves who did escape won degrees of protection and freedom under Spanish sovereignty, the British colonial leaders constantly feared a widespread slave uprising designed to end in a mass exodus to Spanish Florida. Slaves attaining varying degrees of freedom in *La Florida* might well inspire their cohorts in the British lands to try the same.

Treatment of escaped slaves in *La Florida* tended to be more equitable than in the southern British colonies. The relative freedom that escaped slaves encountered in Florida ended abruptly during the British interregnum (1763-1783/84), after which conflicting policies and "property" claims arose as major friction points between British and Spanish officials. Untold numbers of blacks took advantage of the transition of power to flee masters by joining "Negro towns" (maroon communities) and the Native Americans in the reconstituted Spanish colony or by claiming the immunities of freedom by converting to Catholicism. The resurrected Spanish sanctuary policies of 1693 and 1739 became more ambiguous as officials now faced the reality of Americans slave raiding and otherwise harassing the Spanish settlers and fugitive slaves in Florida. The author points out that, while Spain ostensibly supported claims of former slave masters in Florida, the Spanish government often ignored those claims while simultaneously limiting the rights of asylum by creating more rigid color lines in its colony, for example, by issuing proclamations that limited land ownership and business enterprises to only those blacks supervised by whites.

The author uses a rich variety of primary sources in her account and skillfully argues that the changing racial policies of the Spanish had a significant impact on the slave's opportunity and outlook in the British colonies and later the American states bordering Florida. Moreover, she describes why the Spanish acceptance of escaped slaves and their freehanded attitude of granting asylum hinged not solely on altruism and religious beliefs, but more on paternalism and practical concerns—if escaping slaves were harmful to the British, it served Spanish purposes, and when this was no longer the case, the policy was changed and reversed. The author gives an excellent overview of this complicated intersection of race, policy, and international intrigue and how blacks served as pawns in the colonial era's geo-political affairs.

Readers interested in further exploring this issue should take into consideration Spain's own policy of enslaving people of African descent (and Native Americans) in the New World, including *La Florida*. While the record is cloudy on precisely when the first blacks arrived in the colony, historians do know that the Narváez expedition to Florida in 1528 numbered at least one slave, the Moor Estevanico, and that later slave ships visited the coast of Florida. How many Spanish slaves existed in *La Florida* and under what conditions is still open to speculation, but the black determination to resist oppression over time is certainly not a matter of speculation. This notion should be factored into any exploration of early Florida history.

FURTHER READING

Wilbur H. Siebert, "Slavery and White Servitude in East Florida, 1726-1776," *Florida Historical Quarterly*, Vol. 10 (1931);

Dorothy Dodd, "Florida's Population in 1545," *Florida Historical Quarterly*, Vol. 24 (1945);

Edwin L. Williams, Jr., "Negro Slavery in Florida," *Florida Historical Quarterly*, Vol. 28 (1949);

Jeannette Mirsky, "Zeroing in on A Fugative Figure: The First Negro in America," *Midway*, Vol. 8 (1967);

Harry S. Coverston, *The Spanish Colonial System of Justice in La Florida* (1980);

Jane Landers, *Fort Mose: Gracia Real de Santa Teresa de Mose: A Free Black Town in Spanish Colonial Florida* (1992);

Michael Mullin, *Africa in America: Slave Acculturation and Resistance in the American South and the British Caribbean, 1736-1831* (1992);

Molefi K. Asante and Mark T. Mattison, *The Historical and Cultural Atlas of African Americans* (1992);

Jerald T. Milanich, *Native Societies and Spanish Empire in the Sixteenth-Century American Southeast* (1992);

David J. Weber, *The Spanish Frontier in North America* (1994);

Jane L. Landers, "Traditions of African American Freedom and Community in Spanish Colonial Florida," in *The African American Heritage of Florida*, David R. Colburn and Jane L. Landers, eds. (1995), chapter 2;

Michael Gannon, "First European Contacts," Eugene Lyon, "Settlement and Survival," and Amy Turner Bushnell, "Republic of Spaniards, Republic of Indians," in Michael Gannon, ed., *The New History of Florida* (1996), chapters 2-4;

Jerald T. Milanich, *Florida Indians and the Invasion from Europe* (1998);

Jane Landers, *Black Society in Spanish Florida* (1999);
Charlton W. Tebeau and William Marina, *A History of Florida* (1999), chapters 2-4;
Jane G. Landers, ed., *Colonial Plantations and Economy in Florida* (2000);
Daniel S. Murphree, *Racialization and the Middle Ground: Europeans and Indians in the Colonial Floridas, 1513-1783* (2001);
Leigh A. Rosborough, *Settlers and Slaves: A Spatial Analysis of a Colonial and Antebellum Mill Community in Escambia County, Florida* (2004);
Jonathan D. Steigman, *La Florida del Inca and the Struggle for Social Equality in Colonial Spanish America* (2005);
Matthew Restall, ed., *Beyond Black and Red: African-Native Relations in Colonial Latin America* (2005);
Daniel S. Murphree, *Constructing Floridians: Natives and Europeans in the Colonial Floridas,1513-1783* (2006).

THIRTY DOLLARS REWARD:

RUN-AWAY from the Subſcriber, the 16th of September laſt, a Negro Man named BOOD, about 38 Years old, 5 Feet 10 Inches high, yellow Complexion, thin Viſage, has had the Small Pox; his great Toes have been froze, and have only little Pieces of Nails on them: He is much addicted to ſtrong Liquor, and when drunk very noiſy and troubleſome. Whoever takes up ſaid Slave, and brings him home, or ſecures him in Gaol, ſo that his Maſter may get him again, ſhall be intitled to the above Reward of THIRTY DOLLARS, paid by WILSON HUNT.

Any Perſon who takes up ſaid Negro, is cautioned to be particularly careful that he does not make his Eſcape, as he is a remarkable ſtout, cunning, artful Fellow.

Hunterdon-County, Maidenhead, December 20, 1766.

The runaway slave "Bood" may have made his way to the relative safety of Florida. From the *New York Gazette*, December 20, 1766.

Spanish Sanctuary: Fugitives In Florida, 1687-1790

Jane Landers

The Florida Historical Quarterly, Volume 62, issue 3 (1984), 296-313.

Historians of slavery in colonial North America have frequently alluded to the lure of Spanish Florida for slave runaways from the English colonies of South Carolina and Georgia, and contemporary slave owners complained bitterly of the sanctuary provided in St. Augustine. They repeatedly charged the Spanish with deliberate provocation, if not outright theft. Nonetheless, few historians have addressed these issues from the perspective of Spanish Florida. The Spanish policy regarding fugitive slaves in Florida developed in an ad hoc fashion and changed over time to suit the shifting military, economic, and diplomatic interests of the colony, as well as the metropolis.

Although the colony of Florida offered little attraction in terms of wealth or habitat, the Spanish crown had always considered it of vital importance; initially, for its location guarding the Bahama Channel and the route of the treasure fleets, and later, as a buffer against French and English colonization. Throughout the sixteenth and seventeenth centuries Florida was a struggling military outpost, plagued by Indian and pirate attacks, natural disaster, and disease. Had it not been of such strategic significance, the colony might have been abandoned, but Spain would not give up its precarious foothold in North America, despite the costs.[1]

Spain had long claimed the exclusive right to possess colonies on this continent by virtue of the Alexandrine bulls. Her main rivals, France and England, denied this claim, instead basing colonization rights on the principle of effective occupation, and in the seventeenth century they made good their challenge. During this period of Spanish decline, the British established a colony at Charles Town, Carolina, and Spain could do nothing to prevent it. The original charter for Carolina, however, actually included St. Augustine, and therein lay the grounds for serious boundary disputes. From 1670 forward, the Spanish and British contest for control of "the debatable lands" would flare up periodically in Florida itself, and in the larger European theater.[2]

One element in this conflict was the Spanish policy of granting asylum to slaves fleeing British masters. This policy, as with so many others, was not based on crown initiative, but rather, evolved as a response to unforeseen circumstances. The governors of Florida first shaped this policy, the Council of the Indies, after review and analysis, recommended keeping it, and the crown ultimately adopted it. Although the king preferred to stress the humane and religious considerations involved, the statements of the governors and the council reflect the more practical political and military ramifications of harboring runaways. The fugitive slaves were to become pawns of international diplomacy, and yet they gained in the bargain, for in Florida they achieved the freedom for which they had risked so much.

In October 1687, the first known fugitive slaves from the English colonies arrived in St. Augustine. Governor Diego de Quiroga y Lossada's first report stated the group arrived in a boat from St. George, Carolina, and included two females and a nursing-child.[3] English accounts gave the names of the male fugitives as Conano, Jesse, Jacque, Gran Domingo, Cambo, Mingo, Dicque, and Robi, and added that the child was three years old.[4] Governor Quiroga assigned two males to work for a blacksmith and the others to construction on the Castillo. The women worked as domestics, ultimately for the governor himself, and all the slaves were paid for their labor, indicating an ambiguity about their legal condition.[5]

Although an English sergeant major arrived the following fall to retrieve the fugitives, the governor refused to hand them over on the grounds that they had received religious instruction and converted to Catholicism, had married, and were usefully employed. The slaves also purported to fear for their lives, and so the governor offered to buy them. Thus, a fugitive slave policy began to evolve which would have serious diplomatic and military consequences for Spain. The governor and the royal treasury officials repeatedly solicited the king's guidance on the matter, and on November 7, 1693, Charles II issued a royal cédula detailing for the first time the official position on runaways, "giving liberty to all . . . the men as well as the women . . . so that by their example and by my liberality others will do the same."[6]

The provocation inherent in this policy increasingly threatened the Carolinians, for by 1705 blacks outnumbered whites in that colony, and there were chronic fears of slave uprisings. Although Charleston and St. Augustine had on occasion made agreements for the mutual return of runaways, these apparently were ineffective. In 1722 a joint committee of the South Carolina Assembly met to discuss the problem anew and suggested increasing the reward for capturing fugitives.[7] They also considered "a law . . . to oblige all Persons possessing Spanish Indians and Negroes to transport them off the Country."[8] Slave owners from South Carolina charged that successful fugitives even returned from St. Augustine, in the company of Spaniards and Indians, to carry off more slaves.[9]

In March 1725, two more groups of fugitive slaves arrived in St. Augustine, requesting baptism and freedom. The current governor, Antonio de Benavides, sent emissaries north, but the British balked at the proffered payment of 200 pesos per slave, claiming it was insufficient. Governor Benavides reported that "the English will never be satisfied" except by the return of their slaves.[10] Despite British intimations of war, the Council of the Indies recommended against returning the escaped slaves. It was not unmindful of British concerns, however, nor of the vulnerable position of the garrison settlement of St. Augustine. The council acknowledged that the residents feared the English and their Indian allies might invade to recover their slaves by force of arms, that slaves who fled their masters had actually committed a theft of themselves and should properly be returned to their owners, that the Spanish policy might lure great numbers of runaways to Florida who only simulated a desire to convert, and that the British were dependent upon their slaves and had just cause for complaint.[11]

While the Council of the Indies deliberated, Arthur Middleton, the acting governor of Carolina, complained to London that the Spanish, in addition to "receiving and harboring all our runaway Negroes," had "found out a new way of sending our slaves against us, to Rob and Plunder us; . . . they are continually fitting out Partys of Indians from St. Augustine to Murder our White people, Rob our Plantations and carry off our slaves."[12] In retaliation for such raids, Colonel John Palmer of the South Carolina Assembly led a raid against St. Augustine in 1728. Blacks fought bravely in the defense of the Spanish settlement, and in appreciation Governor Benavides freed them and abolished the St. Augustine slave market. Benavides suggested to the council that the freed slaves be sent north to foment revolt and that payment be made to them for English scalps. Although the council rejected this proposal, the incident lends credence to Governor Middleton's accusations.[13]

On October 4 and 29, 1733, Philip V issued two new cédulas which officially amended the crown policy on fugitives, but which, in fact, regularized much that was already standing practice. The first cédula prohibited any future compensation to the owners of fugitives.[14] Although the crown had released funds to reimburse the owners of the first fugitives, Governor Quiroga disbursed these monies to his troops before the English could collect.[15] The English subsequently rejected the payment offered by Governor Benavides, and when several groups of Carolinians tracked their slaves to St. Augustine, the Spanish forced them to leave with neither slaves nor payments.[16] There is no evidence that the crown ever bore the expense of paying for any other than the first known runaways, and even in that case official reports noted that the labor performed by the slaves on royal works more than offset the cost of their purchase.[17]

The king's second cédula commended the valor displayed by the fugitives during the English attack of 1728 and reiterated Spain's offer of freedom to all who fled the cruelty of English masters. It stipulated however that fugitives would be required to complete four years of service to the crown prior to being freed. Although this cédula is the first to specify a required indenture, it only legitimized a policy that had been in effect for nearly half a century. It should be noted that the period of indenture was actually not as long as many required in the English colonies. The king also specifically forbade the sale of fugitives to private citizens, but despite the prohibition, some runaways continued to be re-enslaved in St. Augustine. Such a group petitioned Governor Manuel de Montiano for their freedom in March 1738, and he granted it over the heated protests of their Spanish owners.[18] In gratitude the freedmen vowed to be "the most cruel enemies of the English" and to "spill their last drop of blood in defense of the Great Crown of Spain and the Holy Faith."[19]

Governor Montiano restated the crown's offer of freedom to escaped slaves from the English colonies in a *Bando* issued in1738, and in the same year he established a settlement for the fugitives, called Gracia Real de Santa Teresa de Mose, about one half league north of St. Augustine. He provisioned the settlement and assigned Don Joseph de León to instruct the new residents in Christian doctrine and Sebastián Sánchez to teach them to farm. Montiano reported that twenty-three men, women, and children had arrived from Port Royal on November 21, 1738, and had been sent to live in Mose.[20] These may have been part of the group of nineteen slaves belonging to Captain Caleb Davis and "50 other slaves belonging to other persons inhabiting about Port Royal" that "ran away to the Castle of St. Augustine" in November1738.[21] Captain Davis attempted to recover his slaves in St. Augustine, but the Spanish blocked his efforts, and he later reported that the blacks laughed at him.[22]

The War of Jenkin's Ear led to a new outbreak of hostilities between Spain and England, and in 1740 General James Oglethorpe commanded British troops in an attack against St. Augustine and Mose. The settlement of Mose had to be evacuated, but once again blacks helped defend St. Augustine and the governor subsequently organized a black militia which was maintained throughout the first Spanish period.[23]

Mose was re-established in 1748, but four years later, the interim governor, Fulgencio García de Solís, complained that most of the residents of Mose did not want to stay, and that although their pretext was fear of Indian and English attacks, their real motive was simply a desire "to live in complete liberty." He was forced to oblige them to stay, applying "light" punishments to some, and more severe punishments to the persistently disobedient. He did not specify what these punishments were, but it is evident that the "freed slaves" of Mose were not free to choose where they would live. The governor justified his actions on the basis that Mose was vital to the defense and to the agricultural provisioning of St. Augustine, although he admitted that recurrent illnesses among the blacks prevented the latter.[24] To assuage the fears of the residents, Mose was more heavily fortified in the following years. Cannons were installed, a regular guard of Spanish cavalry was provided, and the black militia was reorganized.[25] Mose survived through the first Spanish period, but when the Spanish left Florida at the end of the Seven Years' War, the Mose residents went with them. Evacuation statistics vary as to whether seventy-nine or ninety-nine free blacks sailed out of East Florida to resettle in Havana, but there is no record that any chose to stay behind.[26]

The fugitive slaves from the English colonies had not escaped all tribulations when they fled to Spanish Florida. The incoming residents were forcibly segregated in Mose where they were subject to debilitating illnesses and to attacks by Indian and British raiders. They served as a kind of early warning system for St. Augustine. The Spanish themselves acknowledged that most residents wanted to leave and live in St. Augustine, although life there was fraught with many of the same hardships encountered at Mose.

Although living conditions were less than ideal, and liberty less than total, the fugitives, nonetheless, made important gains in Spanish Florida. They had achieved de jure freedom, had been welcomed into the Roman Catholic church and given access to its sacraments, and had borne arms in their own defense, proving their military competence. The benefits had not accrued solely to the freedmen, however. The Spanish crown had claimed new souls for the Holy Faith, as was its charge. Religious instruction was conscientiously provided to the former slaves, and careful records were kept on the number of conversions and baptisms.[27] The inhabitants of Mose had also provided added manpower for the Spanish in a variety of useful occupations, and had rendered valuable military services in defensive, as well as offensive, operations against Spain's enemies.

The foremost of these enemies, England, occupied Florida only until 1784, but during this interregnum, there was no haven for blacks in the colony. Encouraged by a generous land policy, the British established rice, indigo, cotton, and sugar plantations around St. Augustine. These were manned by large numbers of slaves. Planters like John Moultrie and Frances Levett transported blacks into the province from South Carolina and Georgia, although the terms of their grants required settlement by white Protestants. Richard Oswald, in 1767, imported Negroes directly from Africa to labor on his Mount Oswald plantation.[28] White immigration did not proceed as rapidly as black, and during the British occupation, blacks outnumbered whites, approximately two to one. This ratio became even further skewed when the British were forced by the course of the American Revolutionary War to evacuate Charleston and Savannah. Many of the loyalist refugees brought their slaves with them to East Florida, adding somewhat over 8,000 blacks to the population.[29]

At war's end, the Treaty of Paris returned Florida to the Spanish, and news of the cession exacerbated problems of slave control and encouraged notorious banditti to raid plantations for slaves and other "moveable" property. Disputes over the ownership of slaves would continue for years and plague not only the departing British but the incoming Spanish administration. Georgians and South Carolinians would contend that the British had stolen their slaves, and loyalists would level similar charges against their accusers. The British army had on a number of occasions promised freedom to blacks joining their ranks, and while many had responded voluntarily to this offer, others were impressed. Some slaves had taken advantage of the wartime chaos to run away from bondage, and others made their break during the British evacuation of East Florida in 1784.

Neither official commissions nor private suits were very successful in sorting out the complicated property claims arising from this confusion, and it was left to the new Spanish governor, Vicente Manuel de Zéspedes y Velasco, to settle matters as best he could. Realizing that quick action was necessary to prevent further theft of slaves, and also desiring to somehow control the blacks he considered to be vagrants, Zéspedes issued a controversial proclamation on July 26, 1784.[30]

This edict prohibited any ships from taking on passengers of any color or status who did not have a license signed by Zéspedes. Should any person be caught trying to ship out slaves, those blacks would be forfeit. Zéspedes also wanted an accounting of the blacks in his province. Any persons having "in their power" Negroes, free or slave, for whom they had no title, was required to register them. Finally, all Negroes or mulattoes without a known owner, or papers attesting to their free status, were ordered to present themselves within twenty days, clarify their status and obtain a work permit, or be apprehended as slaves of the Spanish king.[31]

The outgoing British governor, Patrick Tonyn, was alarmed by these requirements and felt they violated the provisions of the peace treaty. He solicited an opinion of his chief justice, James Hume, who outlined the British objections: the peace treaty of1783 gave all individuals, regardless of color or status, full rights to withdraw from Florida; most slaves were held without virtue of titles, and it was unfair to require owners to produce them; and the slaves who had been freed for service in the British military had no documentary proof and by their illiteracy might not know to secure such.[32]

These British opinions only served to antagonize Zéspedes. He answered that he sought only to protect the property of British citizens from theft and restore law and order, and that he had no desire to impede emigration from East Florida. He maintained that his decree was aimed primarily at "the strolling vagrant Blacks with which this province abounds . . . a pest to the public tranquility."[33] He added, "many Blacks are now beheld passing through the Town with cheerful countenance, who before lurked dismayed in solitary corners, and are now acknowledged free people under the respectable signatures of your Excellency and General McArthur."[34]

Despite the controversy engendered by the proclamation, Zéspedes had his way. The blacks who managed to find out about the new requirements of the Spanish governor, came in to present themselves. Apparently word of the decree spread for the declaration of Juan Gres, a free mulatto from South Carolina, stated that he was a foreman on a ranch near Julianton on the St. Johns River, twenty-eight miles from St. Augustine. He presented himself, his free mulatto wife, and their two sons to the Spanish authorities as required.[35]

A collection of 251 of these declarations have survived. One hundred and fifty simply state the name and race of the presenting slaves who showed papers proving their free status. Of these, eighty-eight are signed by General Archibald MacArthur, commander of the Southern District after the evacuation of Charleston, twenty-one are signed by Governor Tonyn, one by Tonyn's aide-de-camp, Lieutenant Colonel William Brown, and one by Major Samuel Bosworth. The remaining thirty-nine are unsigned. The more complete declarations contain varying amounts of information on the fugitives, including their previous owners, family connections, occupations, reasons for running away, and information on their work contracts in St. Augustine. Those who made these declarations may not be representative of all who ran to Spanish Florida, for unknown numbers of fugitives remained outside St. Augustine in Indian or maroon communities. Nor are there any figures on how many runaways to Florida were re-enslaved by the Spanish or by others along their escape route. Nevertheless, when virtually nothing else is known about them, these declarations are a valuable source of information about blacks in the second Spanish period. Moreover, although scholars like Gerald Mullin, Michael Johnson, and Daniel Meaders have examined colonial newspaper notices on runaways and have provided information on this group of slaves, their data is derived from the accounts of white masters. These declarations represent the fugitives' own accounts, although they are recorded by Europeans. By piecing the fragments together with those gleaned from other sources, one may form a more precise description of a group that comprised "the backbone of East Florida's labor supply" and approximately one-third of the population of St. Augustine after 1784.[36]

An examination of the declarations reveals that some scribes apparently took pride in their penmanship, others did not. Many of the documents are hard to read; two pages had the top portions destroyed. Some of the fugitives' names were missing in part, and in two cases the gender could not be determined. Racial categories of Negro, mulato, and mestizo were entered after almost every name, but if no description of race was included the person was presumed to be Negro. If no direct statement indicated the person escaped as part of a group, he or she is listed as running alone. Fugitives' accounts of former masters, reasons for running away, occupations, and legal status are accepted as being accurate although that may not be true in every case.

The Spanish notaries recording these statements at times doubted their veracity. One complained that he believed Billy, former slave of Benjamin Kenel of Charleston, lied, because he presented a certificate of freedom that had "no formality, whatsoever" and further, that the handwriting was abominable.[37] When Abram, former slave of James Baxall of Charleston, gave his statement, the notary interjected that "everything he says hereafter forms a group of contradictions of which you can credit not one." Abram stated that he had escaped some years before from Mr. Baxall, but that a Mr. William Penn, since departed from the province, claimed ownership of him. Penn's agent, a Dr. Scott, then attempted to sell Abram at auction, but no one would buy him because Dr. Scott could not produce a bill of sale.[38] There is a certificate signed by Governor Tonyn, December 18, 1784, supporting Penn's statement that he transported Abram to St. Augustine from South Carolina, was obliged to leave him when he departed for New Providence, and that Abram was pretending to be free. Tonyn authorized Dr. Scott to attempt to retake Abram, but apparently he was not successful because Abram presented himself to the Spanish sometime in 1787 or 1788.[39]

Certain data from these declarations are less controversial, and yield information about the demographic characteristics of the fugitive population. In this group numbering 251— 165 were male,,eighty-four female, and the gender of two could not be ascertained. Almost twice as many males as females presented themselves. The majority of the group, 206, were Negroes, and twenty four males and twenty females were listed as mulattoes. The only direct reference to possible miscegenation between blacks and Indians was one female, Lucy Black, listed as mestiza followed by the notation black Indian. One cannot tell how many of those listed as Negroes were born in America, and how many were African-born. Only one runaway, Charles, formerly the property of Mr. Drayton of Charleston, stated that he was "brought to America before the last war."[40] However, Jacob Steward, a free black who emigrated to New Providence, stated that he owned a house in which "Negro rites in the style of Guinea" were celebrated.

The ages of adults were not given, but those of children up to the age of fourteen were listed usually as estimates. A total of fifty-five children were presented. Moreover more than half of the slaves presenting themselves (128) were part of a group. Thirteen groups consisted of husbands and wives and ten groups included a mother, a father, and their children. Seven of the units consisted of a mother and her children and five units of a father and his children. One sister and brother appeared without their parents. There were also fugitive groups who ran together from the same owners, but who were apparently not related. Unless a specific relationship was stated, it is assumed that none existed.

The numerous groupings suggest that fugitives sought to maintain family or friendship ties, even in flight. The largest of the family groups consisted of Bacchus, Betty, and their seven children. The two parents are listed as field hands, as are their three children— Andrew, Isaac, and Sally. The ages of these children are not given, but they were probably adolescents. The younger children were Bacchus, age 9; Betsy, age 7 or 8; Kitty, age 5 or 6; and Grace, age 2. Bacchus stated the family fled to escape the bad treatment of their owner, Mr. Cameron of Savannah. In St. Augustine the family, with the exception of Isaac, hired themselves out to Leonardo Roque, an Italian wine merchant. Isaac hired out to the innkeeper, James Clarke.[42]

Although most of the fugitives did not list their occupations there was a wide variety of work skills among those who did. Most were field hands, but there were also carpenters, hostelers, domestics, cooks, seamstresses, laundresses, and menservants, and some said only that they were soldiers or sailors for the British. There were several hunters and fishermen, one overseer and a ranch foreman, and one said he owned an aguardiente shop. Another was a butcher who planned to leave with the British as soon as he completed butchering his cattle.[43]

It is not known if all continued in their former occupations in Spanish Florida, but they were required to hire themselves out and obtain a license when they registered. Apparently the contracts were for a year, but there are numerous notations indicating that the fugitives changed employment frequently, and apparently of their own volition. Particular contracts may have varied, but there are few details. Those of Small and Moris, two slaves who ran to escape the ill-treatment of their owner, William Day of South Carolina, stipulate that their respective renters, James Clarke, and Francisco Amer, dress and feed them and in all else treat them as free.[44] No reference to wages appears in the declarations. Some of the most prominent persons in the colony hired the fugitives. Among these were the governor, his secretary, Captain Carlos Howard, Juan Leslie, of the firm of Panton, Leslie and Company, and the wealthy planter, Don Francis Philip Fatio.

Men of influence also attempted to re-enslave some of these runaways. Lieutenant Colonel Jacob Weed of the Georgia Assembly advertised in December 1786, for the recovery of Prince, described as "6 feet high, strong built and brawny, a carpenter by trade, 30 years of age . . . talkative," his wife, Judy, "a smart, active wench," and their children, Glasgow, "about 8 years of age, a well looking boy of an open countenance and obliging disposition," and Polly, "6 years old, lively eyes and gently pitted with the small pox." Weed had been making arrangements to return this group to the original owners from whom they had been stolen by the British, and he believed that Prince had "carried them off with him to Florida to avoid a separation from his family to which he is much attached."[45] It is not known what transpired the next three years, but Prince presented himself to the Spanish on January 9, 1789, without Judy, Glasgow, and Polly. Prince hired himself out for one year to Francisco Pellicer, who was also a carpenter.[46]

The efforts of one prominent loyalist family to recover their slaves dragged on for more than four years. Major Henry Williams, formerly of North Carolina, fought for the British in North Carolina and Georgia, as did his father and brothers. After the evacuation of Savannah, the family moved to East Florida and Henry established a homestead of 500 acres on the St. Johns River.[47] Williams reported that slaves belonging to himself and to his brother, William, had departed the day after Christmas1784. His notice stated that the runaways included Molly, an "old wench," and "Reynor, wife to Hector and Sam, for they both have her to wife." The date of this notice was May 6, 1785, yet there is a bill of sale for Reynor [Reyna] dated March 17, 1785,showing that William Williams had sold her to Lewis Fatio for twenty pounds sterling. In 1788 Hector, Sam, and Reyna presented themselves to the Spanish, William Williams submitted several memorials to Governor Zéspedes requesting their return.[48]

Hector's statement said that he and his two companions had accompanied Major William Williams to East Florida in Hector's own boat. He claimed the blacks lived as free persons in East Florida as a consequence of their military service. Sam's statement confirms their free status and military service. Yet, when Major Williams prepared to evacuate East Florida, he claimed them as his slaves, and they ran away from him. According to Sam's statement, he was the former property of Henry Alexander of South Carolina, and Hector and Reyna claimed that they had belonged to Diego Devaux. Hector and Sam both identified Reyna as Hector's wife.[49]

On March 5, 1788, Major Williams submitted a petition to Governor Zéspedes for the return of Sam, Hector, Reyna, and Cesar, whom he said ran from him in December 1784, and who were to be found on Fatio's Florida plantation. Zéspedes remembered dealing with the same matter at the time of the British evacuation. He supported Sam and Hector's accounts of their legal status, saying they had never been slaves of Williams, but rather of a Mr. Alexander and a Mr. Devaux. Williams appealed the decision and offered to present bills of sale for the slaves, but once again the governor denied the claim, noting that such items were easily forged.[50] By this time Williams had settled in New Providence in the Bahama Islands, and he finally submitted a claim to the British government for "a Negro woman slave "valued at forty pounds sterling. Henry Williams, also in New Providence, submitted a claim for Sam, a carpenter, valued at fifty pounds, and Cesar, a field hand, valued at forty pounds. There is no record the Williams brothers ever received compensation, and Hector, Reyna, and Sam hired themselves freely to Fatio.[51] In this long and complicated case the Spanish governor consistently supported the claims of the slaves to freedom.

The governor, however, never granted the fugitives absolute equality. On January 15, 1790, he issued a decree approving Manuel Solana's action in forcing free blacks from some land they were cultivating, for "no free black is permitted to cultivate lands, or live in the country side, unless it is with a white man, and with a formal contract and my approval of the conditions."[52] Finally, on May 17, 1790, even the possibility of limited freedom was denied new fugitives, for the king bowed to pressure from the United States government and abandoned the century-old policy of sanctuary for fugitive slaves. The king suspended the cédulas which had been the basis for that policy, and ordered that notice of the change in policy be widely circulated to discourage any further immigration by fugitives.[53] On August 23, 1790, the royal order was forwarded to South Carolina and Georgia to be published in their *gazettes.*[54]

United States Secretary of State Thomas Jefferson in a letter to the new governor of Florida, Juan Nepomuceno de Quesada, expressed his pleasure with the new Spanish policy, and called it "essential" to the good relations between their two nations. Jefferson also wrote that United States Collector of Customs James Seagrove had been appointed to represent the United States in all matters concerning the capture and return of fugitives.[55]

Seagrove's initial proposals called for close cooperation between Spanish and American authorities, but he found the Spanish less dedicated to the pursuit of runaways than he would have liked, despite Governor Quesada's repeated assurances of friendship. Seagrove's correspondence suggests that the Spanish governor found the fugitives a bother, and that American slave owners were doubtful the king's orders were actually being honored.[56]

The fact that Seagrove's own slave, Will, was able to escape, not only from Seagrove's house on the St. Marys River, but from his subsequent captors, seems to indicate deficiencies in the whole effort. Seagrove complained to Quesada that Will had been seen "sculking" around the plantation of John McQueen and that McQueen's slaves were harboring him, but apparently Will remained at liberty.[57]

Ending the official sanctuary in Florida did not resolve the American runaway problem, nor did it fully quiet the border conflicts between Spain and America. Fugitive slaves continued to find shelter in Seminole or maroon settlements outside the reach of Spanish control, and Americans continued their raids into Spanish territory to attempt to recapture them.

Meanwhile, the fugitives who had settled in St. Augustine and had been declared free did not lose this status, but they were less welcome in Spanish Florida than their predecessors had been in earlier years. Whereas runaways in the first Spanish period had been sequestered in Mose, with great pains taken to ensure their proper spiritual development, the fugitives in the second Spanish period lived among the Spanish citizenry, and there was more concern about controlling them. Governor Zéspedes had complained about the problem of black vagrants, "roving this City robbing and even breaking open houses" and declared that their "bad way of life . . . ought to be prevented."[58] He had required registration and work permits for all freed slaves. Quesada also sought to control "the multitude of foreign blacks" by once again ordering them to enter the service of a propertied person within one month of his issuance of a "Proclamation of Good Government" on September 2, 1790.[59]

Fugitives in the first Spanish period had benefited from the international rivalry between England and Spain. The Spanish in Florida harbored and freed them because they had fled the control of Spain's enemy, and because they sought baptism in the "true" faith. The Spanish knew that the slaves were vital to the economic interests of their British competitors in North America and that each fugitive represented a loss to the English and a gain for Spain. These fugitives were also a military asset to the Spaniards attempting to hold Florida in the face of British aggression.

By 1784, however, the fugitives did not enjoy the same leverage with the Spanish, who now viewed them as a source of constant trouble. Not only were they blamed for a variety of social ills, but their presence invited raids by angry American planters. Moreover, the new government of the United States seemed determined to protect the property rights of its citizens. There was little chance of dislodging this neighbor and thus little to gain by antagonizing it by encouraging the flight of American slaves. The usefulness of the fugitives as pawns in international diplomacy had ended, and recognizing that fact, Spain ended their sanctuary in Florida.

Jane Landers is a doctoral candidate in Latin American history at the University of Florida. Ms. Landers read an earlier version of this paper at the annual meeting of The Florida Historical Society, Daytona Beach, May 1983.

1. Robert L. Gold, *Borderland Empires* in *Transition— The Triple Nation Transfer of Florida* (Carbondale and Edwardsville, 1969), 5-8.
2. Charles Loch Mowat, *East Florida as a British Province 1763-1784* (Los Angeles, 1943; facsimile ed., Gainesville, 1964), 3.
3. Diego Quiroga to king, February 24, 1688, Archivo General de Indias, Seville (hereinafter AGI), 54-5-12/44, in Irene A. Wright, "Dispatches of Spanish Officials Bearing on the Free Negro Settlement of Grace Real de Santa Teresa de Mose, Florida," *Journal of Negro History,* IX (April 1924), 150. The governor's initial report to the king stated that only six males, two females, and a nursing child had come in the group, but all subsequent reports change that to read eight males. Most secondary sources do not mention the presence of a nursing child in the group which is a significant oversight. An escape by boat with a small child would presumably be more difficult, indicating close family bonds.
4. Peter H. Wood, *Black Majority--Negroes in Colonial South Carolina from 1670 through the Stono Rebellion* (New York, 1974), 50.
5. Royal officials of Florida to king, March 8, 1689, AGI 54-5-12/74, Wright, "Dispatches of Spanish Officials," 151-52.
6. Royal decree, November 7, 1693, AGI 58-1-2/74, John B. Stetson Collection, P. K. Yonge Library of Florida History, University of Florida, Gainesville (hereinafter SC).
7. Wood, *Black Majority,* 304.
8. Ibid., citing journal of the South Carolina Upper House, December 12.1722, microfilm BMP/D, 487, South Carolina Department of Archives and History, Columbia. Wood gives additional references to slaves escaping to St. Augustine from the same source on June 22, 23, and December 6, 14, 1722.
9. Wood, *Black Majority,* 305.
10. Antonio de Benavides to king, November 2, 1725, AGI 58-1-29/84, Wright, "Dispatches of Spanish Officials," 165.
11. Council of the Indies to the king, April 12, 1731, AGI 86-5-21/33, Wright, "Dispatches of Spanish Officials," 166-72.
12. Wood, *Black Majority,* 305, citing Arthur Middleton to London authorities, June 13, 1728, in W. Noel Sainsbury, comp., "Records in the British Public Records Office Related to South Carolina, 1663-1782," 36 handwritten vols. 1895, XIII, 61-67, South Carolina Department of History and Archives, Columbia.
13. John J. TePaske, "The Fugitive Slave: Intercolonial Rivalry and Spanish Slave Policy, 1687-1764," in Samuel Proctor, ed., *Eighteenth-Century Florida and Its Borderlands* (Gainesville, 1975), 7.
14. Royal decree, October 4, 1733, AGI 58-1-24/256, SC.

15. The royal officials of Florida to king, May 20, 1690, AGI 54-5-12/101, Wright, "Dispatches of Spanish Officials," 154-55; Royal decree, November 7, 1693, AGI 58-1-26/127, SC.
16. Wood, *Black Majority,* 312.
17. Quiroga to king, June 8, 1690, AGI 54-5-12/108, Wright, "Dispatches of Spanish Officials," 156.
18. Manuel de Montiano to king, May 31, 1738, AGI 58-1-31/59, Wright, "Dispatches of Spanish Officials," 172-74.
19. Fugitive Negroes of the English plantations to king, June 10, 1738, AGI 58-1-31/62, Wright, "Dispatches of Spanish Officials," 175.
20. Montiano to king, February 16, 1739, AGI 58-1-31/62, Wright, "Dispatches of Spanish Officials," 176-77.
21. Wood, *Black Majority,* 306.
22. Ibid., 306-07, citing J. H. Easterby and Ruth S. Green, eds., *The Journal of the Commons House of Assembly, 1736-1750,* 9 vols. (Columbia, 1951-1962), I, 596, and "The Journal of William Stephens," in Allen D. Candler and Lucien L. Knight eds., *The Colonial Records of the State of Georgia,* 26 vols. (Atlanta, 1904-1916), IV, 247-48.
23. John J. TePaske, *The Governorship of Spanish Florida, 1700-1763,* (Durham, 1964), 141.
24. Fulgencio García de Solís to king, December 7, 1752, AGI 58-1-33/25, Wright, "Dispatches of Spanish Officials," 187.
25. TePaske, "Fugitive Slave," 9.
26. Gold, *Borderland Empires,* 67.
27. Melchor de Navarrete to the Marques de la Ensenada, April 2, 1752, AGI 86-6-5/114, Wright, "Dispatches of Spanish Officials," 185. In this correspondence, Navarrete reported the baptism of fourteen fugitive slaves living at Mose listing the names as follows: francisco Xavier, Rosa Xaviera, Juan Josseph, Juan Manuel, Antonio Josseph, Ana francisca, franco Xavier, otro franco Xavier, Maria de Loretto, Micaela, Francisco Xavier, Josseph, Juan, Maria Angela. After 1735 religious data on blacks were recorded in a separate book of pardos in the St. Augustine parish registers.
28. Mowat, *British Province,* 67.
29. J. Leitch Wright, Jr., "Blacks in British East Florida," *Florida Historical Quarterly,* LIV (April 1976), 427.
30. Joseph Byrne Lockey, ed., *East Florida 1783-1785: A File of Documents Assembled and Many of Them Translated* (Berkeley, 1949), 21.
31. Proclamation of Vicente Manuel de Zéspedes July 26, 1784, in Lockey, *East Florida 1783-1785,* 240-41.
32. James Hume to Patrick Tonyn, July 26, 1784, Lockey, *East Florida 1783-1785,* 328-30.
33. Patrick Tonyn to Lord Sydney, December 6, 1784, Enclosure 3, 2, Remarks on Hume's Opinion, Lockey, *East Florida,* 339.
34. Zéspedes to Tonyn, August 6, 1784, Lockey, *East Florida,* 335.
35. Statement of Juan Gres, Census Returns, 1784-1814, bundle 323A, microfilm roll 148, East Florida Papers, Library of Congress, microfilm copies in P. K. Yonge Library of Florida History, University of Florida, Gainesville (hereinafter EFP).

36. J. Leitch Wright, Jr., "Blacks in St. Augustine, 1763-1845," typescript at Historic St. Augustine Preservation Board office, 2.
37. Statement of Billy, Census Returns 1784-1814, bundle 323A, roll 148, EFP.
38. Statement of Abram, ibid.
39. Certificate of Patrick Tonyn, December 18, 1784, ibid.
40. Statement of Charles, ibid.
41. Statement of Jacob Steward, ibid.
42. Statement of Bacchus, July 5, 1789, ibid.
43. Statement of Guillermo, ibid.
44. Statements of Small and Moris, July 7, 1788, ibid.
45. Letter of Alexander Semple to McFernan, December 16, 1786, To and From the United States, 1784-1821, bundle 10809, roll 41, EFP.
46. Statement of Prince, January 9, 1789, Census Returns 1784-1814, bundle 323A, roll 148, EFP.
47. Wilbur H. Siebert, ed., *Loyalists in East Florida 1774-1785; The Most Important Documents Pertaining Thereto,* 2 vols. (Deland, 1929), II, 277, 366-67.
48. Runaway notice by Henry Williams, May 5, 1785, and bill of sale by William Williams, March 17, 1785, Papers on Negro Titles and Runaways, 1784-1803, bundle 359; roll 167, EFP; memorial of William Williams to Zéspedes, March 5, 1788, Census Returns 1784-1814, bundle 323A, roll 148, EFP.
49. Statements of Sam and Hector, Census Returns 1784-1814, bundle 323A, roll 148, EFP.
50. Decree of Zéspedes, March 7, 1788, ibid.
51. Siebert, ed., *Loyalists in East Florida,* II, 277, 281; statements of Sam and Hector and Reyna, Census Returns 1784-1814, bundle 323A, roll 148, EFP.
52. Decree of Zépedes, January 15, 1790, Census Returns 1784-1814, bundle 323A, roll 148, EFP.
53. Royal decree in letter from Luis de las Casas to Zéspedes, July 21, 1790, Letters from the Captain General, 1784-1821, bundle 1C, roll 1, EFP.
54. Juan Nepomuceno de Quesada to Leonard Marbury, August 23, 1790, To and From the United States 1784-1821, bundle 10809, roll 41, EFP.
55. Thomas Jefferson to Quesada, March 10, 1791, ibid.
56. James Seagrove to Quesada, December 17, 1790, and August 9, 1791, ibid.
57. Seagrove to Quesada, August 9, 1791, ibid.
58. Fernández to Zéspedes, August 2, 1784 and Tonyn to Zéspedes, September 24, 1784, Lockey, *East Florida,* 360, 340.
59. Proclamation by Quesada, September 2, 1790, Proclamations and Edicts, 1786-1821, bundle 278013, roll 118, EFP.

2

New Contours

J. Leitch Wright, Jr. gleans evidence from scant sources in an attempt to illuminate the significance of the large numbers of blacks in British East Florida. In the process, he acknowledges the difficulty of reaching conclusions derived from partial or inadequate primary sources. Thus, this study is both an exploration into an important period of the black freedom struggle and a historiographical lesson for would-be scholars of the Sunshine State. In Wright's words, "Contemporary historians must utilize the few sources available, and be conscious that, if they are lucky, they may at least see the tip of the iceberg." Here, we learn that even when it is risky to speculate about historical events, scholars are nevertheless bound to do so and in the process add their informed insight to historical literature.

Wright focuses on the culture and activities of blacks in the colonial era. He notes that languages spoken by slaves are uncertain, since so many American slaves traced their roots to the culturally and linguistically diverse regions of West Africa. This diversity of language and dialect sometimes resulted in problems coordinating resistance to the British. The author then discusses why blacks in East Florida manifested little interest in the American Revolution: they generally felt victory by either side would not offer solutions to their racial and class status. For their part, British officials recognized that blacks could play an integral role in military affairs, specifically in their constructing defenses outside major towns and other settlements. This policy led to the British arming slaves, a drastic departure from the prevailing slave codes, many of which made it illegal to arm slaves out of fear of slave insurrections. The author notes that this British willingness to arm slaves out of desperation is analogous to Confederate policies during the American Civil War, which is an interesting point to contemplate.

The author offers a glimpse of the growing numbers of plantation slaves and the expanding slave trade when discussing the blacks during the British era. He notes that in 1775 the black population was around 2,000, but that number had jumped to approximately 10,000 by the end of the American Revolution eight years later. He also notes that during the years of the British period blacks outnumbered whites by nearly 2 to 1—a ratio close to many Southern colonies with similar slave codes (e.g., South Carolina and Georgia) and typical of the British West Indies plantation colonies with their recurring slave revolts. In this discussion, Wright encounters more research roadblocks because of a lack of records demonstrating the origin of both whites and blacks, the economies of the plantations, and the mechanics of slave resistance to mounting oppression. Loyalist claims after the Revolution, as Jane Landers has noted in the first chapter, may provide a more detailed exploration into issues like the value placed on slaves by their white masters, slave work, religions, family cultures, and forms of resistance. Thus, Landers's and Wright's studies complement each other in meaningful ways.

The author makes an interesting point regarding the debate over the disposition of blacks in cases of a capital crime, where occasionally more freedoms and protections were afforded to blacks than in other colonies. Wright notes that in St. Augustine slaves might receive a trial by a judge or jury, a rather lenient system of justice for blacks compared to neighboring colonies. The author further argues that the British councilmen enacting these sorts of protections in East Florida did so largely in opposition to their own best interests, and suggests that they may have been influenced by the rising British abolitionist movement. However, his use of evidence here, as elsewhere in the article, is open to interpretation.

Wright concludes his study with a discourse on why the British refused to return slaves to claimants after the war. This occurred for multiple reasons, such as British honor, spite for the Revolutionaries (many had confiscated Tory property), and the promise of freedom to loyal blacks during the conflict. He ends by providing a valuable discussion on both the internal and external dispersal of blacks in the period, reminding readers that large numbers of them had escaped and joined Indian societies as "Black Seminoles" or resettled in black maroon communities.

Although this article contains many useful observations and well-constructed arguments, the reader may wish that Wright had been able to review more primary sources. To his credit, the author acknowledges that most of his evidence lends itself to inferences rather than to hard conclusion, and therein lies a lesson for students of history regarding the possible uses of limited source material. In the end, Wright's study provides valuable insight and methodological lessons into the nature of race relations and black struggle in an important period of Florida's growth.

FURTHER READING

Wilbur H. Siebert, "Slavery in East Florida, 1776 to 1785," *Florida Historical Quarterly*, Vol. 10 (1932);

Edwin L. Williams, Jr., "Negro Slavery in Florida," *Florida Historical Quarterly*, Vol. 28 (1949);

Robert L. Gold, "The Settlement of the East Florida Spaniards in Cuba, 1763-1766," *Florida Historical Quarterly*, Vol. 42 (1964);

Rembert W. Patrick, *East Florida as a British Province, 1763-1784* (1964);

Laura D.S. Harrell, *Colonial Medical Practice in British West Florida, 1763-1781* (1967);

Robert R. Rea, "'Graveyard for Britons,' West Florida 1763-1781," *Florida Historical Quarterly*, Vol. 47 (1969);

Carole Watterson Troxler, "Loyalist Refugees and the British Evacuation of East Florida, 1783-1785," *Florida Historical Quarterly*, Vol. 60 (1981);

Daniel L. Shafer, "Early Plantation Development in British East Florida," *Escribano*, Vol. 19 (1982);

William S. Coker and Robert S. Rea, eds., *Anglo-Spanish Confrontation on the Gulf Coast During the American Revolution* (1982);

Daniel H. Shafer, "Plantation Development in British East Florida: A Case Study of the Earl of Egmont," *Florida Historical Quarterly*, Vol. 63 (1984);

Carole Watterson, "Refuge, Resistance, and Reward: The Southern Loyalists' Claim on East Florida," *Journal of Southern History*, Vol. 55 (1989);
Daniel L. Shafer, "'Yellow Silk Ferret Tied Round their Wrists': African Americans in British East Florida, 1763-1784," in *The African American Heritage of Florida*, David R. Colburn and Jane L. Landers, eds. (1995);
Robin F. A. Fabel, "British Rule in the Floridas," in Michael Gannon, ed., *The New History of Florida* (1996), chapter 8;
Charlton W. Tebeau and William Marina, *A History of Florida* (1999), chapter 6.

Blacks In British East Florida

J. Leitch Wright, Jr.

The Florida Historical Quarterly, Volume 54, issue 4 (1976), 425-442.

Blacks began arriving in Spanish Florida in the early sixteenth century soon after the appearance of Europeans, and from that point on they constituted a significant minority of the population, if not an absolute majority. During the British era, 1763-1784, blacks outnumbered whites. Except for rare instances, scholars interested in Negro history at any time during Florida's lengthy colonial era will search in vain for published books and articles.[1] A stroll 200 years ago through rice and indigo fields and through sugar houses of St. Johns River plantations or a visit to St. Augustine's public market on the plaza and to the slave auction block would provide much information no longer available. Knowledge which was commonplace two centuries ago has been lost. Contemporary historians must utilize the few sources available, and be conscious that, if they are lucky, they may at least see the tip of the iceberg.

It is risky even to speculate concerning what language most East Florida blacks spoke. Qua appeared briefly in 1777 just before he was executed, and at least, his name is recorded for posterity—which is itself a rarity. But even this fragment is meaningful. Africans named their children for the days of the week. "Qua" represented a male child who had been born on Thursday. Considering the African origins of the few other known East Florida slave names, and taking into account the large scale pre-Revolutionary slave importations into all southern colonies direct from Africa, suggest that Qua was a typical East Florida Negro. Presumably he had been born in West Africa, retained a knowledge of his African tongue and culture, but had been forced to develop a pidgin in order to communicate with whites and fellow blacks alike.[2] The small number of surviving runaway slave notices also shed some light on language, but in no way can these few advertisements be considered a broad statistical sample. Relying on such notices as are available, runaways seemed to be young mulattoes able to speak both French and English.[3]

The problem of language is closely associated with where blacks were born and where they lived before arriving in East Florida. One can consider three major origins: Africa, the West Indies, and the other southern colonies. Though most native Africans presumably came from West Africa, this vast area encompassed many different peoples and cultures. Some, and probably a considerable number of blacks imported into East Florida, came from Jamaica in the West Indies. But where did the blacks described in the runaway notices learn to speak French? Guadeloupe, Martinique and especially Saint Domingue (Haiti) come to mind.[4] East Florida planters such as John Moultrie, master of Bella Vista, had moved into the new province from South Carolina. He had brought slaves with him, but the percentage of his slaves—numbering 180 at the end of the Revolution—which had been born in America and were acculturated and the number who were recent arrivals from Africa is unknown.[5] There is another possible source of French-speaking slaves. During the Revolution French prizes were brought to St. Augustine, where at least some crewmen exchanged a French for a British master.

Yet after all these considerations the original uncertainty about the dominant lan-

This 1893 photograph shows the slave market at the Cathedral Plaza in St. Augustine. State Library and Archives of Florida.

guage of blacks remains. A visitor to East Florida's slave quarters during the American Revolution might have heard English, French, Mandingo, Fulani, Hausa, and Mende, among other languages. In the Indian country there were black Hitchiti and Muskogee speakers. A pidgin, such as Gullah, was emerging and presumably was spoken with varying degrees of proficiency by a majority of East Florida blacks. Regardless of which were the most important languages, at least some blacks, simultaneously thrust into several cultures, became exceptional linguists. Whites employed them in their dealings with other Negroes and with Indians.

Despite the dearth of shipping and plantation records, more is known about the aggregate number of blacks in Florida. There were just over 2,000 Negroes in 1775, and by the end of the Revolution that number had increased to nearly 10,000. Throughout the British period blacks outnumbered whites approximately two to one.[6] This ratio was higher than in other southern colonies but considerably lower than the ratio in the British West Indies. In Jamaica there were at least fifteen blacks for every white.[7] In many respects, including a black majority and numerous absentee planters, East Florida had much in common with the British West Indies.

Population statistics reveal that there were few white yeomen farmers in East Florida. Whites were overseers, civil officials, in the military, or artisans and merchants who catered to their needs. Except for overseers they typically lived in or close by St. Augustine. The largest body of whites were the Minorcan, Greek, and Italian indentured servants at New Smyrna, but this settlement failed early in the Revolution, and the survivors moved to St. Augustine. East Florida produced and exported indigo, sugar, rice, timber, naval stores, and barrel staves, and most of these commodities were grown or manufactured on St. Marys and St. Johns river plantations worked by slaves. One reason so little is known about Florida blacks is because little is known about the British plantation system. Surviving records would allow an enterprising scholar to locate those plantations which existed for some period and to discover more about the crops grown. This basic study has not yet been made, and more is known about plantations which failed than about those which did not.[8]

Some large plantations existed for many years. Governor James Grant, East Florida's first governor, left the province in 1771. He employed an overseer to supervise his sizable holdings, and he did not dispose of his numerous slaves until 1784.[9] The Scottish planter-merchant, Richard Oswald, who helped negotiate the 1783 peace treaty, owned two large East Florida plantations. In 1779 he moved over 100 slaves to his property in Georgia where royal authority had been reestablished, and near the end of the Revolution he returned 170 to Mount Oswald on the Tomoka River.[10] Henry Strachey, an absentee planter who also helped negotiate the 1783 peace, operated his East Florida plantation during the war through an overseer.[11] For seventeen years Robert Bisset and his son managed several plantations on the Hillsborough River employing more than 100 slaves.[12] Taking time out from feuding with his political opponents, Governor Patrick Tonyn periodically inspected his plantation on the St. Johns River.[13] Books have been written about the Minorcans and other white indentured servants who settled in New Smyrna and about the approximately 500 who survived and in 1777 fled to St. Augustine.

Little is known of the blacks at New Smyrna except that 500 shipped over from Africa were drowned just off the Florida coast and that crews from Spanish privateers occasionally landed and spirited away slaves.[14] There is an absence of data on the plantations of Grant, Oswald, Strachey, Bisset, Tonyn, and others who employed 100 or more slaves.

Claims submitted by loyalists after the Revolution to secure compensation for their losses provide the best glimpse of life on an East Florida plantation. These documents reveal that slaves were used extensively in establishing the new British colony to build planters' and overseers' houses, Negro huts, kitchens, barns, fences, and to clear land. Two male field hands were expected to clear one acre every three weeks. Black artisans were in great demand. Perhaps twenty per cent of the slaves were skilled coopers, sawyers, squarers, carpenters, shipwrights, tar burners, and carters, and at times both skilled and unskilled slaves were hired out. Skilled male slaves were valued at between sixty and 100 pounds. Slaves worked in rice, indigo, and sugar cane fields, and operated sugar houses, indigo vats, and rice machines to prepare these crops for export. They boxed many thousands of pine trees to collect turpentine, and upon occasion they picked sweet and sour oranges and prepared juice for sale. Royal bounties for the production of naval stores and indigo served as a stimulus.[15]

Typical plantations employed from seventy to over 200 slaves. They lived in small wooden "Negro houses" holding three to four persons each clustered in a village. The overseer's residence was nearby. Though villages frequently had a common kitchen, it is not clear whether it was essentially an African or European one and whether food was prepared in the African, European, or New World style. Better quarters had built-in wooden beds. After the British period Florida slave houses sometimes were constructed of tabby, but archeologists will have to verify if any were built with this material during the British regime.[16] Based on a few available samples, fifty-seven per cent of the slaves were male and forty-three per cent, female.[17] Because the colony had so recently been acquired by Britain, and because of wartime disruptions, Negro villages never assumed the stability and permanence of those in the West Indies where many black communities became almost a state within a state.

It is an understatement to assert that little is known about plantation slaves in British East Florida, but relatively speaking a veritable cornucopia of documentation survives as compared to sources about blacks in the Indian country. Blacks had lived among the Indians for many decades— probably well over two centuries— before 1763. In the late seventeenth and early eighteenth centuries Carolinians had engaged in a brisk trade in Indian slaves. As a result southern blacks and Indians had labored side by side, intermarried, and sometimes had escaped together to the Indian country. During the Revolution David Black was reimbursed £20 for bringing fugitive Negroes back to St. Augustine.[18] One can only speculate whether the Negroes in question had fled from some harsh East Florida overseer or were homesick and were returning if not to a *zambo* mother at least to *zambo* relatives.

Blacks in the Indian country were either slave or free and lived in separate communities or intimately among the Indians. Two loosely-structured factions seemed to have been evolving: a maroon society and another composed of recent fugitive plantation slaves. Maroons presumably had established themselves at an early date in separate communities and retained much of their African heritage, including agricultural techniques. They adopted some of the Indian culture and perhaps rendered the natives food in return for protection. Because of their superior knowledge of husbandry and ability as interpreters, maroons may have been a far more dominant force in the Indian country than has been generally realized. Maroons partially emerged from their obscurity in the nineteenth century during the course of the Seminole wars. The other group of blacks among the Indians were recent runaways, at least some of whom were looked down upon and enslaved by Indians and maroons alike. *Zambos* were likely to adopt the culture of their mothers and count themselves as either blacks or Indians.[19]

In 1778 John Stuart, Britain's southern Indian superintendent, ordered Moses Kirkland, Seminole Indian agent, into the Indian country to help organize the Indians for the forthcoming campaign. Stuart assured Kirkland that Bully and the Black Factor, who lived near the forks of the Apalachicola River, would furnish horses.[20] At once one wonders about the origins of Black Factor's name. Was it on account of his pigmentation or for some other cause? Along the southern frontier blacks had been employed at cow pens, horse pens, and in various aspects of the Indian trade. Black Factor may have been a mulatto— possibly one of the numerous progeny of the Georgia Indian trader George Galphin— who for some time had raised horses and cattle and had been an enterprising merchant and land speculator.[21] Much of this is conjecture, as are Bully's racial origins and the number of other "black factors," if any, among the Indians.

East Florida had no formal slave code until 1782, but through custom and statutes the lives of slaves were regulated in detail. Blacks were outright chattels, and every Negro and mulatto who clearly could not demonstrate that he was free was deemed a slave. When Qua was publicly executed for robbery in St. Augustine, assessors estimated his value, and the state reimbursed his owner for his property loss.[22] Slaves in and around St. Augustine had their own garden plots and legally could sell their vegetables, fish, etc. only at stalls in the public market. Thirty-nine lashes were to be meted out to violators and also to blacks who congregated and danced after 10:00 P.M.[23]

One searches almost in vain to know what blacks thought about the growing crisis between the American colonies and the mother country concerning taxation and parliamentary sovereignty. Probably these issues, so crucial for white American Whigs, had a low priority among East Florida blacks. Nevertheless, from the very beginning the war was brought home poignantly to East Florida Negroes, and they could not ignore that conflict regardless of what they thought of it.

In 1776, 1777, and again in 1778 Georgians stormed across the St. Marys River in unsuccessful efforts to capture St. Augustine. Exposed plantations on the St. Marys River and Amelia Island were ravaged. Floridians rushed their slaves toward St. Augustine for security, while Georgians captured others and whisked them away to the north. Jermyn Wright hurried his Negroes southward from his several plantations on the St. Marys River. In the ensuing weeks twenty-four slaves roaming about the woods with little to eat died of starvation.[24] After Spain came into the war in 1779 crews from her privateers landed above and below St. Augustine and carried off slaves.[25] Near the end of the Revolution Elias Ball from South Carolina brought 175 Negroes into East Florida and within one month alone over thirty died.[26] These mortality figures help justify the assumption that East Florida was like Jamaica and that the local slave population did not sustain itself in wartime, nor probably at any period.

But one merely has to look at the military sick list in East Florida or at the hundreds of Minorcan deaths at New Smyrna to realize that whites as well as blacks died at an alarming rate in British East Florida. In fact, the "sickle-cell trait," threatening twentieth century black children with anemia, gave Negroes in the eighteenth century a relative advantage over white indentured servants by affording more immunity against malaria.

Despite a high death rate, the scarcity of females, and wartime disruptions, the Negro population in East Florida almost quintupled during the Revolution. This was not due to any advantages of the "sickle cell trait" nor natural increase, but because of war time immigration. William Panton, a Georgia exile and, Indian trader, Jermyn and Charles Wright, brothers of Georgia's last royal governor, James Spalding from St. Simons Island, and many other Georgians and Carolinians fled to East Florida with their slaves during the early years of the Revolution. Their blacks were immediately set to work building Negro houses, growing indigo, rice, and sugar cane, producing naval stores, and packing deerskins for export. Whether blacks also continued to reach East Florida from the West Indies and Africa in appreciable numbers is uncertain.

One new source of slaves was from the sale of Negroes captured aboard ships flying the United States, French, or Spanish flags. St. Augustine had an admiralty court, for long periods the only one in the South, and condemned slaves were routinely auctioned off in the East Florida capital.[27] If any of the admiralty court records ever turn up it may be possible to estimate the numbers and to learn details about the background of the blacks involved and exactly where and how the auction was conducted.

Immediately after the fighting at Lexington and Concord broke out, East Florida lay exposed. Less than 100 untrained militia, neighboring Indians of unpredictable reliability, and a royal navy sloop or two represented the total available force. Minorcans comprised the largest single group of potential white militiamen. But they were Catholics, and it was unclear, particularly after France and Spain came into the war, on whose side they would fight. This made East Florida authorities more aware than ever that blacks were in the majority and that if the province was to be defended Negroes must assist.

One obvious way was by laboring on fortifications. In the neighboring southern colonies pre-Revolutionary laws had stipulated that all able-bodied male slaves between sixteen and sixty years of age must be listed with a local officer. In an emergency they could be called up for service. Owners were paid one shilling a day per slave or were relieved from having to provide labor for construction of public roads.[28] East Florida had no militia law or Negro law until 1781. But even at the beginning of the Revolution it is clear that the governor and council and sometimes individual planters made slaves available to help construct provincial defenses as had been customary in other colonies during the colonial period. The earthen walls surrounding St. Augustine, the parallel lines north of the town, the powder magazine, the redoubts on the St. Johns River, and Fort Tonyn on the St. Marys in part were all constructed by slave labor. Square, wooden Fort Tonyn mounting swivel guns was thrown up in a rush in 1775-1776. Considering the paucity of regular soldiers and militia alike, it is reasonable to assume that blacks provided much of the labor. Tory planters on the exposed St. Marys River likely volunteered their slaves with gusto and did not quibble about prompt reimbursement.

In 1775 white Floridians assumed not only that slaves should be impressed to labor on fortifications but also that if need be they should be armed and employed as ordinary soldiers. Considering the debates during the 1860s in Jefferson Davis's cabinet over arming slaves and the fact that not until a month before Appomattox did the Confederacy agree to enlist slaves as regular soldiers, East Florida's willingness to employ black soldiers at the outset of the Revolution appears surprising. But East Florida's conduct was unique only if it were compared with Confederate policies almost a century later and not with those of Britain's North American colonies earlier in the eighteenth century. South Carolina in the first part of that century had used blacks to fight Indians and. Spaniards alike. After slavery became legal in the 1750s, Georgia made provisions for arming slaves in an emergency. [29] Florida planters, who frequently had come from South Carolina and Georgia, instinctively looked to slaves for assistance when rebels threatened their property. It would have been strange if Jermyn Wright on the St. Marys River and Lord Egmont's overseer on Amelia Island had not done what limited sources indicate other Florida planters did in similar emergencies: i.e. arm and train slaves to defend their lands.[30] At an early date blacks enlisted in the East Florida Rangers and helped garrison Fort Tonyn and protect the St. Marys frontier.[31] When in 1779 Colonel Lewis Fuser counted the number of regular and militia soldiers available to defend the province he found that over one seventh of the total were black.[32]

In 1781 East Florida's first assembly finally met and passed a militia act which generally duplicated earlier militia laws in other American colonies. An unlimited number of slaves could be drafted and used as a labor force or soldiers. Militia captains were to be furnished lists of all able-bodied slaves in their districts, and recalcitrant plantation managers were to be fined fifty pounds. Slave owners received one pound monthly for impressed slaves. For breaches of military discipline slaves were to be whipped rather than fined like their white contemporaries, though for sleeping on duty or betraying the password blacks were treated equally with whites: both were to be executed. For acts of bravery slaves were to be awarded clothing, money, medals, and some relief from service.[33]

Except for provisions authorizing enlisting an unlimited number of slaves and for making no specific mention of freeing slaves who performed outstanding acts of bravery, the East Florida militia act contained no unusual features and merely copied earlier codes of Georgia and South Carolina. When East Florida had refused to revolt in 1775, it had followed precedents, because loyalty to the mother country was the colonial norm. It was the thirteen colonies who, by rebelling, had broken with tradition, and it was these same colonies, i.e. Georgia, the Carolinas, and Virginia, who had departed from colonial custom during the Revolution by refusing to arm slaves to any significant degree. The Revolution held many paradoxes. One was that the southern states for the first time considered it dangerous ever to trust slaves with arms. This was another step in dehumanizing the institution of slavery and depriving blacks of a measure of dignity and independence. It was almost inevitable that blacks and whites, fighting side by side against a determined enemy, must have accorded one another a measure of respect. East Florida blacks, fighting for the white man's liberty, despite the omission of a specific provision in the militia act, in a variety of ways had the opportunity of winning their own freedom.

With neighboring Georgia again under royal control in 1779, with the arrival of many loyalist refugees in East Florida, and with the crushing or expulsion of his most vocal political opponents, Governor Patrick Tonyn assumed that it was safe to hold elections for a representative assembly. It, along with the appointed council (the upper house) and the governor, would share authority. The first assembly was seated in the St. Augustine state house in March 1781, and it met intermittently until the end of 1783. The assembly concerned itself with a multitude of routine affairs—regulating markets and public houses, licensing pilots, building roads, collecting small debts, along with framing a militia law and a law authorizing the governor to impress slaves to work on fortifications. But drawing up a slave code took more time and engendered more controversy than any other issue. Governor Tonyn in a huff even dissolved the assembly in November 1781 on account of this quarrel.

Two centuries later this controversy seems puzzling, because in most respects East Florida's slave code was similar to South Carolina's and Georgia's. It provided that all Negroes, mulattos, and mestizos who could not prove they were free were to be regarded as slaves. Children followed the status of their mother. Negroes and mulattos who were not slaves were to wear a silver armband engraved with "free." Slaves needed a ticket from their master to be absent from the plantation or to carry a firearm in peace time, and masters were to be fined for cruelty to slaves. Authorities compensated any owner of a slave who was legally executed. Companion laws provided for white patrols to keep slaves in check.

The East Florida slave code differed from all others in North America concerning trials of slaves in capital offenses. In the other colonies an accused slave customarily could be tried by two justices of the peace and several local freeholders. They were to meet no later than three days after the commission of the felony, and they had the authority to impose the death sentence and to require that it be swiftly carried out. Based on their knowledge of practices in neighboring colonies, East Florida council members argued that there was no assurance that justices of the peace or freeholders would know much about the law, that torture might be used, and that there was a serious risk of miscarriage of justice. The council demanded that in capital cases the accused slave be brought to St. Augustine and tried before a twelve-man white jury. The presiding judge could properly instruct the jury, and the defendant would be afforded more, but not all, of the protections under the English law.

Members of the lower house, a majority of whom were slave owners, retorted this was unjust and that nowhere else on the American mainland were slaves afforded such guarantees. Assemblymen complained that the accused, representing a valuable investment, might spend six months or more in jail and that witnesses must make a costly trip to St. Augustine to testify. Whether they were white overseers or Negro slaves, the witnesses would not be able to work for long periods. Moreover, assembly men charged such a lenient slave code would discourage loyalist slave-owning planters from immigrating into the province and might prod those already in the colony to leave.[34]

But members of the council were also slave owners, and it is confusing to explain their stance. Few possessed more Negroes than John Moultrie, president of the council and master of Bella Vista on the Matanzas River. The Reverend John Forbes, councilman since 1765, owned fifty-nine slaves, and councilmen Henry Yonge, James Hume, and John Holmes each owned considerably more.[35] All of them would be equally inconvenienced and would suffer financially if slave trials were conducted in St. Augustine. Thomas Brown, colonel of the East Florida Rangers and a slave-owning refugee who joined the council in 1778, might have been the one who suggested that a lenient slave code would help make blacks in his rangers and in the provincial militia more reliable.

There are a number of possible motives to justify the council's action. When the council criticized the assembly's slave code and charged that swift executions and the possible use of torture smacked of Turkish despotism, it may have been thinking less of unfortunate blacks and more of Andrew Turnbull, the proprietor of New Smyrna, and his supporters in the lower house. Turnbull, whose wife was from Turkey, was a leader of the political faction opposed to most if not all council members. Moultrie, Forbes, Yonge, and other councilmen, including Governor Tonyn who agreed with them also must have taken satisfaction in trying to make East Florida's slave code the most humane in America and contrasting it to the thirteen colonies where "liberty" was supposed to be flourishing. Throughout the Revolution Tories delighted in denouncing Thomas Jefferson and Patrick Henry for mouthing liberty while practicing the vilest slavery.

Probably the best explanation of the council's action is that its members were influenced by the growing British abolitionist movement. Slavery had been abolished in the mother country in 1772. Councilman John Forbes had been sent over to East Florida by the Society for the Propagation of the Gospel in Foreign Parts which had something of an anti-slavery tradition. Thomas Brown, who had led black and white soldiers into battle, may have assumed that justice demanded that black soldiers should have the same status as whites not only when bullets were flying but also in peacetime.

Confronted by opposition of the assembly which refused to make any appropriations until the council altered its position and encouraged by authorities in London to become conciliatory, the upper house made concessions. Local justices of the peace and freeholders could still try and convict offenders promptly, but trial proceedings had to be reviewed by the governor and capital punishment administered in St. Augustine.[36]

Near the end of the Revolution East Florida authorities made provisions for building a workhouse. Its primary function was to serve as a jail for fugitive slaves and for itinerant blacks of questionable legal status. Slaves were to be kept in the workhouse until redeemed by their masters; in the interim they labored to help pay for their keep. Whites, such as runaway indentured servants, may also have been assigned to the workhouse. Because East Florida's workhouse was built so late, most fugitive slaves were incarcerated in St. Augustine's jail on the plaza or elsewhere.[37]

East Florida's black religious and medical practices are little understood partly because it is not certain whether Florida blacks were recent arrivals from Africa or had been in the New World for some time. If they had been born in North America, at least a veneer of Christianity represented part of the acculturation. But whether Christ or obeah-men had the greatest influence or whether the white master or the black medicine man treated sick Negroes is unclear. The few surviving records of the Anglican church do not indicate that Anglican ministers overly concerned themselves with black salvation. In fairness to ministers of the Society for the Gospel in Foreign Parts it must be recognized that this missionary arm of the Church of England was overtaxed in East Florida. The needs of white civilians and the garrison were barely attended to, and the Reverend John Forbes, a member of the council, judge of the vice-admiralty court and the court of common law, acting chief justice, and a large planter, had little free time. Anglican priests served as schoolmasters, though there is no record of their ever teaching a black pupil.[38]

At the end of the Revolution the German traveller Johann D. Schoepf visited St. Augustine and discovered a black Baptist minister preaching to a Negro congregation in a cabin outside town.[39] The only fact known about this minister is that he had to be one of the first of his kind in North America. Just before the Revolution Baptists had made numerous converts among Southerners, black and white alike. Negro Baptist churches at Savannah, Georgia, Silver Bluff, South Carolina, and at Williamsburg, Virginia, were all founded in the mid-1770s.[40] Two questions come to mind in connection with the St. Augustine Baptist preacher. Had he established his church in East Florida soon after the British arrived in 1763, or was he a South Carolina or Georgia exile who arrived in the province with thousands of loyalists in 1782-1785? The other unanswered puzzle is was the Baptist congregation typical and were most East Florida blacks if not Baptists at least Christians? This again raises the fundamental issue of language and culture. Were East Florida blacks essentially transplanted Africans or acculturated Americans?

East Florida's Negro population spurted at the end of the Revolution after Britain evacuated Charleston and Savannah. In 1782 and 1783 ships laden with 100 to 300 Negroes each brought approximately 8,300 blacks into the province, a figure almost three times larger than the entire pre-war population, black and white combined.[41] The status of many of these blacks in East Florida was confused, though there was no doubt about their condition as far as South Carolina and Georgia Whig plantation owners were concerned. They charged that the departing British had spirited away thousands of Whig-owned slaves in violation of the peace treaty and basic justice. But it was not that simple, because British commanders had promised freedom to southern blacks who deserted their rebel masters and came into British lines to serve George III.[42] Thousands who had accepted the British offer regarded themselves as free and assumed they had won their liberty at the same time United States republicans had received theirs. Georgians and South Carolinians visited St. Augustine at the end of the Revolution to recover their property but with little success. East Floridians refused to return hardly any blacks partly as a matter of honor—because many slaves had been promised their freedom—and partly out of spite. Southern Whigs had confiscated large amounts of loyalist property, and East Florida loyalists reciprocated by ensuring that few blacks ever returned to Whig owners.[43]

The 1783 peace treaty stipulated that East Florida must be handed over to Spain, and this brought to the forefront the future of East Florida's 11,000 blacks. A majority left, and one can follow the broad pattern of the evacuation. The largest single group went to the neighboring Bahama Islands. Benjamin West, an American expatriate artist in London, painted the *Reception of the American Loyalists by Great Britain in 1783.*[44] Some of his figures were black, and it is safe to assume that at least a few East Florida Negroes ended up in the mother country. Whatever their previous status, they were definitely free after reaching Britain because of Parliament's abolition of slavery in 1772. That Florida masters could not retire with their slave property to the mother country's free soil posed a dilemma for some white loyalists. Other blacks, as slaves, freemen, and indentured servants, went to Nova Scotia, Jamaica, St. Lucia, and the Mosquito Shore in Central America.[45] At least some East Florida blacks who were sailors spent years at sea with no place to call home. A considerable number of Negroes and whites remained in East Florida after the Spaniards returned in 1784. John Leslie and Francis Philip Fatio both stayed, cooperated with the Spaniards, and employed blacks in their St. Augustine houses, on their plantations, and in their trading stores. An undetermined number of blacks fled into the Indian country— sometimes on the same day their surprised white masters sailed away— and the percentage of black "Seminoles" increased in the wake of the Revolution.[46] The fate of St. Augustine's black Baptist minister is unknown, though one might speculate that he moved to Jamaica or the Bahamas like Baptist ministers George Liele and Brother Amos who evacuated Georgia.[47]

One can hope that in the Bahamas, in musty attics or in public archives, papers have been preserved which will illuminate the black experience in British East Florida. Perhaps buried in some Scottish castle or manor house are plantation records and personal correspondence which will better disclose the rhythm of life on an East Florida plantation and tell more about the culture of East Florida blacks. The potential of oral history cannot be overlooked. Among black "Indians" in Florida and Oklahoma, black Bahamians, blacks in Nova Scotia (or Sierra Leone where many subsequently moved), or in black communities in scattered port cities there may be oral accounts of how their ancestors labored and fought for George III in East Florida.[48] From widely scattered written sources, oral traditions, linguistic studies, and archeological investigations scholars in time may discover more about those Floridians who during the American Revolution comprised a majority of the population. Whenever the story of blacks in British East Florida is fully told— and of Spanish Florida as well— it is likely to be an interesting one that will illuminate not only the history of colonial Florida but of the entire Southeast.

Mr. Wright is professor of history, Florida State University, Tallahassee.

1. Those few authors who have made studies of blacks in colonial Florida are: I. A. [Irene Aloha] Wright, ed., "Dispatches of Spanish Officials Bearing on the Free Negro Settlement of Gracia Real de Santa Teresa de Mose, Florida," *Journal of Negro History,* IX (April 1924), 144-95; Kenneth W. Porter, in his articles "Negroes and the East Florida Annexation Plot, 1811-1813," *Journal of Negro History,* XXX (January 1945), 9-29, and "Negroes and the Seminole War, 1817-1818," *Journal of Negro History,* XXXVI (July 1951), 249-80; and John J. TePaske, "The Fugutive Slave: Intercolonial Rivalry and Spanish Slave Policy, 1687-1764," in Samuel Proctor, ed., *Eighteenth-Century Florida and Its Borderlands* (Gainesville, 1975), 1-12.
2. General acc't. of contingent expenses, East Florida, June 25, 1777-June 24, 1778, Great Britain, Public Record Office, Colonial Office 5/559. Hereinafter cited as CO. J. L. [Joey Lee] Dillard, *Black English: Its History and Usage in the United States* (New York, 1972), 124. Approximately one half of the fifty names which I was able to discover were clearly of African origin. This, along with the importation of slaves direct from Africa to East Florida and to adjoining colonies by Richard Oswald, Henry Laurens, and similar merchants, helps demonstrate the strength of the African culture in British East Florida.
3. *Georgia Gazette,* November 15, 1775; *Royal Georgia Gazette,* January 18, March 8, 1781.
4. Philip D. Curtin, *The Atlantic Slave Trade: A Census* (Madison, 1969), 75-84.
5. Memorial of John Moultrie, London, March 24, 1787, Great Britain, Public Record Office, Audit Office 12/3. Hereinafter cited as AO. Most, but not all, of the East Florida loyalist claims are reproduced in Wilbur Henry Siebert, ed., *Loyalists in East Florida, 1774 to 1785: The Most* Important Documents Pertaining Thereto, Edited with an Accompanying *Narrative,* 2 vols. (DeLand, 1929), II.
6. Charles Loch Mowat, *East Florida as a British Province, 1763-1784* (Berkeley, 1943; facsimile edition, Gainesville, 1964), 137; J. Leitch Wright, Jr., *Florida in the American Revolution* (Gainesville, 1975), 13. Population figures are the best estimates available, though they do not include blacks living among the Indians.
7. Alan Burns, *History of the British West Indies,* rev. 2nd ed. (New York, 1965), 511.
8. Three separate books by Epaminondes P. Panagopoulos, Carita Doggett Corse, and Jane Quinn have been written about New Smyrna which survived for a decade. There are no published works about the respectable number of other plantations employing 50 to 200 slaves which lasted much longer. See E. [Epaminondes] P. Panagopoulos, *New Smyma: An Eighteenth Century Greek Odyssey* (Gainesville, 1966); Carita Doggett [Corse], *Dr. Andrew Turnbull and the New Smyrna Colony of Florida* (n.p., 1919); Jane Quinn, *Minorcans in Florida: Their History and Heritage* (St. Augustine, 1975).
9. Patrick Tonyn to Strachey, St. Augustine, December 7, 1784, Henry Strachey Letters, Bancroft Collection, New York Public Library; New York City.
10. Memorial of Mary Oswald, November 11, 1786, AO 12/3.
11. Strachey to Tonyn, London, March 31, 1783, CO 5/560.

12. Memorial of Robert Bisset, London, March 27, 1787, AO 12/3.
13. J. Leitch Wright, Jr., *British St. Augustine* (St. Augustine, 1975), 15, 17, 39.
14. Panagopoulos, *New Smyma,* 58; memorial of Robert Bisset, London, March 27, 1787, AO 12/3.
15. This information is based primarily though not exclusively on the loyalist claims published in Siebert, *Loyalists in East Florida,* II.
16. Charles H. Fairbanks, "The Kingsley Slave Cabins in Duval County, Florida, 1968," *Conference on Historic Site Archeology Papers,* VII (1972), part 1, 62-93.
17. Memorial of John Graham, November 23, 1786, AO 12/3; memorial of Denys Rolle, September 10, 1783, Siebert, *Loyalists in East Florida,* II, 291.
18. General account of contingent expenses, CO 5/559, 66.
19. The best accounts concerning blacks among the southern Indians in the early nineteenth century are Roderick Brumbaugh, "Black Maroons in Florida, 1800-1830," unpublished paper delivered at the annual meeting of the Organization of American Historians, Boston, 1975; Kenneth Wiggins Porter, *The Negro on the American Frontier* (New York, 1971), 182-358. These two scholars, however, do not concern themselves with British Florida.
20. John Stuart to Moses Kirkland, Pensacola, January 30, 1778, AO 13/36A. Bully was also known as Buly or Birli.
21. Tonyn to Stuart, September 8, 1778, CO 5/558.
22. General account of contingent expenses, East Florida, June 25, 1777-June 24, 1778, CO 5/559.
23. *East Florida Gazette,* February 22, 1783.
24. Jermyn and Charles Wright to Lord George Germain, n.d., CO 5/116.
25. Memorial of Bisset, March 27, 1787, AO 12/3.
26. Memorial of Elias Ball, London, August 1, 1784, AO 12/3.
27. East Florida Commons House Journal, St. Augustine, July 20, 1781, CO 5/572.
28. An act for repairing and rebuilding the forts, June 4, 1760, in Allen D. Candler, comp. and ed., *The Colonial Records of the State of Georgia,* 26 vols. (Atlanta, 1904-1916), XVIII, 433-34.
29. Militia Act, January 24, 1755, *ibid.,* 38-44; Peter H. Wood, *Black Majority, Negroes in Colonial South Carolina, From 1670 through the Stono Rebellion* (New York, 1974), 126-29.
30. When the Americans invaded West Florida Adam Chrystie armed and uniformed twenty-two of his slaves. Memorial of Adam Chrystie, Suffolk St., March 4, 1784, AO 13/99.
31. East Florida council minutes, February 2, 1776, CO 5/571.
32. Lewis Fuser to Henry Clinton, September 11 to October 6, 1779, Sir Henry Clinton Papers, William L. Clements Library, University of Michigan, Ann Arbor, Michigan.
33. An act for the establishment and regulation of the militia of this province, St. Augustine, June 7, 1781, CO 5/624.
34. East Florida assembly minutes, July 25, 1781, CO 5/572; East Florida council minutes, July 27, 1781, CO 5/572.
35. Memorial of John Murray in behalf of Dorothy Forbes, London, December 15, 1786, Great Britain, Public Record Office, Treasury 77/6. The totals of Yonge's, Hume's, and

Holmes's slaves are based primarily but not exclusively on documents in Siebert, *Loyalists in East Florida,* II.

36. An act for the better government and regulation of Negroes and other slaves in this province, St. Augustine, May 31, 1782, CO 5/624.
37. Act for granting to the crown £3000 in aid of the support of the government of East Florida, CO 5/624.
38. Wright, *Florida in the American Revolution,* 100, 101.
39. Johann David Schoepf, *Travels in the Confederation, [1783-1784],* transl. and ed. by Alfred J. Morrison, 2 vols. (Philadelphia, 1911), II, 230.

40 Walter H. Brooks, "The Evolution of the Negro Baptist Church," *Journal of Negro History,* VII (January 1922), 15-16.

41. Mowat, *East Florida,* 137.
42. Alexander Leslie to Carleton, Charleston, June 27, 1782, Great Britain, Public Record Office, Sir Guy Carleton (Dorchester) Papers, 4916, microfilm copies in Robert Manning Strozier Library, Florida State University, Tallahassee.
43. James Clitherall to John Cruden, St. Augustine, May 25, 1783, *ibid.,* 7766.
44. Hugh E. Egerton, ed., *The Royal Commission on the Losses and Services of American Loyalists 1783-1785* (Oxford, 1915), reproduces this picture in the frontispiece.
45. The standard account of the loyalist evacuation of East Florida is Siebert, *Loyalists in East Florida,* I, 137-79.
46. Porter, "Negroes and the Seminole War, 1817-1818," 251-52.
47. "An account of Several Baptist Churches, Consisting Chiefly of Negro Slaves: Particularly of One at Kingston, in Jamaica: and Another at Savannah in Georgia," *Journal of Negro History,* I (January 1916), 70-73.
48. Alex Haley is an example of a writer who has utilized oral tradition in his unique forthcoming work, *Roots.*

3

SPANISH, BRITISH, SPANISH, AMERICAN

Patrick Riordan's study of the complex relationship between Native Americans and free blacks in Florida from 1670-1816 builds on the ideas explored in the first two chapters of this book. While Landers and Wright investigate what escaping slaves saw in a lenient Spanish policy of asylum and a British plantation-based model of slave codes, Riordan focuses on the motivations of blacks and Indians to seek autonomy in the back country of Florida and the resulting dynamics of that often shared relationship. Of particular significance is how the author suggests certain linkages between a rising market economy in the southeastern quadrant of the continent and the propensity for Native Americans and blacks to seek refuge in Florida's "Indian country." For much of this period, Native Americans wished to maintain trade and other ties with the British, but this desire proved vexing for them: should they assist fugitive slaves, incorporate them into Native American society, or return them for bounty? In the end, the author concludes that the Native Americans maintained dynamic responses to these dilemmas until the American destruction of the Negro Fort in 1816. He seems to suggest, as well, that the long shadow of white hegemony over Indians and blacks invariably created inter-group empathy and association. This is, indeed, a significant aspect of Florida's freedom struggles that deserves attention.

Early in his study, Riordan demonstrates that the ebb and flow of slaves fleeing the British colonies to the north correlated with shifts in Native American demographics in Florida and border lands. He then explores the ambiguity and contradictions in the Native Americans' responses to British attempts to enlist Seminoles as slave-catchers. This policy, in particular, moved freedom-loving Native Americans to friendship with a people seeking to escape bondage. It is plausible that the Indian and black migration from the Carolinas and later Georgia resulted from similar cravings for freedom by both populations and, therefore, logically resulted in cross-group alliances. This sort of brotherhood of experiences and visions would certainly have made it difficult for Indians to eschew black cries for shelter and bonding. Such bonding, as the historical record reflects, did occur in Florida.

The author proceeds to argue that British intrusions into Spanish Florida resulted in new Spanish attacks on North Florida native villages that were considered British allies. After a number of native villages were destroyed in the early eighteenth century for trading with the British, the Indians shifted northward, thus eliminating or diminishing their support in upper Florida for escaping slaves. The Yamassee War in North Carolina and the founding of the new British colony of Georgia (which initially forbade slavery) in 1733 led to a re-occupation of North Central Florida by native peoples, who, in the process, established north-south migration routes for both Indians and blacks. Significantly, the new migration into Florida included many land-hungry whites as well.

Riordan then notes, as have the earlier authors in this work, that the increasing number of American settlers brought new attempts to appropriate Indian lands as well as to eliminate Florida as a slave haven. As American expansion southward brought settlers into conflict with the escaped slaves, the number of "black Seminoles" in Middle Florida decreased as they retreated into the inhospitable swamplands of Central and Southwest Florida. Riordan surmises that this demographic shift occurred concurrently with that of Native Americans, but the lack of hard data makes it difficult to gauge the depths of this joint movement. It appears, however, that this southward migration further strengthened the bonds between the two groups and weakened white efforts to pit Indians against blacks.

As the British era dawned in1763, their rule in Florida had three significant implications for blacks. First, Florida ceased to be a territory where religious and diplomatic rivalry produced sanctuary. Second, British racial practices and slave codes became more subjective than they had been during the first Spanish period. And third, that British stress on instituting new market economies in Florida (including a slave trade) eliminated Florida as a haven for blacks and Indian allies, at least across the upper peninsula. Finally, the slaves the British brought to Florida to work on new plantations now fled in tandem with many Seminoles to the southern back country. This further strengthened the bonds between the two groups and prompted an Indian aversion to returning blacks to white claimants. Through statistical analysis, the author finds that increasing numbers of slaves now came to take advantage of their Native American brotherhood in their own unending search for freedom. Riordan skillfully dissects this issue and others in the article, in the process revealing the complex and not fully understood nexus between Native American and African-American migration, bonding, and resistance in colonial Florida.

FURTHER READING

Mark F. Boyd, "Events at Prospect Bluff on the Apalachicola River, 1808-1818," *Florida Historical Quarterly*, Vol. 16 (1937);

Kenneth Wiggins Porter, "Negroes and the East Florida Annexation Plot, 1811-1813," *Journal of Negro History*, Vol. 30 (1945);

Kenneth Wiggins Porter, "Negroes on the Southern Frontier, 1670-1763," *Journal of Negro History*, Vol. 33 (1948);

Edwin L. Williams, Jr., "Negro Slavery in Florida," *Florida Historical Quarterly*, Vol. 28 (1949); Marion Francis Shambaugh, *The Development of Agriculture in Florida during the Second Spanish Period* (1953);

Richard K. Murdoch, "The Return of Runaway Slaves, 1790-1794," *Florida Historical Quarterly*, Vol. 38 (1959);

Robert L. Gold, *Borderland in Transition: The Triple Nation Transfer of Florida* (1969);

Howard Francis Cline, *Notes on Colonial Indians and Communities in Florida, 1700-1821* (1974);

Samuel Proctor, ed., *Eighteenth-Century Florida and the Caribbean* (1976);

J. Leitch Wright, Jr., *Florida in the American Revolution* (1976);

Michael H. Getzler, Bruce S. Chappell, and Loren D. McWatters, "New Access to the History of Spanish Florida: The Spanish Florida Borderlands Project," *Escribano*, Vol. 15 (1978);

William Hilton Graves, *The Evolution of American Indian Policy: From Colonial Times to the Florida Treaty (1819)* (1982);

Jane Landers, "Spanish Sanctuary: Fugitives in Florida, 1687-1790," *Florida Historical Quarterly*, Vol. 62 (1984);

James Covington, "The Negro Fort," *Gulf Coast Historical Review*, Vol. 5 (1990);

Michael Mullin, *Africa in America: Slave Acculturation and Resistance in the American South and the British Caribbean, 1736-1831* (1992);

Jane Landers, "Slave Resistance on The Southeastern Frontier: Fugitives, Maroons, and Banditti in The Age Revolutions," *Escribano*, Vol. 32 (1995);

Charles W. Arnade, "Raids, Sieges, and International Wars," William S. Coker and Susan Parker, "The Second Spanish Period in the Two Floridas," and Daniel L. Shafer, "U.S. Territory and State," in Michael Gannon, ed., *The New History of Florida* (1996), chapters 6, 9, and 12;

Colin A. Palmer, ed., *The Worlds of Unfree Labour: From Indentured Servitude to Slavery* (1998);

Charlton W. Tebeau and William Marina, *A History of Florida* (1999), chapters 2-12;

Jennifer Lynn Baszile, *Communities at the Crossroads: Chiefdoms, Colonies, and Empires in Colonial Florida, 1670-1741* (1999);

Rosalyn Howard, *Black Seminoles in the Bahamas* (2002);

Kiley Mallard, *The Kingsley Plantation: Slavery in Spanish Florida* (2007).

Finding Freedom In Florida:

Native Peoples, African Americans, And Colonists, 1670-1816

Patrick Riordan

The Florida Historical Quarterly, Volume 75, issue 1 (1996), 24-43.

The entry of the lower south into a world marketplace wrought transformations on its European, native, and African American populations. As production demands increased after the turn of the 18th century, African laborers began to escape their European masters in greater numbers and more frequently sought permanent freedom. When they entered "Indian country," African Americans confronted native peoples with a difficult choice. Native Americans could assist them in escape, incorporate them into native groups, or return them to the Europeans with whom Native Americans maintained a delicate balance of diplomacy and trade.

The interpenetration of these populations created spaces where fleeing slaves might find an escape route, a temporary hiding place, and even a permanent home. Slaves in the British colonies of Carolina and Georgia became aware that, if they reached St. Augustine, they could achieve a degree of freedom. Eighteenth-century Native Americans, by contrast, discovered in Spanish Florida's uninhabited and fertile back country an escape from European influences. From the founding of Carolina in 1670 until the destruction of the Negro Fort in 1816, native and African people sometimes found in colonial Florida's remoteness a haven from white settlers.[1]

Migration varied over time, gradually increasing as working and living conditions worsened for laborers in the early 18th century. Initially South Carolina's agricultural economy was based on provision gardening, naval stores, and cattle raising rather than monocrop plantations. The social distance between blacks and whites was comparatively small at first. Blacks generally lived in accommodations similar to those of whites, experienced a relatively acceptable work regime, and some African Americans apparently even voted in 1703. After the 1710s, work regimes worsened and migration rates increased. For the remainder of the period under study, African American laborers in South Carolina generally faced conditions of life and work that tended to promote flight, if not outright rebellion.[2]

By the 1720s, the mix of the worker population was richer in newly-arrived Africans, who were more likely to run away. A recent study of the runaways advertised in South Carolina newspapers from 1732 to 1782 shows that of nearly 3,000 escaped slaves, two out of three were born in Africa. Significantly, the Stono uprising of 1739 was led by slaves fresh from Africa, who headed south toward Florida. A study of 453 runaways advertised in Georgia during a shorter period, 1763 to 1775, found that three of every four runaways were African-born.[3]

Word of Florida's potential as a sanctuary probably reached Carolina blacks as early as 1685, when several slaves captured by Spanish raiders returned and recounted their adventures in St. Augustine. Runaways began arriving the following year and continued irregularly thereafter.[4]

This migration led Spain to initiate the policy that made Florida a magnet for slave migration. In 1693 the Spanish king offered limited freedom to any slave escaping from British territory who would accept Christian conversion. To be sure, the Spanish restricted the freedom of movement of the former British slaves, and required them to work on the huge stone fort known as San Marcos. Other Carolina slaves petitioned for freedom upon arrival in1688, 1689, 1690, 1697, 1724, and 1725. In the early years of the18th century the number of African Americans rose and fell, reaching several hundred by the 1740s including free people of color.[5]

The apparent decline in migration between the late 1680s and 1724 may be due to missing records, but shifts in native American demography provide a likely explanation. In the 1680s Spain countered British military probes of its territory with violence against native settlements it considered as British allies. One such group, located north of the Spanish fort at St. Mark's in Apalachee, was trading with the British, who offered better goods, lower prices, and a more reliable supply than the Spanish. Antonio Matheos, commander of St. Mark's, burned those villages which refused to switch their trade to Spain. When he torched the leading towns, Coweta and Kasihta, their leaders organized a general movement of Creeks, or Muscogulges, eastward.[6]

This Muscogulge relocation had three consequences. First, it removed them from the Chattahoochee River watershed, which flowed into Spanish territory, and put them outside the sphere of Spanish influence. Second, it placed them on the headwaters of the Altamaha River, within trading range of the British. Third, it placed them strategically between Carolina and Florida, where they or the British traders they attracted might cut off the flow of escaping slaves, if they chose to do so. The Muscogulges' new location was undoubtedly a factor in the drastic reduction in black migration between 1690 and 1724.[7]

Soon after their removal to British territory, the Muscogulges became involved in a three-way colonial fight for hegemony in North America that broke out in 1702, known as Queen Anne's War. The British formed an alliance with the Muscogulges to counter a French eastward advance. British and Muscogulge troops attacked Spanish Florida, and, in the words of Thomas Nairne, "destroy'd the whole Country, burnt the Towns, brought all the *Indians,* who were not kill'd or made Slaves, into our own Territories, so that there remains not now, so much as one Village with ten Houses in it, in all Florida, that is subject to the Spaniards…."[8]

The British had reason to believe that they had co-opted or destroyed all the native peoples within 700 miles of Charles Town. This British-native alliance had the effect of cutting off the escape route to Florida. In fact, net migration briefly ran in the opposite direction. The Carolina forces, including a thousand Yamassee Indians, burned Spanish missions and enslaved at least 1,000 and, according to some interpretations, up to 4,000 Apalachee and other Indians. As a result, many Florida Indians were taken to Carolina, the Apalachee territory was left virtually uninhabited, and Indian slaves became the fastest-growing segment of the South Carolina population in the 1708 census. North Florida was left with few if any Native American settlements where newly arriving refugee slaves could seek assistance.[9]

Violent conflict erupted periodically in the region until the war played out in a series of skirmishes between native allies of European powers. In 1713, the Tuscarora attacked colonists in North Carolina who encroached on their lands, opening a prolonged period of conflict. After years of abuses at the hands of Indian traders—ranging from rum-running to rape, enslavement, and murder—the leaders of Coweta inspired the Yamassee Indians to revolt. The Yamassee took many African Americans as captives, and carried some of them to St. Augustine. Although the Yamassee War failed to achieve the goal of a pan-Indian rebellion to expel all Europeans from the southeast, it did result in the Muscogulges' capture of numerous African laborers and the re occupation of north central Florida by native peoples.[10]

After the Yamassee War several important Muscogulge towns pulled up stakes a second time—relocating this time to the west, out of the path of black migration. Coweta, the town whose leaders had instigated the war, moved back to the headwaters of the Chattahoochee, along with Kasihta and several other towns. At about the same time, the British Lords of Trade and Plantations recast its policies toward Native Americans. Seeking to rebuild lost alliances, the board decided to liberalize the terms of Indian trade by supporting "honest and reasonable prices," and to require colonial governors to regulate traders, whose abuses had provoked the Yamassee War. While the new policy did reinforce British trade alliances, it came too late to prevent the Muscogulge from relocating. Their movement created a buffer zone between Muscogulge territory and British Carolina-one through which African American refugees could travel safely, particularly when native peoples aided them.[11]

After Coweta led the westward movement back to the Chattahoochee valley, they found themselves at the center of a three-cornered international power struggle. The Spanish sought to make peace with as many of the Muscogulge groups as possible and to isolate the British. In 1717, the French established Fort Toulouse near present-day Montgomery, Alabama, to facilitate trading with the Muscogulges. The British, meanwhile, constructed Fort King George at the mouth of the Altamaha River in 1721. The construction of these forts defined a triangular contest for native friendship that handed the regional balance of power to the Muscogulges. The Muscogulges developed internal factions, each oriented toward one of the European powers, learning its language and manipulating it to native advantage. Such power politics led native groups sometimes to help runaways and other times to capture and return them for pay.[12]

Uncertainty immediately following the Yamassee War created turmoil, generally unfavorable to black migration. Spanish records suggest that the flow of African Americans did not resume until well after the westward movement of native peoples. By 1724, freedom-seeking blacks once again found their way to St. Augustine and petitioned for freedom. In September 1725, Spanish negotiators came to Charlestown to discuss the return of runaway slaves, but talks failed.[13]

By the late 1720s, the barriers had become much less formidable, and St. Augustine's population of freedom-seeking blacks began to rise. British subjects returning from Spanish captivity to Carolina told tales of African Americans and Yamassees selling British scalps for 30 Spanish pieces-of-eight in St. Augustine. Sometimes the fugitives joined forces with the remnant of the Yamassees who lived near St. Augustine, and raided Carolina.[14]

In 1733, as the British established a new buffer colony in Georgia, Philip V formally restated the policy of offering runaways freedom at the price of conversion to Roman Catholicism, and a term of four years of public servitude. Georgia's founders initially banned slavery, realizing that conditions favored escape. If slavery had been permitted from the colony's outset in 1732, the Earl of Egmont wrote in his diary, "there would not be 50 out of 500 remain in two months time, for they would fly to the Spaniards [in Florida] . . ." His colleague William Stephens, the colonial secretary, agreed that any slaves in Georgia "would march off when they pleased," southward to the Spanish. By the 1750s however, the slave population was growing as Carolina planters moved in.[15]

In a few years time, Georgia's leader, General James Edward Oglethorpe, successfully cultivated a military alliance with the Muscogulge. The Spanish reacted to the increasing British presence by establishing an outpost north of St. Augustine, Gracia Real de Santa Teresa de Mose. The town of Mose became home to 75-to-100 former English slaves, and the first self-governing community of free African Americans in North America.[16]

As new fugitives arrived, the Spanish governors placed them in Mose, under the care of the escaped Carolina slave known to the Spanish as Francisco Menendez. In November 1738, a group of 23 arrived from Carolina, including 19 who worked for a planter named Caleb Davis. Davis' experience demonstrated Spain's commitment to the policy of attracting British laborers. When Davis journeyed to St. Augustine seeking their return, his laborers laughed and jeered at his efforts to force them to return with him. Oglethorpe arrested and imprisoned Spaniards he found negotiating with blacks in Georgia, but the flow continued. In 1749, James Glen, the governor of South Carolina, complained that "both in peace and war, [the Spanish] protect the negroes that desert from this province." The black town of Mose was maintained until 1763,when Florida became British territory and its residents evacuated to Cuba.[17]

Throughout Florida's first Spanish period, the British encouraged the native peoples of the southeast to catch escaping slaves, offering rich bounties for live escapees and lesser goods for their scalps or severed heads. Results were inconsistent, however. A talk from the Cherokees in 1730 shows the thinking of some Native Americans, and demonstrates their unreliability as slave catchers. The Cherokees agreed to return slaves in general, for free, but balked at agreeing to return all runaways in exchange for payment. Their language is significant: ". . . [T] his small rope which we show you is all we have to bind our slaves with, and may be broken; but you have iron chains for yours; however, if we catch your slaves, we shall bind them as well as we can, and deliver them to our friends again, and have no pay for it. . . ."[18]

Such discourse— rejecting pay and retaining a measure of discretion—clearly should be read as a negotiating ploy intended to empower the speaker to make independent decisions. Impossible as it is to enter the consciousness of the Cherokee negotiators of 1730, nevertheless one can discern several levels of meaning in their representations of themselves and Europeans. First, the Cherokees were referring to differing social definitions of slavery. Their slaves were bound lightly (with small rope) while those of the British were more stringently secured, with metal chain. This distinction corresponds the contrast between Cherokee slaves or captives, who might become free by adoption, marriage, ransom, or exchange, and English chattel slaves, whose condition was hereditary and perpetual. Second, the speaker questioned how the Cherokees could be expected to hold, with mere rope, slaves that had already escaped their British chains. At this level, the speaker was underlining social differences, raising a practical question, and perhaps making fun of the British.[19]

Crucially, the Cherokees were likening the "iron chain" to a formal relationship which would bind them as surely as a chain would secure an escaped slave. They preferred a looser, more informal relationship with the English. Significantly, the Cherokees' discussion of chains to bind slaves follows immediately a reference to the "Chain of Friendship" between themselves and the British. While the image of the chain of friendship is a common one in native American diplomatic rhetoric, this juxtaposition suggests that the Cherokees saw similarities between their own relations with Europeans and the situation of African Americans. In any case, the agreement, as they amended it, did not require them to return every escaped slave, but instead gave them the right to decide which to capture and which to ignore.

The complex issue of the relationship between native peoples and runaway slaves arose at the Augusta Congress in 1763, as the British and the native peoples negotiated their new living arrangements after the Seven Years' War. Speaking for the Upper, Middle and Lower Creek towns, the native leader Captain Aleck proposed a new policy. In the past, he said, Muscogulges returned "any negro, horse, etc." found on their side of the Savannah River. ". . . But now the Ogeechee is the boundary, any negro, horse, cattle, etc., that exceeds such bounds he declares openly and in the presence of all the governors he will seize and keep." The British representative offered £5 or the equivalent for the continued return of runaways, observing, "You know it is very difficult to prevent Negroes from running away and cattle and horses from rambling." Although the final, English-language version of the treaty reflects agreement on the slave-catching plank, Captain Aleck's forceful position suggests that at least some of the Muscogulge continued to regard the practice of slave catching as optional— a potential source of income, but not an obligation.[20]

A third example of native attitudes comes from Seminole territory. In 1777, Seminoles living on the Flint River sent a highly direct message to British authorities in East Florida. Offering to support the British cause during the American Revolutionary War, the Seminoles set out their terms: "Whatever Horses or Slaves or Cattle we take we expect will be ours."[21]

For the black refugees from British colonies living in Florida in1763, the coming of British rule had two significant implications. First, the racial attitudes of Florida's new rulers were very different from those of the Spanish. The British world included black slaves and white masters, but no in-between groups like free people of color, the middle social layer that two centuries of Spanish culture had created. Awareness of the new reality doubtless encouraged the acknowledged free blacks in Florida to emigrate. In Georgia, runaway slave advertisements only rarely reflect laborers joining existing back country maroon communities.[22]

Second, Florida ceased to be a territory where religious and diplomatic rivalry produced a policy of religious sanctuary. On the contrary, the leaders of British East Florida actively encouraged plantations on the model of Carolina, and British settlers brought slaves with them in large numbers. The result was a demographic shift in the African American population, which grew in numbers and declined in status. By July 1782 Governor Patrick Tonyn estimated the population of East Florida at 3,000 African Americans and 1,000 Europeans. During the chaos of the American Revolutionary War, the total official population expanded more than fourfold.[23]

By the time of the revolution, Florida's Indian country had been accumulating a population of African Americans and their progeny for many years. By mid-century, the Lower Creek Indians, in the process of differentiating into the Seminoles, had moved south from Georgia. Hemming in the Spanish between the St. John's River and the coast, these native peoples created a human screen that the British acknowledged by treaty. Their presence blocked both the Spanish and the British from controlling an immense, fertile, and well-drained territory, accessible from Georgia, into which some runaways obviously found refuge. They established several villages of maroons with a black population of at least 430, living alongside and among the Seminoles.[24]

Slaves on plantations in pre-war British East Florida lived under conditions similar to those of their counterparts elsewhere in the Lower South. Indeed, Governor James Grant recruited South Carolina planters to East Florida with the distinct goal of replicating the onerous Carolina plantation work regimes that pushed so many workers to flee. At least one insurrection occurred in British East Florida, resulting in the drowning of an overseer known as Mr. Hewie. Escapes were far more frequent. A slave named Peter was never found after fleeing James Penman's plantation in October1769. A slave named Phyllis fled in 1780 in search of her husband whom her master Robert Robinson had sold. John Moultrie wrote, "It has been a practice for negroes to run away from their Masters and to get into the Indian towns, from whence it proved very difficult and troublesome to get them back." Despite a bounty of £2 ahead, native peoples in Florida did not always return laborers who reached their territory. Not surprisingly, hundreds of East Florida laborers were unaccounted for after the Revolutionary War, and may be presumed to have fled to Seminole country.[25]

Wartime chaos provided cover for escaping African Americans, and white colonists expected many to take advantage of it. Suspecting that some escapees reached Indian country, the British offered Native Americans a reward of 100 chalk marks per prisoner, white or black. (One chalk mark represented one pound of deer skins, convertible to British trade goods.) On the other side, both South Carolina and Georgia cited the fear of rebellion as an excuse for their lack of enthusiasm for the revolution. They reported to the Continental Congress that their militias could not be counted upon to fight the British, because they were needed to prevent slave rebellion and flight.[26]

Loss claims filed by British Loyalists after the war opened a window onto the lives of African laborers in British East Florida. At least 38 claimants mentioned slaves, although not all claimed slaves as lost property. If these African laborers are typical, then most workers in British East Florida spent their lives on large plantations. Of the 1,493 slaves mentioned in these 38 claims, 1,038 (representing more than two out of every three) lived on plantations with 100 or more slaves. Overall, 92 of every 100 of the laborers mentioned in these East Florida Loyalist claims worked on plantations with a total of least 20 laborers. Only 15 workers-one percent-worked with two fellow slaves or fewer, and only three worked on a farm where they were the only slave around.[27]

Those on plantations with 100 or more workers were likely to find a permanent mate or spouse. For them the odds were no worse than three to two, with sex ratios ranging from 1.52 to 1.16. On the other hand, those who lived on farms with ten or fewer workers faced highly uneven sex ratios ranging as high as four men for every woman. For those in between, sex rations were far from ideal: seven men and 13 women worked on Alexander Paterson's farm, one woman and four men on Stephen White's farm. Two farms were home to two women workers each, three others to two men each. Only one had exactly one man and one woman laborer.[28]

Some African Americans underwent involuntary migration as the result of war. Two women named Sarah and Asserina, claimed by East Florida settler Mary Webb, were seized on a voyage to New York in 1779, when an American privateer raided their ship and took them to Boston. Rebels carried off a shipwright named Tom and a laborer named Jacob when they raided John Imrie's homestead in East Florida. In September 1776, American Rebels seized 30 blacks from Florida plantations, and an American Man of War seized 200 slaves from Georgia. In 1779, the British captured 200 Georgia slaves and brought them to St. Augustine. Some slaves lost their lives when their masters evacuated. Claims show that 42 of Denys Rolle's workers and at least three laborers claimed by Francis Levett died en route to new homes in the Caribbean.[29]

After the war, the Commission for Sequestered Estates in South Carolina advertised for runaways in the East Florida Gazette. He wrote that he had "received information that many negroes, the property of gentlemen of Carolina whose estates were sequestered in my hands, have made their escape to this province" between September 1780 and May 1783.[30]

Black and white refugees poured into East Florida before beginning the long process of evacuating in 1783, and many slaves profited from the ensuing confusion to give their masters the slip. As Table 1 shows, approximately 42 percent of all blacks in British East Florida—some 4,745 people—were unaccounted for at the conclusion of the evacuation. These totals include the handful of documented escapes, such as that of three laborers who fled Alexander Paterson's farm as he prepared to evacuate, and Francis Levett's 24-year old "compleat servant" named Monday, who refused to evacuate without his wife.[31]

After the war, Florida's new Spanish government recognized the continuing presence of African Americans in Indian country, and sought half-heartedly to eject or recover them for their owners. In 1781, in peace talks at Pensacola, the Spanish requested that Creeks and Seminoles return fugitive slaves. Again in September 1789, the Spanish asked "that all negroes, horses, goods and American citizens, taken by the Indians, should be restored." And, in1802, at the conclusion of hostilities with native warriors led by William Augustus Bowles, the Spanish sought to require Mikasukis and Seminoles to return blacks taken from Spanish owners during the conflict. For once, the Seminoles appeared to have complied: in September 1802, the Seminole leader Payne and Jack Kanard, the leader of the Hitchiti, met a Spanish official in the town of Mikasuki to turn over the blacks.[32]

DESTINATION	WHITES	BLACKS	TOTALS
Europe/England	246	35	281
Nova Scotia	725	155	880
Jamaica	196	714	910
Dominica	225	444	669
Bahamas	1,033	2,214	3,247
United States	462	2,561	3,023
Other Foreign	61	217	278
Did Not Depart	450	200	650
Missing	2,692	4,745	7,437
Total	6,090	11,285	17,375

The "Missing" category reflects estimates by Governor Patrick Tonyn and others that approximately 4,000 people fled to the north and west in early 1784. The racial composition of this back country group is unknown. My estimate for missing blacks is computed by subtracting the number of blacks who remained or were reported as leaving East Florida for known destinations from the total who were resident in East Florida. Other estimates are taken from British emigration reports in Siebert, 1: 168, 174, 208.

In Georgia, meanwhile, African laborers continued to make their way into Indian country, slipping away sometimes silently and occasionally after a fire fight. The *Georgia Gazette* of May 1, 1788 reported that, in Savannah, "a few Negroes, belonging to Mr. Girardeau, were carried off from Liberty County, by the Indians, the beginning of last week.[33]

Although the record furnishes little direct information about the lives of African Americans in Seminole country, certain inferences can be drawn. For example, once African Americans had lived in freedom among the Creeks and Seminoles, slave traders considered them a poor business risk, because— even when captured and re enslaved— they were extremely likely to run away. In 1794, the Panton Leslie Co. was sued when slaves shipped from Florida escaped from their New Orleans buyer, who sought reimbursement under Spanish law. When William Panton learned he might have to make good the loss, he expressed his frustration: "Pray was it not made known to the purchaser that the negroes were from the Indian Country[?]"[34]

Panton's comment sets blacks living in Seminole country apart from all others. Clearly, Panton's remark reflects his awareness that "negroes . . . from the Indian country" were likely to escape, and that a prudent trader would protect himself by disclosing their origin to a subsequent buyer.

Panton's comment further reveals his awareness of two realities. First, he was familiar with the everyday conditions of life for blacks among the Seminoles. Native American and African American villages extended from near St. Augustine to west of the Apalachicola River. Blacks lived in habitations similar to those of their Indian hosts, surrounded by fields of up to 20 acres. They dressed like the Seminoles, owned and used hunting rifles, and planted their fields in common as the native peoples did. Although some blacks were in submissive relationships to Indians, it is misleading to describe the relationships as slavery in the sense understood by Americans in the early 19th century. In some cases, these blacks merely shared their harvests with a dominant village, such as a tributary native village would do with its dominant neighbors.[35]

Panton also knew that many of these black Seminoles had not themselves escaped from plantation slavery, but were the children, grandchildren and even great-grandchildren of refugees. Capture would bring not the bitterness of slavery's return, but the shock of its first impression. It is hardly surprising that African American people who had grown up freely on Seminole lands would reject a life of slavery. What is significant is Panton's recognition that a competent slave dealer would protect his company's interest by acknowledging the deep hunger for freedom that such people had acquired.

If blacks in Seminole country were a high-risk business for William Panton, they were also a danger to the leaders of the new United States. The growth of settlements of runaways in conjunction with Indians, tolerable when Florida was a remote frontier, became unacceptable as American settlers drew near. During the period between the Revolutionary War and the War of 1812, such enclaves drew the attention of President George Washington, who noted them in his diary of 1791. The issue further occupied his secretary of State, Thomas Jefferson, and was an element of this first treaty signed by the new United States government in 1790.[36]

Florida's attractiveness to runaways increased during the first two decades of the 19th century. During the War of 1812, the British attempted to entice slaves way from their American masters, offering them two alternatives— a job in a British regiment, or freedom, transportation to new homes, and free land. Many accepted: more than 60 abandoned the East Florida plantation of the American John Forbes, sailing on a British ship to Bermuda.[37]

After the war, British agents continued to undermine the United States by helping the Seminoles and their African American allies. About 1,000 escaped slaves and Native Americans lived along the banks of the Apalachicola River between Apalachicola Bay and the Georgia border, near a fort which the British had conveniently abandoned, fully armed and equipped. The maroons cultivated the fields on either side of the stronghold, known as the Negro Fort, for 50 miles on both sides of the river. Living in the fort or nearby were about 100 men and 200 women and children.[38]

The world of Florida maroons fell into eclipse on the morning of July 27, 1816, when the powder magazine of the Negro Fort exploded. United States Naval personnel bombarded the fort at five a.m., aiming for the maroon village located just behind it. When the fort exploded, the Naval officers in charge promptly took the credit; glowing reports expressed amazement at their lucky shot, although the Army version cautiously attributed the explosion to causes unknown. The Naval reports also contain evidence for the possibility that the blacks, themselves, were responsible for the destruction of the fort. Their leader, an African American man named Garson, threatened to destroy the fort if he could not hold it.[39]

One thing the military did destroy was the hopes of the maroons. For several years, Garson and the other maroons had invested their labor and dreams in an experimental, multicultural world. These marginalized people lived in a self-governing society of their own making, developing sufficient social order to plant and harvest a field crop. The maroons' population had grown; they were living in family groups, and their children were growing up in a richer, freer life than their parents had known. In the siege before the explosion, the military destroyed their crops, trained 18-pounders on their stronghold, and made it impossible to leave or enter the fort.[40]

After the explosion, black and native peoples reestablished themselves precariously in the area between the Suwanee and the Apalachicola Rivers. More raids followed in 1818, causing the black population of north Florida to decline to approximately 430. By the mid 1830s, the number of African Americans living with Seminoles was estimated to have climbed to 800, of whom 150 were men and 650 were women and children. Since many in this population had a motive to remain in hiding, official estimates are probably low.[41]

The explosive destruction of the Negro Fort, then, serves as a violent punctuation point separating two epochs. After that point, the Muscogulge in North Florida were as good as "annihilated," in the words of trader James Innerarity, and so were their free black allies. White American settlers flowed in, established hegemony, and pushed the surviving native-black alliance southward. The cycle of American economic expansion, black escape, and native resistance began again, clashing in the violence of the Second Seminole War. Within a few years, involuntary laborers picked cotton on lands where native peoples and free blacks once had lived very different kinds of lives.[42]

Patrick Riordan, who will receive his Ph.D. from Florida State University in August, is a lecturer in American Studies and History at Middlesex University, London.

1. The fear of a native-African alliance led colonists to ban Indian traders from using African Americans as laborers in Indian country. For the Georgia statute, see *An Act for Maintaining the Peace with the Indians in the Province of Georgia,* January 9, 1734, British Public Record Office, Colonial Office, Class 5, piece 681 (hereinafter CO5/681) f. 34. Similarly, in April 1758, South Carolina colonists refused a Cherokee offer to trade two French POWs for black slaves, because of the policy against Indians owning slaves. Ludovick Grant, "Historical Relation of Facts Delivered by Ludovick Grant, Indian Trader, to His Excellency, the Governor of South Carolina," *South Carolina Historical and Genealogical Magazine* 10 (January 1909) 54-69, as cited in R. Halliburton, Jr., *Red over Black: Black Slavery Among the Cherokee Indians,* Contributions in Afro-American and African Studies 27, ed. Hollis R. Lynch (Westport, CT: 1977), 10.
2. Peter Wood expressed the ambiguity facing escaping African Americans in these terms: "The prospect of total absorption into a compatible culture had to be balanced against the risk of betrayal, captivity, or death." Peter H. Wood, Black Majority: Negroes in Colonial South Carolina from 1670 Through the Stono Rebellion (New York, 1975), 230-31. For the harsh conditions slaves experienced while escaping, see Daniel L. Schafer, "'Yellow Silk Ferret Tied Round Their Wrists:' African Americans in British East Florida, 1763-

1784," in *The African American Heritage of Florida,* eds. David R. Colburn and Jane L. Landers (Gainesville, FL., 1995), 93.

3. David Richardson, "The British Slave Trade to Colonial South Carolina," *Slavery and Abolition,* 12 (December 1991) 3, 125-171, esp. Table 2 and p. 160; Philip D. Morgan, "Colonial South Carolina Runaways: Their Significance for Slave Culture," *Slavery and Abolition,* 6 (December 1985) 60; "An Account of the Negroe Insurrection in South Carolina," *Colonial Records of the State of Georgia* (hereinafter CRG) v. 22, part 2, 1737-1740, 232-236; John K. Thornton, "African Dimensions of the Stono Rebellion," *American Historical Review* 96:4 (October 1991), 1102; Betty Wood, *Slavery in Colonial Georgia 1730-1775* (Athens, GA, 1984), 173.
4. Edward Randolph to Council of Trade and Plantations, March 16, 1699, CO5/1258, ff. 88-89v; Lords Proprietors of Carolina to Governor James Colleton, March 3, 1687, CO5/288, ff. 53v-54; Lords Proprietors of Carolina to Governor James Colleton, London, December 2, 1689, CO5/288, f. 81. It is likely that the ten slaves of whom Governor Quiroga wrote were the survivors of the 13 taken from Governor Morton's estate. Two of the slaves are said to have escaped from the Spanish and returned to Governor Morton. Another may have died in the storm which killed the Spaniard, DeLeon, who seized them. It is also possible that the ten slaves were true runaways who arrived in September 1687. Juan Marques Cabrera a Su Majestad, April 15, 1685, as cited in Herbert E. Bolton and Mary Ross, *The Debatable Land: A Sketch of the Anglo-Spanish Contest for the Georgia Country* (1925, reprint; New York, 1968), 40; John J. TePaske, "The Fugitive Slave: Intercolonial Rivalry and Spanish Slave Policy, 1687-1764," in Samuel Proctor, ed., *Eighteenth-Century Florida and its Borderlands* (Gainesville, FL, 1975), 3. See also "William Dunlop's Mission to St. Augustine in 1688," *South Carolina Historical and Genealogical Magazine* 34 (January 1933) 24, 3.
5. Archivo General de Indias, Santo Domingo (Audencia de Santo Domingo), Legajo 842. Carta del gobernador de la Florida al rey, November 2, 1725, as cited in TePaske, "The Fugitive Slave," 3; Jane Landers, "Gracia Real de Santa Teresa de Mose: A Free Black Town in Spanish Colonial Florida," *American Historical Review* 95 (1990) 14-15; Robert LaBret Hall, "'Do, Lord, Remember Me:' Religion and Cultural Change Among Blacks in Florida, 1565-1906" (Ph.D. diss., Florida State University, 1984) 26-7.
6. Mark F. Boyd, "Diego Peña's Expedition to Apalachee and Apalachicola in 1716," *Florida Historical Quarterly* 28 (July 1949) 2-4.
7. William Bartram wrote that the Muscogulges believed that their ancestors had migrated eastward in the mid-17th century, reaching the Ocmulgee River in central Georgia in the 1680s. Basing his accounts on elderly male oral informants, Bartram wrote that the Muscogulge first contacted the Spanish. After receiving abuse, "[t]hey joined their arms with the Carolinians," defeated native peoples allied with Spain, "and in the end proved the destruction of the Spanish colony of East Florida." Bartram, "Observations on the Creek and Cherokee Indians," in Gregory A. Waselkov and Kathleen E. Holland Braund, eds., *William Bartram on the Southeastern Indians* (Lincoln, NE, 1995), 140. For a later version, heavily edited after Bartram's death, see *Transactions of the American Ethnological Society* V. III., Part 1. For the burning of Coweta and Cassita, see Mattheos to Cabrera, Caveta, January 12, 1686; San Luis, March 14, 1686; San Luis, March 14,

1868, and Cabrera to the Viceroy, March 19, 1686, as cited in Bolton and Ross, *The Debatable Land,* 51. For the movement to the Oconee and Ochese Creeks, see Crane, *Southern Frontier,* 35-36.

8. [Thomas Nairne], *A Letter from South Carolina; Giving an Account of the Soil, Air;* Product, Trade, Government, Laws, Religion, People, Military Strength, &c., of That Province; Together with the Manner and necessary Charges of Settling a Plantation there, *and the* Annual profit *it will produce. Written by a Swiss Gentlemen, to his Friend at Bern* (London, 1710), 33-35.

9. Col. Robert Quarry to the Council on Trade and Plantations, May 30, 1704, CO324/5, f. 51; Crane, *The Southern Frontier,* 80, 161; James Adair, *The History of American Indians* (1775, original; 1930, reprint; Samuel Cole Williams, ed., Nashville, TN, 1971), 277; Alexander Moore, ed., Nairne's *Muskhogean Journals:* The 1708 Expedition to the Mississippi River (Jackson, MS, 1988), 14. John Hann has noted discrepancies in published versions of letters from Moore in 1704. From these and his readings of various Spanish sources, Hann doubts that Moore captured many more than 1,000 native slaves. John H. Hann, *Apalachee: The Land Between the Rivers* (Gainesville, FL, 1988), 279. For the growing number of Indian slaves in Carolina, see Letter from the Governor and Council of Carolina [to the Board of Trade], September 17, 1708, CO5/1264 ff. 152-54, also Verner W. Crane, *The Southern Frontier 1670-1732* (1928; reprint, New York), 113, and Wood, *Black Majority,* 143-45.

10. Letter from the Lords Proprietors of Carolina . . . relating to the massacre in North Carolina, St. James' Square, December 4, 1711, CO5/1265 f. 247; Wood, *Black Majority,* 144; *Journal of the Commissioners of the Indian Trade* (1955; reprint, Columbia, SC, 1992), September 12, 1710 1:4, July 27, 1711,1:11; David Crawley to William Byrd, July 30, 1715, CO5/1265, f.2; Lords Proprietors of Carolina to the Council of Trade and Plantations, June 4, 1717, CO5/1265, ff. 133-34; Copies of Certificates from Col. Robert Daniel, Deputy Governor of South Carolina, August 13, 1716, CO5/1265, f. 94; John H. Hann; "St. Augustine's Fallout from the Yamassee War," *Florida Historical Quarterly* 68 (October 1989), 180-200; Bolton and Ross, *The Debatable Land,* 57-63, Crane, *The Southern Frontier,* 74-97.

11. C. O. Maps, North American Colonies General 7, *c.* 1722; Copy of a Representation of the Lords Commissioners for Trade and Plantations to the King Upon the State of His Majesty's Colonies and Plantations in the Continent of North America, September 8, 1721, Kings MSS 205 f. 39v; see also CO324/10, 296-431, and *Calendar of State Papers Colonial, American and W. I. 1720-1721,* 424-28.

12. Marcel Giraud, *A History of French Louisiana,* Vol. 1 *The Reign of Louis XIV, 1698-1715* Joseph C. Lambert, trans. (1953, translation; Baton Rouge, LA, 1974), 201-212; Daniel H. Thomas, *Fort Toulouse: The French Outpost at the Alabamas on the Coosa* (1960, reprint; Tuscaloosa, AL, 1989), 1; Barnwell to Nicholson, July 21, 1721, in *South Carolina Historical and Genealogical Magazine* 27 (October 1926), 189-203.

13. Crane, *Southern Frontier;* 241-44.

14. Thomas Geraldino to Duke to Newcastle, enclosure in Duke of Newcastle to the Council of Trade and Plantations, September 21, 1736, CO5/365, ff. 120-23.

15. The king lifted the labor requirement in 1740, and his successor, Ferdinand VI, broadened the policy to cover all Spanish provinces of the Americas in 1750. TePaske, "The Fugitive Slave," 5-7. For Georgia slavery laws, see *An Act for Rendering the* Colony *of Georgia more Defencible by Prohibiting the Impartation and use of Black Slaves or Negroes in the same,* January 9, 1734, PRO CO/5/681 ff. 39-44; Wood, *Slavery in Colonial Georgia,* 31. For commentary on likelihood of escapes, see Journal of the Earl of Egmont, February 20, 1738. *CRG 5:315:* Journal of William Stephens, December 15, 1738, *CRG* 4:248. For white Carolinians in early Georgia, see David R. Chesnutt, *South Carolina's Expansion into Colonial Georgia, 1720-1765* (New York, 1989), 56-9, 82, 125-26, 170-71, 211.
16. A Ranger's Report of Travels with General Oglethorpe, 1739-42, Stowe Manuscripts 792, British Library MSS Collection, f. 10v. The best accounts of the lives of blacks in Spanish and British Florida are those of Jane Landers, who has published two seminal articles: "Gracia Real de Santa Teresa de Mose," *American Historical Review* 95 (1990), 9-30, and "Spanish Sanctuary: Fugitives in Florida, 1687-1790," *Florida Historical Quarterly* 62 (January 1984), 296-313; and J. Leitch Wright, "Blacks in British East Florida," *Florida Historical Quarterly* 54 (April 1976), 425-442.
17. Journal of William Stephens, December 15, 1738, in *Colonial Records of the State of Georgia,* IV, 247-48; Charles C. Jones, *The History of Georgia,* (Boston, 1883) v. 2, p. 300, as cited in Chatelaine, *Defenses of Spanish Florida;* James Glen, Answers of James Glen, Esq., Governor of South Carolina, to the Queries Proposed by the Lords of Trade, 1749, Kings MSS 205, f. 302v.
18. In 1775, Gen. William Shirley instructed officials to offer "Certain Rewards" to Southern Indians in exchange for the scalps of Britain's enemies. General William Shirley to His Majesty's Principal Secretary of War, New York, December 20, 1775, WO1/4, ff. 5-9. In 1721, South Carolina colonists offered the Creeks four blankets and two guns for every slave captured beyond the Oconee River, half as much for those found closer to home, and if only the head could be provided, one blanket, redeemable at any trader. Wood, *Black Majority,* 260-61. For test of talk comparing rope and chains, see Answer of the Indian Chiefs of the Cherokee Nation, September 9, 1730, CO5/4, part 2, ff. 215-16. See also Crane, *Southern Frontier;* 300, and Tom Hatley, *The Dividing Paths: Cherokees and South Carolinians Through the Era of Revolution* (New York, 1993), 103-04.
19. The Journal of Antoine Bonnefoy, 1741-42, describes a European's experience of Cherokee slavery. It can be found in Newton D. Mereness, ed., *Travels in the American Colonies* (New York, 1916), 241-260, and Samuel Cole Williams, ed., *Early Travels in the Tennessee Country, 1540-1800* (Johnson City, 1928). See also Theda Perdue, *Slavery and the Evolution of Cherokee Society* (Knoxville, TN 1979 3-18, and Gregory Evans Dowd, *A Spirited Resistance: The North American Indian Struggle for Unity, 1745-1815* (Baltimore, 1992), 13.
20. Fenwicke Bull, Journal of the Proceedings of the Southern Congress at Augusta from the Arrival of the Several Governors at Charles Town South Carolina the 1st October to their Return to the Same Place etc. the November 21, 1763, CO5/65, part 3, ff. 51v-52, 55v-57; John Stuart to Lord George Germain, Pensacola, September 15, 1777, CO5/79, No. 19, p. 13.

21. Copy of a Talk from the Seminollie Indians dated Flint River 3d September 1777, in Stuart to Germain CO5/79, f. 37.
22. Betty Wood cited the Georgia *Gazette* of November 22, 1769, for the escape of two women— Minda, 20 and Esther, 21— who escaped from Governor Wright's Ogeechee plantation, crossed the Ogeechee River, and were believed to have joined "a parcel of Mr. Elliot's Negroes who have been runaway for some time." Wood, *Slavery in Colonial Georgia,* 173.
23. The increase included working slaves but not escapees. Charles Loch Mowat, *East Florida as a British Province* 1763-1784 (Berkeley, CA, 1943), 8, 126.
24. Report of an Inspection Tour Made by Lieutenant-Colonel James Robertson late 1763, CO5/540 ff. 36-51; Carita Doggett Corse, *Dr. Andrew Turnbull and the New Smyrna Colony of Florida* (Jacksonville, FL, 1919), 14. For black settlements between the Suwanee and Apalachicola Rivers, see Laurence Foster, "Negro-Indian Relationships in the Southeast" (Ph.D. thesis, University of Pennsylvania, 1935), 20.
25. Moultrie to Lord Hillsborough, June 29, 1771, CO5/552, ff. 55-56v (erroneously cited as CO5/551 in Schafer, "African Americans in British East Florida," 93; see also 73); Wilbur Henry Siebert, *Loyalists in East Florida 1774 to 1785, The Most Important Documents Pertaining Thereto Edited with* an *Accompanying Narrative,* 2 vols. (Deland, FL, 1929), 2: 20-21. The originals of most of this material can be found in the British Public Record Office in Audit Office Class 12, piece 3. Citations will include a Siebert page number and an AO12/3 folio number where available. AO 12/3 ff. 13-18.
26. W. C. Ford, ed., *Journals of the Continental Congress* 13:385, as cited in Herbert Aptheker, *America Negro Slave Revolts (1943,* 5th ed., New York, 1987), 22; Charles Lee to John Hancock, July 2, 1776, Conference with the Georgia Delegation, *The Lee Papers,* Vol. 2, Collections of the New York Historical Society for the Year 1872 (New York, 1873), 115; Thomas Brown to the Superintendent, Chechaws, September 29, 1776, CO5/78, ff. 34-77b.
27. Siebert, *Loyalists in East Florida,* 2, *passim.*
28. Author's analysis of Loyalist data.
29. Siebert, 2: 371,229, 61-2, 104, 162 (AO12/3 ff. 186v-'95v, 45, 75-7); Robert Rae to Samuel Thomas, May 3, 1776, CO5/77: 269-71, ff. 137-138v; Letter from Governor Patrick Tonyn to John Stuart, St. Augustine, December 20, 1779, CO5/559, pp. 211-15, ff. 106-108v.
30. *East Florida Gazette,* May 3, 1783.
31. Siebert, 1: 127-28, 232 (AO12/3 ff. 91-94, 186v-195v).
32. Albert James Pickett, *History of Alabama and Incidentally of Georgia and Mississippi from the Earliest Period,* 2nd ed. (Charleston, SC, 1851), Vol. 2, 61, 98; Juan Ventura Morales to Miguel Cayentano soler. Nueva Orleans, 30 Septiembre 1802, Archivo General de Indias, (Baltimore, 1979), pp. 1-30, Santo Domingo 2645, fo. 177; Vicente Folch to Governor and Captain General, [Fuerte San Marcos de Apalache], 10 septiembre 1802, AGI, Santo Domingo 2569, ff. 662.
33. *The Gazette of the State of Georgia,* No. 275, Thursday, May 1, 1788, Savannah, PRO AO13/36A, 2.

34. G[uillermo] Butler to William Panton, New Orleans, March 19, 1794, University of South Florida Library, Special Collections, Cruzat Papers, MSS file 93-2; William Panton to [John Forbes], Pensacola, March 30, 1794, Cruzat Papers, MSS 93-2; Don Bartolome Fabre Daunoy Vs. Don Guillermo Butler, March 20, 1794, Judicial Records of the Spanish Cabildo, March 15, 1794 to April 7, 1794, microfilm: LDS #1290483, Roll #242.
35. Joshua R. Giddings, *The Exiles of Florida, or, the Crimes Committed by Our Government* Against the Maroons, Who Fled from South Carolina and Other Slave States, Seeking *Protection Undo, Spanish Laws* (Columbus, OH, 1858), 97; William Hayne Simmons, *Notices of East Florida* (1822, reprint; Gainesville, FL, 1973), 44, 76; Richard Price, ed., *Maroon Societies: Rebel Slave Communities in the Americas*, 2d. ed. *passim;* Herbert Aptheker, "Maroons Within the Present Limits of the United States," in Price, *Maroon Societies,* 151-167; Jack D. Forbes, *Black Africans and Native Americans: Color, Race and Caste in the Evolution of Red-Black Peoples* (London, 1988), 62; Rebecca Bateman, "Africans and Indians: A Comparative Study of the Black Caribs and Black Seminole," *Ethnohistory* 37 (Winter 1990), 3; Kenneth Wiggins Porter, "Negroes and the Seminole War, 1817-1818," in *Four Centuries of Southern Indians,* edited by Charles Hudson (Athens, GA, 1975), 160-61.
36. John C. Fitzpatrick, ed., *The Diaries of George Washington, 1748-1799* (Boston, 1925), May 20, 1791, 4:180-81; Thomas Jefferson to Jose Ignacio de Viar, October 27, 1790, Jefferson Papers, Library of Congress, as cited in *Diaries of Washington,* 4: *n.* 1,181. See Treaty of New York, 1790, between the United States and the Creek Nation.
37. Sebastian Kindelán y Oregón to Rear Admiral George Cockburn, January 31, 1815 WO 1/144:31-32, as cited in William S. Coker and Thomas D. Watson, Indian Traders of the Southeastern Spanish Borderlands: Panton, Leslie & Company *and John Forbes & Company, 1783-1847* (Gainesville, FL, 1986), 292; Kindelán to Thomas Llorente, St. Augustine, February 25, 1815, bundle 150G12, microfilm reel 62, East Florida Papers, Library of Congress (hereinafter, EFP); Llorente to Kindelán, San Nicolas, February 26, 1815, bundle 150G12, reel 62, EFP.
38. Patterson to Secretary of Navy, New Orleans, August 15, 1816; John Lee Williams, *A View of West Florida* (1827, reprint; Gainesville, FL, 1976), 98.
39. Lt. Col. D. L. Clinch wrote to his commanding officer that "The black chief heaped much abuse on the Americans and said he had been left in command of the fort by the British government, and that he would sink any American vessels that should attempt to pass it; and blow up the fort if he could not defend it." D. L. Clinch to Col. R. Butler, Adjutant General, Camp Crawford, August 2, 1816, *Army and Navy Chronicle* 2:115, microfilm: American Periodical Series 1800-1850 A85 775 Vols. 1-2, Reel 469. The official account of the "lucky shot" version is that of Jairus Loomis: "At 4 A.M., on the morning of the 27th, we began warping the gun-vessels to a proper position; at 5, getting within gun-shot, the fort opened upon us, which we returned, and after ascertaining our real distance with cold shot, we commenced with hot . . ., *first* [emphasis in original] one of which, entering their magazine, blew up and completely destroyed the fort." J. Loomis to Commodore Patterson, U. S. Gun-vessel No. 149, Bay St. Louis, August 13, 1816, in American State Papers: Foreign Relations (Washington, DC, 1834), 559-60. Rebutting the "lucky shot" theory is a letter published by the *Savannah Republican* (reprinted by the

National Intelligencer), and apparently written by Col. Clinch. It is signed "C," is accompanied by copies of personal letters to Cal. Clinch, and offers a defense of Clinch's role. The letter states, "The commandant was requested to fire a few shots in order to ascertain the distance with more accuracy, and the practicability of bettering them from that point— four or five shots were accordingly fired, when the explosion took place; from what cause is unknown— opinions on that source are varied." "The Negro Fort in Florida," *National Intelligencer,* April 27, 1819, Library of Congress Photo duplication Service, Microfilm Reel 25. Adding to the improbability of a lucky shot in the predawn darkness is the uncertain distance of the bombardment. While some sources placed the Naval gun not far from the fort, one account located it at a distance of two miles away. Item entitled "New Orleans, Aug. 16," *National Intelligencer* September 18, 1816, Reel 20.

40. John D. Milligan, "Slave Rebelliousness and the Florida Maroon," *Prologue* 6 (Spring 1974): 7.

41. One source, with an obvious anti-British bias, states that the British were responsible for transporting 300-400 blacks from Louisiana to the Apalachicola River after losing the War of 1812. Deposition of Samuel Jervais, May 9, 1815, as cited in John W. Monette, *History of the Discovery and Settlement of the Valley of the Mississippi by the Three Great European Powers Spain, France and Great Britain,* and *the Subsequent* Occupation, Settlement and Extension of Civil Government by the United States *Until the Year 1846,* Vol. 1, (New York, 1848), 88. Another possibility, supported by military correspondence of Andrew Jackson, is that the African Americans were runaways from East Florida, Georgia and Carolina. Andrew Jackson to Governor of Pensacola, April 23, 1816, *ASPFR* 4499. See also James Grant Forbes, *Sketches Historical and Geographical of the Florida; More Particularly of East Florida* (1821, reprint; Gainesville, FL, 1964), 121. For the extent of fields cultivated by runaways, see Monette, 90, and Williams, *A View of West Florida,* 98, 101-02. For population estimates, see Horatio Dexter to His Excellency William P. Duval, Governor and Superintendent of Indian Affairs of the Territory of Florida, St. Augustine, August 20, 1823, in Letters Received by the Secretary of War Relating to Indian Affairs, 1800-1823, S-4 (Microform, Library of Congress Publication M27-1, frame 508); and John T. Sprague *The Origin, Progress and Conclusion of the Florida War* (New York, 1848), 19.

42. James Innerarity to John Forbes, Mobile, August 12, 1815, in "The Panton Leslie Papers," *Florida Historical Quarterly* 12 (January 1934), 127.

4

Refuge Among Native Americans

George Klos's article succinctly describes the three-way relationship among whites, Native Americans, and African-Americans in the Jacksonian Era. In the new territorial days of Florida (1821-1845), and in the wake of General Andrew Jackson's incursions into the Spanish lands in 1816 and 1818, it became clear to Seminoles and blacks that the American policy of Indian removal would possibly end their mutual, small measure of autonomy and opportunity in the territory. In this regard, Klos's study is particularly significant for illustrating how blacks struggled to preserve whatever freedom they had or hoped to aspire to at the very time in Florida's history when it transformed into a bona fide slave society, with its harsh, all- encompassing, and exploitative racial codes and culture.

When Jackson became the first territorial governor of U.S. Florida, he simply continued his slavemaster's determination to punish and recapture escaped slaves—Klos states that at least 400 blacks resided in Seminole communities at the time Jackson raised the American flag in the former Spanish possession. Jackson's tenure in Florida proved short-lived, but his successor as governor, William P. DuVal, quickly solidified and even expanded Jackson's official policy of removing Indians from the "rich soil" of Florida. As a result, blacks faced both the loss of Seminole allies in their freedom struggle and the thorny question of what role they should play in the white efforts at Indian removal: should they become integral players in the struggle to prevent Indian removal and thereby endanger their own freedom struggle, or should they pursue a separate path in an effort to protect their own well-being? In addressing these issues, the author also provides rich detail regarding the working alliances between blacks and Indians and the many ways African-Americans in territorial Florida sought to ensure and prolong their own tenuous hold on self-determination in the Jackson Era's new frontal attacks on people of color.

The author begins with the debatable proposition that the Seminoles, a marginalized people themselves, paradoxically owned and used black slaves in their communities, albeit more humanely than the white masters. The belief that Seminole slavery would be less harsh than American slavery led many African-Americans to flee white subjugation in hopes of a better life with the Indians of Florida. According to the author, some of these black Seminoles found sanctuary and opportunity among the Indians while others ended up as Indian "slaves," who were nevertheless treated better than the slaves of South Carolina and Georgia. Despite this "Florida distinction," it should be noted that slavery is slavery, and this is what the author may be accused of not fully accentuating.

During the Indian removal period, disputes between whites and Seminoles over the disposition of blacks overarched most of the era. What resulted were internecine disagreements between blacks and Seminoles that increasingly fractured their alliances of convenience. A particularly interesting point the author makes is that many black Seminoles served as trusted translators of white dispatches and meetings for the Seminoles, and that it was not unusual for black translators to provide inaccurate interpretations to Indian councils in attempts to further their own interests. If this were the case, then it underscores the creative ways blacks sought to secure and retain freedom in Florida over the centuries.

The author also makes an interesting point regarding the legal status (in white society) of Seminoles and blacks—they were more similar than dissimilar, leading to a camaraderie of the oppressed. Seminoles seldom submitted to legal summons outside their tribal lands because they anticipated white chicanery, especially in any white-mediation involving the custody of fugitive slaves. Government efforts to retrieve escaped slaves were often hampered by the personal motives of Indian agents—often themselves speculating in the slave trade—who acted as interlocutors between white and native leaders. As is frequently the case, self-interest overpowered probity. As President Andrew Jackson pursued his "Indian Removal" policy in the 1830s, black-Indian alliances in Florida faced new challenges in the reality of the U.S. determination to eliminate Indians from the Florida peninsula. This article shows how free and enslaved blacks faced the new dilemma.

This article carefully navigates a complicated series of motivations and relationships that had as much to do with the freedom struggle of black Floridians as any other event in the period between 1821 to 1845, save the rise of chattel slavery. The author is clear in arguing that Seminoles, for many reasons, protected and provided varying degrees of refuge for blacks in Florida, even through such nefarious practices as slavery. For their part, blacks found many reasons to ally with Indians, a situation that became palpably strained as Jacksonian Era officials increasingly pursued a policy of Indian Removal from "white lands." Moreover, like most good scholarship, this article raises important questions regarding the dynamics of black life with the Indians. For instance, how did intermarriage affect a black slave's status in Seminole society? Did the children of miscegenation inherit the status of their parents or the traditional status of free Seminoles? Did Seminoles fear losing slaves to unprincipled whites or did they actually fear losing in-laws and relatives? If the Seminoles did not see African-Americans as anything other than slaves, why did they allow them to create distinct "Negro towns" in Indian Territory and permit uncounted blacks to rise in the Seminole social and political hierarchy?

In the end, these types of historical inquiries, like the ones raised in the preceding three chapters, further complicate any understanding of black "refuge" and status in Florida and how those issues affected the black freedom struggle. Nevertheless, digested in tandem with the past analyses, readers should certainly gain important insight into the momentous and continuous struggle for black freedom in the long years from colony to statehood.

FURTHER READING

Wilton M. Krogman, "The Racial Composition of the Seminole Indians of Florida and Oklahoma," *Journal of Negro History*, Vol. 19 (1934);

Kenneth W. Porter, "Notes on Seminole Negroes in The Bahamas," *Florida Historical Quarterly*, Vol. 24 (1945-1946);

John M. Goggin, "The Seminole Negroes of Andros Island, Bahamas," *Florida Historical Quarterly*, Vol. 24 (1946);

Kenneth Wiggins Porter, "The Negro Abraham," *Florida Historical Quarterly*, Vol. 25 (1946);

Kenneth W. Porter, *Negro on the American Frontier* (1971);

James E. Sefton, "Black Slaves, Red Masters, White Middlemen: A Congressional Debate of 1852," *Florida Historical Quarterly*, Vol. 51 (1972);

John D. Milligan, "Slave Rebelliousness and the Florida Maroons," *Prologue*, Vol. 6 (1974);

Kenneth Wiggins Porter, "Africans and Seminoles: From Removal to Emancipation," *Pacific Historical Review*, Vol. 48 (1979);

Kenneth Wiggins Porter, "Africans and Creeks: From the Colonial Period to the Civil War," *Florida Historical Quarterly*, Vol. 59 (1980);

Elliot J. Gorn, "Black Spirits: The Ghostlore of Afro-American Slaves," *American Quarterly*, Vol. 36 (1984);

George Klos, *Black Seminoles in Territorial Florida* (1990);

Kenneth W. Porter, *The Black Seminoles: History of a Freedom-Seeking People* (1996);

Cheryl Race Boyett, *The Seminole-Black Alliance during the Second Seminole War, 1835-1842* (1996);

Martha Condray, "The Introduction of African Slavery into the Creek Indian Nation," *Georgia Historical Quarterly*, Vol. 22 (1998);

Claudio Saunt, "'The English Has Now a Mind to Make Slaves of Them All': Creeks, Seminoles, and the Problem of Slavery," *American Indian Quarterly*, Vol. 22 (1998);

Edward Twyman, *The Black Seminole Legacy and North American Politics, 1693-1845* (1999);

Rosalyn Howard, *The Promised Island: Reconstructing History and Identity among the Black Seminoles of Andros Island, Bahamas* (1999);

Rosalyn Howard, *Black Seminoles in the Bahamas* (2002);

Joe Knetsch, *Florida's Seminole Wars, 1817-1858* (2003).

Blacks and the Seminole Removal Debate, 1821-1835

George Klos

The Florida Historical Quarterly, Volume 68, issue 1 (1989), 55-78.

The rise of Jacksonian democracy in the United States during the 1820s and 1830s led to a national program of Indian displacement for the benefit of white settlers and land speculators. Disputes between whites and Indians over the possession of black slaves was a very prominent feature of Indian removal from Florida. Unlike Indian removal in other parts of the United States, land was not the main issue; thousands of acres of public land could be had in Florida without dispossessing the Seminoles. Mediation of white-Seminole slave disputes failed, in part, because the federal Indian agents often owned and speculated in slaves themselves and thus were compromised by personal interests. Also, many blacks worked for the Seminoles as influential interpreters and advisors.

Even before the acquisition of Florida by the United States in 1821, blacks were involved in white-native conflicts. The combination of blacks and Seminoles was important in the international affairs of the region, from the 1810-1814 plot to take East Florida from the Spanish by force, to the 1816 Negro Fort incident on the Apalachicola River and Andrew Jackson's Florida campaign of 1818.[1] After 1821, the problems between whites, Seminoles, and black allies of the Seminoles changed from an international issue to an internal one; the Florida Indians could now be dealt with unilaterally by the Americans.

Settlers coming into Florida found, according to a correspondent in *Niles' Weekly Register*, "the finest agricultural district within the limits of the United States." He described the area between the Suwannee and St. Johns rivers as "combining the advantages of a mild and healthy climate, a rich soil, and convenient navigation."[2] William P. DuVal, Jackson's successor as territorial governor of Florida, warned Secretary of War John C. Calhoun that "it will be a serious misfortune to this Territory if the Indians are permitted to occupy this tract of country." DuVal recommended moving the Indians of Florida to the domain of the Creeks, "to whom they properly belong," or to land west of the Mississippi River.[3] Writing to Florida Indian agent John R. Bell, Calhoun noted, "The government expects that the Slaves who have run away or been plundered from our Citizens or from Indian tribes within our limits will be given up peaceably by the Seminole Indians when demanded." Calhoun instructed Bell to convince the Seminoles either to join the Creeks or "to concentrate . . . in one place and become peaceable and industrious farmers."[4]

Governor DuVal, along with Florida planters James Gadsden and Bernard Segui, met with Indian representatives in September 1823 at Moultrie Creek south of St. Augustine. The Seminoles agreed to cede their land in north Florida to the United States and to receive a large tract farther south with recognized boundaries. Part of the negotiations required the listing of Indian towns and a census of their inhabitants. Neamathla, the leader of the Seminole delegation, listed thirty-seven towns with 4,883 natives. He objected, however, according to Gadsden, to specifying "the number of negroes in the nation." [5]

The Moultrie Creek agreement reserved for the Seminoles the area from the Big Swamp along the Withlacoochee River south to the "main branch of the Charlotte [Peace] river," some fifteen to twenty miles inland from the coast. The Indians were to receive $5,000 per year for twenty years. Article seven bound the Indians to be "active and vigilant in preventing the retreating to, or passing through, of the district assigned them, of any absconding slaves, or fugitives from justice" and to deliver all such people to the agent and be compensated for their expenses.[6]

The United States government representatives, in their report accompanying the treaty, recommended that military posts be established around the contours of Indian country "to embody such a population within prescribed limits, and to conquer their erratic habits . . . [and to] further induce an early settlement of the country now open to the enterprise of emigrants."[7]

In giving up their north Florida land, the Indians were relinquishing an area of fertile soil, good rainfall, and temperate climate. Many of the early settlers migrated from elsewhere in the South and, with slaves that they brought with them, established cotton, sugar, and tobacco plantations and farms. Many Piedmont and Tidewater elites moved to Florida and created a new hierarchy in the territory.[8] Between 1825 and 1832, 433,751 acres of public land were sold in Florida. Some 5,000,000 acres were still available in 1833. The territorial Legislative Council, in an 1828 resolution to Congress, requested that the price per acre for public land be reduced to attract more settlers. The legislators argued it was a national security move to increase population.[9]

The 1830 census listed 34,730 Floridians, 15,501 of whom were slaves and 844 "free colored."[10] The Comte de Castelneau, a French visitor to Florida in the 1830s, observed the local planter as "accustomed to exercise absolute power over his slaves[;] he cannot endure any opposition to his wishes." Whites of modest means, he said, were "brought up from childhood with the idea that the Indians are the usurpers of the land that belongs to them, and even in times of peace they are always ready to go hunting savages rather than deer hunting. . . . [T]hese men know no other power than physical force, and no other pleasure than carrying out their brutal passions."[11]

Blacks living with the Seminoles became a point of contention for whites because the Seminole system of slavery was not as harsh or rigid as the Anglo-American system: a comparatively lenient system in such close proximity might offer slaves of whites an alternative that their owners could not tolerate. A Seminole was more a patron than master, for the Seminole slave system was akin to tenant farming. Blacks lived in their own villages near Indian villages and paid a harvest tribute consisting of a percentage of the yield from their fields to the chief. Blacks, an Indian agent reported, had "horses, cows, and hogs, with which the Indian owner never presumed to meddle."[12]

In the 1820s, there were approximately 400 blacks living with the Seminoles. Only about eighty could be identified as fugitive slaves. Jacob Rhett Motte, an army surgeon stationed in Florida in the 1830s, noted, "They had none of the servility of our northern blacks, but were constantly offering their dirty paws with as much hauteur, and nonchalance, as if they were conferring a vast deal of honor."[13] They could "speak English as well as Indian," the trader Horatio Dexter reported, "and feel satisfied with their situation. They have the easy unconstrained manner of the Indian but more vivacity, and from their understanding of both languages possess considerable influence with their masters."[14] Only a few black Seminoles were bilingual, and those who were became influential in Indian councils. Furthermore, much has been made of the "equality" of the black Seminoles, but it would be more accurate to say that some blacks were more equal than others. Seminole society had blacks of every status whether they were born free, the descendants of fugitives, or perhaps fugitives themselves. Some were interpreters and advisors of importance; others were warriors and hunters or field hands. Intermarriage with Indians further complicated black status. But even a black of low status among the Seminoles felt it was an improvement over Anglo-American chattel slavery.

People living near the Seminoles became acquainted with the Indians and their black interpreters usually through trade. Seminoles visited stores and plantations despite the legal prohibition on leaving the reservation. Blacks often crossed the prescribed boundaries, and some white-owned slaves had spouses and other relatives living in Indian country. John Philip, a middle-aged "chief negro" to King Philip, leader of an Indian band, had a wife living on a St. Johns River plantation. Luis Fatio was owned by Francis Philip Fatio, one of the most prominent planters in East Florida. Luis's first contact with the Seminoles was on the plantation. His older brother ran away to Indian country, and Luis learned one of the Indian languages during his brother's periodic visits to the slave quarters. One day Luis went on a visit to Seminole country and never returned.[15]

There were others like Luis. Alachua County slave owners estimated 100 runaways among the Seminoles, complaining that black Seminoles (the planters apparently saw a difference between them and runaways) "aided such slaves to select new and more secure places of refuge."[16] Owen Marsh visited several "Negro Villages" looking for runaways, and he noted that the number of runaway slaves among the Seminoles could not be determined "from the Circumstances of their being protected by the Indian Negroes. . . . [T]hese Indian Negroes are so artfull [sic] that it is impossible to gain any information relating to such property from them."[17]

Governor DuVal admonished the Seminoles in January 1826 for not returning runaway slaves. "You are not to mind, what the negroes say; they will lie, and lead you

Many runaway slaves from the north chose to live among the Seminole Indians of Florida. From the Stetson Kennedy collection.

astray, in the hope to escape from their white owners, and that you will give them refuge and hide them. Do your duty and give them up. They care nothing for you, further than to make use of you, to keep out of the hands of their masters." DuVal further rebuked the Indians telling them that "thus far the negroes have made you their tools, and gained protection, contrary to both justice and the treaty, and at the same time, laugh at you for being deceived by them. Your conduct in this matter is cause of loud, constant, and just complaint on the part of the white people. . . . Deliver them up, rid your nation of a serious pest, and do what, as honest men, you should not hesitate to do; then your white brothers will say you have done them justice, like honest, good men." Should the Seminoles refuse, DuVal warned, the army will take the blacks by force, "and in the confusion, many of you may lose your own slaves.[18]

Tuckose Emathla (John Hicks), a principal spokesman for the Indians, replied to DuVal's criticisms. "We do not like the story that our people hide the runaway negroes from their masters. It is not a true talk. . . . We have never prevented the whites from coming into our country and taking their slaves whenever they could find them and we will not hereafter oppose their doing so." At another meeting that year, Tuckose Emathla voiced the main Indian complaint regarding slaves. "The white people have got some of our negroes, which we expect they will be made to give up."[19]

Besides the black communities on Seminole land, other groups of blacks and Indians lived outside the treaty boundaries, and still others left Florida altogether. Owen Marsh, in his investigation of Seminole country, reported that many runaway slaves had departed for the Bahamas and Cuba, and a Darien, Georgia, slave owner complained to the secretary of war that his escaped slaves left Florida via "West India wreckers" working the Atlantic coast.[20] Two other settlements in southwest Florida were described by John Winslett who was tracking three slaves of a Georgia planter. He was told at Tampa Bay, "it would not be safe to pursue them much farther without force; that a band of desperadoes, runaways, murderers, and thieves (negroes and Indians, a majority runaway slaves)" lived on an island south of Charlotte Harbor. Blacks and Indians who had been there told Winslett of "another settlement of lawless persons (Indians and absconded slaves) on a creek between Manatia [Manatee] River and Charlotte's Harbor, some miles west of the latter."[21] The island community was a haven for some survivors of the Negro Fort incident on the Apalachicola River, and it existed up to the war for Seminole removal.[22] The residents cut timber and fished, shipping their goods to Havana where they were traded for rum and firearms. The Seminoles also traded with Cuban fishermen, and Indian agent Gad Humphreys reported that runaway slaves were shuttled to

Havana this way, sometimes for freedom and sometimes for sale.[23]

The legal mechanisms for settling slave disputes between whites and Indians failed. DuVal proposed that the government buy Seminole slaves, as individual whites were prohibited from slave trading with Indians, but he was told by Superintendent of Indian Affairs Thomas L. McKenney that agents should not involve themselves in slave trade with their charges. When whites took Indian slaves, Florida agents were instructed to use due process to get the slaves back. When Indians held slaves claimed by whites, the burden of proof was on the white. In accordance with the Moultrie Creek treaty, the Seminoles did return some runaway slaves, and in other cases, Humphreys explained to the representative of a Georgia slave owner, they welcomed investigation "by a competent tribunal."[24] For the most part, however, the Seminoles refused to surrender the slaves in question before the trial. "Their own negroes that have been taken from them are held by white people who refuse to dilliver [sic] them up," DuVal told the superintendent of Indian Affairs, "I have felt asshamed [sic] while urgeing [sic] the Indians to surrender the property they hold, that I had not power to obtain for them their own rights and property held by our citizens. . . . To tell one of these people that he must go to law for his property in our courts with a white man is only adding insult to injury."[25]

Indians resisted surrendering slaves to public (white) custody as a precondition for resolving disputes because they knew they had no rights in court. "The Indian, conscious of his rights, and knowing that he paid the money, though incapable of showing the papers executed under forms of law, as he had received none, and relying upon the honesty of the white man, protested most earnestly against these demands, and resolutely expressed a determination to resist all attempts thus to wrest from him his rightfully acquired property," explained John T. Sprague in his history of the Second Seminole War. "Deprived as they were of a voice in the halls of justice, the surrender of the negro at one dispossessed them, without the least prospect of ever getting him returned." The commander of the army post at Tampa Bay, Colonel George M. Brooke, observed in 1828 that "so many claims are now made on them, that they begin to believe that it is the determination of the United States to take them all. This idea is strengthened by the conversations of many of the whites, and which they have heard."[26]

Whites, however, saw it differently. Samuel Cook, Abraham Bellamy, and other planters complained that "whilst the Law furnishes to the Indians ample means of redress for the aggressions of Whitemen, we are Constrained to look with patience, whilst they possess and enjoy the property most justly and rightfully Ours." They also objected to being prevented from taking from Indian country "even those negroes that are unclaimed and unpossessed by the Indians."[27] Cook also voiced another frontier slave owner's complaint, that slaves purchased from the Seminoles often slipped back to Indian country. DuVal reported to Superintendent Thomas McKenney that "the persons who have been most clamorous about their claims on the Indians and their property are those who have cheated them, under false reports, of their slaves, who have since gone back to the Indians."[28] Alfred Beckley, an army lieutenant stationed in Florida in 1825, noted that planters sought any opportunity to use force against the Seminoles "so that the whites might possess themselves of many valuable negroes."[29]

DuVal favored withholding treaty annuities until the Indians returned runaway slaves, and the Indian Office did so in 1828, but later reversed the policy and forbade it in the future. Since some white claims were indisputable, DuVal said, the slave in question ought to be given by the Indians to the agent, or the owner "ought to receive the full value of him from the nation."[30] Local slave owners, however, advocated "adequate military force" to "recover pilfered property" from the Seminoles.[31]

If, in the critical role of the agents as mediators between Indians and frontier whites, "the success of the work depended upon the character of the man," then the agents assigned to the Seminoles exacerbated rather than allayed conflict.[32] Ample evidence shows that, contrary to orders, Gad Humphreys engaged in slave trade with his charges, and planters accused him of dragging his feet on their complaints about runaways. In one case, a woman in St. Marys, Georgia, claimed that a slave and the slave's children were living with the Seminoles. A man dispatched to retrieve them found it "next to an impossibility" to get them back due to the Seminoles' "natural reluctance to give it up and the wish of their agent to speculate."[33] "The negroes this man is after are ours, and the white people know it is so," said the subchief Jumper to Humphreys.[34] When Humphreys reported the Seminoles' determination not to allow the contested slaves out of their possession, interested parties petitioned Washington for an investigation, charging Humphreys with colluding with a local planter to prevent transfer of the slaves so that the claim would be abandoned with the passage of time and as expenses mounted.[35]

McKenney also received accusations that Humphreys had worked fugitive slaves on his own land for several months before returning them to their owners. Secretary of War Peter B. Porter informed President John Quincy Adams of allegations that Humphreys had "connived with the Indians in the concealment of runaway slaves, and in that way affected purchases of them himself, at reduced prices."[36]

Humphreys explained to Alex Adair, the investigator of the allegations, that he bought slaves from Indians so that claimants could prove ownership in court, an impossibility as long as the slaves were in Indian possession.[37] Adair concluded that while Humphreys probably did bill the government for sugar kettles installed on his land, the other charges were difficult to prove since "those who had been most clamorous appeared most disposed to evade the inquiry." Humphreys apparently had made reasonable settlements with his accusers when he learned that he was to be investigated. Zephaniah Kingsley, who claimed that Humphreys had held one of his slaves for over a year, "stated he had settled his business with the Agent in his own way. . . .[H]is property had been surrendered to him some months back and he cared no more about it."[38]

An Alachua County resident reported to Governor DuVal that Humphreys possessed blacks belonging to Indians, and that he bought Indian cattle with IOUs he later refused to honor. Humphreys was a liability, McKenney noted, because those opposing him in Florida "make his services in that quarter of but little, if any, use to the Government, whilst his dealing in slaves is in direct violation of an express order forbidding it." Both Governor DuVal and the territory's Congressional delegate Joseph White wanted Humphreys replaced, and he was dismissed in March 1830.[39]

Humphreys's slave problems continued. DuVal received complaints from Indians that Humphreys held their slaves. Humphreys's replacement, John Phagan, attempted to return the slaves, but Humphreys refused to release them unless Phagan was willing to purchase them.[40] In another case, stemming from his role as Indian agent, Humphreys sought government assistance in recovering two black men claimed by an Indian woman named Culekeechowa. She had inherited from her mother a slave named Caty, who later bore four children. Horatio Dexter, a trader, persuaded Culekeechowa's brother and Caty's husband to trade Caty and her two daughters and two sons in exchange for whiskey. Humphreys, as agent, agreed to help the Indian woman, so he went to St. Augustine where Dexter was offering the slaves for sale. Humphreys maintained that he had to buy them to prevent their sale to a Charleston buyer. But then, instead of returning them to Culekeechowa, he kept the slaves for himself. When the boys grew older and became aware of what had happened, they left for Seminole country in 1835.[41]

Slave disputes between Seminoles and whites frequently went unresolved because the interpreters in these negotiations sometimes were former slaves themselves. DuVal observed that Seminole blacks were "much more hostile to the white people than their masters," and were "constantly counteracting" advice to the Indians. In several instances, he said, chiefs had agreed to a white demand in council but later were talked out of compliance by their black advisors.[42] The problem, as Humphreys saw it in 1827, was that "the negroes of the Seminole Indians are wholy independent, or at least regardless of the authority of their masters; and are Slaves but in name." Indians considered blacks "rather as fellow Sufferers and companions in misery than as inferiors," Humphreys wrote, and the "great influence of the Slaves possess over their masters" enabled them to "artfully represent" whites as hostile to people of color.[43] The first step in moving the Seminoles out of Florida, DuVal told the commissioner of Indian Affairs in 1834, "must be *the breaking up of the runaway slaves and outlaw* Indians."[44]

When Andrew Jackson was elected president, public opinion in the South was demanding stricter control over Indians. Whites wanted land, of course, but they also saw Indians as possible allies of foreign powers (as in the War of 1812), and the presence of fugitive slaves among them was viewed as a threat to internal security. Jackson urged Indian removal legislation in his December 1829 annual message to Congress, and he tried to soothe opposition by assuring that removal would be voluntary and peaceful. In May 1830, Congress appropriated $500,000 for the negotiation of removal treaties. The territory north of Texas and west of Arkansas that was designated for resettlement was considered at the time the only available location where the Indians would not be in the way of white expansion. [45]

Floridians had been voicing removal sentiment since early in the territorial period.[46] As indicated in a message to Congress, the main reason for ousting the Seminoles from Florida never changed through the years. "A most weighty objection" to the presence of Indians in the territory was "that absconding slaves find ready security among the Indians and such aid is amply sufficient to enable them successfully to elude the best efforts by their masters to recover them."[47]

Territorial government wholeheartedly supported the white slave interests. The Legislative Council requested removal in July 1827, and Acting Governor James Westcott asked the council to strengthen the militia because "we have amongst us two classes who may possibly at some future period, be incited to hostility, and . . . it behooves us always to be prepared." He believed the only humane solution was to move the Indians away from whites and without their slaves.[48]

An 1826 Florida law to regulate Indian trade imposed the death penalty on anyone who "shall inveigle, steal, or carry away" any slave or "hire, aid, or counsel" anyone to do so. That this section— which does not mention Indians— appears in a bill relating to Indian trade shows slave owners' concern over the black Indian connection. In 1832, the territory prohibited "Indian negroes, bond or free," from traveling outside the Indian boundaries. Also, in light of the Gad Humphreys episodes, the council set limits to the amount of the reward Indian agents could collect for capturing runaway slaves, established accounting requirements in slave cases, and required agents to advertise fugitive slaves in their custody.[49]

In January 1832, Secretary of War Lewis Cass instructed James Gadsden, Florida planter and Jackson supporter, to arrange a treaty with the Seminoles agreeing to their removal west to the new Creek country, with all annuities in the West to be paid through the Creeks.[50]

Gadsden met with the Seminole leaders at Paynes Landing on the Ocklawaha River. Among the first orders of business was selection of interpreters satisfactory to the Seminoles. Gadsden brought along Stephen Richards for that purpose, while the Seminoles chose Abraham, "a faithful domestic of Micanope, the Head Chief. In addition the interpreter of the agent, Cudjo, was present."[51] As advisors and interpreters in Indian-white negotiations, these two men were perhaps the most influential blacks in Florida at the time.

Abraham was regarded as more than an interpreter; he was frequently called a "chief Negro" in official dispatches, and army surgeon Jacob Rhett Motte described him as "a perfect Tallyrand of the savage court."[52] How he arrived among the Seminoles is speculative, but judging by his manners and knowledge of English, he may have been an Englishman's house servant prior to the United States' acquisition of Florida. His wife was Bowleg's half-black widow, by whom he fathered three or four children.[53] Abraham's influence is usually described in comparison to his "master" or patron, Micanopy, "a large, fat man, rather obtuse in intellect, but kind to his people and his slaves."[54] Micanopy was described by General George McCall as "rather too indolent to rule harshly"; he tended to leave official business to what he called his "sense-bearers," one of whom was Abraham.[55] Despite the prevailing opinion of Micanopy, no one underestimated Abraham. John Lee Williams, one of the first Florida historians and a figure in territorial politics, said Abraham had "as much influence in the nation as any other man. With an appearance of great modesty, he is ambitious, avaricious, and withal very intelligent."[56] Thin and over six feet tall with a broad, square face and a thin moustache, Abraham was "plausible, pliant, and deceitful," according to Mayer Cohen, who also noted, "and, under an exterior of profound meekness, [he] cloaks deep, dark, and bloody purposes. He has at once the crouch and the spring of the panther."[57] Captain John C. Casey, who spent much time with Abraham during the war and knew him better than most whites, described him as having "a slight inclination forward like a Frenchman of the old school. His countenance is one of great cunning and penetration. He always smiles, and his words flow like oil. His conversation is soft and low, but very distinct, with a most genteel emphasis."[58]

Cudjo was described as a "regular interpreter at the Seminole agency," although it is not known when his relationship with the government began. As late as 1822 he was "one of the principal characters" of a black Seminole town in the Big Swamp area, according to William Simmons who spent a night in his house.[59] One Indian agent complained of his "very imperfect knowledge of the English language," and John Bemrose, a soldier in Florida in the 1830s, described his speech as "the common negro jargon of the plantation." Bemrose mentioned that partial paralysis afflicted Cudjo.[60] Another contemporary caustically remarked of the "little, limping figure of *Cudjoe* . . .with his cunning, squinting eyes; and his hands folded across his lap, in seemingly meek attention to the scene around him."[61] Of all the blacks to figure prominently in Seminole removal and the ensuing war, Cudjo was the first to side with the government. Kenneth Porter, in his account of black interpreters who served before the Second Seminole War, attributes this to "his physical deficiency of partial paralyais [that] predisposed him toward association with those who could give him the medical attention and comforts which his condition called for and which would have been inaccessible among the hostile Indians and Negroes."[62] By the time of the meeting at Paynes Landing, Cudjo was drawing a salary and rations from the Indian agency at Fort King, and probably living there as well.

Gadsden's main obstacles to a successful conclusion of the treaty negotiations were slave claims and the idea that the Seminoles should combine with the Creeks. He told the assemblage that as bad as emigration sounded to them, their situation would only be worse under local jurisdiction, which would be their fate if they refused to sell their land. He offered to include an article earmarking $7,000, over and above the main payment for relinquishing their land, for the government to settle property claims against them. The sum "will probably cover all demands which can be satisfactorily proved," Gadsden said "Many claims are for negroes. . . . The Indians allege that the depredations were mutual, that they suffered in the same degree, and that most of the property claimed was taken as reprisal for property of equal value lost by them."[63] Finally, Gadsden conferred privately with Abraham and Cudjo and added $400 to the Seminole payment specifically for the two black men. It was "intended to be a bribe," recalled one disgusted army captain; Gadsden "could not have got the treaty through if he had not bribed the negro interpreter."[64]

The Seminoles believed they had forestalled giving up their land. All they had agreed to, they thought, was to send a delegation to the Indian territory to examine the proposed new land. The group would report back to the larger body of Seminoles, and then the final decision would be made. This interpretation was also held at the highest levels of the federal government. The secretary of war, in his annual report to the president, said the treaty was "not obligatory on [the Indians'] part" until a group examined the land "and until the tribe, upon their report, shall have signified their desire" to move. "When they return, the determination of the tribe will be made known to the government." [65]

Seven Seminoles, Abraham, and agent John Phagan went to the proposed new Seminole land during the winter of 1832-1833. At Fort Gibson on the Arkansas River, Phagan and three other federal agents prepared a document for the group's signatures. It stated that the group was satisfied with the country to be assigned to the Seminoles, that they would live within the Creek nation but have a separate designated area, and that they would become "a constituent part of the Creek nation."[66] The Seminoles balked. They had no authority to sign anything, and it is reasonable to assume that Oklahoma in the winter was not very appealing to natives of Florida. According to one version, Phagan threatened to refuse to guide them home until they signed. Jumper, Holata Emathla, and Coi Hadjo later claimed never to have signed, but they probably said that to protect themselves from Seminoles violently opposed to removal. Abraham's part at Fort Gibson went unrecorded and is unclear, but obviously a combination of trickery and duress was employed to hasten emigration. Ethan Allen Hitchcock, who later had to fight in the resulting war, called the Seminole treaty process "a fraud on the Indians."[67]

When the group returned and reported to the Seminole council what they had seen, Micanopy informed agent Wiley Thompson that the Seminoles decided to decline the offer. Thompson told him that the delegation had signed away Florida and to prepare his people for emigration. Abraham brought the chief's answer the next day. "The old man says today the same he said yesterday, 'the nation decided in council to decline the offer.'" Captain McCall, with several years' service in Florida, knew the interpreter to be "crafty and artful in the extreme" and thus did not doubt that he had "as usual, much to do in keeping the chief, who was of a vacillating character, steady in his purpose."[68] Abraham, however, was not the only influence on Micanopy; "not an Indian would have consented to the relinquishment of their country" had the Paynes Landing agreement worked the way they thought it would, according to John Sprague. The Seminoles who signed at Fort Gibson were, in fact, "ridiculed and upbraded by all classes, male and female, for being circumvented by the whites." Resistance sentiment was so strong that the Fort Gibson signatories feared for their lives.[69]

Aside from the overt fraudulence of the recent treaties, the two major obstacles to Seminole removal remained living with the Creeks and the designs of others on their slaves. The first problem was destined to continue as a part of the removal treaties; the second was supposedly settled in the stipulation that the United States settle property claims against the Seminoles. Nevertheless, plans were still afoot to keep the blacks in Florida as the Indians were moved out.

The Seminoles gradually separated themselves from the Creek Confederacy, a process virtually complete by the Red Stick War, but the Creeks, however, often included the Seminoles in their treaties even though no Seminoles were signatories. [70] The Seminoles, in fact, adamantly denied the Creeks' right to do so. These treaties usually had articles indemnifying American citizens out of the Creek annuity for slaves taken by Indians; thus the Creeks claimed black Seminoles as their own, and these demands for the "return" of slaves further complicated Indian removal. Though the Seminoles recognized a political separation between themselves and the Creeks, clan ties still bridged the two groups.[71]

Even Seminoles who favored emigration objected to uniting with the Creeks. The Creeks wanted, according to Lieutenant Woodbourne Potter, to bring the Seminoles into their nation "evidently with a view to dispossess the Seminoles, in the easiest manner, of their large negro property, to which the former had unsuccessfully urged a claim."[72] Colonel Duncan Clinch, leader of the United States forces in the 1816 Negro Fort battle and now owner of 3,000 acres in Alachua County, explained that the Seminoles feared for their property because the Creeks were much more numerous than they were. They also believed they would have no justice in the West without a separate agent to attend to their interests. However, the authorities in Washington did not heed the advice of those at the scene and continued to plan combining the Creeks and Seminoles on the same land under one agency.[73] The Seminoles argued that the slave claims made by the Creeks were covered by the sixth article of the Paynes Landing treaty in which the United States agreed to pay for such claims. "As it would be difficult, not to say impossible, to prove that the negroes claimed by the Creeks, now in the possession of the Seminole Indians, are the identical negroes, or their descendants. . . . I cannot conceive that the Creeks can be supposed to have a fair claim to them," said agent Thompson.[74]

The Creeks were but one group asserting the right to enslave black Seminoles. After President Jackson agreed with his Florida supporters that it might be a good idea for the government to permit the selling of the black Seminoles to whites, Thompson expressed his fear to the acting secretary of war that such a policy would "bring into the nation a crowd of 'speculators,' some of whom might resort to the use of improper means to effect their object, and thereby greatly embarrass our operations."[75]

Governor Richard Keith Call, who had served under Jackson in the Florida campaign of 1818, initiated the plan to sell the blacks. "The negroes have a great influence over the Indians; they are better agriculturalists and inferior huntsmen to the Indians, and are violently opposed to leaving the country," he explained to Jackson. "If the Indians are permitted to convert them into specie, one great obstacle in the way of removal may be overcome." Carey A. Harris, head of the Office of Indian Affairs, explained to Thompson that such a move would rid the Seminoles of one certain point of conflict in the West "which. . . would excite the cupidity of the Creeks." Harris believed, furthermore, that it would not be an inhumane act as "it is not to be presumed the condition of these slaves would be worse than that of others in the same section of the country."[76] To Thompson, a policy of allowing Seminole slave sales was one more problem blocking peaceful removal. He had to counteract rumors spread by "malcontent Indians" that he had his own designs on the blacks, "and the moment I am called upon to meet this new difficulty, a party of whites arrives at the agency with what they consider a permission from the War Department to purchase slaves from the Indians." Should this continue, he warned, "it is reasonable to suppose that the negroes would en masse unite with the malcontent Indians." Instead, he proposed using the blacks "to exert their known influence" to work for removal by assuring the security of their existing relations with the Indians and not "classing them with skins and furs." In the end, Thompson was permitted to deny entry to Seminole country of any trader without a license from him, and he could issue licenses at his own discretion.[77]

Army officers in Florida agreed with Thompson that black opposition to being sold to whites would bring energy to the Seminole resistance, as blacks did not see themselves benefiting by coming under white control. The commander of American troops in Florida, Lieutenant Colonel A. C. W. Fanning, worried that "the cupidity of our own citizens" might ruin removal plans because the blacks, "who are bold, active, and armed will sacrifice some of them to their rage."[78] When Thompson asked chiefs friendly to removal to conduct a pre removal census of their people, including slaves, blacks became alarmed that the compilation of their names and numbers was the first step in the effort to put them under white control. At the same time, Thompson said, whites came to the agency with the War Department's affirmative response to Call's inquiry about Seminole slaves.[79]

The majority of Indians opposed emigration, regardless of the agreement made by a handful of chiefs. As General Thomas S. Jesup explained in the midst of the war, "even when a large portion of the heads of families should assent to a measure, those who dissented did not consider themselves bound to submit to or adopt it." Some headmen, including Jumper, Coi Hadjo, Charley Emathla, and Holata Emathla, knew American power made resistance futile and thus privately favored emigration, but their people so opposed it that they threatened the lives of any Indians complying with the removal plan. Osceola emerged as a leader of the militant resistance and, though not a hereditary Seminole leader, collected followers who agreed with what he said. His ascent to leadership also owed as much to action as talk; Thompson jailed him briefly for threatening him with a knife, and a month before the onset of the Second Seminole War he killed Charley Emathla for preparing for removal regardless of the sentiment of the people.[80]

Thompson tried to explain to the Seminoles how much worse their condition would be if they remained in Florida without federal protection. He also offered assurances that the government would protect their property from the Creeks. Micanopy held firm on the twenty-year term of the Moultrie Creek treaty which did not expire for nine more years. Other Indian speakers complained that the Paynes Landing treaty had not been explained to them correctly, that they only meant to look at the western land, and that the western land was no good. Nothing was resolved at this October 1834 meeting, and Thompson noticed that the Indians, "after they had received their annuity, purchased an unusually large quantity of powder and lead."[81]

Duncan Clinch met with the Seminoles in April 1835 and got no further than had Thompson. Jumper proceeded to make a lively two-hour speech, and Bemrose recorded "Cudjo's short and abrupt elucidation of doubtless a noble harangue. . . . 'When he look upon the White man's warriors, he sorry to injure them, but he cannot fear them, he had fought them before, he will do so again, if his people say fight.'. . . When asked to elucidate more fully the speaker's meaning, it tended only to his imperfect grunt of 'he say he no go, dat all he say.'" Clinch, exasperated, finally told the council if they did not emigrate voluntarily it would be done by force. A number of chiefs agreed, but not Micanopy or Jumper.[82]

Abraham, who had interpreted the removal treaties, was now counseling resistance, and Thompson believed the cause lay in the actions of his predecessor at the Seminole agency, John Phagan.[83] Abraham fumed that he had never been paid. As Thompson explained, "He has (in my possession) Major Phagan's certificate that he is entitled for his service to $280 for which Major Phagan, on the presentation of Abraham's receipt at the Department received credit. Abraham says he never gave a receipt; that he has been imposed upon; and he is consequently more indifferent upon the subject of emigration than I think he would otherwise have been. I have little doubt that a few hundred dollars would make him zealous and active." The money, Thompson said, should not be given "but on the production of the effect desired."[84]

Secretary of War Cass declined this opportunity to influence a useful ally. "Major Phagan having filed here the proper receipt for Abraham for his pay as interpreter, and received credit for the amount, it would be unsafe and inconsistent with the rules of the Department to set aside the receipt, and pay the claim now presented," he told Thompson.[85]

With the blacks, especially the influential ones, siding with the resistance, the murder of Charley Emathla by Osceola as an example for those Indians inclined to cooperate with removal, and the sudden abandonment of the Seminole communities, Clinch and Thompson perceived that trouble was imminent. The Florida frontier could be destroyed, Clinch told the adjutant general of the army, "by a combination of the Indians, Indian Negroes and the Negroes on the plantations." Reinforcements arrived in December, and a plan was made to move by force on the Seminole country after New Year's Day to round up the Indians for emigration.[86]

The eruption of hostilities in the last week of 1835 owed much to the alliance of blacks with the Seminoles. Luis Pacheco, the former slave of the Fatio family who had subsequently lived in Indian country, was the guide for Major Francis L. Dade's fateful encounter with the Seminole warriors who were determined to resist removal. Whether or not he colluded with the attackers, as he denied to his death, other blacks assisted the warriors who ambushed Dade's troops. Major F. S. Belton published in *Niles' Weekly Register* his account of the battle in which he stated that "a negro . . . named Harry, controls the Pea Creek band of about a hundred warriors, forty miles southeast of [Fort Brooke] . . . who kept his post constantly observed, and communicate with the Mickasukians [sic] at Wythlacoochee [sic]."[87]

At the same time Dade's force was wiped out, blacks and Indians assaulted plantations near St. Augustine, and approximately 300 slaves joined them. One leader of the raids, John Caesar, was a black Seminole with family connections on one plantation. Another was John Philip who lived with King Philip and had a wife on Benjamin Heriot's sugar plantation.[88]

Thus began the longest and most expensive Indian war the United States government was to wage. Ultimately the war for removal could not be resolved without a guarantee by Major General Thomas Jesup that blacks would be permitted to go to the West with the Seminoles rather than sold into slavery. Obviously, the events leading up to the war were distinctly influenced by blacks sympathetic to Seminole resistance.

George Klos is a graduate student in history at Florida State University and is employed at the Florida State Archives.

1. Kenneth W. Porter's *Negro on the American Frontier* (New York, 1971) is a compilation of articles first published in the *Florida Historical Quarterly* and *Journal of Negro History,* among others. Rembert W. Patrick, *Florida Fiasco* (Athens, 1954), covers the East Florida campaign of 1811-1813 and includes a chapter on the blacks living with the Seminoles of Alachua. Mark F. Boyd, "Events at Prospect Bluff on the Apalachicola River, 1808-1818," *Florida Historical Quarterly* 16 (October 1937), 55-96, and John D. Milligan, "Slave Rebelliousness and the Florida Maroon," *Prologue* 6 (Spring 1974), 4-18, cover the Negro Fort incident.
2. *Niles' Weekly Register* 21 (September 29, 1821), 69.
3. William DuVal to John C. Calhoun, September 22, 1822, in Clarence E. Carter, ed., *Territorial Papers of the United States,* 27 vols. (Washington, DC, 1934-1969), *Florida Territory,* XXII, 533-34. (Hereafter cited as *Territorial* Papers.)
4. Calhoun to John R. Bell, September 28, 1821, *Territorial Papers,* XXII, 219-21.
5. *American State Papers,* 38 vols. (Washington, DC, 1832-1861), *Indian Affairs,* II, 439.
6. The treaty is printed in full in Charles J. Kappler, ed., *Indian Affairs: Laws and Treaties* (Washington, DC, 1904-1941), 5 vols., II, 203-06.
7. Indian commissioners to Calhoun, September 26, 1823, *Territorial Papers,* XXII, 750.
8. Julia F. Smith, *Slavery and Plantation Growth in Antebellum Florida, 1821-1860* (Gainesville, 1973), 18. Michael G. Schene, *Hopes, Dreams, and Promises: A History of Volusia County, Florida* (Daytona Beach, 1976), 30-39, details the sugar enterprises set up in a county near the Seminole boundary.
9. *American State Papers: Public Land,* VI, 630, 663; ibid., V, 46.
10. *Abstract of Returns, 5th Census* (Washington, DC, 1832), 44. Indians, and the blacks living among them, were not counted.
11. Arthur R. Seymour, trans., "Essay on Middle Florida, 1837-38," *Florida Historical Quarterly* 26 (January 1948), 236, 239.
12. Wiley Thompson to Lewis Cass, April 27, 1835. *American State Papers: Military Affairs,* VI, 534.
13. Jacob Rhett Motte, *Journey into the Wilderness: An Army Surgeon's Account of Life in Camp and Field during the Creek and Seminole Wars, 1836-1838,* James F. Sunderman, ed. (Gainesville, 1953), 210.
14. Mark F. Boyd, "Horatio Dexter and Events Leading to the Treaty of Moultrie Creek with the Seminole Indians," *Florida Anthropologist* 6 (September 1958), 81-92.
15. Porter, *Negro on the American Frontier,* 240-41; Kenneth W. Porter, "The Early Life of Luis Pacheco Nee Fatio," *Negro History Bulletin* 7 (December 1943), 52.
16. House Exec. Doc. 271, 24th Cong., 1st Sess., 31.

17. Owen Marsh to Thomas L. McKenney, May 17, 1826, Office of Indian Affairs—Letters Received, National Archives Microcopy 234, roll 800. (Hereafter cited as OIA-LR.)
18. House Exec. Doc. 17, 19th Cong., 2d Sess., 18.
19. Ibid., 20; Tuckose Emathla to James Barbour (transcribed by Gad Humphreys), May 17, 1826, OIA-LR, roll 800.
20. Marsh to McKenney, May 17, 1826, and John N. McIntosh to Calhoun, January 16, 1825, OIA-LR, roll 800. See also, John M. Goggin, "The Seminole Negroes of Andros Island, Bahamas," *Florida Historical Quarterly* 24 (January 1946), 201-06; Kenneth W. Porter, "Notes on the Seminole Negroes in the Bahamas," *Florida Historical Quarterly* 24 (July 1945), 56-60; and Harry A. Kersey, Jr., "The Seminole Negroes of Andros Island Revisited: Some New Pieces to an Old Puzzle," *Florida Anthropologist* 34 (December 1981), 169-76.
21. Statement of John Winslett, sworn to by Augustus Steele, Jr., December 21, 1833, OIA-LR, roll 290.
22. James Forbes and James Innerarity searched for slaves known to have been at the Negro Fort. They reached Tampa Bay where they learned that the runaways were in the Charlotte Harbor area. William Coker and Thomas Watson, *Indian Traders of the Southeastern Spanish Borderlands* (Pensacola, 1986), 309.
23. DuVal to Calhoun, September 23, 1823, *Territorial Papers,* XXII, 744: Gad Humphreys to Calhoun, January 31, 1826, *Territorial Papers,* XXIII; 203; James W. Covington, "Life at Fort Brooke, 1824-1836," *Florida Historical Quarterly* 36 (April 1958), 325-26.
24. Humphreys to Horatio Lowe, September 17, 1828, OIA-LR, roll 800.
25. DuVal to McKenney, March 20, 1826, *Territorial Papers,* XXIII, 483; McKenney to DuVal, May 8, 1826, *American State Papers: Indian Affairs,* II, 698; Mark F. Boyd, *Florida Aflame* (Tallahassee, 1951), 36.
26. John T. Sprague, *Origin, Progress, and Conclusion of the Florida War* (New York, 1848; facsimile ed., Gainesville, 1964), 34, 43, 52-53.
27. *Territorial Papers,* XXII, 763.
28. Ibid., XXIII, 473, 483.
29. Cecil D. Eby, Jr., ed., "Memoir of a West Pointer in Florida," *Florida Historical Quarterly* 41 (October 1962), 163.
30. *Territorial Papers,* XXIV, 452; Boyd, *Florida Aflame,* 42; DuVal to Cass, May 26, 1832, OIA-LR, roll 288.
31. "Memorial to the President by Inhabitants of St. Johns County," March 6, 1826, *Territorial Papers,* XXIII 462-63. Three members of the Fatio family signed the memorial.
32. Francis Paul Prucha, *American Indian Policy in the Formative Years* (Cambridge, 1962), 56.
33. James Dean to Archibald Clark, September 20, 1828, OIA-LR, roll 800.
34. Sprague, *Origin, Progress, and Conclusion,* 51. The Indians maintained, and white witnesses later confirmed, that the slave woman in question had been sold to an Indian by the claimant's father twenty years earlier.
35. Clark to McKenney, October 20, 1828, OIA-LR, roll 800.
36. McKenney to Peter Porter, November 1, 1828, *Territorial Papers,* XXIV, 95-97; Porter to John Quincy Adams, December 6, 1828, OIA-LR, roll 800.

37. Humphreys to Alex Adair, April 27, 1829, OIA-LR, roll 800.
38. Adair to John Eaton, April 24, 1829, ibid.
39. Marsh to DuVal, May 29, 1829, *Territorial Papers,* XXIV, 234; McKenney to Porter, November 1, 1828, ibid. 95-97.
40. DuVal to Phagan, October 9, 1830, OIA-LR, roll 800; Phagan to Cass, February 6, 1832, ibid. The blacks in this case were claimed by an Indian woman named Nelly Factor and by two whites named Floyd and Garey. DuVal told Phagan to seize the slaves and deliver them to Floyd and Garey. DuVal to Phagan, February 7, 1832, ibid.
41. Wiley Thompson to Cass, July 19, 1836, *American State Papers: Military Affairs,* VI, 460. A copy of the bill of sale is in the Florida Negro Collection, Florida Historical Society Archives, University of South Florida Library, Tampa. Later, Caty and one of her daughters also ran away, as Humphreys listed them (and the sons) as slaves "taken" by the Indians in the war. Caty, one son, and one daughter are listed in 1838 muster rolls of captured blacks en route to Indian Territory.
42. If the Seminoles were to be removed from Florida and transported west, DuVal recommended, "the Government ought not to admit negros [sic] to go with them. . . . I am convinced the sooner they dispose of them the better." DuVal to McKenney, January 12, 1826, *Territorial Papers,* XXIII, 414; DuVal to MKenney, March 2, 1826, ibid., 454.
43. Humphreys to Acting Governor William McCarty, September 6, 1827, ibid., 911.
44. DuVal to Elbert Herring, January 26, 1834, House Exec. Doc. 271, 24th Cong., 1st Sess., 18. (Emphasis in original.)
45. Ronald N. Satz, *American Indian Policy in the Jacksonian Era* (Lincoln, 1975), 3-11; Prucha, *Formative Years,* 225-38.
46. Joseph Hernandez to Thomas Metcalfe (chairman, House Committee on Indian Affairs), February 19, 1823, *American. State Papers: Indian Affairs,* II, 410. Hernandez, like many Florida slave owning petitioners to the government, was a naturalized American citizen who had been living in Florida since the Spanish period.
47. Memorial to Congress by Inhabitants of the Territory, March 26, 1832, *Territorial Papers,* XXIV, 679.
48. *Territorial Papers,* XXIII, 897; St. Augustine *Florida Herald,* January 26, 1832.
49. *Acts of the Legislative Council,* 5th Sess. (1827), 79-81; ibid., 6th Sess. (1828), 104-07; St. Augustine *Florida Herald* July 1, 1830, February 2, 1832.
50. *American State Papers: Military Affairs,* VI, 472.
51. James Gadsden to Cass, November 1, 1834, OIA-LR, roll 806.
52. Woodbourne Potter, *The War in Florida* (Baltimore, 1836; facsimile ed., Ann Arbor, 1966), 9; Motte, *Journey into the Wilderness,* 210.
53. Porter, *Negro on the Frontier,* 296-305.
54. John Lee Williams, *Territory of Florida* (New York, 1837; facsimile ed., Gainesville, 1962), 214.
55. George A. McCall, *Letters from the Frontiers* (Philadelphia, 1868; facsimile ed., Gainesville, 1974), 146.
56. Williams, *Territory of Florida,* 214.
57. Myer M. Cohen, *Notices of Florida and the Campaign* (Charleston, 1836; facsimile ed., Gainesville, 1964), 239.

58. Casey quoted in Charles H. Coe, *Red Patriots* (Cincinnati, 1898; facsimile ed., Gainesville, 1974), 46.
59. William Simmons, *Notices of East Florida* (Charleston, 1822; facsimile ed., Gainesville, 1973), 41.
60. Thompson to Herring, October 28, 1834, House Exec. Doc. 271, 24th Cong., 1st Sess., 154; Lt. Joseph W. Harris to Cass, October 12, 1835, ibid., 217; John Bemrose, *Reminiscences of the Second Seminole War,* John K. Mahon, ed., (Gainesville, 1966), 17.
61. Quoted in Kenneth W. Porter, "Negro Guides and Interpreters in the Early Stages of the Seminole War," *Journal of Negro History* 35 (April 1950), 175.
62. Ibid., 177.
63. Quoted in Potter, *War in Florida,* 31-32.
64. W. A. Croffut, ed., *Fifty Years in Camp and Field: Diary of Major-General Ethan Allen Hitchcock* (New York and London, 1909), 79; John K. Mahon, "Two Seminole Treaties: Paynes Landing, 1832, and Fort Gibson, 1833," *Florida Historical Quarterly* 41 (July 1962), 1-11; Paynes Landing treaty printed in Kappler, *Indian Affairs,* II, 394-95.
65. *Niles' Weekly Register* 43 (January 26, 1833), 367.
66. Fort Gibson treaty printed in Kappler, *Indian Affairs,* II, 394-95.
67. Mahon, "Two Treaties," 11-21; Croffut, *Fifty Years,* 80, 122; Grant Foreman, *Indian Removal* (Norman, 1932), 322.
68. McCall, *Letters,* 301-02.
69. Sprague, *Origin, Progress, and Conclusion,* 79.
70. The treaty the Creeks made in New York in 1790 and the Indian Springs treaty of 1821 are two examples.
71. Gadsden warned Gad Humphreys that "disaffected" Creeks were prone to move to the Seminoles "whenever their irregularities earned them to chastizement." Gadsden to Humphreys, November 11, 1827, OIA-LR, roll 806. Creeks unwilling to move west, he said, will seek refuge in Florida. The letters of the Office of Indian Affairs during the war and the diary of Major General Thomas Jesup (Florida State Archives, Tallahassee) show that many did indeed seek their escape in Florida. Cases also exist, such as Chief Neamathla, of Florida Indians moving to Creek country in Alabama to forestall removal.
72. Potter, *War in Florida,* 43.
73. Boyd, *Florida Aflame,* 52; Duncan Clinch to Cass, August 24, 1835, House Exec. Doc. 271, 24th Cong., 1st Sess., 104; Acting Secretary of War C. A. Harris to Thompson, May 20, 1835, OIA-LR, roll 806; Rembert W. Patrick, *Aristocrat in Uniform: General Duncan L. Clinch* (Gainesville, 1963), 61.
74. Potter, *War in Florida,* 41; Thompson to DuVal, January 1, 1834, *American State Papers: Military Affairs,* VI, 154.
75. Thompson to Harris, June 17, 1835, *American State Papers: Military Affairs,* VI, 471.
76. Call quoted in Potter, *War in Florida,* 46-49; Harris to Thompson, May 22, 1835, OIA-LR, roll 806.
77. Thompson to Cass, April 27, 1835, House Exec. Doc. 271, 24th Cong., 1st Sess., 183-84; Harris to Thompson, July 11, 1835, OIA-LR, roll 806.
78. Alexander C. W. Fanning to Adjutant General, April 29, 1835, *Territorial Papers,* XXV, 133.

79. Potter, *War in Florida,* 45-46; Thompson to Harris, June 17, 1835, OIA-LR, roll 800.
80. Boyd, *Florida Aflame,* 47-56; Williams, *Territory of Florida,* 216; Thomas S. Jesup to Joel Poinsett, October 17, 1837, *American State Papers: Military Affairs,* VII, 886.
81. Thompson to Herring, October 28, 1834, House Exec. Doc. 271, 24th Cong., 1st Sess., 54-65.
82. Bemrose, *Reminiscences,* 17-24; *American State Papers: Military Affairs,* VI, 75.
83. Phagan had been fired in 1833 when a treasury department comptroller found in Phagan's accounts twelve invoices that had been altered $397.50 over the true amount, with Phagan paying the contractor the true amount and the agent pocketing the remainder. J. B. Thornton to Cass, August 29, 1833, OIA-LR, roll 800. The year before, Phagan was in trouble for openly campaigning against Joseph White in the delegate election, conducting card games in the office, and hiring his own slave in the agency smithery at government expense. Phagan to Cass, February 6, 1832, ibid.
84. Thompson to George Gibson (commissary general of subsistence), September 21, 1835, House Exec. Doc. 271, 24th Cong., 1st Sess., 214.
85. Cass to Thompson, October 28, 1835, ibid., 227. The Paynes Landing treaty stated that Abraham and Cudjo were "to be paid on their arrival in the country they consent to remove to"; thus Phagan had no business invoicing the government for Abraham's payment while the Seminoles were still in Florida. Cudjo also had been victimized by Phagan, as the agent sent to Washington a bill for $480 (although Cudjo was due only $180) from which the interpreter received nothing. Cudjo complained that in three years with Phagan he had received only $175. Thompson to Herring, March 3, 1835, OIA-LR, roll 800.
86. *American State Papers: Military Affairs,* VI, 61; Patrick, *Aristocrat in Uniform,* 71.
87. *Niles' Weekly Register* 49 (January 30, 1836), 367.
88. Motte, *Journey into the Wilderness,* 118.

5

PROTEST THROUGH ALL MEANS

The author herewith explores the irony of white masters in Florida maintaining that their slaves were tractable, happy, and ever loyal to "Ol' Massa" and his family, despite the fact that the white slaveocracy promulgated some of the most inhumane slave codes and restrictive measures in the South. Although the author does not note it, in good part this pattern arose from what noted historian John Hope Franklin maintained in his classic book, *From Slavery to Freedom: A History of African Americans,* that in reality slaves resisted at all times through all means possible. As Granade's study underscores, not only was this true in Florida, but the territory/state presented additional fear elements for whites: vast hinterlands ideal for sanctuary, maroon communities, asylum with Native Americans, and a strong pull for restless slaves from contiguous territories/states. When the inevitable slave resistance surfaced in Florida, whites were quick to blame external influence and Seminole scheming rather than to acknowledge the roots of black struggle in their own myths about docile slaves. A close perusal of this study reveals that slavery in Florida was often as brutal and exploitative as in other entities of the Deep South, and that the unrest and resistance of bondsmen in Florida was as persistent and threatening to whites as in any other place that enslaved people of African descent.

As Larry E. Rivers in "A Troublesome Property . . ." and Horace Randall Williams in *No Man's Yoke on My Shoulders* have noted in their respective studies, slaves continually sought measures of autonomy in

Florida through religious behavior, interpersonal relations, and labor subterfuges. Rivers and Williams could have easily added "pulling foot," as large numbers of slaves in Florida sought or accomplished escapes to the "Indian lands." As Franklin has noted, there were myriad forms of personal and collective slave defiance, and as Granade suggests, almost all of them surfaced among the "docile" slaves of Florida. He also, like Rivers, finds that slaves were anything but submissive and that their masters repeatedly found them to be "troublesome property." This property (which accounted for nearly half the population in Florida by the Civil War) undertook repeated individual actions to impair their master's possessions and psyche, such as murder, burglary, arson, sabotage, malingering, "insolence," and, most notably, "pulling foot" into the Indian lands. He also finds that key characteristics of Florida—in particular, the high ratio of blacks to whites, the vast wilderness, the disruptions of the Indian Wars, and the Native American encouragement for flight and brotherhood—provided a peculiar advantage to rebellious bondsmen.

Whites sought to counteract these advantages by codifying their control measures, to include prohibiting bondsmen from unsupervised travel, requiring passes when off the master's property, criminalizing literacy and assembly, instituting white patrols, limiting blacks' access to firearms and weapons, forbidding seditious speech, and by promoting a general sense of isolation and powerlessness to prevent what slave owners feared most—slave insurrections. Although the author claims no large-scale uprising took place within Florida, he acknowledges that rumors of them did circulate in Florida, mainly in Elba in 1856 and in Quincy that same year. By the outbreak of the Civil War, whites had even reduced the small number of free blacks into a quasi-servile status out of fear of their inspiring bondsmen to flee or worse. Not only did the legislative bodies coordinate the oppression of the "free Negro," but the newspapers of the day also attempted to paint free blacks as slothful, despicable, and as threats to the established order. As the author suggests, none of these repressive actions eliminated the deep-rooted black determination to struggle for freedom and dignity in a racist society.

The author then shifts the article from a focus on large-scale insurrections to the ever-present personal acts of rebellion that formed the true (and arguably most effective) slave protestations. He finds that theft, arson, sabotage, murder, and violence were the most frequent modes of defiance (as they were across most of Dixie). The local press heavily publicized slave "insubordination" but couched stories in language suggesting that these types of events were aberrations and not related to a widespread slave discontent. On the other hand, Granade effectively examines the importance of these seemingly isolated acts as evidence of a widespread slave struggle and as evidence that bondsmen pursued, as John Hope Franklin argued, resistance *at all times through all means possible.*

FURTHER READING

Edwin L. Williams, Jr., "Negro Slavery in Florida," *Florida Historical Quarterly*, Vol. 28 (1949);

George P. Rawick, ed., *The American Slave: "A Composite Autobiography,"* Vol. 17, *Florida Narratives* (1972-79);

Julia Floyd Smith, *Slavery and Plantation Growth in Ante-Bellum Florida, 1821-1860* (1973);

Dianna Zacharias, *An Interpretation of the Florida Ex-Slaves' Memories of Slavery and the Civil War* (1976);

Larry Rivers, "'Dignity and Importance': Slavery in Jefferson County, Florida, 1827 to 1860," *Florida Historical Quarterly*, Vol. 61 (1983);

Gary R. Mormino, "Florida Slave Narratives," *Florida Historical Quarterly*, Vol. 66 (1988);

Christopher Morris, "Challenging the Masters: Recent Studies on Slavery and Freedom," *Florida Historical Quarterly*, Vol. 73 (1994);

Jane Landers, "Slave Resistance on The Southeastern Frontier: Fugitives, Maroons, and Banditti in The Age of Revolutions," *Escribano*, Vol. 32 (1995);

Larry E. Rivers, "'A Troublesome Property': Master-Slave Relations in Florida, 1821-1865," in *The African American Heritage of Florida*, David R. Colburn and Jane L. Landers, eds. (1995), chapter 5;

Christopher E. Linsin, "Skilled Slave Labor in Florida, 1850-1860," *Florida Historical Quarterly*, Vol. 75 (1996);

Larry E. Rivers, *Slavery in Florida: Territorial Days to Emancipation* (2000);

Lori Ann Garner, "Representations of Speech in the WPA Slave Narratives of Florida and the Writing of Zora Neale Hurston," *Western Folklore*, Vol. 59 (2000);

Loren Schweninger, ed., *Race, Slavery, and Free Blacks. Series II, Petitions to Southern County Courts, 1775-1867. Part A, Georgia (1796-1867), Florida (1821-1867), Alabama (1821-1867), Mississippi (1822-1867)* (2003);

Donn C. Worgs, "'Beware of The Frustrated . . .': The Fantasy and Reality of African American Violent Revolt," *Journal of Black Studies*, Vol. 37 (2006);

Horace Randall Williams, ed., *No Man's Yoke on My Shoulders: Personal Accounts of Slavery in Florida* (2006);

Irvin D. S. Winsboro, "Give Them Their Due: A Reassessment of African Americans and Union Military Service in Florida During the Civil War," *Journal of African American History*, Vol. 92 (2007).

SLAVE UNREST IN FLORIDA

Ray Granade

The Florida Historical Quarterly, Volume 55, issue 1 (1976), 18-36.

WHITE FLORIDIANS, like other Southerners in the years before the Civil War, usually spoke of slave revolts in low, fearful voices. While their words indicated concern for the security of the group, their interest was essentially a personal one. They wondered how really safe they and their families were in the constant presence of vast numbers of servile blacks. Yet slave unrest involved more than insurrection. Murders, burglary, arson, rape, trespass were all crimes that an individual slave might commit even though he was not involved in an organized revolt. Floridians recognized these threats to their lives and property, yet their greatest fear was the possibility of slave insurrection.

Before Florida became an American territory in 1821, slave unrest occurred largely outside her borders. Carolina and Georgia residents complained of intruders from Florida enticing blacks to escape, and runaways often sought sanctuary among the Indians in the Spanish borderlands.[1] The aborted attempt to seize East Florida in 1812-1813 by Americans was fomented in part by the desire to control this slave refuge.[2] Southern whites warned: "Our slaves are excited to rebel, and we have an army of negroes raked up in this country . . . to contend with." Spanish Florida, they claimed, dispatched "emissaries" to encourage "a revolt of the black population in the United States."[3] Andrew Jackson later stated that the area was filled with a "desperate clan of outlaws" who had "drawn into their confederacy many runaway negroes."[4] The persistent American effort to acquire Florida, amounting "almost to a disease," was motivated by Southerners who sought to protect their economic interests and to guard against armed maroons.[5]

Once the sovereignty of Florida passed from Spain to the United States in 1821, the problem of slave unrest became an internal one. Despite this, it did not admit of an easy solution. The juxtaposition of white, black, and Indian caused many of Florida's troubles. Anti-American Seminoles proved a major source of aggravation. A slave could easily slip into the woods or swamps and make his way to one of their camps. The Indians offered refuge, and their presence encouraged runaways.

The black-white ratio was another difficulty. In 1845, the year Florida became a state, slaves outnumbered their masters in five of the twenty-six counties, and a significant minority of blacks existed in ten other counties.[6] The Tallahassee Floridian in 1846 provided statistics: white males over twenty-one in Marion County numbered 247, slaves of all ages, 523; in Gadsden County only 746 whites were old enough to help oversee 4,150 bondsmen.[7] The 1850 census revealed 39,310 slaves in a total population of 87,445; a decade later, there were 77,747 whites and 61,745 slaves.[8] The seven counties which contained over half of Florida slaves in 1860 (Alachua, Gadsden, Jackson, Jefferson, Leon, Madison, and Marion) had overwhelming black majorities, and in eleven others slaves formed a significant percentage of the population.[9]

R. B. Smith and W. Bartlett, editors of the Tallahassee *Southern Journal,* noted in April 1846, "there will never be a heavy slave population throughout the state" because the character of the land "insures us just the population which we desire. There will be a preponderance of whites."[10] Though technically correct about a statewide numerical superiority of whites, Smith discounted transportation difficulties which denied whites in some sections the safety of ruling numbers. Another reason for Smith's and Bartlett's error was the sparseness of the population. Florida remained frontier throughout the era of slavery. As late as 1850, only three counties— Dade, Holmes, and Wakulla— could claim more improved than unimproved land within their borders.[11]

Runaways found large areas everywhere in the state in which to hide. The relation of people to specific portions of Florida, and the relative scarcity of white inhabitants throughout the state, meant an ease of escape unmatched in most other regions of the South.

Faced with population and physical problems, white Floridians worked to insure continued control. The first territorial legislature established a strict legal system to minimize the effects of unrest, and subsequent legislatures increased the slave code's severity.[12] Bondsmen were not allowed to move about freely— it was too easy for them to slip into the wilds and join other maroons in troubling isolated plantations.[13] Blacks could not possess transportation, and a written pass was prerequisite to off-plantation movement.[14] Slaves could not engage in riots, routs, unlawful assemblies, commit trespass, or make seditious speeches.[15] The main deterrents to violence were prohibitions against the possession of firearms or any type weapon, and a system of patrols— the chief method of enforcing slave code stipulations.[16]

Florida legislators provided for a system of patrols in late 1825 and again in early 1831. Composed of male volunteers from various neighborhoods, the patrols were supposed to visit each plantation at least once every two weeks. Any slave outside the owner's fence or cleared ground would be questioned, and the patrol could search slave houses for firearms and disperse any gathering of seven or more bondsmen.[17] The law, however, did not guarantee that the patrols would remain active. It was a time consuming duty. Often whites became complacent, and patrols almost ceased to function. Newspapers constantly chided the citizenry to keep the search parties alive. The Tallahassee *Floridian* pointed out that local stores were open until church services began at ten o'clock Sunday mornings to "avoid the greater evil" of slaves going to town at night, or under cover of darkness bartering with stolen property "at half its value" for things like coffee and sugar in "disreputable establishments." The paper implied that patrols should insure that the system fulfilled its purpose by carefully accounting for all slaves.[18] Just before the Civil War, William Babcock of the *East Floridian* noted the ease with which blacks obtained illegal rum. Fernandina "needs a corrective in this respect," he wrote, calling for increased surveillance.[19]

At times, government officials or an alarmed populace acted on the patrol question. The Benton County grand jury in the spring of 1846 called for adherence to the patrol law "as we are of the opinion that that important law is much neglected." There port warned citizens and officials that slaves had "too much privilege in carrying arms, and more particularly violating the Sabbath day."[20] As in Leon County in 1835, vigilance committees were occasionally formed. to supplement regular patrols.[21]

The vigilance committee proved particularly active just prior to 1861. During the two years before the war, "suspicious individuals" supposedly lurked in Florida, enticing slaves to flee or revolt. These people were sought with a vengeance. Speaking for Floridians, one newspaper urged: "If they are caught, let them be consigned instanter to the tender mercies of Judge Lynch."[22] Editors warned the committees of any rumored agitator and reported the formation of committees throughout the state.[23] Tensions of the times and worries over slave unrest were demonstrated by one Florida editor who criticized the New York *Tribune's* "gloating over the expectation of a servile insurrection at the South." "If any individual is *convicted* of tampering with our slave population," the Florida man wrote, "let him die the death of a felon." Such punishments as whipping and tar and feathering "do not incapacitate the offenders from renewing their dangerous efforts." He concluded that "such scoundrels should be 'wiped out.' If they are ambitious of wearing the crown of martyrdom, place it upon their brows. If they furnish necks, hemp is cheap and live-oak limbs numerous."[24]

Other efforts were made to implement and facilitate control measures. In 1844, a letter in the Apalachicola *Commercial Advertiser* voiced concern over slaves being sent to town by owners who "allow them to act as free." This communication reminded readers that "Negro slaves are forbidden, by the ordinances of this city, from living separate and apart from their owners, employers or overseers."[25] Alone or in large groups, Negroes caused additional precautions, as in the Pensacola Navy Yard, where the numerous Negro laborers were quartered near the gate, where the marine guard was stationed.[26]

To whites, the presence of the free black posed one of the major obstacles to control. So clearly was his very freedom a threat that many efforts were made to curtail that freedom. The Tallahassee *Floridian & Journal* echoed the Alabama *Journal* in calling free Negroes "the most dangerous incendiary element to our existing institution of society," whose influence was "prejudicial on the slaves."[27] This paper had already denounced the freeman's "abandoned and dissolute lives" and their bad example for the slaves.[28] The greatest threat posed by the free black was the possibility that slaves "should grow to a sense of equal rights" on seeing freemen and "should become more restive under the chains of servitude, and thus become less valuable to their owners, and more troublesome and dangerous to the community." The aim was to prevent the "evil" of contact between free Negroes and slaves.[29] Occasionally Floridians handled the problems without recourse to the law. At Fernandina, the local jail was forced late in 1860, and three free Negroes, part of the crew of a brig then in port, were "removed and have not since been heard of." There were rumors about their fate, and the fate of six blacks seized from the bark *N. W. Bridge* a short time before, but no one really knew what had happened to them.[30]

News of slave unrest outside Florida sometimes added to the white fears. Reports of revolts in Jamaica and Puerto Rico circulated widely.[31] Yet the prospect of such violent deeds in Florida was usually discounted. Prior to the 1840s, the attitudes of most Floridians were ambivalent. In 1829, Governor William P. DuVal warned of both slave insurrection and of "predatory excursions of the Indians." Floridians should always be ready to defend themselves, he cautioned.[32] A Tallahassee editor noted that "unless they [Northerners] aim to kindle a civil and servile war amongst us— unless they intend . . . to hurl the midnight torch into our dwellings, unsheath the relentless dagger against men, women and children, reposing in defenseless sleep, and wave the flag of humanity drenched in blood over a desolated land they had better cease their clamors."[33] On the other hand, an Apalachicola paper claimed, "No! no! we have nothing to fear from that source— the idea is ridiculous and not worth noticing." It would be best, both papers did agree, to be ever "on the alert."[34]

The concern of Floridians over abolitionist activities had increased by 1844. The Apalachicola paper warned its readers against their treacherous depredations. Hopefully, Southerners will "wake from this lethargy in time to save themselves from a general massacre," a letter signed "Patriot" observed. Abolitionists are merely awaiting the proper moment, the author claimed, and "They are every day exciting the slaves to discontent and disobedience."[35] As sectional tensions increased and abolitionists intensified their work, Florida's equanimity on the topic of slave unrest declined. Outside agitators were constantly decried as the cause of slave unrest. John Brown's 1859 raid on Harper's Ferry received much attention in Florida. An editor queried, "Can we any longer shut our eyes to the glaring fact, that a large and influential portion of our Northern brethren, would heartily rejoice to see the negro elevated, even should it be necessary, to shed the *blood* of the people of the South. . .?" All persons convicted of inciting slave insurrection should receive punishment "prompt and certain, 'a short shift and a stout cord.'"[36] A public meeting in Fernandina warned after the Harper's Ferry episode, "that in the most safe and quiet places in slave territory, our homes and homesteads are unsafe." The citizens agreed that "it is fit and proper that we should throw around us such safeguards as our means will allow."[37]

By the time of the 1860 elections, most Floridians overreacted to every mention of abolitionists. Newspapermen called for the South to arm "to resist every form of insurrection and incendiaryism which Northern hatred can inflict."[38] The ladies of Broward's Neck near Jacksonville sent a post-election address to the *Weekly East Floridian* and warned of abolitionists "illuminating our country occasionally from Texas to Florida."[39] Rumors of insurrection flourished amid such fears. Late in 1860 the *Madison Messenger* contradicted reports that an uprising was imminent there.[40] Most rumors centered on the nefarious deeds of abolitionists who would stop at nothing, the paper claimed, to free slaves. Reporting a servile revolt in Texas under the heading "Abolition Outrages," the Fernandina *Weekly East Floridian* noted the activities of "certain white miscreants," and warned that such "fiendish designs" were plotted to reenact on American soil the "sanguinary scenes" of the St. Domingo insurrection.[41] Fear of abolitionists had definitely risen-fear of losing property as well as of facing insurrection bred by "fiends."

Though Florida never faced a full-blown slave insurrection, many of its citizens believed they had cause to fear. The Second Seminole War was sometimes called the Negro War by some participants. Reportedly there had been an uprising in March1820, put down by American troops when the "Patriots" of Talbot Island called for help.[42] Despite these two examples of direct violence, fear of slave revolt generally remained groundless. A letter to the Cincinnati (Ohio) *Citizen* in May 1846, and substantially reproduced in the June 5, 1846 issue of the Boston *Liberator,* spoke of slaves conspiring to rebel as soon as "a sufficient number" of white men went to the Mexican War. The letter mentioned many arrests and the Pensacola Navy Yard's strictures under Commodore Latimore's proclamation of martial law. "Everybody is armed, and some of the ladies are so frightened that they keep pistols loaded," the missive concluded.[43] Florida newspapers contained no reference to this incident. Yet the Tallahassee *Floridian & Journal* noted similar occurrences as "links in the chain of passing events," and indicated that unrest was not unusual and rumors frequent.[44]

Local as well as northern papers recorded the greatest fright of the antebellum period in 1856. That September, the town of Elba, Florida, was shaken by turmoil, and reports of disquiet continued for several weeks.[45] The main panic occurred in December, sparked by stories of revolt in Texas. The *Floridian and Journal* noted that the "alarm occasioned at certain points in distant States by vague rumors of negro insurrections widens and amplifies as a natural result."[46] The editor should have included his own state: James Stirling, traveling in Florida in 1856, observed white uneasiness in Jacksonville.[47]

An anonymous letter from Quincy, Florida, in 1856, brought news that "a bloody conspiracy is now ripening with a certain class of the population of this State," allegedly to occur some time between Christmas Day and January 1.[48] The New York *Tribune* version was particularly lurid.[49] In the original, the tone was largely disbelief, mingled with warning: "We frankly confess that we place but little confidence in the statement, yet such a thing is possible." Floridian editor James S. Jones had received a letter from a dozen of "the most respectable citizens" of Gadsden County denying the validity of the anonymous letter signed "Floridian." They wrote that the subject was "one of an extremely delicate character," and bandying it about in the public prints was "calculated to produce unnecessary excitement." They regretted the letter's publication even more "from the conviction that the 'conspiracy' alluded to has not the slightest foundation." Adding a comment, Jones noted the communication with satisfaction, reminding his readers that he had "placed no confidence in the real or imaginary revelations of an unknown correspondent. "Excusing himself for mentioning the letter at all, he perhaps unconsciously emphasized the thoughts in Floridians' minds: "The specifications were distinctly made in the letter, and had they been verified, without a premonition from us, we should have felt afterwards self-reproved, and doubtless, would have incurred the condemnation of all."[50]

Fear of slave unrest in Florida continued throughout the Civil War. In April 1862, Confederate Brigadier General R. F. Floyd appealed to Governor John Milton to declare martial law in Clay, Nassau, Duval, Putnam, St. Johns, and Volusia counties "as a measure of absolute necessity, as they contain a nest of traitors and lawless negroes."[51] The problem intensified as slaves deserted their plantations for Union lines.[52] In August 1864, Confederate General John K. Jackson observed that "Many deserters . . . are collected in the swamps and fastnesses of Taylor, La Fayette *[sic]*, Levy, and other counties, and have organized, with runaway negroes, bands for the purpose of committing depredations upon the plantations . . . of loyal citizens and running off their slaves."[53]

During the period of the Seminole Wars, more slave problems had existed than were even feared during the Civil War. As soon as hostilities broke out in 1835, blacks began joining the Seminoles.[54] Osceola recognized the validity of the American officer's observation that ten "resolute negroes, with a knowledge of the country, are sufficient to desolate the frontier," and worked to make it a reality.[55] Early in 1835, General Duncan L. Clinch foresaw the danger and warned that without sufficient military protection, "the whole frontier may be laid waste by a combination of the Indians, Indian negroes, and the negroes on the plantations."[56] By October, Clinch was reporting that "some of the most respectable planters" feared "a secret and improper communication" between the three groups.[57] The planters had cause to worry, for Osceola, actively recruiting, had detailed a war chief, Yaha Hajo, to coordinate slaves' escape and enlistment.[58]

Recognizing Negro participation in the war, the Florida legislature in January 1836 passed an act to sell blacks caught working with the Indians.[59] All available force was utilized to prevent Indian-slave communications and cooperation. During the first week of 1836, Captain F. S. Belton advised the adjutant general from his post at Fort Brooke: "This place is invested by all the Florida Indians in the field, with a large accession of Negroes, particularly from the plantations of Tomoka & Smyrna."[60] Six months later Major Benjamin A. Putnam informed Secretary of War Lewis Cass: "Many have escaped to and joined the Indians, and furnished them with much important information and if strong measures were not taken to restrain our slaves, there is but little doubt that we should soon be assailed with a servile as well as Indian War."[61] General Thomas Sidney Jesup informed his superiors that "depredations committed on the plantations east of the St. John's were perpetrated by the plantation negroes, headed by an Indian Negro, John Caesar . . . and aided by some six or seven vagabond Indians."[62] In what proved one of the best assessments of the war (aside from Joshua Giddings's figure of a slave hunt carried on by the United States Army), Jesup noted at the end of 1836: "This, you may be assured, is a negro, not an Indian war; and if it be not speedily put down, the South will feel the effects of it on their slave population before the end of the next season."[63] A large portion of the militia remained at home to guard against just such a sudden uprising.

St. Augustine illustrated the tension resulting from fear of slave unrest during the Second Seminole War. Inside the town resided several hundred Negroes who had once lived with the Seminole and had spoken with him daily in his own tongue. Occupants of St. Augustine feared that slaves would fire the town, then admit Indians to the scene while defenders fought the flames.[64] Residents attempted to institute an active patrol system. However, an ordinance issued June 23, 1836, to strengthen the patrols was not put into force until May 1839.[65] Patrols were organized, but few arms and little ammunition were available; in the preceding weeks the Seminoles had, unnoticed, purchased nearly all available munitions.[66] Protective measures occasionally proved insufficient. Two free Negroes, Stephen Merritt and Randall Irving, were accused of selling arms to the Indians, but were cleared of the charge. Merritt's son Joe was not so fortunate; caught in the act, he paid with his life.[67] In early 1840, several of John M. Hanson's slaves were arrested for supplying the enemy with powder and information.[68]

Aside from these few instances, Florida was not troubled by major slave violence. In this respect, Governor Richard Keith Call had nothing to fear, and could correctly boast on the eve of the Civil War: "I sleep soundly with my doors unlocked, unbarred, unbolted, when my person is accessible to the midnight approach of more than two hundred African slaves." Call then spoke of "some few individual cases of shocking murders of masters and overseers by slaves," but decided they were "by no means so frequent, nor have they been marked by greater treachery and ferocity, than the murders committed by white men on both races within the same time."[69] Here was the crux of the slave unrest matter. Most slave unrest in Florida took the form of runaways, theft, arson, and personal violence. Yet, the result was the same, whether the violence was protest against enslavement or a very personal kind of individual retribution directed, not against an enslaving master, but against another man.

Theft was so common that Floridians were even able to joke about it. Except for the nuisance, pilfering was easier overlooked than punished. Viewing two evils—theft and literacy— with equanimity, Florida papers avidly copied the humorous tale of a pilfering slave.[70] Arson was another matter; few persons laughed at its frequent and often tragic occurrence. Incendiaries ignited houses, public buildings, stores, gin houses, warehouses, corncribs, corn, and cotton. Florida papers often commented on these incidents. On September 8, 1829, an editor noted Tallahassee's "combustible nature," and the next year called for the organization of a fire department.[71] For thirty years before the Civil War, many Floridians viewed most fires as the work of arsonists. For example, when Tallahasseeans read of plantation fires in 1834 and the great Apalachicola holocaust of 1846, they laid the blame on incendiaries.[72]

Fear of arson was one reason for Floridians' concern over runaways. In the eyes of slave owners and their supporting society, the problems of slave stealing, runaways, and personal violence were heinous and interrelated. Absent slaves were economic debits for the owner; worse was the runaways' threat to property and person. Often banding together in outlaw areas, maroons caused consternation throughout the region.

Runaways were generally blamed on slave-stealers. Whites believed that blacks were not intelligent enough to leave on their own, nor would they forsake their carefree existence unless lured away. And if a slave had to be lured away, he certainly could not find his way back. Examples of "scapegoating" were rampant. Governor Call wrote of the problem of Negro-stealing: ". . . if the white man will not corrupt the virtue, or seduce the fidelity of the faithful African slave," slaves would never leave their masters. They were too dependent.[73] According to Southerners, however, slaves were constantly importuned by Negro-stealers. The Apalachicola paper in 1844 told of "Samuel Walker," who supposedly had helped seven Negroes escape and lived with a price of $1,000 on his head.[74] Two years later the *Pensacola Gazette* reported the lynching of the "notorious negro thief Yeoman." An assembled mob had voted, sixty-seven to twenty-three, to hang and had summarily executed the culprit at noon because of "the insecurity of their jails, and the fact of his having a band of accomplices in the community."[75] As the antebellum period drew to a close, Floridians began blaming almost all slave disappearances on lurking Negro-stealers. Denunciation of the thieves also increased in venom. In 1859, the *East Floridian* berated such "enemies— those who are not only attempting the destruction of our interests, but applying the torch to our homesteads, exciting insurrections and murdering our people."[76]

Floridians recognized the ever-present runaway problem. Florida planter George Noble Jones's papers include numerous references to runaways.[77] Florida's newspapers contained many evidences of and advertisements for runaways. Judging from casual references, the fugitive population was much larger than anyone acknowledged. In 1830, the Tallahassee *Floridian and Advocate* admonished the citizens to watch their kitchens more closely; runaways could obtain food too easily. Lax planters not issuing proper passes compounded the problem. Only a "more strict observation of every individual over his own premises" could solve the problem.[78] Again in 1834, the paper called citizens' attention to this evil, and chided masters for not being more active in securing slaves who disappeared. Plundering the public "with singular audacity in their predatory expeditions," runaways must be curtailed.[79]

Runaways had to be caught because they represented danger. Plundering was one thing; increased personal violence was another. In 1844, the *Commercial Advertiser* complained that British authorities had refused to extradite some runaways who had murdered and stolen in East Florida, then fled to the Bahamas: "our negro slaves are not only encouraged to commit murder and theft, but every facility is offered them for escape, and protection extended to them when they are successful." Such activities, the paper held, would only encourage other slaves to commit atrocities and run for British territory.[80] Floridians may have remembered an earlier incident which supported this contention. Christopher Smith, living about seven miles from Magnolia, had been attacked in 1837 "by a straggling party of Seminoles, or by a gang of runaways, of whom it is reported there are a number out from some of the frontier plantations." The house and its contents were burned.[81] Florida faced violence from maroons throughout the period, but during the 1860s this proved a particular problem. Either violence increased or it was more faithfully reported.[82] Regardless of the reason, violent fugitive slaves received more attention.

Runaways were incidental to the possibility of unexpected slave violence. Often runaways and violence were interrelated, as James Stirling indicated in his 1856 warning to the South that repression would merely increase "the explosive force" of slavery and change "complaint into conspiracy."[83] Examples to prove Stirling's point surfaced throughout the era of slavery. At El Destino Plantation in Leon County, overseer Moxley whipped four female slaves who had run away, then been caught and returned. Aberdeen, the brother of one, seized an axe and tried to kill Moxley.[84] George Evans, Chemonie Plantation's overseer, had his life threatened under similar circumstances.[85] In 1829, Hagan, Governor Call's plantation overseer, was stabbed in the back by a slave when Hagan attempted to chastise him. A second man, answering Hagan's calls, was likewise stabbed before the slave fled.[86] In another instance, William Pierce, a Madison County slave-owner, was murdered when he started to whip a slave. Presumably as Pierce approached, the Negro uncovered an axe he had hidden and "split in twain the head of his master, scattering the brains in every direction."[87]

Often a slave's violence occurred in conjunction with another crime, most often theft. Examples proliferated during the antebellum era. Thomas P. Trotter and Richard Bolton, two Negro traders from North Carolina, were murdered in Georgia by a pair of their own slaves. As the men slept, the blacks cut their owners' throats with razors, though Trotter had to be axed when he refused to die. The slaves took money, burned the papers which proved them chattel, then fled toward Florida.[88] In another instance, an unnamed slave murdered Fish, driver of the Tallahassee-Quincy stage, but lost most of the stolen loot to Holloman and Caruthers, two white accomplices.[89] In 1860, Albert Clark of Hernando County was shot when he returned from taking his daughter to school in Brooksville. Hampton, one of Clark's slaves, had secreted himself in a hammock near the road, shot his master, and robbed the body.[90] In another instance, a seaman named Curry had his throat cut and "a considerable sum of money" taken from him. A slave of Colonel J. Gamble had given the sailor a ride from St. Marks in Gamble's wagon, then murdered him.[91] Another case occurred when Joe and Crittenden, two slaves, murdered a Mr. Roundtree near the Georgia line. The editor of the *Floridian* claimed that "The object of the perpetrators is supposed to have been money, of which the deceased was known to have a small sum."[92]

Murder for money and violence to escape punishment were understandable; murder without apparent motives was not. Perhaps officials felt constrained to provide solutions for open cases and obtained admissions of guilt from slaves. A stranger named Ferguson was found dead in a Calhoun County pond in 1859. No clues existed, but the Fernandina East Floridian intimated that perhaps a slave should be questioned.[93] Equally mystifying were the murders of masters known to be kind, or of respected overseers.

M. D. Griffin, overseer for Major Watts of Madison County, was murdered by eleven of his charges in March 1860.[94] Just the previous month, Lewis, slave of Dr. W. J. Keitt, had cut his master's throat. Local authorities near Ocala claimed that Allen, Issac, John, Zelius, and Melvina, all Keitt's slaves, had participated in the murder. Kitt was known as a kind man, gentle with his chattel, and people across the state wondered at his killing. No one could, or would, offer any explanation for the murder.[95]

In Florida, favorite slave weapons were axes, razors, knives, and occasionally guns. Poison was less frequently employed, perhaps because of its scarcity. As in the attempt to poison John Harris's whole wedding party in Georgia in 1837, the measure often failed.[96] American slaves, like their masters, seemed to prefer a more personal, face-to-face violence. Slaves might murder masters in a fit of temper or to escape punishment. Runaways might simply be escaping the consequences of earlier actions. Murder might be for money, arson for revenge, and non-production due to chronic laziness. Suicide and the murder of one's family might signal insanity, as freemen sometimes committed the same irrevocable act.

One proof of causation appeared in the Florida papers in 1856. A slave woman in Cincinnati had cut the throat of one child, and told slave catchers that she wished she had been able to do the same to her others. She had rather kill her children than have them return to slavery.[97] The *Florida News* told of James E. Humphrey's Negro woman and her two children. Though Humphrey was a "lenient and kind" master, the woman had drowned her five-year-old son and three-year-old daughter in a nearby well. She then returned to her house, burned it, and fled. No motive other than insanity could be assigned to the "unnatural and diabolical act."[98] Insanity was one possible explanation for suicide too, but "fatal accident" was more common. Such was the verdict when one of S. B. Thomas's slaves was found dead a short distance from Fernandina. Supposedly the gun he was carrying discharged accidentally as he stepped over a log, although the lead hit his forehead.[99]

Causation was not a primary concern to antebellum Floridians—violence was. Rationally, Floridians seemed to realize that an insurrection was only remotely possible; the evidence of 1820, the Seminole wars, and continuing slave unrest shook their assurance. Ambivalence toward the probability of black revolution was the result. When warned that England might send black regiments to the Gulf states in case of war, a Tallahassee editor echoed the *Montgomery Journal's* belief that, "Three or four thousand negroes to be had for the catching" would only prove "the tallest sort of *hunt.*"[100] This was Florida's answer to the belief that abolition was the cure for unrest. What Floridians could not easily understand was the daily resistance to the institution. Slaves seldom fought openly in revolt, despite the Seminole wars. The razor or axe was most liable to drip with the master's blood in an individual act, either out of pique or a search for freedom. Theft, arson, fugitive slaves, murder, suicide, and slave-to-slave violence should have convinced Floridians that they would have no rest so long as slavery existed. Despite the adaptation of the black to servitude, the willingness to take freedom by "pulling foot" or express his emotions by violence was always below the surface, waiting for expression.

Mr. Granade is assistant professor of history, Ouachita Baptist University, Arkadelphia, Arkansas.

1. Kenneth Wiggins Porter, "Negroes on the Southern Frontier, 1670-1763," *Journal of Negro History,* XXXIII (January 1948), 58, 62, 64. M. Foster Farley, "The Fear of Negro Slave Revolts in South Carolina, 1690-1865," *Afro-American Studies,* III (December 1972), 199, mentions the problem of Florida and Spanish proclamations offering freedom to fugitive slaves.
2. Herbert Aptheker, *American Negro Slave Revolts* (New York, 1943), 30.
3. Kenneth Wiggins Porter, "Negroes and the East Florida Annexation Plot, 1811-1813," *Journal of* Negro *History,* XXX (January 1945), 24.
4. Quoted in Nicholas Halasz, *The Rattling Chains* (New York, 1966), 107. Brevard's background for Jackson's activities in Florida is especially important, considering the rumor that the Seminoles and Negroes would unite under Lieutenant Ambrister, seize St. Marks from the Spanish garrison, and fortify themselves as the band of Garcia had done earlier in the St. Marys River "Negro Fort." Caroline Mays Brevard, *A History of Florida, From the Treaty of 1763 to Our Own Times,* ed. James Alexander Robertson, 2 vols. (DeLand, 1924-1925) I, 49.
5. Porter, "Negroes and the East Florida Annexation Plot," 9.
6. Dorothy Dodd, "Florida's Population in 1545," *Florida Historical Quarterly,* XXIV (July 1945), 29.
7. Tallahassee *Floridian,* March 14, April 18, 1846.
8. U. S. Bureau of the Census, *A Century of Population Growth, From the First Census of the United States to the Twelfth, 1790-1900* (Washington, 1909), 223; U. S. Census Office, *Population of the United States in* 1860; Compiled from the Original Returns of the Eighth Census, Under *the Direction of the Secretary of the Interior* (Washington, 1864), 51, 53.
9. *Eighth Census, 1860, Population,* 50-53.
10. Tallahassee *Southern Journal,* April 21, 1846.
11. U. S. Census Office, *Statistical View of the United States, Embracing Its* Territory, Population— White, Free Colored, and Slave— Moral and Social Condition, Industry, Prop-

erty, and Revenue; The Detailed Statistics of Cities, Towns, and Counties; Being a Compendium of the Seventh *Census* (Washington, 1854), 208.

12. *Acts of the Legislative Council of the Territory of Florida, Passed at Their First Session, 1822* (Pensacola, 1823), 181-85.
13. *Acts of the Legislative Council of the Territory of Florida, Passed at Their 6th Session, 1827-8* (Tallahassee, 1828), 99-100.
14. *Acts of the Legislative Council of the Territory of Florida, Passed at Their Third Session, 1824* (Tallahassee, 1825), 291.
15. *Ibid.,* 290.
16. Thelma Bates, "The Legal Status of the Negro in Florida," *Florida Historical Quarterly,* VI (January 1928), 163.
17. *Acts of the Legislative Council of the Territory of Florida, Passed at Their Fourth Session, 1825* (Tallahassee, 1826), 52-56; *Acts of the Legislative* Council of the Territory of Florida, Passed at Their Ninth Session, Commencing January Third, and Ending February Thirteenth, 1831 (Tallahassee, 1831), 23-25.
18. Tallahassee *Floridian,* March 8, 1834.
19. Fernandina *East Floridian,* December 8, 1859. Under laws of 1828 and 1853, intoxicating liquors were taboo. *Acts of the Legislative Council, 1827-8,* 104; *Laws of Florida,* 1852-1853, 117.
20. Tallahassee *Floridian,* June 13, 1846. Benton replaced "Hernando as the name of the twenty-second county from March 6, 1844, until December 24, 1850, when the former name was restored. Named for Thomas Hart Benton (1782-1853), U. S. senator from Missouri for 30 years (1821-51). His vociferous opposition to paper money and a national bank earned Benton the nickname 'Old Bullion.' Florida's recognition of Benton was, however, the result of his sponsorship of the Armed Occupation Act of 1842, which opened central Florida to settlers." Allen Morris, *Florida Place Names* (Coral Gables, 1974), 23.
21. Tallahassee *Floridian,* October 3, 1835.
22. Fernandina *East Floridian,* December 15, 1859.
23. *Ibid.,* January 5, 1860; Fernandina *Weekly East Floridian,* October 4, 1860.
24. Fernandina *Weekly East Floridian,* October 24, 1860. Such actions by northern papers may have been one reason for the silence over slave unrest in southern journals. Northern exaggerations could fuel abolitionist sentiment and undercut southern defenses of the peculiar institution. The "extremely delicate character" of the information could also produce "unnecessary excitement" at home. Tallahassee *Floridian and Journal,* December 13, 1856. Such excitement might prove useful, however, in trying to unify southern public opinion against the "enemy" in the North.
25. Apalachicola *Commercial Advertiser,* March 11, 1844. For more insight into this situation, see Peter D. Klingman, "A Florida Slave Sale," *Florida Historical Quarterly,* LII (July 1973), 62-66.
26. Ada Lou Cherry, "The United States Navy Yard at Pensacola, Florida, 1823-1862" (M.A. thesis, Florida State University, 1953), 57.
27. Tallahassee *Floridian & Journal,* January 11, 1851.
28. Tallahassee *Floridian,* September 25, 1832.

29. Apalachicola *Commercial Advertiser,* January 25, February 1, 1849.
30. Fernandina *Weekly East Floridian,* November 21, 1860.
31. Tallahassee *Southern Journal,* September 11, December 25, 1848. While some historians believe that Florida, along with the rest of the South, panicked after the Nat Turner rebellion in 1831, such does not appear to have been the case. The new laws either reenacted earlier measures or were one more step in the gradual, constant tightening of restrictions throughout the era. Evidently Virginia seemed far away. Local newspapers gave no indication of undue alarm. Of the periodic revisions of the Florida slave code, none took place immediately after Nat Turner's revolt, and the legislative records (although not recording debate) indicate no great concern. Perhaps John W. Cromwell realized this when he excluded Florida from his list of those states which did significantly strengthen their slave codes in his "The Aftermath of Nat Turner's Insurrection," *Journal of Negro History,* V (April 1920), 208-34.
32. Quoted in Tallahassee *Floridian & Advocate,* October 13, 1829.
33. "Southern Times," 11, 1830. quoted in Tallahassee *Floridian and Advocate,* May
34. Apalachicola *Commercial Advertiser, Floridian,* August 8, 1835. September 30, 1844; Tallahassee
35. Apalachicola *Commercial Advertiser,* September 30, 1844.
36. Fernandina *East Floridian,* November 10, 1859.
37. *Ibid.,* January 5, 1860.
38. Fernandina *Weekly East Floridian,* October 31, 1860.
39. *Ibid.,* December 5, 1860.
40. *Madison Messenger,* quoted in *ibid.,* November 28, 1860.
41. *Ibid.,* August 16, 1860.
42. Helen Tunnicliff Catterall, ed., *Judicial Cases concerning American Slavery and the Negro,* 5 vols. (Washington, 1926-1937; facsimile edition, New York, 1968), II, 327-28. A lack of records makes the reality and extent of this uprising seem questionable. Both Harvey Wish, "American Slave Insurrections Before 1861," *Journal of Negro History,* XXII (July 1937), 318n; and Aptheker, *American Negro Slave Revolts,* 266n, get their information from Catterall.
43. Boston *Liberator,* June 5, 1846.
44. Tallahassee *Floridian & Journal,* August 31, 1850.
45. Aptheker, *American Negro Slave Revolts,* 111. Aptheker's source is the Richmond (Virginia) *Daily Dispatch,* September 30, 1856, citing "local newspapers." See also, Harvey Wish, "The Slave Insurrection Panic of 1856," *Journal of Southern History,* V (May 1939), 206-22, for an overview.
46. Tallahassee *Floridian and Journal,* December 27, 1856.
47. James Stirling, *Letters from the Slave States* (London, 1857; facsimile edition, New York, 1969), 299.
48. Tallahassee *Floridian and Journal,* December 6, 1856.
49. New York *Tribune,* December 20, 1856.
50. Tallahassee *Floridian and Journal,* December 6, 13, 1856.
51. Quoted in Herbert Aptheker, "Maroons Within the Present Limits of the United States," *Journal of Negro History,* XXIV (April 1939), 183.

52. Catterall, *Judicial Cases,* III, 125. To avoid this problem, many owners sent their slaves to the interior. See John E. Johns, *Florida During the Civil War* (Gainesville, 1963), 146.
53. Quoted in Aptheker, "Maroons Within the Present Limits of the United States," 183.
54. Edwin L. Williams, Jr., "Negro Slavery in Florida," *Florida Historical Quarterly,* XXVIII (October 1949), 104.
55. John T. Sprague, *The Origin, Progress, and Conclusion of the Florida War* (New York, 1849; facsimile edition. Gainesville, 1964), 309. For further information, see Kenneth W. Porter, "Osceola and the Negroes," *Florida Historical Quarterly,* XXXIII (January-April 1955), 235-39. There were perhaps between 250 and 800 slaves with the Seminoles. Sprague, *Origin, Progress, and Conclusion of the Florida War,* 19, 97.
56. Quoted in Kenneth Wiggins Porter, "Florida Slaves and Free Negroes in the Seminole War, 1835-1842," *Journal of Negro History,* XXVIII (October 1943), 393
57. Ibid.
58. *Ibid.,* 394.
59. Acts of the Governor and Legislative Council, of the Territory of Florida. Passed at the Fourteenth Session. Begun and Held at the City of Tallahassee, on Monday January 4th, and Ended Sunday February 14th, *1836* (Tallahassee, 1836), 13-15.
60. Quoted in Porter, "Florida Slaves and Free Negroes in the Seminole War," 395.
61. *Ibid.,* 398.
62. *Ibid.,* 409.
63. Quoted in Russell Garvin, "The Free Negro in Florida Before the Civil
64. War," *Florida Historical Quarterly,* XLVI (July 1967), 6.
65. Porter, "Florida Slaves and Free Negroes in the Seminole War," 397. *Ibid.,* 416. Two years later, the city council was forced to decrease night patrols because of "general unwillingness" to participate. *Ibid.,* 419.
66. *Ibid.,* 397. The purchases continued despite a January 23, 1837, city ordinance forbidding such sales— especially ammunition— to slaves, free blacks, or mulattoes. *Ibid,* 402.
67. *Ibid.,* 414-15. The question which most needs answering is why a free Negro would risk the consequences of such an act. Perhaps in the answer lies another clue to slave unrest.
68. *Ibid.,* 416-17.
69. Quoted in Brevard, *History of Florida,* II, 224-25.
70. Apalachicola *Commercial Advertiser,* September 2, 1844. "A slave was brought before a magistrate charged with pilfering; the magistrate began to remonstrate: 'Do you know how to read?' 'Yes massa, little.' 'Well, don't you never make use of the bible?' 'Yes, massa, *I trap my razor on it sometime.'"*
71. Tallahassee *Floridian & Advocate,* September 8, 1829; Tallahassee *Floridian and Advocate,* May 4, 1830. Arson was made a capital offense in 1840. *Acts and Resolutions of the Legislative Council of the Territory* of Florida, Passed at its Eighteenth Session, Which commenced on the sixth day of January, and ended on the second day of March, 1840 (Tallahassee, 1840), 39-40. An 1848 law distinguished between misdemeanors (minor dwellings) and felonies (public buildings) and set new penalties— thirty-nine lashes and one hour in the pillory, and up to 100 lashes plus one-half hour with ears nailed to posts. *Laws of Florida,* 1847-1848, 10-11.
72. Tallahassee *Floridian,* March 22, 1834, October 24, 1846.

73. Quoted in Brevard, *History of Florida,* II, 224-25.
74. The Apalachiocola *Commercial Advertiser's* July 6, 1844, reference to "Samuel Walker" was probably an error. The story is most likely based on the experience of Jonathan Walker, a Massachusetts native who took seven slaves from the Pensacola area on June 22, 1844, and headed for the Bahamas in his boat. The $1,000 reward was offered by the owners of the slaves. For the complete story, see his *Trial and Imprisonment of* Jonathan Walker, at Pensacola, Florida, for Aiding Slaves to Escape from *Bondage* (Boston, 1845; facsimile editions, New York, 1969, Gainesville, 1974).
75. *Pensacola Gazette,* January 24, 1846.
76. Fernandina *East Floridian,* December 8, 1859.
77. Ulrich Bonnell Phillips and James David Glunt, eds., *Florida Plantation Records from the papers of George Noble Jones* (St. Louis, 1927), passim.
78. Tallahassee *Floridian and Advocate,* October 5, 1830.
79. Tallahassee *Floridian,* January 18, 1834.
80. Apalachicola *Commercial Advertiser,* March 11, 1844.
81. Tallahassee *Floridian,* July 1, 1837.
82. See, for example, the Fernandina *East Floridian,* March 15, 1860, Fernandina *Weekly East Floridian,* August 23, 30, 1860. Passage of the Fugitive Slave Act in 1851 may have encouraged reports of runaways.
83. Stirling, *Letters from the Slave States,* 301.
84. Kathryn T. Abbey, "Documents Relating to El Destino and Chemonie Plantations, Middle Florida, 1828-1868. Part I," *Florida Historical Quarterly,* VII (January 1929), 196.
85. Edwin L. Williams, Jr., "Negro Slavery in Florida," Part II, *Florida Historical Quarterly,* XXVIII (January 1950), 191.
86. Tallahassee *Florida Advocate,* March 14, 1829.
87. Julia H. Smith, "The Plantation Belt in Middle Florida, 1850-1860" (Ph.D. dissertation, Florida State University, 1964), 138-39.
88. Tallahassee *Southern Journal,* February 14, 1848.
89. *Ibid.,* September 22, 29, 1846.
90. Fernandina *Weekly East Floridian,* October 18, 1860.
91: Tallahassee *Floridian,* July 22, 1837.
92. *Ibid.,* March 29, May 3, November 15, 22, 1834.
93. Fernandina *East Floridian,* July 28, 1859.
94. *Ibid.,* March 15, 1860.
95. Ocala *Fla. Home Companion,* quoted in *ibid.,* March 3, 1860; *Ocala Home Companion,* quoted in *ibid.,* March 8, 1860; *Home Companion,* quoted in *ibid.,* March 29, 1860.
96. Tallahassee *Floridian,* September 9, 1837.
97. Tallahassee *Floridian and Journal,* February 9, 1856.
98. Fernandina *Florida News,* February 10, 1859.
99. *Ibid.,* March 10, 1859.
100. Tallahassee *Southern Journal,* February 24, 1846.

6

Quasi-Freedom

In the antebellum era most free blacks lived in Maryland, Delaware, and Virginia, but by the time of the Civil War all states of the Deep South had free black populations, including the 932 living in Florida. Like its neighboring states, Florida had developed a social, four-caste system: white planters, poor whites, free blacks, and chattel slaves. On the face of it, free blacks seemed to occupy a stratum one step above slaves; in reality, free blacks in Florida suffered much of the same denigration and restrictions as bondsmen, rending them by the 1850s as little more than "quasi-free." This racial fault line of colonial and U.S. Florida is a long and engaging subject of the state's freedom struggle yet remains a somewhat obscure topic. As Russell Garvin notes in one of the few studies devoted to this subject, history discloses "precious little" about free blacks in colonial, territorial, and antebellum Florida. Without a full appreciation of the daunting challenges and varied roles free blacks faced and played, students of the Sunshine State's past will find it difficult to understand the depths and lessons of this story.

Proceeding from that premise, this article sheds light on the evolving history of free blacks' roles in Florida, beginning with the Spanish governor (Zuniga) opening the colony to fugitive slaves in 1704. The author recalls the record of the growth of free blacks up to the antebellum era, but readers should be aware that much new work on the subject has been done since the publication of this study, especially by scholars like Larry E. Rivers and Jane L. Landers.

The bulk of Garvin's article addresses the vicissitudes of life for free blacks (most of whom were mulattoes) in pre-Civil War decades. The author explains how white legal measures deprived free blacks residing in Florida of even the smallest semblance of self-determination. The free black community in Pensacola may be the exception to this pattern, as blacks there seemed to enjoy a more respected place in society than in other areas of Florida. The author quoted from the local newspapers attesting to the regard for blacks in that western panhandle city; however, it would have been helpful if he had further delved into the root causes of Pensacola's permissiveness. Another topic that demands further exploration is that of the "secret" origins of numerous free mulattoes in Florida: many resulted from white masters' sexual predation on slave women and their subsequent manumission of mixed-race children as masters faced death. As with free blacks in general, this is a particular topic that is yet submerged in the history books.

The heart of Garvin's article is his analysis of 19th-century demographics and restrictive legislation. The author recounts how white society promulgated measures to dissuade free blacks from migrating into Florida and to force them into a menial status in the state. One of the telling statistics is that the number of freed blacks remained static through four decades of censuses—not static percentage-wise but as a raw figure. When juxtaposed with the exponential growth of other sectors of the population, Garvin notes that the number of free blacks within the state remained dramatically lower than that of the slave states of the Upper South.

While Garvin's discussion is illuminating, readers may wish to learn more about the role of and successes of free blacks. For example, free blacks, despite racist shackles, supported themselves and their families through an incredibly wide-range of occupations, such as trade and transportation, dock workers, skilled craftsmen, construction hands, and as skilled and semi-skilled workers in Florida's urban centers. Free black women also seized opportunity in a variety of fields (e.g., manufacturing and mechanical pursuits, textiles, and seamstresses and tailoresses) and did not work solely as domestics as is commonly believed. Indeed, most free blacks congregated in urban milieus, with the largest percentage in Key West. Based on the Eighth Census of the United States in 1860, Key West included 156 free blacks (almost one-ninth of the state's total free black population) who owned property worth over $12,000. If reflective of the state at-large, free blacks in Key West secured important measures of self-control and financial success despite white attempts through various and persistent means to restrict opportunity.

Garvin concludes that free blacks recognized that imperfect freedom was worth the hardships of white racism, but readers should consult other sources for timely examinations of this subject. The final paragraph is particularly pithy—the author acknowledges that the evidence is scarce but it does seem to suggest a historical and endless struggle by free blacks to overcome their status of "near slave." Although this article dovetails nicely with preceding sections of this book, its greatest asset may be whetting the reader's appetite to further understand free blacks' personal and collective struggle for dignity and rights in pre-Civil War Florida.

FURTHER READING

Eugene P. Southall, "Negroes in Florida Prior to the Civil War," *Journal of Negro History*, Vol. 19 (1934);

Ruth B. Barr and Modeste Hargis, "The Voluntary Exile of Free Negroes of Pensacola," *Florida Historical Quarterly*, Vol. 17 (1938); Kenneth Wiggins Porter, "Florida Slaves and Free Negroes in the Seminole War, 1835-1842," *Florida Historical Quarterly*, Vol. 28 (1943);

Kenneth Wiggins Porter, "The Negro Abraham," *Florida Historical Quarterly*, Vol. 25 (1946);

Herbert J. Doherty, Jr., ed., "A Free Negro Purchases His Daughter: Two Letters From The Richard Keith Call Collection," *Florida Historical Quarterly*, Vol. 29 (1950);

F. Bruce Rosen, "A Plan To Homestead Freedmen in Florida in 1866," *Florida Historical Quarterly*, Vol. 43 (1965);

Leedell Neyland, "The Free Negro in Florida," *Negro History Bulletin*, Vol. 29 (1965);

Peter D. Klingman, "A Florida Slave Sale," *Florida Historical Quarterly*, Vol. 52 (1973);

William Warren Rogers, "A Great Stirring in The Land: Tallahassee and Leon County in 1860," *Florida Historical Quarterly*, Vol. 64 (1985);

Daniel H. Shafer, "'A Class of People Neither Freemen Nor Slaves': From Spanish to American Relations in Florida, 1821-1861," *Journal of Social History*, Vol. 26 (1993);

Jane Landers, "Free and Slave," in Michael Gannon, ed., *The New History of Florida* (1996), chapter 10;

Jane G. Landers, ed., *Against the Odds: Free Blacks in the Slave Societies of the Americas* (1996);

Loren Schweninger, ed., *Race, Slavery, and Free Blacks. Series II, Petitions to Southern County Courts, 1775-1867. Part A, Georgia (1796-1867), Florida (1821-1867), Alabama (1821-1867), Mississippi (1822-1867)* (2003);

David Barry Gaspar and Darlene Clark Hine, eds., *Beyond Bondage: Free Women of Color in the Americas* (2004).

The Free Negro In Florida Before The Civil War

Russell Garvin

The Florida Historical Quarterly, Volume 46, issue 1 (1967), 1-18.

FREEDOM FOR NEGROES in a society where race was the only qualification for slavery was at best an anomaly and at worst an illusion. In either case though, freedom survived alongside slavery. Florida first acquired free Negroes early in the seventeenth century. In 1704 the Spanish governor, Zuniga, opened the territory to fugitive slaves from British plantations to the North.[1] Thus established, potential liberty across the border tempted Carolina blacks and tormented their white owners. It was hoped that the colonization of Georgia would serve as a buffer region to prevent the escape of slaves to Florida. Carolina benefited, but Georgia, once slaves had been imported, found the runaway problem its biggest nuisance,[2] and it remained for Georgia a continuous problem. Spanish correspondence of the period reveals a regular flow of Negroes into Florida.[3] Once in the region the blacks lived as free subjects of the Bourbon king. They were soon numerous enough to be formed into companies to aid in the defense of the territory.[4] A refuge for the Negroes, Gracia Real de Santa Teresa de Mose, was established three miles north of St. Augustine by the accommodating Spanish authorities in 1739. Provisions were made for military and religious instruction, and food was to be supplied by the government until a crop could be harvested.[5] But there was no harvest. In the summer of 1740, James Oglethorpe led a group of British colonists into Florida. They attacked St. Augustine and drove the Negroes from their fort, which was destroyed. In the city the blacks found safety, and there they remained until 1763, when they were transferred to Cuba.[6]

At the same time, in the western parts of Florida, Negroes were immigrating along with those factious Creek Indians called Seminoles. Spanish law extended its protection over them and gave them the right of land ownership.[7] The Negroes associated with the Indians can be separated roughly into two groups: those who were legally slaves, and those who were free and who served as allies.[8]

The Indians had obtained slaves as gifts from the British government or had purchased them in imitation of slave-owning whites. What to do with them once the novelty wore off posed an insuperable problem for the Seminoles. The Negroes were allowed to build their own farms, paying a moderate rent in kind to their Indian masters. A type of democratic vassalage was created completely devoid of feelings of racial superiority. Intermarriage was common. Some who possessed a knowledge of English and Spanish became useful interpreters. The most astute gained the confidence of the Indians and served as valued councilors of much influence. When necessary the males willingly fought alongside the braves for the protection of their homes and independence.[9]

Many a slave longed to exchange his position for this kind of servitude. When Georgia settlements wee attacked by the Creeks, Negro escapes were given further encouragement.[10] The seventeenth century slave owners could do little more than fume and complain to the government. After the Revolution, a few abortive expeditions were launched to capture runaways, but these were singularly unsuccessful. The power of the Creeks effectively stood in the way of attempts to return Negroes to their owners, and the blacks worked harmoniously near the Indians. They settled on good land along the Apalachicola and Suwannee rivers and many owned large flocks and herds.[11]

Tranquility could not last forever, however, and beginning in 1811 American raids into Florida increased. Indian and Negro property was destroyed, including two or three Indian towns, but neither the Seminoles nor Florida was conquered.[12]

Active participation in the American-British war came in 1814 when two English ships landed Lieutenant Colonel Edward Nicholls, his regular troops, Negro and Indian allies, and about 100 Negro slaves in Apalachicola Bay. At a point on the east bank of the Apalachicola, some fifteen miles upstream, the English constructed a military stronghold. Eight cannons were placed in it. From the fort, the British could control river commerce and operate against the Georgia-Alabama frontier. They also used it as headquarters to confer with the Red Stick Indians, the Seminoles, and refugee Negroes. The troops stayed through the winter, but with spring they withdrew at the request of a disapproving British ministry. The fort was left stocked with arms, ammunition, and artillery.[13] The residents of Georgia and Alabama looked upon the fort with little equanimity. It housed 300 Negroes, including women and children, and it became know as Negro Fort. Perhaps another thousand Negroes settled "under the guns of the fort" in the surrounding area. Opposition increased until finally in July 1816, after the Spanish governor at Pensacola indicated that he could do little to stop the fort's activities, General Andrew Jackson ordered the destruction of the fort. On July 20 an attack was launched under the command of Colonel Duncan L. Clinch. Seven days later, on the morning of July 27, a battery of American vessels attacked the fort, and a hot shell found its target, exploding the fort's central magazine. The resulting explosion reportedly was heard all the way to Pensacola. One observer estimated that 270 men, women, and children were killed, and nearly all the rest were mortally wounded. Only three persons escaped injury. The Americans and friendly Indians confiscated all of the fort's remaining contents, the Indians receiving the greater part of the booty. Many refugee Negroes had already sought protection in the Seminole Indian villages when they learned of Clinch's movement down the river. The others were captured and returned to the Spaniards and Americans who claimed them. On August 2 the campaign against the Negro Fort officially ended.[14]

Runaways, however, continued to filter into Florida, and in time Indians and Negroes reoccupied many of the farms, and their settlements again served as resting places for slaves fleeing South. There were Negro villages scattered across Florida almost to St. Augustine. Contemporary accounts give estimates of well over 1,000 free Negroes in Florida in the two decades following the destruction of Negro Fort. They lived in log and palmetto huts surrounded by fields up to twenty acres in size. The greatest numbers were found on the islands of the Great Wahoo Swamp, along the Withlacoochee River, in the Big Cypress Swamp, in the St. Johns River, and on the Suwannee where their Old Town was located.[15]

Since Indian raids and slave escapes persisted along the Georgia-Alabama frontier, General Jackson in March 1818 led Regulars and Georgia militia into Florida. He moved against the Indians and Negroes living along the east side of the Apalachicola River, and several small villages in the area, inhabited almost entirely by blacks, were destroyed. For the next several days Jackson pursued the Indians. Finally, a skirmish was fought at Old Town on the Suwannee. Very few Indians were captured and no Negroes. Jackson could not follow the remainder into more southerly parts of the territory and withdrew. In May 1818, he declared the war at an end.[16] The remaining Negroes and Indians for the most part settled around Tampa Bay or moved south to Cape Florida where many were carried by Bahama wreckers to remote islands.[17] With the end of fighting the Indians and Negroes tried hard to return to pre-1816 conditions, but raids and immigration by whites prevented this.

That part of the First Seminole War which had aimed at quelling the Indians and capturing Negroes had been a failure for the United States. Apart from those wounded at Negro Fort in 1816, few slaves had been captured. Many Negroes thus remained at liberty, increasing in numbers as they were joined by escapees from Georgia and Alabama. Their presence was tempting to whites, who ventured into Indian lands intent on capturing slaves and fugitives. The incursions were especially bad along the Apalachicola River, and probably few had escaped the Georgia raiders by the late 1830s.[18]

Penetration of the wilderness by farmers also served to thwart a reversion of the Indians and Negroes to former modes of living. White husbandry pushed the Indians deeper and deeper into the peninsula. In 1832, some of the tribal chiefs signed a treaty providing for emigration to western lands where the Creeks were already settled. Orders to move came three years later, but dissenting Indians and Negroes began warfare anew.[19] They hoped first of all to persuade the government to grant them lands not coveted by white settlers, but if forced to move West, they wanted a treaty which would allow the Negroes to move with them. The Negroes for their part were farmers, and they were not averse to settling the land west of the Mississippi if guarantees for their freedom could be secured. The only way each group could secure its goals was to wear down the government until it made a reasonable offer.[20]

Negroes played an important roll in the resistance, and many participated in the actual fighting. According to some interpreters, they excelled the Indians as warriors. They exercised superior caution and attended to many important details.[21] So involved were they in the Second Seminole War, that General Jesup, commanding general in Florida, in 1836 wrote the war department that the "negroes rule the Indians."[22] In another letter he elaborated: "This, you may be assured, is a negro, not an Indian war; and if it be not speedily put down, the South will feel the effects of it on their slave population before the end of the next season."[23]

The part played by Negro leaders in the Second Seminole War was hardly mentioned at all except by contemporary Indians. Part of the reason for this was the reluctance of a Seminole Negro, who was legally a slave, to give information to a white questioner. But more of the reason was found in the southern mind; the Negroes were considered as a body which threatened the existence of slavery in Florida and adjacent states. To picture the Negroes as individuals with human emotions could evoke sympathy in many quarters, so whenever mention was made of a Negro, particularly one who was a leader, it was usually kept brief and unfavorable.[24]

There were some free Negroes not associated with the Indians who also participated in the Seminole War. Even though they had less to gain and more to lose than either slaves or Indian Negroes, they fought in the field and worked behind the line. Some operated as spies and secret agents to obtain recruits, supplies, and information. The general atmosphere of discontent and brooding hostility produced by all these operations kept a large part of the militia at home to guard against any sudden outbreak, thus relieving pressure on the Indians and Negroes in the field and contributing to the prevention of their utter defeat.[25]

The Seminole War was nearing its end, and by 1841 it was believed that nearly all the Negroes that had cooperated with the Indians had been moved to the West. One observer estimates that 500 persons had been "seized and enslaved" during the war.[26] Many Negroes had intermarried with the Indians and half-breeds, and others had been enslaved by the Indians. Whatever the relationship, these Negroes left with the Indians.[27] But by no means did all free Negroes live with the Indians. It is believed that there were a number of others living in Florida, but information about them is scarce.

Comparatively few free Negroes lived among the white citizens of ante-bellum Florida, and those living with the Indians were ignored by census takers.[28] While Florida's population quadrupled in the four federal censuses taken before the Civil War, the number of free Negroes remained nearly static: 844 Negroes, making up 2.4 percent of the population in 1830; 817, or 1.5 percent in 1840; 932, 1.1 percent in 1850; and 932, or 0.6 percent in 1860.[29] Compared with other states on the number of non-slave blacks, Florida ranked near the bottom throughout the ante-bellum period.

The average Florida free Negro, as shown by the following statistics from the population census of 1860 was decidedly older than either slaves or whites:

AVERAGE AGE IN FLORIDA

Year	Free Negro	Slave	White
1830	23.8	20.3	20.9
1840	24.8	21.3	21.5
1850	26.6	21.6	21.4
1860	25.0	21.3	21.2

Florida did not differ in this respect from the rest of the United States except that Florida whites were younger than most in the nation. This was due probably to the influx of young settlers. According to census reports literacy was not too low. In 1850, thirty percent of free Negro males and forty percent of the females over twenty years old could read and write, as compared with seventy-five percent white women and eighty-six percent white men. In the same year sixty-six free Negroes were attending schools in Escambia, Monroe, and St. Johns counties. [30] Ten years later only nine free Negroes were in school.[31]

It should be explained that the term free Negro includes mulattoes, who were defined by law as "every person other than a negro, who shall have one fourth part or more of negro blood... ."[32] Beginning with the census of 1850 officials noted this distinction. In that year there were 703 of mixed blood to 229 blacks. When contrasted to the 8:100 ratio of mulatto to Negro among Florida slaves, the disproportion is staggering.[33] Certainly legal freedom for a few blacks seemed to indicate sexual license for some whites. Indeed, it was not uncommon for a black mother to have mulatto children living with her; the census schedules abound with examples.

Only a few areas of the state had free Negroes in any concentration. Two-thirds of them lived in Duval, Escambia, Monroe, and St. Johns counties; most of the others were located in north-west Florida, particularly along the Apalachicola River and in Leon County.[34] Hillsborough County had few free Negroes because of the recency of its settlement and its distance from borders and other Negroes.

While the total number of free Negroes in the state remained fairly constant in the years prior to 1860, this should not be interpreted as meaning life was stable for them. Indeed, it must have been anything but tranquil. While women outnumbered men, the margin fluctuated greatly; in 1830 and 1850 there were almost a hundred more women, yet in each of the subsequent enumerations the difference almost disappeared.[35] The changeableness of their lives makes it difficult to follow a name through the censuses. For example, no name appears more than twice in any of the four relevant censuses of

St. John's County-one of the most peaceful regions for free Negroes. Only fifteen out of 200 names are the same in both 1850 and 1860 when the list included all members of a family and not just heads of families.

Why this constant change? Deaths certainly claimed many, but births served to replace the dead. More of an answer lies in the unpopularity the free Negro as a group faced from white sources. When whites chose to make it so, life became difficult in many ways. Movement away from Florida and away from the United States was encouraged and enslavement was always a real possibility. Many free Negroes had already known compulsory servitude in their lives, and they knew how easy it would be to return to this status.

Some of the free Negroes were runaways or descendants of runaways who had chosen to live among the whites or had fate choose it for them. The seventy-five to a hundred free blacks who lived along the banks of the Apalachicola River were probably among this group. However, since most lived in the old Spanish port cities, it is reasonable to assume that they owed much to the liberal Spanish laws which required a master to free any slave offering him $300,[36] and which made children of unmarried black mothers free.[37] Legal immigration and manumission also may be assumed to have played their part in creating the free Negro population.

Immigration of Negroes was exceedingly unpopular with settlers in Florida. An early legislative act made it unlawful for any free Negro to come on his own or to be brought into the Florida Territory. A guilty offender had to put up $500 recognizance that he would leave within ten days, and if the bond could not be paid the Negro was to be sold out for one year's service to the highest bidder.[38] According to an 1828 enactment sailors on foreign or American vessels in territorial waters around Florida were specifically excluded.[39]

So important was this issue that the Constitutional Convention of 1838 could not overlook it. The drafting committee for the document which became effective with statehood in 1845 wanted to make it the "duty" of the legislature to prevent free Negro immigration.[40] The full delegation found it too extreme to charge the General Assembly with this specific task, but it still gave the legislature "power" to pass such laws.[41]

For the remainder of the pre-Civil War period immigration was illegal. The law of 1827 was reenacted on February 10, 1832,[42] and that date, a decade later, was made the legal cut-off time, for the movement of free Negroes and mulattoes into Florida. All free Negroes brought into the territory after that time were to be sent out by the sheriff, and any culprit who refused to leave could then be sold into slavery for a period of ninety-nine years.[43] That this penalty was too harsh was immediately perceived, and in 1846, at the next session of the legislature, it was repealed.[44] The old act of 1832 remained on the books, however. Yet even in this attenuated degree, enforcement was light enough for the legislature in 1855 to pass the following act: "Whereas, Doubts have been expressed as to whether the act approved February 10, 1852 [*sic,* 1832], entitled an act to prevent the future migration of free negroes or mulattoes into this State, and for other purposes is in force; Therefore, Section 1, *Be it enacted by the Senate and the House of Representatives of the State of Florida in General Assembly convened,* That the said act . . . be and the same is hereby declared to be in full force, operation and effect, and applies to the migration and importation of the persons therein mentioned since the date of the approval of said act."[45]

These anti-immigration laws did serve to keep new free Negroes for the most part out of Florida, but they were not completely effective. Their success can be shown if the age of the Negroes born outside of the state was decidedly greater than those born in Florida; those born in other places would have entered the state in the years before enactment of the law, while Florida residents would include all born since. Thus the latter's age would be lower. Statistics computed from census reports show that this was the case. In 1850, the average Negro born in Florida was 17.2 years old as compared to 42.0 years for non-state births. In 1860, the figures were 18.4 and 41.6 respectively. The laws against entry were not totally successful. If they had been, the average age of out-of-state Negroes would be increasing, but this was not the case. Positive proof of lax enforcement is contained also in the census schedules. In 1850, there were thirty-six free Negroes under twenty-one that had been born outside Florida, and the number increased to thirty-eight ten years later.

In addition to prohibiting movement in, the legislature tried to limit manumission, but like the former law, this was also only partially successful. The first regulations on the matter allowed emancipation of any sane and healthy adult slave so long as he was younger than forty-five, which was an unlikely event.[46] Evidently this was not improbable enough; later legislation required a $200 forfeiture for each slave freed.[47] But even with these restrictions, manumission did occur, and in 1850, twenty-two are recorded, and in 1860, seventeen.[48] While these are small numbers, they do represent two percent of the total free Negroes living in Florida at the time.

Little can be definitely said about the relation of the Negroes and whites. Only a couple of specific examples come down to us. Free Negroes living in Pensacola seemed to have had the greatest amount of security. Called "creoles" because of their large portion of Spanish blood, they formed an active property-owning class, served on city juries with whites, and held a respected place in the community.[49] When many of them left the United States in 1857 because of the growing restrictions on their life, the *Pensacola Gazette* expressed a common sentiment: "It was a painful sight to see them parting from their friends and their native country to seek homes in a foreign land. They take with them the sympathy of all our citizens on account of the causes which have led them to leave us, and also their best wishes for their future happiness and prosperity in their new home."[50] Pensacola was an exception to the general rule, however. Whites and free Negroes did not get along so cordially elsewhere in Florida. Even Key West, another old Spanish port city, complained about the lax enforcement of the anti-immigration laws in a Grand Jury "List of Grievances," announced December 5, 1834.[51]

A unique insight into the life of another class of Negroes is given by the following annotation of the last page of the 1860 census schedules for Calhoun County: "The Free Negroes in this County are mixed blooded almost white and have intermarried with a low class of whites-Have no trade, occupation or profession. They live in a Settlement or Town of their own, their personal property consists of cattle and hogs. They make no produce except Corn Peas and Potatoes and very little of that. They are a lazy, indolent, smooth afs [sic] race."[52]

More balance can be presented by adding up the estimates of wealth the census takers made. Negroes throughout Florida owned property - $36,480 worth in 1850 ($25,900 in Escambia County), and $56,500 worth in 1860 ($19,750 in Escambia, $12,250 in Monroe). Martha Baxter, a Duval County Negro farm owner, had $5,000 real estate and a personal estate estimated at $52,000. When this is added to that of other free Negroes in the state in 1860, the total personal estate figures were $97,985 ($10,865 in Monroe, $7,800 in Escambia).

Occupations of the free Negroes tended to be unskilled and semi-skilled jobs like farmers, servants, seamstresses, and laundresses. But there were also carpenters, dressmakers, barbers, musicians, overseers, shoemakers, tavern keepers, bakers, cabinet makers, brickmasons, fishermen, mariners, merchants, raftmen, midwives, teamsters, mechanics, cooks, and clerks.

Florida law continued to be harsh on the free Negro. The white legislators wasted no time in modifying the liberal Spanish law which governed the early days of the new American territory;[53] the action of the Legislative Council placed the new state on a road of strict regulation.

The specter of slave revolt obsessed Florida no less than it did the rest of the South.

Free Negroes were regarded as a source of discontent for Negro slaves and as a means whereby abolitionist propaganda could be spread. To some extent the free blacks were even held responsible for the number of runaways among slaves.[54] On this subject, a Tallahassee paper in 1851 quoted the *Alabama Journal:* "The opinion in Alabama is quite equivalent, that the free negro population is the most dangerous incendiary element to our existing institution of society. Their example is prejudicial on the slaves, and the opinion is very general that the steps adopted by Virginia, to remove them, would be the best policy which could be pursued here."[55]

Fear of rebellion prompted a law which made illegal "riots, routs, and unlawful assemblies, quarrels, fighting, trespasses and seditious speeches by free Negroes and Mulattoes, or slave or slaves."[56] Black gatherings to hear preaching or "exhorting" were illegal unless they were worship services held in white churches. Patrols had authority to enter any establishment where such activity was going on and disperse the "illegal assembly."[57] Control was easier when negroes attended the same churches as whites; closer check could be kept on what went on before and after the service. In this instance, integration provided a better means of control than segregation.[58] Certain restraints were also placed on Negro commerce. Intoxicating liquors could not be sold to slaves by free Negroes, and nothing at all could be vended on Sundays.[59] In 1853 free Negroes were brought under the temperance law, and alcoholic beverages could not be given them in any quantity.[60]

Weapons, of course, were under careful legal superintendence. An early law prohibited any free Negro from "hunting by firelight outside of his inclosure."[61] There could be no good reason it was argued, for blacks to be stalking around at night. A couple of years later no free Negro or mulatto, except in St. Augustine and Pensacola, could carry any firearm without a license from a local justice of the peace.[62] The inevitable was not far behind. In 1833 it became unlawful for any Negro to keep in his house any firearms whatsoever.[63] After this no Negro was permitted to be armed except for his own defense, and then under white supervision.[64]

Still another way of controlling free Negroes was to place them in an inferior legal and political position. From the very beginning there was no question of political equality with white citizens. Legislation setting up the qualifications for suffrage in the Florida Territory excluded mention of all Negroes,[65] Jury duty was also prohibited to free colored persons; the congressional act setting up the territorial government saw to it,[66] and the Legislative Council wasted no time incorporating the debarment into the statutes.[67] A Negro, mulatto, or Indian could give evidence in a trial only where no whites were involved.[68] Where they could testify, and Negro who perjured himself was to have his ears nailed to posts, and he would be forced to stand like that for one hour, then his or her back was to be bared and thirty-nine lashes applied.[69] Feelings ran strong on the issue of Negroes being witnesses against whites, since that tacitly implied equality. In 1845, State Representative W. H. Brockenbrough was accused of supporting a bill which would have allowed Negroes to testify against whites. In his rebuttal, he claimed he was falsely accused, and he called the idea "shocking and absurd."[70]

One of the few rights free Negroes did have was property ownership. An 1828 letter from the commissioner of the General Land Office to the secretary of the treasury reports that one free person of color had had his claim to preemption suspended because of race. Feeling that this was unjust, the commissioner wrote, "I know of no law of the U. States which prohibits a free negro from *purchasing* lands, unless there be some express law of the Territory by which they are excluded from *purchasing,* I perceive no reason why a patent should not be issued."[71] The law did not forbid property ownership and it was relatively widespread.

Of more concern and less certainty was the Negro's right to own himself. Whenever a free Negro was apprehended as a slave, the burden of proof of his liberty rested with him; he was presumed slave.[72] Indiscriminate seizure was not allowed though, and if anyone should be convicted of stealing or selling a free person, he was to suffer death without the benefit of clergy.[73] The law was later reconsidered and the penalty lightened; the maximum punishment became a $500 fine and standing in the pillory for not more than three hours.[74] Anyone sold into slavery, though, could appeal to the governor for pardon. Freedom was actually achieved by this method in 1842, and again ten years later.[75]

Debt further jeopardized the Negro's liberty; his person served as ultimate security. A lender could get a court to issue a writ of *capias ad satisfaciendum* against a defaulting Negro for the money and all costs thereon attached. If the judgement was not paid, the officer issuing such a writ would "advertise the sale of the services of such defendant or defendants, to any such person who will pay or discharge such execution . . .for the shortest space of time . . ." at public auction. The Negro could then be sold and held as a slave subject to the same penalties, treatment, and duties which could be exacted from slaves. Should the Negro try to escape, his time would be doubled and continued to be doubled at every instance of attempted runaway.[76] Continuous residents since transference from Spain were exempted.[77] The same procedure could be used when fines for misdemeanors had been levied against free Negroes.[78]

The black man had to be kept in his place. Florida law prohibited mixed marriage; any such marriage was null and void and any children were "regarded as bastards and incapable of. . . receiving any estate . . . by inheritance." Any white man fornicating with negroes was to be fined up to $1,000, and he was disqualified from exercising any office of profit or trust in the territory, serving as a juror, or giving evidence in any case against whites.[79] No black could use "abusive and provoking language to, or lift his hand in opposition to" a white person except in cases where the offender was "wantonly assailed and lifted his hand in his or her own defense." Punishment was up to thirty-nine lashes.[80] After 1855, whites and Negroes were prohibited by law from playing card or dice games with each other.[81]

Free Negroes were subject to head taxes. At first they were brought under the general twenty-five cent head tax for all males of the state,[82] but in 1832, this was raised to a punitive level of $5.00 on all free persons of color over fifteen years of age.[83] Seven crimes were made capital offenses in the first laws of the territory: arson, burglary, manslaughter, poisoning, murder, rebellion, and rape.[84] Later on, even the attempt of that most "heinous of crimes" against white femininity would doom a Negro to be "cropped, branded, or suffer death."[85] In 1848, punishment was compounded on free Negroes convicted of a felony when they were required either to pay the expense of prosecution or to be sold temporarily into service for that purpose.[86]

in 1842, it was stipulated that guardians were to be placed over all free colored persons who were not living in the territory prior to its cession to the United States. The judge of the county court was to issue a certificate, at a fee of one dollar a head, to "proper and discreet" guardians who would enjoy full privileges of master except regarding property. The entire slave code would be applicable except again in the matter of property ownership.[87] Although the act was repealed the next year,[88] a similar statute was enacted in 1848.[89] Even more strenuous efforts to enforce the law came after 1856. Negroes without a guardian were to be fined not less than $10.00.[90] Anyone convicted of buying or selling to a free Negro without the written consent of his guardian could be fined $100 to $500.[91]

There was only one more step to be taken. An act of 1859 provided that a free person of color over the age of fourteen could choose his own master or mistress and become a slave. To make the loss of liberty more attractive, such a master would be prohibited from selling the slave, and he could not allow him to be taken for his debts or judgements against his property. Any free Negro found by a judge of probate to be "of idle and dissolute habits" could be sold for a term of years to the highest bidder.[92]

The guardian requirements struck Pensacola's free Negroes most harshly. Sympathetic white friends offered to be come guardians as a legal formality. Many followed this course, but others found even this too degrading. Some free Negroes, believing that they would never be able to improve their position, sailed for Mexico in April 1857.[93] They left behind many others to face the trials of war and the uncertain triumph of victory.

This then is what is known about the free Negro in pre-Civil War Florida. It is a precious little. We see through the past darkly a group without a face. That freedom was thought worth a struggle is evident from the life they lived among the perils of the Florida swamps and in the jungles of the white man's law. That many gained much against great odds is signaled by the century-old census registers. But that unobtrusiveness was the key to survival shows up in their anonymity. That most were kept from living a whole life is shouted by the silence of history.

1. Mark F. Boyd, "The Seminole War: Its Background and Onset," *Florida Historical Quarterly,* XXX (July 1951), 22.
2. Eugene P. Southall, "Negroes in Florida Prior to the Civil War," *Journal of Negro History,* XIX (January 1934), 79.
3. "Documents of Spanish Officials Bearing on the Free Negro Settlement of Gracia Real de Santa Teresa de Mose, Florida," *Journal of Negro History,* IX (April 1924), 144-95.
4. Joshua R. Giddings, *The Exiles of Florida* (Columbus, 1858), 2. See also facsimile edition with introduction by Arthur W. Thompson (Gainesville, 1964). Throughout his life Joshua Giddings was ardent in his defense of Negro rights. His stand on slavery, which he develops extensively in *The Exiles of Florida,* has been the subject of much controversy and disagreement. His fundamental thesis, however, has stood the test of time, as well as the scrutiny of recent historians. See Kenneth W. Porter, "The Episode of Osceola's Wife: Fact of Fiction?" *Florida Historical Quarterly,* XXVI (July 1947), 93; Edwin L. Williams, Jr., "Negro Slavery in Florida," *Florida Historical Quarterly,* XXVIII (October 1949), 104; and Edwin L. Williams, Jr., "Florida in the Union, 1845-1861" (unpublished Ph.D. dissertation, University of North Carolina, 1951), 116.
5. Southall "Negroes In Florida," 78-79; Zora Neale Hurston, "Communications," *Journal of Negro History,* XII (October 1927), 664.
6. Southall, "Negroes In Florida," 78-79; Hurston, "Communications, 6 6 4.
7. Giddings, *Exiles of Florida,* 3-4.
8. Kenneth W. Porter, "Relations Between Negroes and Indians Within the Present Limits of the United States," *Journal of Negro History,* XVII (July 1932), 325.
9. Boyd, "Seminole War," 22-23; Kenneth W. Porter, "Negroes and the East Florida Annexation Plot, 1811-1813," *Journal of Negro History,* XXX (January 1945), 12-14.
10. Boyd, "Seminole War," 22.

11. Giddings, *Exiles of Florida,* 5-29.
12. *Ibid.,* 29-31.
13. John K. Mahon, "British Strategy and Southern Indians: War of 1812," *Florida Historical Quarterly,* XLIV (April 1966), 300; Mark F. Boyd, "Events at Prospect Bluff on the Apalachicola River, 1808-1818," *Florida Historical Quarterly,* XVI (October 1937), 79-81.
14. Rembert W. Patrick, *Aristocrat in Uniform: General Duncan L. Clinch* (Gainesville, 1963), 27-33.
15. Giddings, *Exiles of Florida,* 19, 47, 52, 70, 97, 282-83; John T. Sprague, *The Origins, Progress, and Conclusion of the Florida War* (New York, 1848), 19, 97. See also facsimile edition with introduction by John K. Mahon (Gainesville, 1964).
16. E. Dolorus Preston, Jr., "The Genesis of the Underground Railroad," *Journal of Negro History,* XVIII (April 1933), 150; Rembert W. Patrick, *Florida Under Five Flags* (Gainesville, 1960), 28; Giddings, *Exiles of Florida,* 50-55.
17. Kenneth W. Porter "Notes on Seminole Negroes in the Bahamas," *Florida Historical Quarterly,* XXIV (July 1945), 57-58.
18. Giddings, *Exiles of Florida,* 57-58, 88-93, 253.
19. Patrick, *Florida Under Five* Flags, 34; Porter, "Notes on Seminole Negroes," 58; Giddings, *Exiles of Florida,* 252.
20. Kenneth W. Porter, "Three Fighters for Freedom," *Journal of Negro History,* XXVIII (January 1943), 56.
21. Giddings, *Exiles of Florida,* 54.
22. *American State Papers,* VII, *Military Affairs* (Washington, 1861), 832.
23. U. S. Documents, 25th Cong., 2nd Sess., No. 78, p. 52.
24. Porter, "Three Fighters for Freedom," 54-55.
25. Kenneth W. Porter, "Florida Slaves and Free Negroes in the Seminole War, 1835-1842," *Journal of Negro History,* XXVIII (October 1943), 421.
26. Giddings, *Exiles of Florida,* 315.
27. Porter, "Florida Slaves and Free Negroes," 418-20.
28. The Seminole Indian Agent in 1830 attached a report to the census schedules stating that the council of that tribe refused to permit the enumeration of the Negroes residing on Seminole lands. U. S. Census Schedules, 1830, Florida, Sheet 53, p. 105.
29. J. D. DeBow, *Statistical View of the United States,* (Washington, 1854), 63-65; *Population of the United States in 1860* (Washington, 1864), 53.
30. Computed from figures in *The Seventh Census of the United States: 1850* (Washington, 1853), 369-99, 405-06.
31. *Statistics of the United States in 1860* (Washington, 1866), 507.
32. *Acts of the Legislative Council of the Territory of Florida*, 6th Session, January 19, 1828, pp. 97-110. Cited hereafter as *Acts of Council.*
33. DeBow, *Statistical View of the United States,* 83.
34. "Population Schedules, Territory of Florida," *Fifth Census of the United States, 1830;* "Population Schedules, Territory of Florida," *Sixth* Census of the United States, 1840; The Seventh Census of the United States; *1850,* 400-01; *The Population of the United States in 1860,* 50-54.

35. DeBow, *Statistical View of the United States,* 66; *Population of the United States in 1860,* 52
36. Porter, "Florida Slaves and Free Negroes in the Seminole War, 1835-1842," 390.
37. Clarence E. Carter, ed., *The Territorial Papers of the United States: The Territory of Florida,* 26 vols. (Washington, 1959-1962), XXIII, 801.
38. *Acts of Council,* 5th Session, January 3, 1827, 81-84.
39. *Ibid.,* 7th Session, November 21, 1828, 186-87.
40. *Journal of the Proceedings of a Convention of Delegates to Form a* Constitution for the People of Florida, Held at St. Joseph, December, *1838* (St. Joseph, 1839), 30.
41. *The Constitution of 1838,* Article XVI, Sec. 3.
42. *Acts of Council,* 10th Session, February 10, 1832, 143-45.
43. *Ibid.,* 20th Session, March 5, 1842, 34-35.
44. *Ibid.,* 21st Session, 1843, 50.
45. *Acts of the General Assembly of the State of Florida,* 7th Session, December 15, 1855, 10. Cited hereafter as *Acts of Assembly.*
46. *Acts of Council,* 1st Session, September 17, 1822, 181-85.
47. *Ibid.,* 8th Session, November 21, 1829, 134-35.
48. *Statistics of the United States in 1860,* 337.
49. Ruth B. Barr and Modeste Hargis, "The Voluntary Exile of Free Negroes of Pensacola," *Florida Historical Quarterly,* XVII (July 1938), 3-4, 10-11.
50. *Ibid.,* 3.
51. Jefferson B. Browne, *Key West: The Old and the New* (St. Augustine, 1912), 67.
52. "Population Schedules, State of Florida," *Eighth Census of the United States in 1860.*
53. U.S. Congress, "An Act for the Establishment of a Territorial Government in Florida," reprinted in *Acts of Council,* 1st Session, 1822, xxxvii.
54. Thelma Bates, "The Legal Status of the Negro in Florida," *Florida Historical Quarterly,* VI (January 1928), 164.
55. Tallahassee *Floridian and Journal,* January 11, 1851.
56. *Acts of Council,* 6th Session, January 19, 1828, 97-110.
57. *Ibid.,* 10th Session, February 10, 1832, 143-45.
58. Jesse J. Jackson, "The Negro and the Law in Florida, 1821-1921" (unpublished Master's thesis, Florida State University, Tallahassee, 1960), 30-31.
59. *Acts of Council,* 6th Session, January 1828, 97-110.
60. *Acts of Assembly,* 6th Session, January 10, 1853, 116.
61. *Acts of Council,* 4th Session, December 10, 1825, 79-81.
62. *Ibid.,* 6th Session, January 19, 1828, 97-110.
63. *Ibid.,* 11th Session, March 21, 1833, 26-30.
64. *Ibid.,* 18th Session, February 25, 1840, 22-23.
65. *Ibid.,* 1st Session, August 12, 1822, 9-12; *The Constitution of 1838,* Article VI, Sec. 1.
66. U.S. Congress, "An Act for the Establishment of a Territorial Government in Florida," reprinted in *Acts of Council,* 1st Session, 1822, xxxvii.
67. *Acts of Council,* 2nd Session, June 29, 1823, 110.
68. *Ibid.,* 1st Session, August 31, 1822, 33-46
69. *Ibid.,* 6th Session, January 19, 1828, 97-110.

70. W. H. Brockenbrough, *Wm. H. Brockenbuough's Vindication* (n.p.,n.d.), 4.
71. Carter, *Territorial Papers,* XXIII, 1047.
72. *Acts of Council,* 3rd Session, December 30, 1824, 289-92.
73. *Ibid.,* 1st Session, September 17, 1822, 181-85.
74. *Ibid.,* 5th Session, January 19, 1827, 34-49.
75. Jackson, "The Negro and the Law in Florida," 27.
76. *Acts of Council,* 10th Session, February 4, 1832, 32-33.
77. *Ibid.,* 13th Session, February 13, 1835, 315.
78. *Ibid.,* 10th Session, February 6, 1832, 75.
79. *Ibid.,* 10th Session, January 16, 1832, 4-5.
80. *Ibid.,* 6th Session, January 19, 1828, 97-110.
81. *Acts of Assembly,* 7th Session, January 6, 1855, 62.
82. *Acts of Council,* 2nd Session, July 4, 1823, 140; *ibid.,* 6th Session, January 10, 1828, 49-50.
83. *Ibid.,* 10th Session, February 12, 1832, 128-29.
84. *Ibid.,* 1st Session, September 17, 1822, 181-85.
85 *Ibid.,* 7th Session, November 21, 1828, 174-90.
86. *Acts of Assembly,* 3rd Session, January 7, 1848, 111.
87. *Acts of Council,* 20th Session, March 5, 1842, 34-36.
88. *Ibid.,* 21st Session, February 22, 1843, 50.
89. *Acts of Assembly,* 3rd Session, January 8, 1848, 27.
90. *Ibid.,* 8th Session, December 23, 1856, 27.
91. *Ibid.*
92. *Ibid.,* 9th Session, January 15, 1859, 13-14.
93. Barr and Hargis, "Free Negroes of Pensacola," 4, 11-14.

7

Strength From Religion

Throughout Florida's history, blacks have turned to religion for solace and camaraderie in the face of injustice. In the antebellum and Reconstruction periods, African-Americans increasingly embraced religion and the black church for intra-group support and sustenance. As Albert Raboteau and other scholars of the subject have noted, in pre-Civil War years this "invisible intuition" not only sustained the black spirit of resistance but also assisted bondsmen in more aggressive forms of struggle via the "grapevine telegraph." The use of code words and elliptical song lyrics had long been an effective tool in the slaves' creative ways of struggle. With the coming of the war, this took on a new significance as songs and hymns cheered the coming of the "Lord" in place of "Yankees." During Reconstruction, the creation of new black churches and independent denominations helped build a sense of black community by sponsoring funeral and burial rites, creating schools, benevolent and fraternal societies, and numerous mutual-aid societies. This trend has lasted well into modern times. Without question, the institution of the African-American church is a significant aspect of the uninterrupted black struggle against oppression in Florida.

Robert L. Hall's study of the transformation of religion is an interesting and useful look at the rise in importance of religion to blacks from the plantation era through the socio-political upheavals of the Civil War and Reconstruction. The author sums up the reason for slaves feeling the necessity to create their own invisible institution by quoting John Hope

Franklin, "slavery had become as much a part of the religious orthodoxy of the South as the Creation in the Book of Genesis or Armageddon in the Book of Revelations. The work of promulgating and defending slavery, when entrusted to the southern clergy, could not have been in safer hands." Yet, as noted, slaves and free blacks, although circumspect in their approach, refused to be duped by the master's biblical validation of slavery. While Rabotou has characterized black resistance to white-interpreted religion as an underground factor of plantation life, other historians have seen this form of dissent as simply another survival method of what former slave Robert Smalls termed, "the secret life of the colored people."

With the disruptions of the war, blacks seized the opportunity to expand on their own devotion and to reject white churches in favor of black-led churches and denominations. Occupation by Union forces also laid the groundwork for predominantly black congregations to break away from white congregations and found new churches. Often black women were the moving forces behind the new black church movement and readers may perceive, as well, that it was at this time that black males assumed unprecedented respect and status in the black community as ministers and elders, a dual paradigm that has lasted into the new millennium.

Reconstruction and the increased participation by blacks in the political and legal affairs of the postwar years resulted in renewed efforts by freedmen to establish independent black churches. The author quotes Florida historian Joe A. Richardson in claiming the establishment of black churches as the single most important development for freedmen and their families during Reconstruction. The sprouting black churches, in many cases Baptist and Methodist, notably helped freedmen reconstitute families torn apart under slavery and to create schools for children, always a priority in the black community. The author notes the importance of literacy both for religious practice and for socio-political activity—literacy strengthened the freedmen's standing in both areas. In addition, the author finds that black religious leadership set a priority on legitimizing marriage rites for blacks. As slaves, marriages did not hold legal standing, but black churches blessed and legalized marriages between freed blacks. In short, the swift transition from slavery to freedom catapulted the emerging black religious movement into the forefront of the black struggle: the new churches and congregations provided emancipated persons an unprecedented and critical opportunity for assistance in securing work, housing, education, and other forms of self-actualization during a challenging time of transition.

Hall presents a compelling argument that independent churches and committed ministers served as beacons of hope and aspiration for the newly freed and added an unusual, if not unique, dimension to the historical black male and female freedom struggle in Florida. Readers may want to build on this article by exploring how black churches of the 1860s and 1870s mirrored those of the modern civil rights movement of the 1950s and 1960s in terms of serving as a rally point and source of leadership. Moreover, interested readers may also wish to explore the deep roots of black religious practices in the Sunshine State, and how those practices have manifested themselves right down to the new millennium, for example, Santeria and other Caribbean-influenced religious practices of the recent stream of immigrants into South Florida.

FURTHER READING

Charles Summer Long, *History of the A.M.E. Church in Florida* (1939);

A. Verot, *Slavery and Abolitionism: Being the Substance of a Sermon, Preached in the Church of St. Augustine, Florida, on the 4th day of January, 1861, Day of Public Humiliation, Fasting and Prayer* (1861);

Joe M. Richardson, "Jonathan C. Gibbs: Florida's Only Negro Cabinet Member," *Florida Historical Quarterly*, Vol. 42 (1964);

Joseph D. Cushman, Jr., *A Goodly Heritage: The Episcopal Church in Florida, 1821-1892* (1965);

H. Shelton Smith, *In His Image, But . . . Racism in Southern Religion* (1972);

Edward Earl Joiner, *A History of Florida Baptists* (1972);

Joseph D. Cushman, Jr., *The Sound of Bells: The Episcopal Church in South Florida, 1892-1969* (1978);

Mechal Sobel, *Trabelin' On: The Slave Journey to an Afro-Baptist Faith* (1979);

Robert L. Hall, "Tallahassee's Black Churches, 1865-1885," *Florida Historical Quarterly*, Vol. 58 (1979);

John B. Boles, ed. *Masters and Slaves in the House of the Lord: Race and Religion in the American South, 1740-1870* (1988);

Diana González Kirby and Sara María Sánchez, "'Santeria': From Africa to Miami Via Cuba: Five Hundred Years of Worship," *Tequesta*, Vol. 48 (1988);

Walter T. Howard and Virginia M. Howard, "Family, Religion, and Education: A Profile of African-American Life in Tampa, Florida, 1900-1930," *Journal of Negro History*, Vol. 79 (1994);

Robert L. Hall, "African Religious Retentions in Florida," in *The African American Heritage of Florida*, David R. Colburn and Jane L. Landers, eds. (1995), chapter 3;

James F. Findlay, Jr., *Church People in the Struggle: The National Council of Churches and the Black Freedom Movement, 1950-1970* (1997);

Mark Newman, "The Florida Baptist Convention and Desegregation, 1954-1980," *Florida Historical Quarterly*, Vol. 78 (1999);

Larry Rivers and Canter Brown, Jr., *Laborers in the Vineyard of the Lord: The Beginnings of the AME Church in Florida, 1865-1895* (2001) chapter 2;

Ernest F. Dibble, "Religion on Florida's Territorial Frontiers," *Florida Historical Quarterly*, Vol. 80 (2001).

"Yonder Come Day": Religious Dimensions Of The Transition From Slavery To Freedom In Florida[1]

Robert L. Hall

The Florida Historical Quarterly, Volume 65, issue 4 (1987), 411-432.

The Confederate firing on Fort Sumter in 1861 was a watershed not only in the political and military history of the United States, but also a turning point in its social history. The heady wine of secessionism and the rupturing of lines of communication and calm moral discourse were experienced in some religious polities for more than a decade before the fateful military event. Southern Methodists and Baptists had parted company with their non-southern counterparts by 1845, when, as John Hope Franklin has written, "slavery had become as much a part of the religious orthodoxy of the South as the Creation in the Book of Genesis or Armageddon in the Book of Revelations. The work of promoting and defending slavery, when entrusted to the southern clergy, could not have been in safer hands."[2] On the eve of secession, bishops of the Episcopal and Catholic churches in Florida were urging secession and preaching fiery pro-slavery sermons. Bishop Frances Huger Rutledge of the Episcopal Church was so enthusiastic in his exhortations on behalf of southern independence that Edmund Ruffin, an eyewitness observer of the Florida secession convention, was impressed with Rutledge's "ardent and active patriotics entiments."[3] Not only did he refuse to attend church services on the national day of humiliation and prayer proclaimed by President Buchanan, but Rutledge also pledged $500 to help defray the new government's expenses if the ordinance of secession passed.[4]

There were nearly 400 black Catholics living and worshipping in St. Augustine on the eve of the Civil War. Three months before the firing on Fort Sumter, many of them were undoubtedly present when Augustin Verot, vicar apostolic of Florida, preached a sermon advancing the traditional Catholic theological position that slavery was not in itself evil and vigorously defending the property rights of those who owned slaves. Bishop Verot's sermon, "Slavery and Abolitionism," delivered in the parish church at St. Augustine on January 4, 1861, was soon printed and disseminated widely throughout the South, and it became a popular Confederate pro-slavery tract.[5] In other regards, however, Verot's biographer believed "he had a compassionate regard for the Negro slave."[6] Unquestionably, Bishop Verot did demonstrate a profound concern for the religious instruction of black Floridians during the years immediately after the Civil War.

During the Civil War, rumblings of black religious assertions began to be heard even more loudly than during the antebellum period. Shortages of both human power and financial resources rendered these black assertions nearly irresistible, and converted the war years into a period of incubation for local and regional black religious leadership even before the missionary invasions from the north.

Although he made no specific mention of Florida, Bell I. Wiley devoted a chapter in his study, *Southern Negroes,* to the "Religious Life" of southern blacks during the Civil War. He suggested that the interest of white Southerners in the spiritual welfare of slaves may actually have intensified during the Civil War for a number of reasons. A primary factor must have been "the realization of the value of religious training in preserving submissiveness and loyalty amid the disturbing influences of the war."[7] Florida Methodists concurred with the judgement of the South Carolina Conference of the

Methodist Episcopal Church, South, that slave missions had considerable value in "securing the quiet and peaceful subordination of these people."[8] In 1861,the Florida Conference reported that about forty-three per cent of its 15,453 members were black.[9] However, changes occurring in southern society were obvious statistically to Florida Methodists. In 1863, there was a net loss of 987 black members, and in 1865, a net loss of 560.[10]

Other factors cited by Wiley that may have contributed to expanded religious opportunities for southern blacks during the Civil War included the scarcity of white ministers, the shrinking incomes of churches, and the physical deterioration of church properties. Florida's Protestant Episcopal Church, for example, suffered several setbacks during the Civil War. Among them was the loss of four of its thirteen pre-war churches. The buildings of three of the parishes were burned and a fourth was sold for debt." The lack of white ministers also may have created a leadership vacuum which left room for black preachers,[11] class leaders, and would-be preachers to address black religious gatherings and, occasionally, racially-mixed meetings.[12] Helen Moore Edwards recalled that during the Civil War her father, Kidder Meade Moore, let the slaves on his Pine Tucky plantation in Jefferson County "preach in our school house. They put seats outside and "we would often go and listen to them," she wrote. Edwards also recalled that Joe Curry, "a negro refugee," did the preaching.[13]

The wartime–Union occupation of the Jacksonville area enabled such black evangelists as Ivey Barnes to travel about. Sometime during the early 1860s a small band of black Protestants in St. Augustine held meetings in the home of Deacon John Newnan. Barnes frequently journeyed from Jacksonville to St. Augustine to exhort the faithful gathered at Newnan's home, but attracted little attention. Later, Hammie Williams organized a Baptist Sunday School consisting of ten children, seven of whom were Catholic. The Sunday School continued to grow, and on March 13, 1864, the First Baptist Church in St. Augustine was organized. The church called Reverend Barnes as its first pastor. Eventually, a lot on the corner of St. Francis and St. Benedict streets was purchased, and a wooden shack was erected as a house of worship.[14]

St. Mary's Primitive Baptist Church in Tallahassee may have been founded as early as June 1861, by the Reverend Henry Griffin, a minister from Virginia. During the war a site for the church building, located on Call Street between McComb and Boulevard (renamed Martin Luther King, Jr. Boulevard in1980), was purchased from a white man for $250 and a small frame building was erected. [15] During the Civil War when white Baptists in Key West shifted or drifted to other churches, their building was taken over by black Baptists who continued to hold services there until as late as the fall of 1879.[16]

When, on June 10, 1865, Reverend William G. Steward organized Florida's first African Methodist Episcopal Church under an authorized pastor in Midway, a settlement east of Jacksonville, he was besieged by numerous requests from black Floridians to start churches in their locales. Henry Call of Cottondale, who organized a black congregation with the approval and presence of white overseers during the war, is said to have walked over 240 miles from Marianna to Jacksonville to persuade Reverend Steward to return with him to incorporate officially a two-year old congregation into the A.M.E. Church.[17]

Not all black Floridians, of course, were able to attend local congregations led by black preachers. Throughout the Civil War the vast majority of the slave population was probably involved in the cycle of becoming members in, and occasionally being excommunicated from, racially-mixed congregations affiliated with southern white-controlled denominations. Slaves in Madison County, for example, continued to join the Concord Missionary Baptist Church much as they had before the outbreak of the war. Nineteen slave members were received into the church during 1862. In July, Jeptha (the property of James Wilson), Dick, Mack, and Dorcas (Parramore estate) were received into membership. In June, Charles, Vina, Catherine, Lucy, Luke, Sam, Jack, and Claracy all "came in by experience."18 In October1862, the following Parramore estate slaves became members of Concord Missionary Baptist Church: Lydia, Emaline, Rachael, Henrietta, Amy, and Sarah, and Sarah, owned by Brother Lloyd. On the third Sunday in January 1865, twenty-four more slaves became members of this church. In September 1865, only months after the close of the Civil War and fully five years before a mass exodus from the church, Prince, one of the twenty-four blacks who had joined earlier that year, was charged with theft, found guilty, and excommunicated from the church for his transgression.[18]

In those instances where slaveholders did not build chapels on their own land, slaves from several farms might travel by foot or wagon to country churches where slaves and masters from several farms would worship together.[19] These gatherings, sometimes followed by "dinner on the grounds," especially during revival season after the crops had been laid by, provided more than spiritual enlightenment. There was also the chance to meet friends and kinfolks who lived on other farms and, not to be overlooked, the opportunity to meet members of the opposite sex and to court. Many a match was made as a result of such a meeting at a Sabbath outing. The parents of Emma Porter, who lived on separate farms in Wakulla County, met and courted at church during the Civil

War. Their daughter was born before the end of the war, and in the 1960s she was remembered by the *Magnolia Monthly* as "The Last Slave in Wakulla County."[20]

During the Civil War, Florida's Episcopal churches continued to minister to some slaves. In 1863, Reverend William J.Ellis, rector of St. John's Church, Tallahassee, reported three baptisms of "colored" infants (three of forty-seven or 6.3 percent of all the infant baptisms reported for that year from the parish). Half of the eighteen people confirmed in 1863 were black.[21] On July 18, 1863, Reverend Owen P. Thackara of Christ Church, Monticello, recorded the baptism of fifty-seven "colored" infants. All eleven of the adults baptized at Christ Church that year were black. Thirty-nine of the eighty-five members listed for Christ Church in 1863 (or about forty-six per cent) were black Episcopalians. Reverend Thackara reported that "the Sunday services were divided between Monticello and Aucilla. Part of each Sunday is devoted to the servants. The children, both white and colored, are catechized every Sunday before service."[22] The slaves on the plantations owned by John Bradley, William Bailey, Dr. John Eppes, and Dr. Bythewood were, according to Thackara, regularly instructed once a month. "The slaves on these plantations," wrote Thackara, "seem interested in the services, and having been taught the prayers, the creed, the chants, and some of the selections of the psalms, join heartily in the responses." Successful religious instruction resulted in the slaves memorizing the creed, the Lord's Prayer, the Ten Commandments, and the responses in the baptismal service.[23] Four of the twenty-three infants baptized by Episcopalian missionaries at Lake City in 1863 (or 17.4 per cent) were black. Christ Church, Pensacola, also reached a few blacks, mostly infants.[24]

In his report to the 1867 convention of the Protestant Episcopal Church in Florida, Reverend Osgood E. Herrick, rector of St. Paul's Church, Key West, enumerated the transactions that had occurred since his previous report of April 1861.Twelve of the 201 individuals baptized between 1861 and 1867,or about six per cent, were listed as "colored." Twenty-two of the ninety-seven marriages performed during the same period, about 22.7 per cent, involved black couples.[25]

The year 1865 was one of uncertainty and emotional peaks and valleys for both blacks and whites throughout the South. A telling capsule of these emotions comes from the April 29, 1865,letter of an agent of the American Missionary Association in Florida: "But this week, our hearts too were made to rejoice at glorious intelligence [the news of Lee's surrender] and the Freedmen of this place seemed to feel doubly sure of their freedom which their old task-masters, especially mistresses, seemed to feel for the first time that there were signs of . . . [word illegible] and that all was lost! And they wept and groaned saying we shall never have our niggers back again. But when the news of the President's death came two or three days after, they took heart again— taunting the colored people about their dark prospect of being free and some of our people began to talk of going north to escape enslavement again, for as Massa Lincoln was gone they feared their hope was gone too. But their confidence settled back again into the strong arm of their God, which they said was above all and they would trust Him to carry their cause through."[26]

For those whites who still held on to the dream of antebellum plantation life, the changes wrought by the Civil War were not only momentous but traumatic. "Little did the happy people of Tallahassee and old Leon County dream of the store of trouble and vicissitudes awaiting for them," wrote Captain F. A. Hendry. "These big-hearted wealthy citizens of that day with their hundreds of slaves and broad fields" would see their former slaves participating as freedmen in the processes of government.[27]

One of the most impressive facts of Reconstruction was the strong desire of black people to have churches and preachers of their own. In most instances, independent black churches were successfully established and maintained. Dr. Joe A. Richardson considered the establishment of these independent churches for and by the freed people to be one of the most significant results of Reconstruction.[28] Beside changing personal names, changing church affiliation was one of the major symbolic actions taken by free persons to signify their new status.[29]

The assertion of religious freedom and the establishment of independent churches by blacks, while not marking a change in religious doctrine or ritual, significantly altered black-white social relations. Francis Butler Simkins claimed that "in withdrawing from the white churches he [the Negro] surrendered an element of social intimacy with the white man which he had experienced under slavery."[30] Antebellum Florida laws forbade blacks to hear any preaching that was not delivered either in white churches or under white supervision. After the Civil War, the Florida legislature, as yet unreconstructed, enacted a series of laws which reversed antebellum policies, if not attitudes toward blacks. A law enacted on January 15, 1866, made it a misdemeanor for any Negro, mulatto, or other person of color to "intrude himself" into any religious assembly of whites or any other assembly of whites. The same act also prevented whites from "intruding" into black churches and assemblies. In effect, the law prescribed racial separation during religious worship.[31] The passage of such a law suggests that once slavery had ended the willingness of whites to tolerate antebellum levels of "social intimacy" with blacks had disappeared. Although black Floridians had some pronounced leanings toward separate worship, their decision to "surrender" an element of social intimacy with whites by "withdrawal" from the white-controlled denominations was not entirely unilateral or voluntary. What blacks and whites were experiencing during the liminal years immediately following the Civil War was a kind of re-creation of the conditions facing black members of northern congregations in the late 1700s and early 1800s. Northern blacks, too, had worshipped in the same buildings as the whites, but in specially designated parts of the building. The separate local black congregations which formed the nuclei of the African Methodist Episcopal Church and of the African Methodist Episcopal Zion Church began, at least partially, in protest against such racial restrictions as being required to wait until all the white members were served before taking the sacrament.[32]

Not until months, and sometimes even years after the end of the Civil War, did black

John Henry Dickerson was a leader in Florida's African Methodist Episcopal (AME) church in the late 1800s. He was licensed to preach in Ocala in 1886, ordained a deacon the following year in Palatka, and was named an elder in Gainesville in 1890. He held other subsequent appointments in North Central Florida. From the 1916 *Centennial Encyclopedia of the AME Church.*

Floridians begin their massive exodus from white-controlled southern denominations. In the meantime, a disturbing level of white violence and lawlessness was being unleashed against black Floridians, a circumstance which must surely have strengthened whatever resolve blacks may already have had to avoid whites if possible. Although a significant number of white Christians, often of the upper classes, contributed materially to the development of black churches during Reconstruction, black churches were not immune to the violent rampages of white mobs. On May 8, 1866, the *New York Times* commented on the large number of attacks on the black schools, churches, and other black institutions occurring in Florida.[33]This atmosphere of political flux, legal change, and largely white-initiated racial violence forms the backdrop for understanding the changes in religion that occurred during this period.

A fitting starting point for understanding what freedom might have meant to black Floridians is May 20, 1865, the day which twentieth-century blacks living in north Florida still commemorate as Emancipation Day. It was on that day that Union General Edward McCook gathered the freed people in Tallahassee and read them the Emancipation Proclamation which Abraham Lincoln had issued on January 1, 1863.[34] The areas where the slaves were called together to be told that they were free became almost sacred landmarks and remain so down to the present day. John Byrd's father, who had been a slave in Jefferson County, repeatedly took his son on walks through the fields to show him the big oak tree where they went to "get their freedom."[35] Oral tradition has provided information, and more importantly, a perspective on the bewildering transition from legal slavery to nominal freedom. An anonymous black employee at Florida State University in Tallahassee, whose maternal grandparents and great grandparents were slaves in Leon County, gave the following account of what her mother had told her about her slave great grandmother: "Well, I remember my mother talking about her grandmother. She was in slavery. And how they would have to work, and how the, I guess the old master didn't allow them to associate with one another. They had to work all day long, and then go home and cook for the master and she said after a short while, I guess when freedom was declared, well they [the slave owners] didn't want to believe it, and they still wanted to make them work. Then they came along, and just made them turn them aloose. Then they turned them aloose and they [the slaves] didn't have anything to go upon. Just had to go out and make life by themselves. Didn't have no money, no skills, or nothing of the sort. And they just had to go out and start work all over again to try and make a living for themselves."[36]

Journalist Whitelaw Reid, accompanying Chief Justice Salmon P. Chase and his party on a southern tour, arrived in Jacksonville around May 20, 1865. The blacks of east Florida seemed to Reid "to have a vague idea that they were free; but little change in their relations to their old masters is perceptible. In the back country they remain, as usual, on little cracker plantations, and neither master nor negroes succeed in more than making a rude living."[37]

Douglas Dorsey, the slave of Colonel Lewis Matair, was about fourteen years old at emancipation. On that day he was instructed to tell the driver to summon the slaves. Once gathered, they were told by Colonel Matair's son that they were free and they were offered half of what they raised on the plantation if they remained. Although Dorsey remembered Colonel Matair as "kind," none accepted the offer. Dorsey's father, Charles, who had worked as a mechanic during slavery, found a job with Judge Carraway of Suwannee County for whom he worked one year. Charles Dorsey later homesteaded forty acres of land received from the government and farmed in Suwannee County until he died.[38]

Upon the recommendation of the three–man committee of former slaveholders, the 1866 Florida General Assembly enacted a scheme of legislation known as the "black codes." These laws remained in effect throughout the early months of 1867. In comparison with other former Confederate states, some of which passed mild black codes while others enacted none at all, Florida's policy was exceptional in its harshness and enduring effect upon patterns of race relations in the state.[39] Yet Farley Gilliam contended that, as severe as the Florida black codes were, their passage "was not motivated by the desire of white Floridians to re-enslave the Negro."[40]

Florida freedmen were not so confident that this was the case, for they flocked to the Lincoln Brotherhoods— secret societies whose avowed purpose was to prevent them from being returned to slavery. This determination was, in the words of freedman John Wallace, "sufficient to bring out the old and young, the halt and the blind."[41] The Lincoln Brotherhoods were organized by Thomas W. Osborn of the Freedmen's Bureau. In addition to the laudable activities of feeding destitute freed people and refugees, Osborn advocated black suffrage and kept the proposition before the freed people that their former masters wanted to return them to slavery.[42] The parent lodge of the Lincoln Brotherhoods in Tallahassee became so large it had to be removed from the private home where it was originally organized to a black Baptist church in a part of town seldom visited by whites. John Wallace's politically-jaundiced book makes the intriguing allegation that the meetings in the Baptist church were carefully guarded by sentinels armed with muskets who demanded a countersign before allowing admittance.[43]

Once universal manhood suffrage was extended to freedmen by constitutional amendment, black churches became embroiled in the struggle to encourage, inform, cajole, and capture the black vote. Black church buildings became political meeting halls as well as houses of worship. In addition to serving as meeting places for the Lincoln Brotherhoods, they also served as starting points for political meetings held throughout the state during the spring and summer of 1867. Such was the case in Gainesville on April 27, 1867, when rally goers convened at a black church before parading to a nearby open field to hear political speeches from Captain James H. Durkee, the local Freedmen's Bureau agent, and Captain E. R. Ames, head of the local military force.[44] Many of the political gatherings occurred under the leadership of the black preachers.[45]

In 1867, the Republican National Committee named Daniel Richards, a United States district tax commissioner stationed at Fernandina, to spearhead a major party-organizing campaign in Florida. Richards enlisted William Saunders, a black former Union officer, and Liberty Billings, an ex-officer of a black regiment. The threesome of Billings, Saunders, and Richards was labeled the "Radical Mule Team" by opponents.[46] Richards once stated that Saunders had "done infinitely more for the Republican party in Florida than any other man," but as early as April14, 1868, Richards' perception of Saunders was beginning to change. Writing from Tallahassee, Richards remarked to Congressman Elihu B. Washburne that the black people were becoming exasperated with Saunders and that the feeling was nearly universal that Saunders had "sold out" and "betrayed the best interest of his race." By April 20, 1868, Richards felt Saunders was trying to "bribe and buy up" Reverend Charles H. Pearce, one of the leaders of the African Methodist Episcopal Church in Florida.[47] On the following day, Richards possessed a letter signed by Saunders intimating a threat to assassinate Reverend Pearce, Liberty Billings, and Richards himself.[48] Richards and Billings may have lost faith in Saunders, but they did not lose faith in the Republican-organizing effort. On Tuesday, May 5, 1868, the *Floridian* reported a meeting conducted by Billings and other politicos at the African church in Tallahassee at four o'clock in the morning where, it was presumed, "the colored people were instructed how to vote today."[49]

Also facing the freedmen, their churches, and the public authorities was a complex problem more pressing and more intensely personal than voting rights— marital adjustment and the provision of adequate child support. "Progress" in general behavior, and especially marital relations and family responsibility, has frequently been attributed to the influence of the churches.[50] Although marital relations among slaves were probably not nearly as chaotic as was once generally thought, slave marriages did not have the sanction of law. Furthermore, slave children, being legally defined as property, were treated as "assets" and sustained by their owners without becoming burdens of the state. On January 11, 1866, the Florida legislature passed "An Act to Establish and Enforce the Marriage Relation Between Persons of Color." The act stated, in part, that "colored inhabitants claiming to be living together as husband and wife must, within nine months from the passage of this Act, be legally married by some person authorized to perform [the] ceremony."[51] Certificates of marriage were to be registered with the clerks of the circuit court in the various counties. Whether ex slave couples viewed this law as a mere requirement of their legal condition or as a glorious opportunity to legalize stable matches made during slavery days, the circuit court clerks and persons authorized to perform marriage ceremonies did a brisk business.[52] Among the thousands of black couples who legalized their pre-existing marriage-like bonds was an elderly pair married at Beckett's plantation in Marion County around the middle of September, less than a month before the expiration of the grace period. The 106-year old man and the eighty-year old woman had been living together as man and wife for years without the benefit or the possibility of legal sanction.[53] Then, on December 14, 1866, the law regarding marriage was modified to provide that "persons of color" would be considered legally married if they were living together and had so proclaimed to the world and the children issuing from such relationships would be considered legitimate and legal heirs.[54]

Two additional matters which affected the times were the influx of large numbers of blacks to Florida from other southeastern states, and the marked and often religiously-inspired desire of the recently freed black Floridians for education. Despite Florida's harsh-sounding black codes, it was possible, as one writer has asserted, that "conditions in Florida were better in general for blacks than they were elsewhere in the South. Southern newspapers began to intone the facts of immigration like a grim litany: 'The tide of immigration is unprecedented.. . A thousand freedmen have passed through this city during the past week on their way to Florida. . . . Nearly every day brings trains and wagons to Tallahassee from South Carolina'. "The *New York Times* reported that 50,000 blacks had left South Carolina and that many of them had gone to Florida.[55] While there were surplus laborers in both Georgia and South Carolina, three major circumstances had the combined effect of attracting thousands of black workers from those and neighboring states to Florida. First, those planters who had cotton crops in 1865 reaped high profits which inspired them to expand greatly their cotton acreage the following year, thereby increasing the demand for labor. Second, blacks were attracted to

Florida during the last half of the nineteenth century by the bustling timber and turpentine industry. Among them were many black South Carolinians recruited by labor agents. Mr. Buckner told sociologist Clyde Vernon Kiser that during the 1890s "he had about two hundred Negroes transported to Florida from Colleton and Beaufort Counties to work in the turpentine industry."[56] Finally, linked with the labor demand was the availability of public lands in Florida under the 1866 Homestead Act. According to Claude F. Oubre, "Florida contained more public lands than any of the other states included in the Southern Homestead Act, and was more accessible to the South Atlantic states. For these reasons, Florida became the scene of the most feverish activity on the part of freedmen in search of homestead land. "By the end of 1866, the Freedmen's Bureau alone had furnished transportation from Charleston, South Carolina, to Florida for 602 people under the leadership of a freedman.[57] Sometime between 1867 and 1872, the novelist Harriet Beecher Stowe encountered an aging black man known as Old Cudjo who had been part of "a party of negroes from South Carolina and Georgia" who "had been induced to come into Florida to take up a tract of government land." Characteristically, one of the first acts of this group of former slaves was to build "a prayer booth, where they could hold their weekly prayer-meetings which often seem with the negroes to take place of all other recreations."[58]

Many freedmen who migrated to Florida joined churches there retaining vivid images of the character of the services they had attended and the sermons they had heard as slaves. "Father" Charles Coates was born a slave in Richmond, Virginia, around 1828. Viola B. Muse's paraphrase of her interview with Coates adds yet another chorus to the dreary refrain aimed as much at social control as salvation: "One privilege given slaves on the plantation was appreciated by all and that was the opportunity to hear the word of God. The white people gathered in log and sometime frame churches and the slaves were permitted to sit about the church yard on wagons and on the ground and listen to the preaching. When slaves wanted to hold church they had to get special permission from the master, and at that time a slave hut was used. A white preacher was called in, and he would preach to them not to steal, lie or run away and 'be sure to git all dem weeds outen dat corn in de field and your master will think a heap of you'."[59]

Rebecca Hooks and her husband Solomon left the plantation of William Lowe in Jones County, Georgia, during Reconstruction, and share-cropped on various Georgia plantations before moving to Florida around 1887. One of her early memories was of a sermon in which she was urged to obey her master and to be thankful that she had been removed from darkest Africa.[60] Bill Austin, who settled in Jackson County, Florida, around1882, experienced slavery as a child in Green and Hancock counties, Georgia. Austin recalled that his slave master, Thomas Smith, "On Sunday night would let us go wherever the preacher was holdin' meeting."[61] Thus, many of the individuals who swelled the ranks of Florida's black churches during the decades immediately after the Civil War had acquired their first religious experience as slaves in one of the nearby southeastern states.

The freed people's desire for literacy was motivated, in part, by their religious concerns. Once freedom came and the legal barriers to black literacy disappeared, blacks in Florida, like those elsewhere in the South, actively sought schooling. Although the motivations and outcomes flowing from the educational efforts of northern missionaries have been seriously questioned in some recent scholarship, the genuineness of black motivations and the vigor of black efforts to acquire the secret of letters is beyond question. Early in 1866, in the absence of funds for day schools, E. B. Duncan, assistant superintendent for public schools for freedmen, told the citizens of Florida, "We have gotten and are getting Sabbath Schools all over the State, for our colored Ministers and citizens respond readily to this work."[62] In addition to Tallahassee, Monticello, Houston, Lake City, and Chaires, Duncan reported that "the like work is going on in Gadsden County, besides in almost every place and plantation the blacks are instructed daily."[63] While the inability of the Freedmen's Bureau to set the law in motion to protect the rights of the former slaves is recognized, the introduction of a school system for blacks was, as Richardson indicated, "one of the truly significant accomplishments of Reconstruction."[64]

The impact of this accomplishment was not lost on the freed people. When interviewed by the Works Progress Administration in 1936, Patience Campbell, born a slave on the Jackson County farm of George Bullock around 1853, recalled entering one of the schools established by the Freedmen's Bureau when she was about twelve years old.[65] Some black ministers, like James Smith of Tallahassee, corresponded with officials of the American Missionary Association and pleaded for teachers and aid for education.[66] Freed blacks responded eagerly to the availability of Bibles and the chance to learn to read the Holy Book for themselves. This drive for literacy took place within a religious matrix which reached beyond the fact that church organizations were among the earliest agencies to teach reading. Simon Peter Richardson, an agent for the American Bible Society, stated that "the parent society gave me a wide margin to give or donate large quantities of books to both white and colored." In 1866, it appeared to Richardson that "all the negroes wanted a Bible. They seemed to feel that to own a

Bible made them better."[67] Occasionally, the Bible was used as a physical object in the mysterious rituals of syncretic folk belief. But in the larger number of instances, as one white Episcopalian remarked in 1868, "The height of ambition with the colored children" was not only "to possess a Bible and prayer book," but to "know how to read them."[68]

Many ex-slaves had heard sermons in the white churches or on plantation missions about the clarity of the Gospel, the authority of Scripture, and the desirability of direct access between the believer and the Lord's Word, and they wanted to get the Word straight from the Book for themselves. The Florida Narratives of the WPA contain numerous references to the ex slaves' fondness for sitting on the porch and reading the Bible or having it read to them in their old age. Daytona Beach-born theologian Howard Thurman recalled that his grandmother raised him and had him read the Bible aloud to her repeatedly. When he came to one particular passage which reminded her of the sermons she had heard as a slave, and disliked for their pro-slavery emphasis, Thurman's grandmother stopped him short and admonished him never again to read that passage to her.[69] Even today in Gadsden County, vigorous religious disputes continue to be a front porch and back doorstep pastime. In an ethnohistorical study of religious experience in Midway (Gadsden County), Bruce T. Grindal traced the evolution of black religious life from the 1850s to the present, emphasizing "the highly personal quality of religiosity, in which the authority of religious conviction lies in *feeling* and, at its most intimate level, exists independently of church affiliation or membership."[70] Thus, although much of the information in this study is derived from and reported in a denomination-by-denomination framework, the pervasiveness and intensely personal quality of the religious interpretation of experience in Florida's rural black communities— a religiosity which transcends the fact of church affiliation or attendance-should not be forgotten. Nonetheless, the activities and ritual events of formal churches in much of the rural South, both before and after slavery, whether racially segregated or together, "provided the context in which individual experience is translated into the symbolic meanings of communal religion."[71]

It is against this background of political crisis, legal change, social adjustment, population movement, and vivid memories of the slave experience that the story of the rise of independent black churches in Florida unfolded. Between 1865 and 1868,the southern churches were in as much a state of transition as were the affairs of the nation and of the economy. Emancipation provided blacks with the opportunity to worship publicly without the regular interference of whites. Despite the external pressures of white lawlessness and violence, most blacks viewed this change as a unique opportunity and vigorously-accelerated religious activity ensued. By the early 1870s, most of the galleries and special pews in which the blacks had worshipped as slaves less than a decade before stood empty as separate black churches proliferated.

Robert L. Hall is assistant professor, Department of History and African American Studies, University of Maryland Baltimore County, Catonsville, Maryland.

1. See the jacket liner notes, "In The Old Fashioned Way," Yonder Come Day. *Note Singing and Spirituals From South Georgia,* Front Porch Records 79-001, GA 179. produced and directed by Dennis Coelho.
2. John Hope Franklin, "The Great Confrontation: The South and the Problem of Change," *Journal of Southern History* 38 (February 1972) 10. For details on the Baptist schism, see William Greer Todd, "The Slavery Issue and the Organization of a Southern Baptist Convention," (Ph.D. dissertation, University of North Carolina at Chapel Hill, 1964).
3. Edmund Ruffin, quoted in Dorothy Dodd, "Edmund Ruffin's Account of the Florida Secession Convention, 1861," *Florida Historical Quarterly* 12 (October 1933), 69-70. Rutledge was the Episcopal bishop of Florida from 1851-1866. See also, Joseph D. Cushman, Jr., *A Goodly Heritage: The Episcopal Church in Florida, 1821-1892* (Gainesville, 1965), 27, 42-43, 76.
4. Dorothy Dodd, "The Secession Movement in Florida, 1850-1861, Part II," *Florida Historical Quarterly* 12 (October 1933), 60.
5. A treatment of the anti-Union sentiments of both of the Florida churchmen mentioned in this paragraph is found in H. Shelton Smith, *In His Image, But..Racism in Southern Religion, 1780-1910* (Durham, 1972), 175-77. The title of Bishop Verot's sermon was A *Tract for the Times. Slavery and Abolitionism, Being the Substance of* a *Sermon Preached in the Church of St.* Augustine, Florida, on the 4th Day of January, 1861, Day of Public Humiliation, *Fasting and Prayer* (New Orleans, 1861). In 1864, J. W. Brinckerhoff, who had come to St. Augustine in February 1863 as a United States government superintendent of the colored people, observed that "a large portion of the colored people here are regular attendants and devoted adherents of the Roman Catholic Church," J. W. Brinckerhoff to George Whipple, November 23, 1864, American Missionary Association Papers, microfilm ed., reel 28, Robert Manning Strozier Library, Florida State University, Tallahassee, Florida.
6. Michael V. Gannon, *Rebel Bishop: The Life and Era of Augustin Verot* (Milwaukee, 1964), 33.
7. Bell Irvin Wiley, *Southern Negroes,* 1861-1865 (New Haven, 1938), 98. See also, W. Harrison Daniel, "Southern Protestantism and the Negro, 1860-1865," *North Carolina Historical Review* 41 (July 1964), 338-59.
8. Charleston *Mercury,* November 8, 1861.
9. William E. Brooks, *History Highlights of Florida Methodism* (Fort Lauderdale, 1965), 30.
10. Charles T. Thrift, Jr., *The Trail of the Florida Circuit Rider* (Lakeland, 1944), 160.

11. Jerrell H. Shofner, *Nor is it Over Yet: Florida in the Era of Reconstruction, 1863-1877* (Gainesville, 1974), 145. An example of the loss of white preachers comes from Old Pisgah Methodist Church in Leon County. In his mimeographed study which carries the story up to 1976, the current pastor of Pisgah indicated that the Civil War called "many of the preachers and most of the male members who were of military age into the Confederate Army," Norman Edward Booth, *A History of 'Old Pisgah' Highlights and Happenings, 1830–1976* (1976), 13. Mimeographed copy in the Florida Collection, Robert Manning Strozier Library, Florida State University.
12. Some whites had attended some of the sermons preached by such black ministers as James Page before the Civil War, but during the war, in the absence of white preachers who had gone off to minister to the troops, many more whites had occasion to attend services conducted by black preachers.
13. Helen Moore Edwards, *Memoirs of Helen M. Edwards of Pine Tucky Plantation, Jefferson County, Florida* (1926), 5. This is an eight-page printed booklet, a copy of which is in Special Collections, Robert Manning Strozier Library, Florida State University. Edwards was born on January 27, 1851, in Newport, Florida, and spent much of her childhood on "Pine Tucky" plantation located near Waukeenah in Jefferson County. She was fourteen years old when the slaves were freed.
14. WPA Files, Federal Writers Project, Negro Churches, 1936, carbon copy of typewritten document compiled by workers of the FWP, P. K. Yonge Library of Florida History, University of Florida, Gainesville. The field worker, Wilson W. Rice, secured some of the information about the First Baptist Church through interviews with Mrs. Hammie Williams Jourdan, one of the founders of the church. The interview was conducted in her home on 68 Onida Street, St. Augustine, Florida. The general wartime atmosphere in St. Augustine is treated in Omega G. East, "St. Augustine During the Civil War," *Florida Historical Quarterly* 31 (October 1952), 75-91.
15. WPA Files, Federal Writers Project, Negro Churches, 1936. Alfred Farrell was the fieldworker who prepared the account of St. Mary's Primitive Baptist Church in Tallahassee. Farrell is listed as the interviewer for several of the WPA Slave Narratives consulted in the preparation of this study.
16. Jefferson B. Browne, *Key West, The Old and the New* (1912; facsimile ed., Gainesville, 1973), 44.
17. Charles Summer Long, *History of the A.M.E. Church in Florida* (Philadelphia, 1939), 52. Long, the historian of the A.M.E. Church in Florida, was the son of Thomas W. Long, an A.M.E. minister who served three terms in the Florida Senate. Henry Call is said to have found a church handbill on a battlefield while searching for his master. There were four members in the church when he organized it.
18. Edwin B. Browning, Sr., *History of Concord Baptist Church, 1841-1976* (Madison, FL, 1976), 33.
19. Ibid., 34-35.
20. "The Last Slave in Wakulla County," appeared in the *Magnolia Monthly* (April 1964) and is reprinted in Elizabeth F. Smith, *Waukulla County Pioneers, 1827-1967* (Crawfordville, FL, 1968), I, 37.

21. "Report from St. John's Church Tallahassee, Wm. J. Ellis, Rector, 1863," in Diocese *of Florida Journal of the Proceedings of the Convention held in Tallahassee,* May 8, 1867 in St. John's Church with the sermon preached by the Rev. J. J. *Scott, in memory of the late Bishop Rutledge, including proceedings in* 1863 *and* 1866 (Tallahassee, 1867), 12.
22. Ibid., 12.
23. Ibid., 13.
24. Ibid.
25. Ibid., 53.
26. Harriet B. Greely to Whipple, April 29, 1865, American Missionary Association Papers, microfilm ed., reel 28, Robert Manning Strozier Library, Florida State University.
27. Captain F. A. Hendry, "Tallahassee Before the War," letter to the editor of *The True Democrat,* October 5, 1908, reprinted in *Florida Historical Quarterly* 1 (January 1909), 16-18.
28. Joe M. Richardson, *The Negro in the Reconstruction of Florida, 1865–1877* (Tallahassee, 1965).
29. One example of the changing of names with the advent of freedom is provided in the oral tradition of the McKinney family. During slavery times the family was owned by a man named Smith near Madison, Florida. Since the family considered Smith to be "mean," when freedom came they took the name of McKinney, a "kind" white man in the area. Interview with Richard Ishmael McKinney by Robert L. Hall, Tallahassee, Florida, July 18, 1981.
30. Francis Butler Simkins, "Tolerating the South's Past," in Patrick Gerster and Nicholas Cords, eds. *Myth and Southern History* (Chicago, 1974), 172.
31. "An Act Prescribing Additional Penalties… ," *Acts of Florida Legislatures* 14th Session, January 15, 1866, 23-27.
32. For the history of the A.M.E. Church, see Carol V. R. George, *Segregated Sabbaths: Richard Allen and the Emergence of Independent Black Churches, 1760-1840* (New York, 1973) and, for the A.M.E. Zion Church, see William Jacob Walls, *The African Methodist Episcopal Zion Church: Reality of the Black Church* (Charlotte, NC, 1974).
33. *New York Times,* May 8, 1866. This lawlessness was not to cease with the events of 1866 reported in the *New York Times,* but persisted at least through 1871 and well beyond. The specialist on this episode in Florida history is Ralph L. Peek. See his article, "Lawlessness in Florida, 1868-1871," *Florida Historical Quarterly* 40 (October 1961), 164-85, and "Lawlessness and the Restoration of Order in Florida, 1868-1871" (Ph.D. dissertation, University of Florida, 1964).
34. Dispatched with eight companies by Major General James H. Wilson from Macon, Georgia, it was McCook who accepted the surrender of 8,000 Confederates in Florida. For a general treatment of emancipation celebrations by a folklorist, see William H. Wiggins, Jr., "Lift Every Voice: A Study of Afro-American Emancipation Celebrations," *Journal of Asian and African Studies* 9 (1974), 180-91
35. Charlyn Rainville has helped John Byrd produce a remarkable account of Byrd's life. She first met Byrd on April 12, 1975, having been introduced by William D. Miller, then a resident of Jefferson County and a professor of History and American Studies at the Florida State University. The story of Byrd's life resulted in a loosely edited narrative which

is essentially the verbatim transcript of extended tape recorded conversations conducted on April 14, 15, 23, 29, 1975, May 8, 1975, and December 11, 1975. This document may be found in Charlyn Rainville, "The Story of a Son of a Slave," (Master's thesis, Florida State University, 1976). Although the thesis is Rainville's, the title is Byrd's At the time of the first interview by Rainville, Byrd had been working on his own written narrative for at least two years. Byrd told Rainville, "I want to show you the tree where my father was freed at. I'll show you the big oak tree where they went to get their freedom."

36. Anonymous interview conducted by Sharon Ann Johnson, a student at Florida State University. A typed transcript of the interview is in the author's files.
37. Whitelaw Reid, *After the War: A Southern Tour* (Cincinnati, 1866), 173.
38. George P. Rawick, *The American Slave: A Composite Autobiography,* 22 vols (Westport, CT, 1972), XVII, 93-99 (hereinafter cited as Rawick, *Florida* Narratives).
39. Scholarly treatments of Florida's "black codes" are legion. In addition to the still-standard Theodore B. Wilson, *The Black Codes of the South* (Tuscaloosa, 1965), readers concentrating on Florida should consult Farley M. Gilliam, "The 'Black Codes' of Florida," *Apalachee 6* (1963-1967), 111-20; Joe M. Richardson, "Florida Black Codes," *Florida Historical Quarterly* 47 (April 1969), 365-79; and Jerrell H. Shofner, "Custom, Law, and History: The Enduring Influence of Florida's 'Black Codes'," *Florida Historical Quarterly* 55 (January 1977), 277-98. The members of the three-man committee of ex-slaveholders appointed by Governor William Marvin were C. H. DuPont of Gadsden County and A. J. Peeler and Mariano D. Papy of Leon County. A. J. Peeler had been twice chief clerk of the House of Representatives and was secretary of the 1865 Constitutional Convention, Tallahassee *Semi-Weekly Floridian,* November 14, 1865. M. D. Papy was a law partner of J. P. Westcott with offices located in the Marine Bank Building, Tallahassee see *Sentinel,* October 1, 1868. The full text of the commission's report was printed in the December 26, 1865, issue of the Tallahassee Semi-Weekly Floridian.
40. Gilliam, "The 'Black-Codes' of Florida," 119.
41. John Wallace, *Carpet-Bag Rule in Florida* (1888; facsimile ed., Gainesville, 1964), 42; Wallace's book is generally considered to be politically biased. Rembert W. Patrick said that the book was "a Democratic campaign document, probably written by a white conservative [William D. Bloxham]," and consequently, "should be used with care," *The Reconstruction of the Nation* (New York, 1967), 164.
42. Joe M. Richardson, "The Freedmen's Bureau in Florida," *Apalachee* 6 (1967), 98. Vincent Harding described the Union Leagues, organizations similar in form and function to the Lincoln Brotherhoods as "politico-religious clubs." "The Challenge of the Children: Creating a New Vision of America," *Southern Exposure* 10 (January/February 1982), 75.
43. Wallace, *Carpet-Bag Rule in Florida,* 43.
44. Gainesville *New Era,* May 4, 1867.
45. In many cases the black ministers were the black politicians. This was true for a variety of reasons. First, the number of black men engaged in the professions from which many white politicians came was severely limited. Secondly, most black ministers believed in the inseparability of political creed from religious duties and actions.
46. Daniel Richards to Elihu B. Washburne, November 19, 1867. Washburne Papers, Library of Congress, Washington, DC. These letters were edited by George C. Osborn and

reprinted in "Letters of a Carpetbagger in Florida, 1866-1869," *Florida Historical Quarterly* 36 (January 1958), 239-85.

47. Richards' positive assessment of Saunders is contained in Richards to Washburne, November 19, 1867. Growing black exasperation with Saunders is recounted in Richards to Washburne, April 14, 1868. The effort to bribe Pearce is mentioned in Richards to Washburne, April 20, 1868, Washburne Papers.
48. Richards to Washburne, April 21, 1868, Washburne Papers.
49. Tallahassee *Semi-Weekly Floridian,* May 5, 1868.
50. Richardson, *The Negro in the Reconstruction of Florida,* 31.
51. *Acts of Florida,* 14th Session, January 11, 1866, 31 sectional. Although slave family life in Florida has not yet been systematically studied, occasional glimpses of slave weddings and the disruption thereof can be seen in the primary sources, particularly in travelers' accounts. The following incident, described by the British traveler Francis Tuckett, occurred on the property of Achille Murat sometime during 1829 or 1830: "The evening I spent with Mr. Murat's friends and had an opportunity of witnessing for the first time the festivities of a bridal party among the coloured population. The different members of the family at whose house I stayed felt great interest in facilitating the wishes of the party. The wedding cake was exhibited ornamented with flowers. Friends assembled from a distance of 20 miles around but I am sorry to say the bridegroom was absent, prevented by his subjection to the caprise [sic] of an owner, and the bride consequently absented herself." Francis Tuckett, *A Journey in the United States in the Years 1829 and 1830,* ed. Hubert C. Fox [a great grandson] (Plymouth, England, 1979), 56-57.
52. Among the black "marital auxiliaries," as the historian William W. Davis put it, to gain a wide reputation during this period was the former Gadsden County house servant. Robert Meacham. Early in 1867, Meacham claimed to have married three hundred couples since freedom came. Tallahassee *Semi-Weekly Floridian,* February 5, 1867, cited in William W. Davis, *The Civil* War *and Reconstruction in Florida* (1913; facsimile ed., Gainesville, 1964), 495.
53. St. Augustine *Examiner,* September 29, 1866.
54. *Acts of Florida,* 14th Session, December 14, 1866, 22, Section 1.
55. Gloria Jahoda, *Florida: A Bicentennial History* (New York, 1976), 82.
56. Clyde Vernon Kiser, *Sea Island to City: A Study of Helena Islanders in Harlem and Other Urban Centers* (1932; reprint ed., New York, 1969), 103-4.
57. Claude F. Oubre, *Forty Acres and a Mule: The Freedmen's Bureau and Black Land Ownership* (Baton Rouge, 1978), 137, 143. During three voyages in 1866 the steamer *Dictator* brought about 2,000 blacks from Charleston to Florida, Tallahassee *Semi-Weekly Floridian,* January 29, 1867. See also, Barbara Richardson Cotton, "The Effects of Antebellum Conditions Upon Post-War Economic Adjustment of Blacks in Jacksonville," Negro *History Bulletin* 42 (July-August-September 1979), 68-73.
58. Harriet Beecher Stowe, *Palmetto-Leaves* (1873; facsimile ed., Gainesville, 1968), 270-71. For a discussion of Mrs. Stowe's involvements with blacks in Florida see Marilyn J. Floyd and Harry A. Kersey, Jr., "Harriet Beecher Stowe and Negro Education in Florida," *Negro Educational Review 28* (Januaryt 1977), 19-27.

59. Interview with Charles Coats by Viola B. Muse, December 3, 1936, in Rawick, *Florida Narratives,* 67-68. According to Escott, Viola B. Muse was a black interviewer, Paul D. Escott, *Slavery Remembered: A Record of Twentieth Century Slave Narratives* (Chapel Hill, 1979), 191.
60. Interview with Rebecca Hooks by Pearl Randolf, January 14, 1937, in Rawick, *Florida Narratives,* 172-77. Mrs. Hooks was interviewed in her home in Lake City, Florida. According to Escott, Randolph was black, *Slavery Remembered,* 191.
61. Interview with Bill Austin by Martin Richardson, March 18, 1937, in Rawick, *Florida Narratives,* 23. Austin was living in Greenwood (Jackson County), Florida, when Richardson, a black interviewer, talked with him. Escott, *Slavery Remembered,* 191, identified Richardson as black. In the interview, Austin told Richardson that he had left Greene and Hancock counties "about 55 years ago," which would place his arrival in Jackson County, Florida, around 1882.
62. E. B. Duncan, "An Appeal for Schools for Freedmen," Tallahassee *Semi-Weekly Floridian,* March 13, 1866. An outstanding example of how the conversion experience itself could trigger a desire to learn to read and write is the experience of Lott Carey. The pioneer black Baptist missionary to Africa could not read and write when he was converted through a sermon delivered by the Reverend John Courtney at Richmond's First Baptist Church in 1807. Carey wanted to be able to read the story of Nicodemus (third chapter of John) for himself. As Leroy Fitts put it, "It is significant that Carey's literary education began in his young adult life concomitant with his conversion experience. This is generally consistent with the educational experiences of Black slaves during slavery in America. The limited literary education of the few fortunate Black slaves was primarily biblical instruction. The Bible became the only textbook of Black slaves in America," Leroy Fitts, *Lott Carey: First Black Missionary to Africa* (Valley Forge, 1978), 14.
63. Tallahassee *Semi-Weekly Floridian,* March 13, 1866.
64. Richardson, *The Negro in the Reconstruction of Florida,* 111.
65. Interview with Patience Campbell by James W. Johnson, December 25, 1936, in Rawick, *Florida Narratives,* 58-60.
66. James Smith to Whipple, October 18, 1865, American Missionary Association Papers, microfilm ed., reel number 28, Robert Manning Strozier Library, Florida State University. Smith said: "We have 5 small schools but not one that can teach them the English Language properly. The Colored people is a trying to do what they can for themselves."
67. Simon Peter Richardson, *The Lights and Shadows of Itinerant Life: An Autobiography* (Nashville, 1900), 190-9 1.
68. *The Spirit of Missions* 33 (February 1868), 194-251, quoted in Richardson, *The Negro in the Reconstruction of Florida,* 87.
69. Howard Thurman, *Deep River: Reflections on the Religious Insight of Certain of the Negro Spirituals* (New York, 1945), 16-17, Thurman wrote: "When at length I asked the reason, she told me that during the days of slavery, the minister (white) on the plantation was always preaching from the Pauline letters- 'Slaves, be obedient to your masters,' etc. 'I vowed to myself,' she said, 'that if freedom ever came and I learned to read, I would never read that part of the Bible!"'

70. Bruce T. Grindal, "The Religious Interpretation of Experience in a Rural Black Community," in Robert L. Hall and Carol B. Stack, eds. *Holding on to the Land and the Lord: Kinship, Ritual, Land Tenure, and Social Policy in the Rural South* (Athens, 1982), 89.
71. Ibid.

8

JIM CROW REARS HIS UGLY HEAD

In the 1870s, Florida witnessed the end of Reconstruction and a re-segregation that lasted into the years of the modern civil rights movement. By the 1880s, the Sunshine State had essentially reinstituted or recodified its Old South practices and protocols, chief of which was a rigidly segregated society along color lines. As Florida grew into a more robust population and economy in the late-19th century, it adopted a spate of new policies and priorities, nearly all with a "for whites only" mandate. Many writers trace the origin of Jim Crow rearing his ugly head in Florida to the Supreme Court's "separate but equal" ruling in *Plessey v. Ferguson* in 1896; in truth, as Wali R. Kharif underscores in this study, Tallahassee had institutionalized "separate but *un*equal" well prior to the Court's ruling in *Plessy.* Kharif's article, therefore, helps readers better understand the origins and mechanics of an entrenched system of segregation against which blacks fought "through all means possible" for almost 100 years.

Wali R. Kharif's article illustrates the various and realistic black responses to Jim Crow following the end of Reconstruction in Florida. The author contends that black Floridians met disfranchisement, segregation, discrimination, and racially motivated violence with all manner of legal and personal resistance and protest, including mass demonstrations. He then focuses on transportation segregation as an important early target for black protest, a resistance mode strikingly similar to the protests that launched the modern civil rights movement. Blacks also progressively filed suits in court to protest the resurrection of Jim Crow and associated white assaults on black voting rights. The suits essentially proved meaningless in 1883, when the U.S. Supreme Court declared the federal 1875 Civil Rights Act unconstitutional, thus nullifying the legal undergirding of Florida's own Civil Rights Act of 1873 and similar measures.

The author suggests that after 1883, the state simply codified what had already existed in practice. The result was that freedmen were discriminated against in almost all public facilities and transportation lines, disenfranchised, and barred from jury duty, among other humiliations. The author stresses that blacks bringing suit to protest legal and social injustices had represented viable forms of protest during times prior to the entrenchment of Jim Crow and the horror of blacks facing only white juries. Even so, the spirit of black protest and resistance lived on through personal and collective actions for future generations.

Emigration represented one often overlooked means of protest. The author suggests that some blacks simply fled the state. The number of blacks who could depart the United States for other parts of the world was small, because of financial constraints and the reluctance to sever family and social ties. When resettlement did not prove attractive, many disgruntled blacks, as professor Jerrell Shofner has determined, joined the so-called Great Migration north in the opening decades of the 20th century. He finds that by 1920, 40,000 black Floridians had joined the southern exodus north, with most departing west Florida, Tampa, and Jacksonville for the presumably more tolerant environs of New York, New Jersey, Pennsylvania, and Illinois.

Those who moved about Florida in search of undermining Jim Crow often created self-reliant black communities, sometimes within larger cities like Tallahassee, Jacksonville, Tampa, and Miami by the early 20th century. The internal migration, while attractive to many rural blacks, often laid the foundation for the growth of new forms of segregation in the cities (the one reviewed later in this book is Overtown in Miami). This is a significant point inasmuch as the expanding urban-based black communities of the 20th century would provide numerous sites for attacks on de jure and de facto segregation and perceived white police violence, for example the racial disturbance of Overtown in Miami (1980 and 1989) and in the segregated neighborhoods of St. Petersburg (1996).

The author's thesis is engaging: black response to renewed challenges of Jim Crow following Reconstruction in Florida arose as flexible and realistic means of protest and rejection of segregation that lasted well into the 20th century. Readers should come away from Kharif's study with at least a fundamental understanding of how significantly "ol' man" Jim Crow scarred the socio-political complexion of Florida and how the state's African-American population struggled all too long to bring him down.

FURTHER READING

Hugh Douglas Price, *The Negro and Southern Politics: A Chapter of Florida History* (1957);

David Chalmers, "The Ku Klux Klan in the Sunshine State: The 1920s," *Florida Historical Quarterly*, Vol. 42 (1964);

Derrell Roberts, "Social Legislation in Reconstruction Florida," *Florida Historical Quarterly*, Vol. 43 (1965);

Joseph M. Richardson, *The Negro in the Reconstruction of Florida* (1965);

Edward K. Eckert, "Contract Labor in Florida During Reconstruction," *Florida Historical Quarterly*, Vol. 67 (1968);

Paul S. George, "Colored Town: Miami's Black Community, 1896-1930," *Florida Historical Quarterly*, Vol. 56 (1978);

Jerrell H. Shofner, "Florida and The Black Migration," *Florida Historical Quarterly*, Vol. 57 (1979);

Robert L. Zangrando, *The NAACP Crusade against Lynching, 1909-1950* (1980);

Susan Hamburger, "On the Land for Life: Black Tenant Farmers on Tall Timbers Plantation," *Florida Historical Quarterly*, Vol. 66 (1987);

Leon F. Litwack, *Been in the Storm So Long: The Aftermath of Slavery* (1990);

Robin D. G. Kelley, "'We Are Not What We Seem': Rethinking Black Working-Class Opposition in the Jim Crow South," *Journal of American History*, Vol. 80 (1993);

Maxine D. Jones and Kevin M. McCarthy, *African Americans in Florida* (1993);

"Special Section: Rosewood: Before and After," *Florida Historical Quarterly*, Vol. 76 (1997);

Charlton W. Tebeau and William Marina, *A History of Florida* (1999), chapters 16-25;
Jane Dailey, Glenda Elizabeth Gilmore, and Bryant Simon, eds., *Jumpin' Jim Crow: Southern Politics from Civil War to Civil Rights* (2000);
Leonard R. Lempel, "The Mayor's 'Henchmen and Henchwomen, Both White and Colored': Edward H. Armstrong and the Politics of Race in Daytona Beach, 1900-1940," *Florida Historical Quarterly*, Vol.79 (2001);
David H. Jackson, Jr., "Booker T. Washington's Tour of the Sunshine State, March 1912," *Florida Historical Quarterly*, Vol. 81 (2003);
Irvin D. S. Winsboro and Moses S. Musoke, "Lead Us Not into Temptation: Race, Rhetoric, and Reality in Southern Populism," *The Historian*, Vol. 65 (2003);
Paul Ortiz, *Emancipation Betrayed: The Hidden History of Black Organizing and White Violence in Florida from Reconstruction to the Bloody Election of 1920* (2005);
Robert Cassanello, "Avoiding 'Jim Crow': Negotiating Separate and Equal on Florida's Railroads and Streetcars and the Progressive Era Origins of the Modern Civil Rights Movement," *Journal of Urban History*, Vol. 34 (2008);
Seth Weitz, "Defending The Old South: The Myth of The Lost Cause and Political Immorality in Florida, 1865-1968," *The Historian*, Vol. 71 (2009);
Chris Bray, "'Every Right To Be Where She Was': The Legal Reconstruction of Black Self-Defense in Jim Crow Florida," *Florida Historical Quarterly*, Vol. 87 (2009).

BLACK REACTION TO SEGREGATION AND DISCRIMINATION IN POST-RECONSTRUCTION FLORIDA

Wali R. Kharif

The Florida Historical Quarterly, Volume 64, issue 2 (1985), 161-173.

Equality of protection under the laws, as guaranteed by the Fourteenth Amendment to the United States Constitution, implies that in the administration of criminal justice no person, by reason of his race or color, shall be subjected for the same offense to any greater or different punishment than that to which persons of another race or color are subjected.[1] It also suggests that all citizens are entitled to protection of their civil rights and against discriminatory practices based upon race, color, creed, or religion. Unfortunately, in October 1883 when the United States Supreme Court declared the Civil Rights Acts of 1875 unconstitutional, the legislative framework requiring states to provide for civil rights in public places of accommodation and transportation was dismantled. It further had the effect of nullifying the civil rights act passed by Florida lawmakers in 1873.[2]

Legal segregation was not an overnight development in post-Reconstruction Florida. Lawmakers cautiously approached the establishment of de jure segregation. But once the movement had begun it spread rapidly into every sector of social life within the state. Segregation was established in the regular schools, schools for the deaf and blind, for juvenile delinquents, and in colleges. It was provided for in the prisons— the convict lease and prison system— and the local jails. It was required on the railroads, streetcars, electric cars, at the ticket offices, and in waiting rooms.[3] During this period of Democratic supremacy blacks were also disfranchised and omitted from juries, and they continued to be victims of violence and intimidation. In response to this adversity black Floridians established their own social and cultural institutions. But they also fought back against disfranchisement, racial discrimination, and segregation in other ways. They filed counter suits in the courts, staged protests and boycotts, encouraged some emigration, and established black communities.

The Bell School, located near the Florida-Georgia border, was constructed during Reconstruction to provide an education to newly freed slaves. State Library and Archive of Florida.

Some of the earliest protests were against disfranchisement of black voters who had been dropped from voter registration lists after being convicted of petty crimes.[4] In October 1878 several hundred Jefferson County blacks converged on the courthouse in Monticello unsuccessfully requesting to have their names restored to rolls.[5] Similar actions occurred in Leon, Gadsden, Escambia, and Madison counties where thousands were declared ineligible to vote between 1876 and 1888.[6]

While the earliest protests were in response to disfranchisement, the outcries in opposition to segregation on public accommodations received greatest attention. During the early 1870s it was not unusual to find blacks and whites travelling in the same train cars.[7] But by 1880 there was strong opposition to mixing the races on common carriers. In April 1882, Bishop Daniel A. Payne, then seventy-one years old and the nationally known senior bishop of the African Methodist Episcopal Church, was ejected from a train in Florida when he refused to ride in the car set aside for blacks. The bishop was forced "to carry his baggage several miles in the heat of the day."[8] By 1886 the practice had become widespread enough that black ministers, headed by Bishop Payne, met in Jacksonville and protested the discrimination against blacks in the railroad cars. They resolved that as far as possible they would use their influence to discourage black excursions and all travelling not absolutely necessary on railroads which made distinctions.[9]

In spite of the black response during the following years additional Jim Crow laws were enacted to regulate public transportation. During the first decade of the twentieth century blacks responded by staging organized boycotts. In 1901 two boycotts were sponsored in Jacksonville following that city's passage of an ordinance providing for racial separation on the trolley cars.[10] In further response black hackmen of the Coachmen's Union initiated an emergency system to provide a satisfactory alternative to streetcars, often accepting a loss in profit to help the boycotters.[11] The boycott crippled the transit system and was so effective "that after a few months the city authorities ceased enforcing the ordinance and quietly asked the Negro ministers to spread the word to their congregations."[12]

The victory in Jacksonville was short-lived. Between 1901and 1905 increased emphasis was placed on enforcement of segregation laws. During the Jacksonville mayoral election of 1905 Mayor George M. Nolan was criticized by the opposition for his failure to enforce the ordinance.[13] Further pressure was added by enactment of streetcar segregation laws throughout the South and the eventual passage of such a measure by the Florida legislature in 1905.[14] Blacks organized resistance to the new thrust to segregate the streetcars. Separate boycotts occurred in Jacksonville and Pensacola.[15] Blacks in

Jacksonville walked, rode bicycles, and again were assisted by black hackmen who reduced their fares from a quarter to a dime and gave priority to serving blacks at the reduced price over white patrons at the regular price. On one occasion Jacksonville police arrested Andrew Black "for ordering a white couple out of his hack because he preferred picking up two Negroes waiting for a ride. When the whites became indignant, Black parked the carriage in front of a nearby stable, unhitched the horses, and walked away."[16] In Pensacola blacks began organizing a protest immediately after the streetcar segregation bill was introduced.[17] A committee was selected to go to Tallahassee and urge the legislature to reject the proposal. In addition streetcars were boycotted in much the same manner as in Jacksonville. Notwithstanding black protest, the bill was quickly enacted. Ultimately, the issue was taken to the courts where the state law was declared unconstitutional in the case of *Florida* v *Andrew Patterson.*[18] However, the cities of Jacksonville and Pensacola hurriedly passed streetcar segregation ordinances.[19] These ordinances were tested in the courts and held to be constitutional by the Supreme Court of Florida.[20] In the shadow of these decisions black protest against segregated streetcars dwindled and eventually faded out. There were reportedly no protests in 1909 when the Florida legislature enacted a constitutionally-sound streetcar segregation law.[21]

Black Floridians not only protested against injustices and boycotted segregated facilities, they also brought their cases before the Florida courts. As early as 1873 black Tallahasseeans filed suit against the operator of a skating rink for denying them entry because of race. Ironically, black Justice of the Peace J. W. Toer dismissed the suit on the ground that the rink was private property which its operator could use as he pleased.[22] Blacks also petitioned the courts to restore their voting rights. In the case of the *State of Florida, Ex Rel Charles Scott* v *Board of County Commissioners of Jefferson County,* the state supreme court refused to issue a writ of mandamus on the contention that no specific person had been denied the addition of his name to the voting rolls.[23] In the *State of Florida, Ex Rel Richard Jordan* v *T. E. Buckman,* Jordan sought to have his voting rights restored and argued that he had been purged from the rolls for larceny prior to the 1880 election. The Supreme Court of Florida ruled that under Section 4 of Article XIV of the Constitution of 1868 larceny was grounds for disfranchisement and passed judgement against the plaintiff.[24]

Blacks also initiated legal actions to end discriminatory selection of juries.[25] On March 20, 1906, I. W. Montgomery, a Duval County resident, was convicted of embezzlement in the Criminal Court of Record. He appealed his conviction to the state supreme court challenging the array of jurors. Montgomery contended that the sheriff of

Duval County "did summon only white men to serve as jurors for and during the said week of said court, and did fail and refuse to select any colored men of African descent to serve on the jury as aforesaid, thus discriminating against all colored men of African descent."[26] He went on to present evidence that within Duval County at the time of juror summons "many thousand colored men of African descent of approved integrity, fair character, and sound judgment and intelligence and fully qualified for jury duty" were well known to the sheriff.[27] Additional evidence showed that "for many years . . . when special venires are issued and served. . . the sheriff . . . refuse[d] to select any names of persons of the African race."[28] In its January 23, 1907, opinion, the Supreme Court of Florida ruled unanimously in Montgomery's favor, reversed the criminal court judgment, and ordered a new trial at the cost of the county.[29]

The jury selection for the new trial followed a discriminatory pattern much like that at the earlier trial. The difference was that six of the jurors' names were drawn from the jury box and the other six were selected by the sheriff. Again no black jurors were among the jurors.[30] For the second time Montgomery appealed his case to the state supreme court. The court ruled in a split decision in favor of Montgomery, reversed the lower court judgement, and remanded the case. In its decision the Florida Supreme Court held that "an allegation that the 'refusal of the sheriff to select any men of African race to serve on the jury is on account of their race, color, and previous condition of servitude' is a sufficient charge of discrimination to entitle defendant to prove it."[31] The state supreme court held to this position in its March 11, 1913, decision in the case of *Harry Bonaparte* v *State of Florida.*[32] On June 27, 1916, the state supreme court finally reversed itself in the case of *Charles H. Haynes* v *State of Florida.* Haynes was convicted of first degree murder by an all white jury in the Hillsborough County Circuit Court. He appealed to the Florida Supreme Court and used the same defense as Montgomery and Bonaparte. However, the court ruled unanimously against him. The opinion read in part that "the evidence adduced did not support the allegation . . . that in selecting persons for jury duty the officers 'discriminated against Negroes of African descent because of their race, color, or privious condition of servitude' . . . or show any unlawful discrimination in the selection of jurors of which the accused may complain."[33]

Legal action was sometimes an effective mechanism for challenging white supremacy, but with white judges and juries there were limitations to the extent of any changes made in the behalf of blacks. Against the odds blacks seriously considered emigration as a viable response to racial turmoil. While the number of blacks that actually emigrated from the state was small, many considered emigration as a practical alternative for resolving racial conflict. Some even viewed it as an acceptable means for a family or small colony to leave Florida and start all over somewhere else.[34] A Palm Beach black in applying for departure stated that, "I desire to know what are the sawable timbers of Liberia as I desire to take with me a mill and fixtures for sawing timber. One hundred and thirty-six good families want to go with me. They comprise men of all trades, including experienced farmers. Our object is to form a settlement of our own, and thus lead to success in Liberia."[35] While all along some blacks had left the state, from 1871 to 1910 exactly 100, mostly families, emigrated to Liberia.[36] Forty emigrants were from Alachua County, fourteen from Duval, six out of Escambia, five from Madison County, three Jefferson County residents, and one each from Brevard and Marion counties. Another twenty six were from the state at large.[37] Table One shows the number of black emigrants to Africa by year and the city or residence where known.

The number of blacks who left Florida as colonists to Liberia was small, but not negligible since emigration entailed a financial burden and further required the severing of family and social ties, and the establishing of new roots in a foreign country. Those leaving, no doubt, felt strongly that conditions abroad had to be better than those within the United States. The two most cited reasons for leaving the country were subordination to whites and job shortages.[38] The Jacksonville paper referred to Liberia as "a Paradise for the Negro."[39]

Some blacks who shunned the prospects of emigrating, favorably considered relocating in territorial North America. Will Clemens of Jacksonville, a frequent contributor to the New York *Freeman,* cited economic exploitation, political oppression, and social degradation as the main reasons why some blacks wished to leave Florida.[40] Leon County blacks held a meeting in 1879 to discuss the feasibility of establishing a colony in Kansas or some other western state or territory. Four reasons were given for their desire to leave: unnecessary violence; intimidation and murder of blacks; the absence of governmental protection of their property and of individual rights; and economic abuse of the black worker.[41]

Most black Floridians were content to remain in the state and make the best of their circumstances. Nevertheless, many of these resolved to establish their own residential neighborhoods within Florida cities. Large numbers moved into the developing cities and the established urban centers.[42] Substantial numbers later migrated to central, southern, and southwestern Florida. While churches sprang up and served as symbols of spiritual hope and aspiration, there still was the need for physical protection, Black communities developed, in part, as protection from sometimes hostile white majorities.

TABLE 1
FLORIDA BLACK EMIGRANTS TO LIBERIA

Year	Number of Emigrants	Resident City	County
1871	5	Ellaville	Madison
1873	6	Jacksonville	Duval
1878	6	Pensacola	Escambia
1886	7	Gainesville	Alachua
1887	10	Gainesville	Alachua
1888	19	Gainesville	Alachua
1888	8	Rochelle	Alachua
1888	1	Ocala	Marion
1889	8	Oakland	Duval
1890	3	Monticello	Jefferson
1891	26	Florida at large	–
1895	1	Rockledge	Brevard
Total	100		

Source: American Colonization Society, *Annual Report of the American Society for Colonizing the Free People of Color of the United States*, LV (Washington, 1872), 10; LVII (1874), 9; LX (1876), 6; LXII (1879), 7; LXXI (1889), 6; LXXII (1890), 3;. LXXIII (1891), 4; LXXIV (1892), 4; LXXV (1893), 4; LXXIX (1897), 3.

Inadvertently, such organization perpetrated black social, political, and economic awareness. It also served to create a social structure where the dream of justice and equality could be established among peers.

In 1882 Frenchtown was a developing black community in the northwestern section of Tallahassee.[43] Residential development was also on the rise among blacks in Appalachicola where more blacks than whites were constructing houses.[44] In 1887 a black community was emerging west of Coconut Grove in Dade County.[45] Six years later, housing booms were occurring in East Jacksonville and St. Petersburg, thriving black population centers.[46] On Florida's Atlantic coast communities also sprang up in the newly developing towns and cities. Pompano Beach, Dania, Hallandale and points south each had its designated black quarters. These sections varied in size but generally were small. For example, the black community in Fort Pierce was comprised of a couple of houses isolated from the dominant white segments of the city.[47] In 1904 Fort Lauderdale's quarter consisted of seven houses and two stores.[48]

Discrimination and segregation contributed to the emergence of Black Town, also called "OverTown," in Miami. Black Town was located in Miami's northwest section and expanded in a northwesterly direction. It comprised about fifteen per cent of the city's original area. Blacks owned most of the business district which ran a stretch of one-half mile. At the turn of the century the business district included a grocery and general merchandise store, an ice cream parlor, pharmacy, funeral house, clubhouses, rooming places, soft drink plant, professional offices, and numerous food and entertainment establishments.[49] The Reverend S. W. Brown, formerly of South Carolina, owned and managed the Colored Town Bargain Store; Henry Reeves of the Bahamas published the Miami *Times;* Kelsey Pharr was proprietor of the funeral home and developer of the community's first cemetery; Richard Toomey was the first black lawyer in South Florida and established his office in Colored Town; and Dana A. Dorsey was the recognized leader of the neighborhood, owning extensive land, business, and related holdings.[50] Between 1904 and 1915 there were no fewer than six doctors and three practical nurses in Black Town.[51]

Most black sections of established towns never became very large and were enclosed by white residential developments. Blacks were not legally restricted from living in white neighborhoods until the early twentieth century. Nevertheless, they were excluded in fact from the developing white areas.[52] Such a practice was more by custom than anything else, but black preference in some instances cannot be overruled. The fact that black communities were generally surrounded by white ones limited their expansion. Consequently, new ones began to appear.[53] Unfortunately, wherever it was located black housing was often inadequate. Relatively few blacks could afford to buy or build their own homes, or to pay the high rents requested by white absentee property owners. In St. Petersburg and Miami this accounted for the modest rent housing lived in by most blacks. A large percentage of the available housing was substandard by every definition. Some lived in run-down shanties and shacks. Few had plumbing, and almost none were painted.[54] A few managed to buy homes and properties.[55] These owners placed emphasis on beautifying and increasing the value and appearance of their holdings.[56] In St. Petersburg, William Tanner was reported to have made "quite an addition to his neat home on Ninth Street." J. S. Tanner had "his neat cottage," also located on Ninth Street, "ceiled last week." G. B. McDaniel had "an addition put on his neat cottage on 10th Street," and Grant G. Gray was "having his neat cottage on Ninth Street painted."[57]

In an attempt to protect the neighborhood from white outbursts and criticisms, black community members took it upon themselves to confront internal social ills such as idleness. One anonymous critic wrote: "I am kicking on the young healthy Negroes loafing on the streets of our beautiful little city. They are the fellows that keep us that are trying to elevate ourselves down at the door of poverty. We ask the good people of this place to give them grass to cut on the streets if nothing more."[58] They also provided positive publicity for community successes.[59]

In part it was exclusion from white society that stimulated the emergence of black communities. Blacks in most communities owned the business districts which could run a stretch of one-half mile as in Miami, a few blocks in St. Petersburg, or only a couple of houses in Fort Pierce. These business districts contained grocery and general merchandise stores, ice cream parlors, pharmacies, funeral homes, clubhouses, rooming places, soft drink stands, food and entertainment establishments, and professional offices.[60]

Churches, schools, and social halls were the primary forums within the black community. Social activities such as minstrel shows, bazaars, festivals, parades, athletic contests, and excursions were planned and organized in these institutions. Secret fraternal organizations and orders, civic, business, self-help, and political gatherings used them to hold meetings. As a rule, most prominent blacks came from these institutions. Among them were clergymen, doctors, dentists, lawyers, school teachers, and principals.[61]

Black communities organized for self-help and protection. The merchants, social activists, and politicians joined together to fight against impoverished conditions, congestion, and the associated disease and crime in the cities. These poor and inadequate conditions included unpaved roads, insufficient lighting, uncleared wilderness areas, poor wages, unfair labor practices, lack of sanitary facilities, poor quality schools, and low quantity and quality housing. In Miami several organizations were established to deal with these kinds of social problems. These included the Colored Board of Trade which was founded in 1916; the North Miami Improvement Association, established in 1917; Negro Uplift Association of Dade County organized in 1919; and the Civic League of Colored Town.[62]

In spite of the institutions and community awareness that developed in the black sections of established towns, it must not be forgotten that city administration was in the hands of the whites. However, Florida had at least one black incorporated city during the latter part of the nineteenth century and that city still exists today. The town of Eatonville was first settled in 1883 by a small group of blacks who had fled from Maitland and areas north in response to the pressuring of local blacks to move to another area.[63] On August 14, 1887, twenty-seven registered voters met in the public hall of the town and voted unanimously to incorporate. As a result Eatonville became an all black chartered community. The city had its own city government and provided public services to residents.[64] The establishment of the town of Eatonville gave blacks the opportunity to govern their affairs. Little has been written about this historic community. It is known, however, that the town faced similar problems as those confronted by the black inhabitants of white-controlled cities. County services were poor, expansion was limited, and white injustices were perpetrated against those who ventured outside of the town's boundaries.[65]

Blacks reacted against segregation practices in a number of different ways. They established their own social and cultural institutions within established white-controlled cities; protested against disfranchisement, racial segregation and discrimination; filed suits in the courts; sponsored boycotts of unfair transporters; encouraged emigration; and established black communities. While this is not an exhaustive study of the types and means of the black reaction, it does show that blacks in Florida actively fought against white supremacy in the state. Though in many ways the fight was a losing one, there were several noteworthy successes.

Wali R. Kharif is instructor of history and political science, Southern Georgia College, Douglas, Georgia.

1. *American Law Reports,* 2d, XXXVIII (New York, 1977), 332-39.
2. *Acts and Resolutions of the General Assembly of the State of Florida,* 1873 (Tallahassee, 1873), 25-26.
3. Ibid., 1887-1915. See also Pauli Murray, ed., *State Laws on Race and Color* (Cincinnati, 1950), 77-88. Blacks and whites were also prohibited from cohabiting and intermarrying, and where not otherwise segregated they were discriminated against.
4. Jesse Jefferson Jackson, "Republicans and Florida Elections and Election Cases" (Ph.D. diss., Florida State University, 1974), 28.
5. Monticello Constitution, as cited in Tallahassee *Weekly Floridian,* October 15, 1878.
6. Jackson, "Republicans and Florida Elections," 27-28, 39, 43-44, 325. Voter disfranchisement continued in the years following constitutional revision in Florida. There is no indication, however, that black protests continued during these later years. For further examination of voter disfranchisements and chastisements, calls by Democrats for member turnouts, and further Democratic party attempts to justify the demise of black voters, refer to Tallahassee *Weekly Floridian,* May 21, September 3, November 12, 19, 1878, September 26, October 10, 1882, November 20, 1888.
7. Jacksonville *Daily Florida Union,* March 16, 1876.
8. Huntsville (Alabama) *Gazette,* April 29, 1882; Stanley P. Hirshson, *Farewell* to the Bloody Shirt: Northern Republicans and the Southern Negro, 1877-1893 (Bloomington, 1962), 101-02; Elizabeth Caldwell Beatty, "The Political Response of Black Americans, 1876-1896" (Ph.D. diss., Florida State University, 1976), 58.
9. New Orleans *The Weekly Pelican,* January 1, 1887.
10. August Meier and Elliott Rudwick, "Negro Boycotts of Segregated Streetcars in Florida, 1901-1905," *South Atlantic Quarterly,* LXIX (Autumn 1970), 525. The first black response was to send a group of prominent blacks to the mayor urging a veto of the ordinance. These representatives included Dr. James S. Hills, principal of the Florida Baptist Academy, Nathaniel Collier, Edward W. Robinson, Reverend James Johnson, Reverend

John T. Marks, and the elderly Reconstruction legislator and author *(Carpet-Bag Rule in Florida)* John Wallace.

11. Ibid., 526.
12. Ibid., 527.
13. Jacksonville *Florida Times-Union,* May 3, 16, 20, 30, June 6, 7, 21, 1905.
14. *Acts and Resolutions of the General Assembly of the State of Florida,* 1905, 99.
15. Meier and Rudwick, "Negro Boycotts," 529.
16. Ibid.; Jacksonville *Florida Times-Union,* July 24, 25, 1905,
17. Pensacola *Journal,* April 7, 1905; Tampa *Morning Tribune,* April 7, 1905. The bill providing for segregated streetcars was introduced by J. Campbell Avery, a Pensacola resident. This had the impact of further infuriating blacks in that city.
18. *Florida* v *Andrew Patterson, Florida Reports, L (1905),* 127-33.
19. Jacksonville *Florida Times-Union,* October 18, 1905; Pensacola *Journal,* August 23, 24, 25, September 28, 1905.
20. *Patterson* v *Taylor, Southern Reporter,* XL (1906), 493-97; *L. B. Croom* v *Fred Shad,* ibid., 497-99.
21. *Acts and Resolutions of the General Assembly of the State of Florida,* 1909, 339-40.
22. Jerrell Shofner, *Nor is it Over Yet: Florida in the Era of Reconstruction, 1863-1877* (Gainesville, 1974), 291.
23. *State of Florida, Ex Rel Charles Scott* v *Board of County Commissioners of Jefferson County, Florida Reports,* XVII (1880), 705-22.
24. *State of Florida, Ex Rel Richard Jordan* v *T. E. Buckman, Florida Reports,* XVIII (1881), 267-70.
25. Prior to exclusion from juries black jurors and witnesses were oftentimes targets of abuse. In one instance a black witness against a white man was assaulted with a club by the man he testified against, see Jackson, "Republicans and Florida Elections," 152. In another case, black jurors trying Lieutenant Governor Hull for election tampering were assaulted and jeered on the streets for finding the Democrat innocent. This latter situation is addressed in the Jacksonville *Florida Union,* as reported in the Tallahassee *Weekly Floridian,* June 3, 1879.
26. *Montgomery* v *State, Southern Reporter,* XLII (1907), 895.
27. Ibid.
28. Ibid.
29. Ibid., 897.
30. *Montgomery* v *State,* 2d., *Southern Reporter,* XLV (1908), 880.
31. Ibid., 882.
32. Bonaparte's case was identical to Montgomery's, Both sought relief from convictions of embezzlement in the Criminal Court of Record of Duval County and used the same defenses. See *Bonaparte* v *State, Southern Reporter,* LXI (1913), 633-38.
33. *Haynes* v *State, Southern Reporter,* LXXII (1916), 180-84.
34. Jacksonville *Daily Florida Union,* November 4, 1876.
35. American Colonization Society, *Annual Report of the American Society for Colonizing the Free People of Color of the United States,* LXXII (Washington, 1889), 5. Microfilm in the Robert Manning Strozier Library, Florida State University, Tallahassee.

36. Ibid., LIV (1871)-XCIII (1910). Prior to its demise in 1910, the Society assisted approximately 16,500 blacks nationwide to emigrate to Liberia and Sierra Leone.
37. Ibid., LVII (1874), LXII (1879), LXX (1887)-LXV (1892), LXXIX (1896).
38. Ibid., LXI (1877), 9.
39. Jacksonville *Florida Times-Union,* January 16, 1890.
40. Martin Dann, *The Black Press, 1827-1890: The Quest for National Identity* (New York, 1971), 285-86.
41. Tallahassee *Weekly Floridian,* October 28, 1879.
42. U. S. Bureau of Census, *Ninth Census of the United States,* Florida (Washington, 1871), 18-19, 97-99. In this census, towns of 2,500 and more were classified as urban centers.
43. Tallahassee *Weekly Floridian,* October 28, 1879.
44. Jacksonville *Daily Florida Union,* May 24, 1882.
45. Miami *Herald,* May 6, 1973.
46. Jacksonville *Evening Telegram,* July 27, 1893.
47. Martin County Historical Society, *The History of Martin County* (Hutchinson Island, 1975), 176; Kyle S. VanLandingham, *Pictorial History of Saint Lucie County, 1865-1910* (Fort Pierce, 1976), 38; Bill McGoun, *Hallandale* (Boynton Beach, 1976), 45.
48. Bill McGoun, *A Biographic History of Broward County* (Miami, 1972), 34.
49. Paul S. George, "Colored Town: Miami's Black Community, 1896-1930," *Florida Historical Quarterly,* LVI (April 1978), 432.
50. Ibid., 435, 438.
51. John Gordon DuPuis, *History of Early Medicine . . . in Dade County* (Miami, 1954), 17, 77. The doctors were S. M. Frazier, W. B. Sawyer, J. A. Butler, W. A. Chapman, and Dr. Culp and Dr. Holly. The practical nurses were Hattie Brooks, Fannie Goodwin, and Bertha Turner.
52. Karl H. Grismer, *The Story of St. Petersburg: The History of Lower Pinellas Peninsula and the Sunshine City* (St. Petersburg, 1948), 189.
53. Ibid.; George, "Colored Town," 435, 438, 440.
54. Grismer, *Story of St. Petersburg,* 189.
55. St. Petersburg *Times,* November 8, 1902.
56. Ibid.
57. Ibid., November 29, 1902.
58. Ibid., July 5, 1902.
59. Ibid., September 20, 1902.
60. George, "Colored Town," 438-39.
61. Howard N. Rabinowitz, *Race Relations in the Urban South, 1865-1890* (New York, 1978), 90.
62. Jerrell H. Shofner, "Florida and the Black Migration," *Florida Historical Quarterly,* LVII (January 1979), 271-80.
63. Glatting-Lopez and Associates, A *Comprehensive Plan for Eatonville, Florida* (Winter Park, 1978), 3. The town was named for Josiah Eaton, a white Floridian who had established Maitland. Eaton offered to sell blacks a large parcel of land one mile to the west of Maitland for settlement. Joseph Clarke bought the land and later sold it to any blacks wishing to settle there.

64. Ibid., 3-4.
65. Ibid., 4; Adley Associates, Inc., *Eatonville, Florida: A General Development Plan* (Sarasota, 1973), 4.

9

Gender Knows No Bounds

Florida State University historian Maxine D. Jones argues powerfully in this article that women have played a major role in the struggle against racism and discrimination in Florida, yet they have consistently received less attention than males in the pages of history. In keeping with one of the themes of this book, Jones provides a useful window on lesser-known aspects of the black freedom struggle in the Sunshine State: the deep and multifaceted role women played as a catalyst for change. In the past, the role of females in the fight had been ignored or diminished because of the patronizing notion that women's history was not "real history" or that women simply played supportive roles behind their men folk. Jones's article, and perhaps this book in general, should serve to debunk those notions—if such archaic notions still exist—by helping to make black women more visible, inclusive, and integrated into the human annals of the Sunshine State.

One of Jones's missions is to highlight what some scholars have termed the "double jeopardy" paradox black women have faced: both racial and gender discrimination. Readers would do well to contemplate Jones's point within the context of Shirley Chisholm's (Congresswoman from New York and the first black female to run for the presidency in 1972) response when asked whether she considered her sex or her race to be the greater obstacle to her success as a black female: "I've always met more discrimination being a woman than being black." This has been a dual burden and target of resentment for black women in both white racist society and black sexist society, and it has underwritten the history of Florida since the first black woman set foot there.

Despite the heavy strain of these conjoined prejudices—race and gender—black women have been key contributors through the centuries to the movement for equal rights in Florida. By using case studies, Jones demonstrates that these women were proactive in meeting the needs of the black community and forthright in attacking the inequities of racism, segregation, and discrimination. Jones's article itself is largely a narrative of the lives of some of the key overlooked women who exemplified this type of human struggle beginning in the early 20th century. Jones means for them to be exemplars of the strength and struggles of black women in overcoming repression.

The author first examines the impact of Mary McLeod Bethune, founder of Bethune-Cookman College in the early 1900s, black activist, and eventually an advisor to President Roosevelt during the Great Depression. Jones cites another author's praise of Bethune as the most important civil rights figure in the long period between Booker T. Washington and Dr. Martin Luther King, Jr. Functioning in an era under the shadow of Jim Crow, Jones argues Bethune rose to prominence not only as an educator but also as a vocal critic of voting prohibitions, lynching, segregation, and public health issues, which, she claimed, resulted in overcrowded black ghettos spawned by segregation. Bethune was a tireless advocate, the author maintains, of the need for racial integration, as well as equal economic opportunities in the cities and on the farms, and that her actions set a precedent for the roles of black women in the modern civil rights movement.

The founding of Bethune-Cookman College and other institutions are presented as examples of Mary McLeod Bethune's transformational leadership. Bethune's refusal to segregate seating at public functions held at the college is juxtaposed with the policies of other southern black schools, and the author points out that it took extraordinary courage for black women in the Deep South to challenge state law and social mores. Bethune believed in interracial cooperation rather than confrontation but was more forthright in her criticism of the system than other leaders. For example, when Jones compares Bethune to the famous race leader,

Booker T. Washington, she concludes that Washington was neither as brave nor forthright as Bethune in confronting injustice and racism, including the notorious KKK. Bethune's work on the national level is also reviewed but not in the same detail as her statewide work. The author ends with the statement that between Washington's death in 1915 and the outbreak of the modern civil rights era in and following World War II, Bethune led the fight for racial justice in America.

The author then rounds out her article by illustrating other courageous, and lesser-known, pioneering black women in Florida who have not received their just due. She begins with the contributions of Eartha M. M. White, whom Jones refers to as "the Jane Addams of her race" and proceeds with useful examinations of Blanche Armwood, Viola T. Hill, and Alice Mickens, all of whom reflect moving examples of black female activism in their communities.

Jones's article breaks new ground on the often "hidden" but profound contributions black women made to the Sunshine State's freedom struggle. While only offering a glimpse of the strength and determination of black women, the author, nevertheless, challenges Floridians to understand the deep and particular dual oppression of black women. It is now left to readers and academics to properly research and disclose the full-range of this significant but somewhat neglected aspect of Florida's racial heritage.

FURTHER READING

Zora Neale Hurston, *Dust Tracks on a Road: An Autobiography* (1942);

Lottie Montgomery Clark, "Negro Women Leaders of Florida," M.A thesis, Florida State University (1947);

Theodore Pratt, "Zora Neale Hurston," *Florida Historical Quarterly*, Vol. 40 (1961-1962);

Bruce Ergood, "The Female Protection and the Sun Light: Two Contemporary Negro Mutual Aid Societies," *Florida Historical Quarterly*, Vol. 50 (1971);

O. Sylvia Lamar, *Black Women in Television, 1981: Their Role and Scope in Florida's Network Affiliate Stations* (1981);

Bettye Collier-Thomas, *Black Women in America: Contributors to Our Heritage* (1984);

Jacqueline Jones, *Labor of Love, Labor of Sorrow: Black Women, Work, and the Family from Slavery to the Present* (1985);

James W. Button, *Blacks and Social Change: Impact of the Civil Rights Movement in Southern Communities* (1989);

Roderick D. Waters, "Gwendolyn Cherry: Educator, Attorney and the First African American Female Legislator in The History of Florida," M.A. thesis, Florida State University (1990);

Steve Glassman and Kathryn Lee Seidel, eds., *Zora in Florida* (1991);

Maxine D. Jones and Kevin M. McCarthy, *African Americans in Florida* (1993);

Darlene Clark Hine, *Black Women in America: An Historical Encyclopedia* (1993);

Viki L. Crawford, Jacqueline Anne Rouse, and Barbara Woods, eds., *Women in the Civil Rights Movement: Trailblazers and Torchbearers, 1941-1965* (1993);

Audrey Thomas McCluskey, "Ringing Up A School: Mary McLeod Bethune's Impact on Daytona," *Florida Historical Quarterly*, Vol. 73 (1994);

Maxine D. Jones, "No Longer Denied: Black Women in Florida,1920-1950," in *The African American Heritage of Florida*, David R. Colburn and Jane L. Landers, eds. (1995), chapter 10;

Keith Halderman, "Blanche Armwood of Tampa and the Strategy of Interracial Cooperation," *Florida Historical Quarterly*, Vol. 74 (1996);

Christopher E. Linsin, "Something More Than a Creed: Mary McLeod Bethune's Aim of Integrated Autonomy As Director of Negro Affairs," *Florida Historical Quarterly*, Vol. 76 (1997);

Maxine D. Jones, "The Rosewood Massacre and the Women Who Survived It," *Florida Historical Quarterly*, Vol. 76 (1997);

Belinda Robnett, *How Long? How Long?: African-American Women in the Struggle for Civil Rights* (1997);

Peter J. Ling and Sharon Monteith, eds., *Gender in the Civil Rights Movement* (1999);

Bettye Collier-Thomas and V. P. Franklin, eds., *Sisters in the Struggle: African American Women in the Civil Rights-Black Power Movement* (2001);

Lynn Olson, *Freedom's Daughters: The Unsung Heroines of the Civil Rights Movement from 1830 to 1970* (2001);

Harold Bloom, ed., *Zora Neale Hurston* (2003);

Tananarive Due and Patricia Stephens Due: *Freedom in the Family: A Mother-Daughter Memoir of the Fight for Civil Rights* (2003);

Jessie Carney Smith, ed., *Notable Black American Women* (2003);

Tracy J. Revels, *Grander in her Daughters: Florida's Women during the Civil War* (2004).

"WITHOUT COMPROMISE OR FEAR":

FLORIDA'S AFRICAN AMERICAN FEMALE ACTIVISTS

Maxine D. Jones

The Florida Historical Quarterly, Volume 77, issue 4 (1999), 475-502.

We must challenge, skillfully but resolutely, every sign of restriction or limitation to our full American citizenship . . . we must seek every opportunity to place the burden of responsibility upon him who denies it.

Mary McLeod Bethune[1]

In his study of the civil rights movement in Mississippi, historian Charles Payne observed that "men led but women organized."[2] With few exceptions the same could be said of African American activists in Florida throughout the twentieth century. Women played a major role in combating racism and discrimination, and in seeking first-class citizenship for black Floridians.

Hampered by racial and gender barriers, these women actively sought to secure for blacks the same educational, political, and economic opportunities that most whites enjoyed. They supported those in need by providing food, clothing and shelter, and by creating institutions to strengthen their communities. Students of Florida history are familiar with the names of prominent civil rights leaders C. K. Steele, Edward Davis, Virgil Hawkins, Harry T. Moore, S. D. McGill, C. Blythe Andrews Sr., and John Due. Yet often missing from the pages of journal articles and monographs are the names of the black women who were equally important in eradicating injustice and generating resources and opportunities within their respective communities, women such as Mary McLeod Bethune, Eartha White, Blanche Armwood, Alice Mickens, Viola Hill, Athalie Range, Fannye Ayer Ponder, Olive B. McLin and Patricia Stephens Due. They are just a few of the hundreds of African American women in the Sunshine State who made a difference. Some were known only within their communities and cities, while others were recognized on the state and national levels. They created educational opportunities and influenced federal policy; many worked within the system, others in spite of it. And some were more outspoken than others. Yet all challenged the system and were pro-active in meeting the needs of the black community and pointing out to the white power structure the inequities of segregation, racism, and discrimination. African American female activists and community leaders worked as strenuously and contributed as much to improving the condition of black Floridians as did African American men.

Black women in Florida followed a long tradition of female activism in the African American community. The condition of blacks in twentieth-century Florida required action, and those black women who were in a position to do so eagerly picked up the torch so bravely carried by Sojourner Truth, Harriet Tubman, Maria Stewart, and Ida Wells Barnett decades before. Throughout most of the twentieth century the majority of Florida blacks lived in poverty. Unequal educational, economic, and political opportunities contributed to illiteracy, unemployment, subsistence wages, poor working conditions, and poor health. In 1905 the death rate for black Floridians was 7.3 per 1,000; for whites it was 6.1 per 1,000. Typhoid fever, pneumonia, consumption, and heart disease killed hundreds of Floridians of both races annually. Only 2.2 percent of the state's white population above the age of ten was classified as illiterate in 1925. The black illiteracy rate topped 20 percent. The black illiteracy rate in Dixie County, an alarming 74.5 percent, was the highest in the state.[3]

Such conditions put Mary McLeod Bethune on the path to becoming Florida's most renowned African American activist. A South Carolinian by birth, Bethune adopted Florida as her home when she arrived in Palatka (Alachua County) in 1900. She left Palatka in 1904 to work among destitute blacks in Daytona (Volusia County) and to establish a school similar to the one she had attended in North Carolina-Scotia Seminary. In October 1904, Bethune, with five students and even fewer dollars, opened the Daytona Educational and Industrial Institute.[4]

Mary McLeod Bethune left her mark on Daytona, Florida, and the nation. Clarence G. Newsome concluded that "more than any other black leader during the interregnum between Booker T. Washington and Martin Luther King, Jr., she stood at the helm of the Negro's struggle for racial justice."[5] A natural born and fearless leader, and an independent woman, Bethune quickly earned the respect of many area whites. She believed in racial integration and refused to succumb to southern racial mores. When whites attended events on her campus, which was renamed Bethune-Cookman College in 1923, they sat with African Americans. Harlem Renaissance author and poet Langston Hughes visited the college in 1934 and praised its president for not making "'special provisions' for local white folks." During his lecture there he noticed that "a great many whites were in the audience but they sat among the Negroes." At other black schools in the South, "even the very well-endowed, and famous ones," Hughes found "an amazing acquiescence to the wishes of the local whites and to the tradition of the color-line." He criticized those schools that "set aside whole sections in their own auditoriums for the exclusive use of whites."[6]

Such intermingling between blacks and whites violated state regulations across the South. This was not lost on poet Hughes:

> [I]f you think that is easy to achieve in the South and does not take bravery and gall and guts, try it yourself. Or else be humble like that college president . . . who says he is sorry the white people in his community who wish to hear Mrs. Roosevelt speak on his campus cannot attend because the state law is against it! Thus meekly he accepts an obvious wrong and does nothing— not even verbally. Such men would accept Hitler without a struggle— but Mrs. Bethune wouldn't— not even in Florida. . . .[7]

Indeed it took courage to challenge the South's mores, and Bethune did so, but she also believed that interracial cooperation rather than confrontation was the key to settling the race problem. Thus, she called for "a better understanding between the White and Negro Groups."[8]

Mary McLeod Bethune championed social justice and sought to remove the barriers that prevented Florida's African Americans from participating as full citizens. She frequently spoke out against lynching, barriers to voting, insufficient funding for public education, and "the enactment of measures which in segregating Negroes in unsanitary ghettoes make them a menace to the health and peace of the entire community."[9] Bethune called for the appointment of a statewide committee composed of "the best educated, most cultured, tactful and unselfish leaders" of both races.[10]Because of the "popular disapproval" of a lynching in Ocala in1926, Bethune believed the time was right for such a commission:

> Interracial cooperation in religious [work], education, social service, municipal and State government, is working with splendid effect in other States. Let us have more of it in Florida. The day of selfish, individualistic leadership has passed. We need in Florida a carefully selected interracial committee. Let us have one.[11]

While it is uncertain whether state officials appointed such a committee, several communities, including Jacksonville, eventually did.

Mary McLeod Bethune at Bethune-Cookman College, 1943. Photograph courtesy of the Florida State Archives, Tallahassee.

Bethune-Cookman College faculty and students hosted an interracial student conference in March 1936. Considering the state of race relations in Florida at the time, this was an extremely brave move. Less than two years had passed since the brutal lynching of Claude Neal in North Florida. But on March 3, 1936, white students from Rollins College and the University of Florida convened on the campus of Bethune-Cookman College. The exchange between the students was candid. Rollins College coeds asked their hosts: "What things can white friends do [to] immediately and significantly help improve the condition of Negroes?" Bethune-Cookman students asked those from the University of Florida whether they were willing to integrate their graduate and professional courses. Students from the University of Florida asked how black and white students could best cooperate for their mutual benefit.[12]The students responded to each other's questions honestly and with respect for differing views. All those present pledged to continue to work for better race relations through the Interracial Student Council. President Bethune believed that if the present assembly was any indication, the future for race relations in Florida looked promising.[13] The educator maintained that interracial cooperation at all levels was essential for improvement in race relations, and she facilitated interracial interaction whenever she could.

In February 1931, Bethune addressed an interracial conference in Lakeland, Florida. Dr. Ludd M. Spivey, president of Florida Southern College, directed the meeting and Will W. Alexander of the Commission on Interracial Cooperation gave the opening speech. Alexander declared that objective thinking was the "only sane approach" and key to solving the race problem.[14] Harris G. Sims, a reporter for the *New York Times,* reported that Mary McLeod Bethune "held her head high [and] said she was proud of her own black skin." According to Sims, Bethune "went straight to the heart of the race problem."

> She...pleaded for social justice, pointed out the injustinces that were being practiced upon her race, and did it with such sincerity and zeal that her remarks were followed by applause, instead of derogatory comments that often follows when a Negro speaks with such candor.[15]

Bethune told the delegates that her people deserved social equality, which she defined as equal railroad accommodations as well as educational and economic opportunities. Intimate contact with whites was not the goal. It is uncertain how many "young Southerners" Bethune convinced to support her vision of equal opportunity for all, but she obviously made an impression, as they "made a beeline to the Negro college president after she had made her speech, awaited their turn to shake hands with her and to address her as Mrs. Bethune."[16]

Bethune also made an impression outside the South. A 1926 *New York Times* article referred to her as "the 'Booker Washington' of her sex," while *Time* magazine dubbed Bethune "The Booker T. Washington of Florida" in 1939. The two educators did have much in common. Both were astute black college presidents who knew how to persuade prominent northern whites to contribute vast sums to black educational institutions. Both promoted vocational education and were "adroit politicians" as well, but the comparison probably ends there. Washington was never as brave or as candid as Bethune in pointing out to southern whites the effects of southern injustice, racism, and discrimination. Some may argue that Bethune and Washington lived during different times and indifferent environments, and that Washington had more to lose by being vocal.[17] But violence and lynching were as common in Florida as in other southern states. Between 1889 and 1918 more than150 blacks were lynched in Florida. The Sunshine State led the nation in lynching in 1920 and continued to hold a disgraceful place in the top five for several years.[18] Nonetheless, Bethune refused to be intimidated even by the Ku Klux Klan. When the Klan made an uninvited visit to campus in 1920, she did not gather her students and hide under the cloak of darkness. Instead, according to Dr. Florence Roane, head of the division of education, "Mrs. Bethune made all the girls come out on the steps of Faith Hall and sing 'We are Climbing Jacob's ladder.'" The Klan threatened them, burned a cross, and departed.[19]

Bethune lambasted Florida's treatment of its black citizens, but she did so with poise, dignity, and savvy. For example in one article addressing the disproportionate number of African American men in Florida's prisons, Bethune pointed out the tremendous social costs to whites of "keeping the nigger in his place":

> A large percentage of the Negroes in Florida's penal institutions are there today because of injustice, discrimination in the courts, and inability to secure proper legal aid. They come out hardened, brutalized, hating the society at whose hands they have suffered. They mingle in their community and spread the disease of bitterness among hundreds of others. To keep them inferior they must be huddled in segregated ghettoes without drainage, light, pavements or modern sanitary convenience. They must be denied justice and the right to make a decent living. He must be insulted and bullied and mobbed, discriminated against in public places and denied access to parks and recreational centers. In dollars and cents the cost of this system is tremendous to the Commonwealth which sponsors it. In the effect upon those who put it into practice the price is too high to be paid in this generation. It must be paid by the children of the third and fourth generation.[20]

Booker T. Washington was never as forthright with white Alabamians. Of course, the majority of white Floridians were not swayed by Bethune's candor, even though she described the cost in terms they would understand. But black Floridians were aware of and appreciated her attacks on a system that discriminated against them.

When the National Association for the Advancement of Colored People (NAACP) awarded Bethune its Spingarn Medal in June 1935, the selection committee hailed her national influence, which, it declared, "has always been on a high plane, directed by a superb courage. Mrs. Bethune has always spoken out against injustice, in the South as well as in the North, without compromise or fear."[21]

Mary McLeod Bethune took her campaign for interracial cooperation and first class citizenship for African Americans nationwide. As president of the National Association of Colored Women (NACW) Bethune fought for open seating at the 1925 meeting of the International Council of Women held in the nation's capital. On May 5, 1925, members of the NACW protested the segregated seating arrangements by walking out. An outraged Bethune denounced the seating policy, claiming "it was humiliating to the United States to be segregated in the presence of women from allover the world."[22] Her appointment as Director of the Negro Division of the National Youth Administration (NYA) during Franklin Roosevelt's administration, her friendship with Eleanor Roosevelt, and her presidency of the National Council of Negro Women gave Bethune a wider audience, more power and influence, and an opportunity to expand her work beyond the confines of Bethune-Cookman College and the state of Florida. In 1930 journalist Ida Tarbell named Bethune one of the fifty leading women in the United States. Little did Tarbell know that during the intervening years between the death of Booker T. Washington in 1915 and the birth of the modern day civil rights movement in 1955, Mary McLeod Bethune would assume the leadership of the African American crusade for racial justice.[23]

Bethune was just one of several black female activists working diligently for positive change for Florida's black citizens. Eartha M. M. White had as much influence and impact in Jacksonville as Bethune had in Daytona. White, known as "the Angel of Mercy" and the "Jane Addams of her race," was Jacksonville's first African American social worker and an advocate for the downtrodden. A native Floridian born in 1876, White, like her friend Mary McLeod Bethune, began her career as an educator. Her work eventually extended beyond the confines of the classroom to that of the broader Jacksonville community, and she became a bridge between Jacksonville's black and white residents. Eartha White's mother, Clara English White, taught her to "do all the good you can, in all the ways you can, in all the places you can, for all the people you can, while you can."[24] Until her death in 1920, Clara White worked alongside her daughter, helping those in need.

A fire in Jacksonville in 1901 left thousands of blacks and whites homeless and destitute. The two White women came to their aid. From their home they fed and clothed many of the dislocated. They solicited and raised funds to establish an Old Folks Home in1902 for African Americans. Because blacks did not receive their fair share of social services in Jacksonville, Clara and Eartha White operated a mission from their home on First Street to meet the immediate needs of the poor. In 1928, as a memorial to her mother, Eartha White officially established the Clara White Mission. With the help and financial contributions of friends, White moved the mission from its First Street location to a permanent site on Ashley Street in 1932.[25]

Mary McLeod Bethune called Eartha White "a great humanitarian" and an advocate for "the needy and the unfortunate."[26] Only five feet tall, White earned the reputation and gained the admiration and respect of influential whites that allowed her to establish institutions to aid the black community. Even though her primary clientele was African American, she assisted the "unfortunates of all races and all creeds, without pay and with loving kindness." According to Matilda O'Donald, Chairman of the Interracial Committee in Jacksonville, "Miss White knows no racial differences when it comes to helping those who need help. Many young white persons both men and women have risen up and called her blessed."[27]

In addition to establishing the Old Folks Home in 1902, White, through the Clara White Mission, operated a much needed Tubercular Rest Home in the black community. Tuberculosis was the leading cause of death among blacks in Duval County in 1920.[28]The "Angel of Ashley Street" also established an orphanage and child placement service, a home for unwed mothers, an unemployment agency, and a nursery for working mothers. The city of Jacksonville and Duval County failed to provide such services to their black citizens, so White assumed the responsibility. A successful businesswoman in her own right, White lobbied local politicians and influential whites and blacks for support and funds. Using her own money and that donated by others, including Mrs. Arthur J. Cummer and Mrs. Alfred I. DuPont, White established and sustained institutions that met the health, educational, and social welfare needs of Jacksonville's blacks. Eventually White received aid from both the city and the county governments.[29]

By the 1930s, White had helped thousands, but she may have accomplished her most important work during the Great Depression. The Clara White Mission operated a

Eartha M. M. White, n.d. Photograph courtesy of the Eartha M. M. White Collection, University of North Florida

soup kitchen that fed hundreds daily without benefit of government funds. No one was turned away. Although the federal government did not support the soup kitchen, it chose the Clara White Mission to direct its various projects designed to help blacks in Jacksonville and Duval County. With the help of government funds, the mission operated a sewing room that hired unemployed black women, provided art and music programs for youth, and housed the Negro Unit of the Florida Writers Project.[30] Mary McLeod Bethune may have persuaded government officials to select White to head this project.

Eartha White accomplished much in meeting the needs of the black community with a leadership style quite different from that of Bethune. White, to a degree, adhered to Booker T. Washington's philosophy. She attended the organizational meeting of Washington's National Negro Business League in 1900 and was active in the Jacksonville chapter. She almost certainly was in the audience of 2,500 when Booker T. Washington spoke in Jacksonville in 1912.Although White sought to dismantle racism and discrimination, she was not outspoken and did not vocally challenge the system. According to Altermese Bentley, whose parents were friends of White's, Eartha White was "very strong" but "not overly assertive."[31] However, she used her influence with Jacksonville's powerful whites and policy makers to achieve for blacks those opportunities and services that they were denied. She used their financial contributions to establish Mercy Hospital, and she persuaded local politicians to provide a playground and other facilities for black neighborhoods. White established a network of supporters and admirers across the state, including Secretary of State R. A. Gray, Attorney General Richard Ervin, United States Senator Claude Pepper, and Governor Fuller Warren, all of whom wrote glowing testimonials in honor of her seventy-fifth birthday.[32]

Although cautious, White was not necessarily accommodating, and she often led by example. She was active in politics at a time when race and gender kept thousands from voting in Florida. She was active in the local Republican Party, serving as president of the Duval County Republican Executive Committee in 1920 and the state chairperson of the National League of Republican Colored Women in 1928. When women finally gained the right to vote in 1920 she actively encouraged black women to register to vote. As a direct result of the efforts of White and others, African American women registering to vote outnumbered white women in several wards. Threats from the Ku Klux Klan, which marched to discourage blacks from voting, did not prevent black women from turning out in large numbers in the 1920 fall elections.[33]

White and Bethune were friends and were members of many of the same clubs and organizations. Both were members of the National Association of Colored Women

(NACW), a national organization that Bethune chaired from 1924 to 1928, and the Florida State Federation of Colored Women (FSFCW). With the power of the FSFCW behind them, White and Bethune lobbied state officials to provide a home for wayward and delinquent girls. In fact, White chaired the Education and the Industrial Home for Colored Girls Committees and received credit for securing the passage of the measure that established an institution for black female youth in Marion County.[34] Through national, regional, state, and local clubs and organizations, White and Bethune were able to influence policy that benefitted blacks outside of their respective communities.

Blanche Armwood was also affiliated with the club movement in Florida and was a contemporary and friend of Eartha White and Mary McLeod Bethune. She, too, sought first-class citizenship for African Americans and eloquently articulated the needs of those who had no voice. A Tampan by birth, Armwood emerged as an outspoken leader in the early struggle for civil rights in Florida. In 1922 this woman, described as a "rebel," became the first executive secretary of the Tampa Urban League. In this position and as Supervisor of Negro Schools for Hillsborough County, "she did not ask favors—she demanded rights— the same rights for all American citizens," for the county's more than 20,000 African Americans. Buttressed by her membership in the NACW, the NAACP, and the FSFCW, Armwood sought to make blacks in Tampa "politically conscious, educationally alert, socially constructive [and] economically independent."[35]

Blanche Armwood's stint as a school teacher and principal prepared her for the position of Supervisor of Negro Schools in Hillsborough County (1922-1930) where she sought to erase the inequality of black and white schools. Educational opportunities for blacks in Tampa were poor. White students attended school for nine months, blacks for only six. Black schools were congested and unsanitary, and black teachers received substantially less pay than their white counterparts. It was obvious to Armwood that under such conditions black youth stood "a very slim chance for development into strong, intelligent manhood and womanhood." "Dynamic, aggressive, zealous, [and] enthusiastic for whatever cause she espoused," Armwood took action. Reputedly, within less than two years, the glaring inequities were at least slightly mitigated. African American students received instruction for nine months, the county dramatically improved school facilities, and black teachers welcomed an increase in salary.[36]

Armwood was the first African American in Florida to serve as a county Supervisor of Negro Schools. Whites generally held this position. During her eight-year tenure the county constructed five new brick school buildings and additions to two existing black schools in Tampa. She encouraged parents' participation in their children's education by establishing a parent-teacher organization in every black school in the county. Additionally, Armwood played a major role in creating Booker T. Washington High School—the first accredited school for blacks in the county.[37]

Ironically, Armwood, like Bethune, was considered a "Female Booker T. Washington." Perhaps it was because of her reputation for organizing successful schools of household arts, not only in Tampa, but also in Athens, Georgia, New Orleans, Louisiana, and Rock Hill, South Carolina. Maybe it was because in these schools, African American women learned "how to work with their hands while they trained their minds" and departed imbued with the gospel of "industry, thrift, self-reliance, and self-respect." She firmly believed that such skills ensured a degree of economic independence that could lead to improvements in other areas.[38] Armwood, however, was more of a militant than an accommodationist.

Tampa Club Women in 1925. Blanche Armwood is seated in the front row, far right. Photograph courtesy of the Florida State Archives, Tallahassee.

Unlike Booker T. Washington she actively joined the NAACP and the struggle against racism, discrimination, and lynching. While probably not as outspoken as Bethune, Armwood was not one to hold her tongue. She denounced mob violence and lynching, fervently supporting the NAACP's anti-lynching campaign and the Dyer Anti-Lynching bill. When a white reader of the *Tampa Tribune* suggested that the "money, time, and determination" spent by advocates of anti-lynching would be better spent on "a campaign to eradicate the cause for which lynching in the South is the remedy,"—what he called the "bad nigger" who is "usually of 'high color' and 'high eddication'"—Armwood could not help but respond:

> The Negroes of this community feel that the editorial referred to shows such a spirit of antagonism to Negro education and advancement as we are reluctant to characterize as the Tribune's real attitude . . .The premium that white men put on their womanhood is worthy of the commendation of any people. Making criminals of hundreds of fathers of the future womanhood of their race who participated in mob murders is rather inconsistent, however. Please let us say further, Mr. Editor, that we do not know any case where educated Negroes have been lynched save in race riots like the ones in Arkansas and Oklahoma, where the bloodthirsty mob found pleasure in destroying the lives and property of the best Negro citizens as a means of humiliating the entire race. Nor do we understand what is meant by the Negro of "high color." Surely, the writer does not refer to mulattoes whose color proves the disregard our Southern white men have had for racial purity and the value of virtuous womanhood even among the Negroes, their humble loyal friends . . . Yours of peace and civic righteousness. Blanche Armwood Beatty. [39]

This exchange took place around the time of the racial incident at Rosewood, Florida, in January 1923, which resulted in the deaths of at least six African Americans and the complete destruction of their community. May white Tampans respected Armwood and worked alongside her at the Urban League and other interracial groups. In a sense she accomplished for race relations in Tampa what Eartha White did for Jacksonville's black and white citizens - she served as a bridge. Mary Burke concluded that Armwood's "conservative and diplomatic policy toward race relations led to acceptance by the white power structure."[40] Armwod's shrewd diplomacy definitely paid off for the black community, but the above letter to the editor throws her alleged conservatism into question. Her gender probably offered some protection, but often such bluntness resulted in a loss of respect and influence among whites, warnings, and even physical violence. Armwood demonstrated her boldness in challenging southern injustice not only by responding to the white reader, but also by including her name.

Likewise, she joined fellow Floridians Eartha White and Mary McLeod Bethune in supporting the Anti-Lynching Crusaders and helping to establish the Florida branch of that organization. She was also a member of the Republican Party and active in the National and State League of Colored Republican Women.[41]

Her actions and affiliations indicate that Blanche Armwood was not as conservative as she might have appeared. While Armwood aided African Americans in Tampa much as did White in Jacksonville— by working for daycare, health care, recreational facilities, better housing, equitable education— she was not quiet and retiring. Although she obviously needed the assistance of influential whites to bring about tangible changes in the black community, she did not turn her back when she saw racial injustice. Armwood openly criticized southern whites for their treatment of African Americans and consistently called attention to the inhumane conditions under which blacks were forced to live. She was unafraid to point out the discrepancies in almost every aspect of life between black and white Tampans.

Mary McLeod Bethune, Eartha White and Blanche Armwood were only the most prominent of the black activists in early to mid twentieth-century Florida. Many other women such as Viola T. Hill of Orlando and Alice Mickens of West Palm Beach were active as well. Hill was appointed to direct the Negro branch of the NYA in Orlando in 1941. She also organized the first nursery for blacks in that city. Many of her activities were designed to strengthen the black community. Hill was particularly interested in developing leaders among black youth and women. Mickens, who believed there was "strength in union" became heavily involved in the club movement in Florida. She was elected president of the Florida Federation of Colored Women's Clubs in 1938. She truly believed that equal rights and opportunities would be achieved for African Americans via colored women's clubs. For more than ten years Mickens worked to secure a playground for black children in West Palm Beach. "White children had nine or ten playgrounds and athletic fields," she pointed out, and "colored children had none." Black children needed a safe place to play and Mickens believed that playgrounds kept them out of trouble. Because of her persistent efforts the city eventually erected a playground for blacks on Fifteenth Street.[42]

Mickens' biggest battle, however, was with the West Palm Beach (Palm Beach County) Board of Public Instruction. It was common in Florida and other southern states for black school children to attend school in the summer. Often referred to as "Strawberry Schools," such a practice made it possible for black children to harvest crops or, as in the case in West Palm Beach, to caddy for white golfers during the winter months.

This arrangement also made it impossible for teachers to improve their credentials by attending summer school. Mickens lobbied the school board to change its policy and to lengthen the school year for black students. It refused. But as Lottie Clark Montgomery observed, "when Mrs. Mickens sets out to achieve an objective she doesn't rest until she accomplishes it." Although it took several years of struggle the county Board of Public Instruction changed the discriminatory policy. Black students began the school year in September and attended school for 9 months as did white students.[43] "Poised, patient, tolerant and benevolent," Mickens fought for equal opportunities for African Americans. She, too, was associated with various New Deal programs and encouraged blacks to take advantage of the opportunities offered through the NYA and the Civilian Conservation Corps. Whites apparently had high regard for Mickens and depended upon her "to interpret the Negro to the white race." When speaking before interracial groups she called for "better understanding and greater cooperation between the races."[44]

These African American activists often worked together on projects and called on each other for support when needed. White, Mickens, Bethune and Armwood helped secure the home for delinquent black females; White and Armwood were delegates to the Second National Conference on the Problems of the Negro and Negro Youth chaired by Bethune in January 1939. At the Washington, D.C., conference, delegates attacked the poll tax and discrimination in the military and New Deal agencies. They were actively involved in the NAACP's national anti-lynching campaign and advocated interracial cooperation. Armwood, Bethune, and White continued their activism and humanitarian efforts until their deaths. Armwood died in 1939, two years after completing a law degree at Howard University. Bethune, who became a national leader, spent much of her time in the nation's capital from 1934 until her death in 1955 campaigning against racism, sexism, and discrimination. Her position in the NYA enabled her to influence policy that benefitted blacks in Florida. She played a significant role in securing recreational facilities for the black communities in Bradenton and Daytona Beach, and the Durkeeville Housing Project in Jacksonville.[45] Eartha White lived for another nineteen years after Bethune's death. In 1941 she along with Bethune supported A. Philip Randolph's threat to lead a March on Washington unless President Roosevelt issued an edict condemning discriminatory hiring practices in the nation's defense industries. Ironically, she did attend the March on Washington in August 1963. Born into a segregated society that oppressed those with dark skin, Eartha White outlived legal segregation and overt discrimination in Florida. By the time of her death in 1974, Florida society had changed considerably. The government— local, state and federal—

helped provide for the needy and enforced federal laws that outlawed segregation and discrimination. She had played a part in bringing about such changes.[46]

In a sense, White linked Florida's early female activists with those of the modern civil rights movement. Through their activism these women built institutions that strengthened black communities across the state. The result was a more educated African American populace with the confidence and courage to follow in their footsteps. The Colored Women's Club movement and the examples set by Bethune, White, Hill, and Armwood, generated a new cadre of black female activists who were unafraid to challenge racism and discrimination. Their modes of operation differed considerably from earlier activists. They openly protested injustice, marched against discrimination, and were willing to go to jail to bring about change in the black community. Undoubtedly, many of them had met or had been influenced by those women who had laid the groundwork.

In 1956, Carrie Patterson and Wilhelmina Jakes inadvertently catapulted the state of Florida into a new phase of the struggle for first class citizenship. Like Mary McLeod Bethune before them, Patterson and Jakes refused to accept southern rules. The two Florida Agricultural and Mechanical University (FAMU) students disobeyed a white city bus driver's order to leave the only available seats on the bus to go stand in the "colored" section. Patterson and Jakes refused to be publicly humiliated and offered to leave the bus if their fares were returned. Instead of returning their fares, the bus driver called the police, and the two young women were arrested for "placing self in position to incite a riot." Emboldened by their bravery FAMU students confronted the racist seating policy by organizing a boycott of the City Transit Company. The ultimately successful bus boycott forced the bus company to change its seating policy and thrust the Reverend C. K. Steele into the national limelight.[47]

FAMU students initiated the civil rights movement in the state capital, and black women were at the forefront. Patricia and Priscilla Stephens were especially determined in their efforts to challenge segregation. In 1959, the FAMU sophomores organized a campus branch of the Congress of Racial Equality (CORE).CORE, an interracial organization established in 1942, confronted racism using nonviolent tactics.[48] In February 1960, Patricia and Priscilla Stephens, along with nine other students (including Mary Gaines, Barbara Broxton, and Angelina Nelson), launched a sit-in at the downtown Woolworth and were arrested for "disturbing the peace and tranquility of the community and inciting a riot." On March 17, Judge John A. Rudd found the students guilty and sentenced them to sixty days in jail or a three-hundred-dollar fine. Three students appealed and were released on bonds. Three others paid the fine so that they could "carry on the fight." Patricia and Priscilla Stephens, Barbara Broxton, William Larkin, and John Broxton chose the sixty-day jail sentence.[49] Although they missed classes and fell behind in their school work, their parents supported them. Patricia Stephens explained, "Our parents came up and offered to pay the fine. But we felt if we paid any more money to the city, we would be supporting segregation." The student activists spent forty-nine days in jail and were released on May 5, 1960.This was the first of several arrests for student activist Patricia Stephens who asserted, "when I get out, I plan to carry on this struggle. I feel that I shall be ready to go to jail again, if necessary."[50]

People across the country were impressed with the students' determination to end racism and discrimination, and with their willingness to be incarcerated in a southern jail. They gained national attention and soon after their release embarked on a national tour. They spoke to a variety of groups including a congregation in Harlem pastored by Adam Clayton Powell. Former First Lady Eleanor Roosevelt welcomed them and hosted a luncheon in their honor in New York. They were also received by Jackie Robinson. More importantly, CORE presented them with the Ghandi Award for "outstand-

Patricia and Priscilla Stephens confront police officers while picketting and boycotting stores in downtown Tallahassee in December 1960. Photograph courtesy of the Florida State Archives, Tallahassee.

ing service in the field of civil rights and human relations."[51] Patricia Stephens continued her activism, picketing and protesting in Miami and Washington, D.C. Between 1960 and 1965, Stephens, CORE, FAMU students, and white students from Florida State University and the University of Florida targeted Tallahassee's Trailways Bus Station, Neisner's, and the Florida Theater. After a long and bitter encounter the students forced the establishments to make concessions. Tallahassee lunch counters were desegregated in January 1963. After mass arrests and numerous dates with Florida judges, the Florida Theater finally integrated its facilities in 1965. The victories, however, were won at a great cost. Campus leader Patricia Stephens and fellow student Rubin Kenyon were suspended from FAMU during the 1963 fall semester. Patricia and Priscilla Stephens emerged as campus leaders and eagerly assumed prominent roles in the Tallahassee movement. They, along with hundreds of others, suffered many indignities—jail, tear gas, in addition to being spit on, called nigger, and dragged through the capital city's streets.[52] But none was as humiliating as the second-class citizenship that sentenced them to a life of inferiority.

Patricia Stephens Due continues the struggle but in a different arena. While her goals are the same as they were in the 1960s, her activism has shifted "from the street to the places of personal encounter—homes, schools, neighborhoods."[53] Other black females emerged from FAMU and other black institutions in the state as strong advocates for equal educational, political, and economic opportunities for African Americans, for women's rights, and for racial justice. They continued to work in their communities, churches, and schools and to articulate the needs and concerns of the poor and oppressed. Some took their platform for change to the people and were elected as representatives at all levels of government.

Interestingly, women who attended FAMU a decade before Patricia and Priscilla Stephens evolved into influential leaders during the 1970s and 1980s, and took the concerns of their constituents directly to the policy makers. Gwendolyn Sawyer Cherry, Mary Littlejohn Singleton, C. Bette Wimbish, and Carrie Meek, all FAMU graduates, became outspoken advocates for women, minorities, and the poor. All were educators, and all had been victims of racism and sexism. Cherry, Singleton, Wimbish, and Meek were older and more established than the Stephens sisters. They had families and successful careers, and because of the gains of the civil and women's rights movements, were, while not necessarily welcomed, able to seek and win elected positions in city and state government.

Gwendolyn Sawyer Cherry became the first African American woman elected to the

Florida legislature. Born and raised in Miami, Cherry represented Florida's 96th district. From 1970 until her untimely death in 1979, Cherry sought equal rights for women and minorities, and prison reform. She was also a strong advocate for children's rights and became a "legislative pioneer in the quest for statewide affordable child care centers."[54] A feminist, Cherry was not afraid to tackle controversial issues. She supported abortion rights, asserting that it was "a matter between a woman and her doctor." She disagreed with the 1977 United States Supreme Court decision that ruled that states were not required to pay Medicaid benefits for non-therapeutic abortions and that public hospitals did not have to provide such services. Cherry claimed the ruling discriminated against poor, particularly African American, women. She also called for prison reform, the establishment of rape centers for victims of sexual assault, and an end to capital punishment.[55]Cherry did not have Bethune's reputation or White's influential white friends, but her legacy was as important. She laid the groundwork for the African American women and men who would follow. Carrie Meek completed Cherry's term after her death in 1979.

According to Meek, "Gwen was strong: she cut a wide swath up here. And she made it much easier for another black woman to come into the Legislature and be accepted."[56] Mary McLeod Bethune had served as Carrie Meek's heroine and role model. Meek became friends with Bethune when she worked at Bethune-Cookman College. Though Meek "experienced extreme, rigid and very painful segregation and racism from childhood," she asserted, "I don't see myself as a victim—Carrie Meek is a fighter." Meek, a Tallahassee native, earned her stripes in the civil rights struggles in Tallahassee during the 1950s.[57]

Meek was elected to the Florida Senate in 1982. The first African American woman to serve in that body, Meek achieved another first when, in 1992, she and Corrine Brown of Jacksonville became the first African American congresswomen from Florida. Meek became an effective politician and an excellent advocate for women and minorities. She worked diligently to provide affordable housing for the poor and to improve education, and also introduced bills to aid women and minority business owners. Bethune's influence on Meek was evident in the causes that she championed.[58]

Mary Littlejohn Singleton joined Cherry in the Florida House of Representatives in 1972. She had been elected to the Jacksonville City Council in 1967 along with Sallye Mathis, the first African Americans to serve on the council for more than half a century. The Jacksonville community considered Singleton "a trailblazer and a bridge builder." In the state legislature Singleton, a former teacher, became a strong advocate for education and worked to improve race relations.[59]

C. Bette Wimbish, educator, attorney, and civil rights activist, continued the struggle against segregation and discrimination. She endured the humiliation of segregation and the hurt, anger, and helplessness of "trying to explain to her children why they could not

State Representative Gwendolyn Sawyer Cherry, Florida's First African American female legislator. Photograph courtesy of the Florida State Archives, Tallahassee.

have an ice cream cone in a downtown drugstore" in St. Petersburg.[60] Wimbish and her husband, physician Ralph Wimbish, challenged racial inequities and slights, and along with other prominent St. Petersburg blacks, provided housing for professional African American baseball players who trained in the Sunshine City as well as black entertainers. Blacks, regardless of their status, were not welcomed in the city's hotels and restaurants. Wimbish also held "sit-ins" at downtown lunch counters. "It was a very frightening experience," she recalled. "There was always the threat of shooting, beating or spitting. But it was a thing that had to be done." Crosses were burned on her lawn when she ran for a seat on the Pinellas County School Board in 1960. Undaunted by the cross burnings and her failure to gain a seat on the school board, Wimbish continued to seek means to improve conditions for blacks and to destroy segregation. In 1969 she became the first African American to serve on the St. Petersburg City Council, which enabled her to influence public policy, improve conditions in the black community, and to dismantle unfair laws. Wimbish served as vice mayor of St. Petersburg, from 1971 to 1973. Even though her bids to become an advocate at the state and national levels were unsuccessful, her most important work had already been achieved in the trenches.[61]

The historical record shows that hundreds of black women willingly and sometimes unknowingly served as active, effective, and outspoken advocates for African Americans in Florida. Whether individually or through clubs, churches, or other institutions, these women, to the best of their abilities, articulated the concerns of the poor and disabled. They fed the hungry, clothed the naked, and provided health care for the sick. In addition, they attempted to change the laws that made it nearly impossible for Florida's African Americans to enjoy the benefits of a democratic society. These female activists gave hope to many and built institutions that served and strengthened the black community. Their encouragement persuaded many to not give up, to continue to battle for access to equal education, political rights, and economic opportunities. It should be noted that whites sometimes assisted black female activists in Florida. Bethune, White, Armwood, Mickens, and Hill depended on financial contributions and support from sympathetic whites. The same was true during the more recent struggle. Patricia Stephens acknowledged white support. White students marched, demonstrated, and picketed segregated businesses, and were gassed and arrested alongside black students.[62]

Scores of other African American women deserve attention. Carrie Mitchell Hampton, Clara Frye, Lydia Pettis, Johnny Ruth Clarke, Olive Beatrice McLin, Mary McRae, Athalie Range, Aquilina Howell, and others emerged as leaders in their communities as doctors, nurses, educators, and business women and in the process shielded African Americans to some extent from the malignant cancer of racism. They were positive role models who encouraged race pride and provided the indomitable spirit and courage needed to continue the struggle for equal rights. African American women were the backbones of Florida's black communities.

Maxine D. Jones is professor of history at Florida State University

1. Mary McLeod Bethune, "Viewing the Facts Objectively," Mary McLeod Bethune Papers: The Bethune Foundation Collection, Part I, Reel 2, Frame 612.
2. Charles Payne, "Men Led, but Women Organized: Movement Participation of Women in the Mississippi Delta," in Vicki L. Crawford, Jacqueline Anne Rouse, and Barbara Woods, eds., *Women in the Civil Rights Movement: Trailblazers and Torchbearers, 1941-1965* (Brooklyn, 1990), 1-11.
3. *The Third Census of the State of Florida, 1905* (Tallahassee, 1906), 142, 144, 146-49; *The Fifth Census of the State of Florida, 1925* (Tallahassee, 1926), 94.
4. Henry Flagler employed hundreds of African American men to build the Florida East Coast Railroad. These men and their families lived in a destitute environment. Bethune hoped to educate their children so that they might know a better life. *The Christian Advocate,* February 4, 1937; Dorothy C. Salem, ed., *African American Women: A Biographical Dictionary* (New York, 1993), 47-51; *Crisis* 26 (September 1923), 222-23; Gerda Learner, ed., *Black Women in White America: A Documentary History* (New York, 1973), 134; Leedell Neyland, *Twelve Black Floridians* (Tallahassee, 1970) 17-18.
5. Clarence G. Newsome, "Mary McLeod Bethune in Religious Perspective: A Seminal Essay" (Ph.D. diss., Duke University, 1982), iv.
6. Langston Hughes, "Cowards from the Colleges," *Crisis* 41 (August 1934), 227-28.
7. Langston Hughes, "The Need for Heroes," *Crisis* 48 (June 1941), 185.
8. Mary McLeod Bethune, "Interracial Cooperation in Florida," typescript, n.d., Mary McLeod Bethune Papers, 1875-1955, Amistad Research Center, Tulane University, New Orleans, Louisiana (hereafter MMBP).
9. Ibid.
10. Ibid.
11. Ibid. In April 1926, a group of "masked men" seized Charles Davis, an African American accused of killing a Pasco County deputy sheriff, as he was being transferred from Ocala to Brooksville for trial. Sheriff W. D. Cobb believed Davis had been lynched and thrown into the Withlacoochee River. Papers of the NAACP, Part 7, The Anti-Lynching Campaign, 1912-1955, series A: Anti-Lynching Investigative Files, 1912-1953, reel 8, group 1, series C, Administrative Files, box C-351.
12. The University of Florida student did not give a direct response to the question asked. He asserted that the students in attendance would be willing to accept a Bethune-Cookman graduate into their academic programs. He pointed out, however, that all graduate pro-

grams were already "overcrowded." "Interracial Student Conference in Florida," *Crisis* 43 (April 1936), 109.

13. Ibid., 110.
14. *New York Times,* February 18, 1931, news clipping, in MMBP.
15. Ibid.
16. Ibid.
17. *New York Times,* November 11, 1926, news clipping, MMBP; Lottie Montgomery Clark, "Negro Women Leaders of Florida" (master's thesis, Florida State University, 1942), 25.
18. National Association for the Advancement of Colored People, *Thirty Years of Lynching in the United States, 1889-1918,* with appendices for years 1919-1922 (New York, 1919), 35, 41.
19. Dr. Florence Roane and Bethune were close friends. Another account of the same incident claims that the students sang, "'Be not dismayed whate'er betide, God will take care of you."'*St. Petersburg Times,* December 28, 1975; Newsome, "Mary McLeod Bethune in Religious Perspective," 244-45.
20. Mary McLeod Bethune, untitled typescript, n.d., MMBP.
21. "Mrs. Bethune: Spingarn Medalist," *Crisis* 42 (July 1935), 202; *Philadelphia Tribune,* June 6, 1935, news clipping, MMBP; Monroe N. Work, *The Negro Year Book* (Tuskegee, 1937), 11.
22. Elaine Smith. "Mary McLeod Bethune" in Darlene Clark Hine, Elsa Barkley Brown, Rosalyn Terborg-Penn, eds., *Black Women in America: An Historical Encyclopedia* (Bloomington & Indianapolis, 1994), 118-19.
23. Bethune died in May 1955. Clark, "Negro Women Leaders of Florida," 28; "Along The Color Line," *Crisis* 37 (November 1930), 380; Newsome, "Mary McLeod Bethune in Religious Perspective," iv.
24. "Biography of Clara White," in *75th Diamond Birthday Observance of [the] Useful Life of Eartha Mary Magdalene White,* souvenir program, 1951, Eartha White Collection, Clara White Mission, Jacksonville, Florida; *Florida Times-Union* (Star Edition), March 12, 1952, March 25, 1951; Neyland, *Twelve Black Floridians,* 38, 40-41; Paul Diggs, "Little Angel of Ashly Street— Miss Eartha M. M. White," typescript, 1938, Florida Writers Project, Special Collections, University of South Florida (hereafter FWP).
25. James B. Crooks, *Jacksonville After the Fire, 1901-1919* (Jacksonville, 1991), 16-18, 89-90; Wilson Rice, "Negro Churches" unpublished manuscript, 1936, FWP; "History of Clara White Mission," *75th Diamond Birthday Observance of [the] Useful Life of Eartha Mary Magdalene White.*
26. Mary McLeod Bethune to Eartha M. M. White, October 25, 1951, in *75th Diamond Birthday Observance of [the] Useful Life of Eartha Mary Magdalene White,* Crisis 49 (September 1942), 289.
27. Matilda O'Donald, chairman, Interracial Committee, to Whom It May Concern, March 29, 1951, in *75th Diamond Birthday Observance of [the] Useful Life of Eartha Mary Magdalene White.*
28. Council of Social Agencies, *Jacksonville Looks at its Negro Community, a Survey of* Conditions Affecting the Negro Population in Jacksonville and Duval County, Florida (Jacksonville, May 1946), 2-3.

29. *75th Diamond Birthday Observance of [the] Useful Life of Eartha Mary Magdalene-White.*
30. Diggs, "Little Angel of Ashly Street"; Rice, "Negro Churches"; *75th Diamond Birthday Observance of [the] Useful Life of Eartha Mary Magdalene White,* 289.
31. Crooks, *Jacksonville After the Fire,* 85, 89, 94; Mrs. Altermese Bentley, interview with author, August 21, 1998.
32. Robert T. Thomas, "Interracial Relations," *Crisis* 49 (January 1942), 19; *75th Diamond Birthday Observance of [the] Useful Life of Eartha Mary Magdalene White.*
33. Walter F. White, "Election Day in Florida," *Crisis* 21 (January 1921), 106, 109; Barbara H. Walch, "Sallye B. Mathis and Mary L. Singleton: Black Pioneers on the Jacksonville, Florida, City Council" (master's thesis, University of Florida, 1988), 47-48.
34. Fannye Ayer Ponder, "A Salutation to a Friend to Man," in *75th Diamond Birthday Observance of [the] Useful Life of Eartha Mary Magdalene White;* Clark, "Negro Women Leaders of Florida," 30.
35. Clark, "Negro Women Leaders of Florida," 63, 64, 67, 70-71; Blanche Armwood Family Papers, Special Collections, University of South Florida; John R. Durham, "Blanche Armwood: The Early Years, 1890-1922" (master's thesis, University of South Florida, 1988), 13; *Fifth Census of the State of Florida,* 59; Mary Burke, "The Success of Blanche Armwood, 1890-1939," *The Sunland Tribune* 15 (November 1989), 40, 41.
36. Clark, "Negro Women Leaders of Florida," 65, 66, 70; *Tampa Tribune,* February 26, 1983.
37. Clark, "Negro Women Leaders of Florida," 66; Burke, "The Success of Blanche Armwood," 41-42; *Tampa Tribune,* February 26, 1983.
38. Clark, "Negro Women Leaders of Florida," 65-66; Burke, "The Success of Blanche Armwood," 40.
39. Ibid.
40. Burke, "The Success of Blanche Armwood," 43.
41. *Tampa Tribune,* February 26, 1983; Blanche A. Beatty to Eartha White, April 28, June 16, 1928, Eartha M. M. White Collection, University of North Florida, Jacksonville.
42. Clark, "Negro Women Leaders of Florida," 83, 85, 57, 60.
43. Ibid., 60.
44. Ibid., 61-62.
45. Ibid., 30, 68; 69; Mary Claire Clark, "'In Unity There is Strength': Women's Clubs in Tampa during 1920s," *Tampa Bay History* 11 (Fall/Winter 1989), 15-16.
46. Smith, "Mary McLeod Bethune," 123; Audreye Johnson, "Eartha Mary Magdalene White," in Hine, et al., eds., *Black Women in America,* 1257; Clark, "Negro Women Leaders of Florida," 69; Walch, "Sallye B. Mathis and Mary L. Singleton," 53.
47. *Tallahassee Democrat,* May 27 and 28, 1956; Glenda A. Rabby, "Out of the Past: The Civil Rights Movement in Tallahassee, Florida" (Ph.D. diss., Florida State University, 1984), 10, 21-27; Gregory B. Padgett, "C. K Steele and the Tallahassee Bus Boycott" (master's thesis, Florida State University, 1977), 25-27; Gregory Padgett, "C. K. Steele, A Biography" (Ph.D. diss., Florida State University, 1994), 60-62; Leedell W. Neyland, *Florida Agricultural and Mechanical University: A Centennial History—1887-1987* (Tallahassee, 1987), 421; *Tallahassee Democrat,* February 20, 1994, May 25, 1997.

48. Aldon D. Morris, *The Origins of the Civil Rights Movement: Black Communities Organizing for Change* (New York, 1984), 128-29; *St. Petersburg Times,* May 26, 1963.
49. *Tallahassee Democrat,* February 21 and 22, March 17 and 18, 1960; *St. Petersburg Times,* May 26, 1963; Padgett, "Steele, A Biography," 169-72; Rabby, "Out of the Past," 100-104, 139.
50. *St. Petersburg Times,* May 26, 1963; Neyland, *Florida Agricultural and Mechanical University,* 424; *The Southern Patriot* 19 (September 1961), 3, and Ibid., 21 (April 1963), 2.
51. *St. Petersburg Times,* May 26, 1963.
52. *St. Petersburg Times,* May 26, 1963; *Miami Times,* October 6 and 26, 1963; *Miami Herald,* May 31, 1963; Neyland, *Florida Agricultural and Mechanical University,* 425.
53. *Tallahassee Democrat,* February 2, 1993.
54. Roderick Dion Waters, "Sister Sawyer: The Life and Times of Gwendolyn Sawyer Cherry" (Ph.D. diss., Florida State University, 1994), 108.
55. Waters, "Sister Sawyer," 112-14.
56. Waters, "Sister Sawyer," 220.
57. *Jet,* September 28, 1992, 34-37; *Time,* November 2, 1992, 46.
58. Allen Morris, *A Changing Pattern: Women in the Legislature,* 4th ed. (Tallahassee, 1991), 114-16; *Time,* November 2, 1992, 46; *Florida Flambeau,* April 30, 1979.
59. Marianna W. Davis, ed., *Contributions of Black Women to America* (Columbia, S.C., 1982), 222; *Florida Times Union,* February 1, 1991, February 9, 1992; *Tallahassee Democrat,* November 28, 1976.
60. *St. Petersburg Times,* March 9, 1998.
61. *St. Petersburg Times,* June 28, 1970, March 18, 1979, March 9, 1998; Davis, *Contributions of Black Women to America,* 200-201; The Associated Press Political Service, AP Bids, @ (http://web.lexis-nexis...7c88c12517986161aa8479); *Who's Who Among African Americans,* 111th ed. (New York, 1998) @ (http//web.lexis-nexis... Of850bca0734c94822d2ec); *The Southern Patriot* 18 (June 1960), 2.
62. *St. Petersburg Times,* May 26, 1963; *New York Times,* April 3, 1960; *Miami Times,* October 5 and 26, 1963; *Miami Herald,* May 31, 1963.

10

No Looking Back

In this study, noted Florida historian Gary R. Mormino constructs an important story of how the Sunshine State offered a microcosm of events in the national civil rights struggle during the World War II era. By focusing on Florida's history of racial discrimination and on the state's racist coverage (e.g., in the state's newspapers) of black soldiers and sailors, the author illustrates an important—and persistent—gap between America's promise of equality for all and caste treatment for some. The ultimate value of this article is that it highlights at the state level the very issues that moved blacks in Florida, in the region, and in the nation to focus greater attention on their subordinate status, even as they sacrificed and died in America's military callings. Significantly, the practice of Jim Crow during the time of the Second World War served as a catalyst for renewed black protest in Florida, as it did nationally. A close reading of Mormino's study on racial incidents and the military in World War II-era Florida discloses how and why African-Americans undertook a renewed collective and individual resistance in an effort to finally and permanently put the racial protocols of the past behind them.

World War II itself fostered a reborn spirit of protest designed to bring race concepts into conformity with America's democratic creed, much as had been the experience of blacks in the military since their notable service in the American Revolution, War of 1812, Civil War, Indian Wars of the West, Spanish-American War, and World War I. At the outset of the next war in the late 1930s and early 1940s, many industries refused to drop their color line against the hiring of nonwhite males, while the Army, Army Air Corps, Navy and Marines continued to restrict nonwhites to "mess duty" or to "general services" units (a euphemism for segregated corps). Additionally, blacks faced the usual unemployment disparity, particularly in the burgeoning defense industries. A wide range of black leaders voiced concerns. The NAACP spoke directly to the domestic issues of World War II: "This is no fight merely to wear a uniform. This is a struggle for status, a struggle to take democracy off of parchment and give it life."

Against this backdrop, Florida native and labor leader A. Philip Randolph called on blacks to unite in a March on Washington Movement (MOWM), an all-black effort to create "faith and confidence of the Negro people in their own power for self-liberation." Reacting to Randolph's assertion that he could march "100,000 strong" on Washington, President Roosevelt promised him an executive order with "teeth in it." Roosevelt soon signed Executive Order 8802, which established a Committee on Fair Employment Practice in the Office of Production Management to ensure that defense industries hired on a non-discriminatory basis. The FPEC remained silent on racism in the armed forces, however. In retrospect, Randolph's MOWM presaged what would become the symbol of major social protest in the 1950s and 1960s, namely mass, nonviolent demonstrations of unity and power designed to push the federal government to new levels of awareness and commitment.

During the 1940s the NAACP also continued to seek reform through legal and judicial means. It underwrote numerous amicus briefs and initiated or backed a number of important court cases, including the precedent-setting *Mitchell v. U.S.* (1941), which stated that blacks holding first-class passenger tickets had to be provided accommodations equal to those provided whites, and *Smith v. Allwright* (1944), which declared all-white primary elections unconstitutional. These and similar actions propelled blacks into a broader freedom struggle that, as Mormino notes in his state-level study, resulted in new civil rights forces in the Sunshine State.

Mormino's case study examines a number of incidents and black reactions that took place on and off military bases around the state, many caused by military segregation policies and inequity in basic services and recreational facilities. Northern, black GI Joes, unaccustomed to rigid, Old South segregation often raised their voices to protest Florida's deep-seated brand of Jim Crow. Old South Florida simply was not accustomed to such "insolence" and would not brook it. The author includes valuable information on an NAACP investigation of conditions at McDill Airbase in Tampa. The report disclosed a system of endemic segregation, lack of black officers, and lack of adequate health care and services for African-American servicemen. The report also found that the large black civilian population in Tampa was actually a detriment to the servicemen because police relations with the community were poor and police corruption allowed crime to flourish. Mormino goes on to explain how these Jim Crow practices and problems even seeped into service athletic and USO events.

Mormino recounts a litany of other violence, unfair arrests, and racial indignities black GIs faced in Deep South Florida. The author further demonstrates how small incidents or misunderstandings at times escalated into riots. He concludes that when evaluated together, these incidents exposed deep flaws in military policies and civilian attitudes. White newspapers often attributed black protest to communist propaganda and northern meddling, a smear tactic that would reappear more nefariously in the 1950s an 1960s. When these measures did not satisfy reactionary whites, they turned to violence and lynching, such as those that occurred in Marianna in 1943 and Live Oak in 1944. Florida U.S. Senator Claude Pepper perhaps best summed up the state's reaction to the new black activism in World War II, "The South will allow nothing to impair white supremacy." But, the rising tide of resentment and protest fostered by the injustice of World War II in Florida and in the nation would soon add new dimensions and meanings to Pepper's words. "GI Joe Meets Jim Crow" aptly outlines how the war in Florida set the stage for these ensuing events, both locally and nationally.

This article may be best understood within the context of historical black struggle in times of war as presented throughout the pages of this book and by reading Willard B. Gatewood's "Negro Troops in Florida, 1898," in the 1970 *Florida Historical Quarterly*, Irvin D. S. Winsboro, "Give

Them Their Due: A Reassessment of African Americans and Union Military Service in Florida During the Civil War," in the 2007 *Journal of African American History,* and Thomas P. Honsa's "Doing the Job: The 1964 Desegregation of the Florida Army National Guard," in the 2008 *Florida Historical Quarterly.*

FURTHER READING

Carey McWilliams, "The Klan: Post-War Model," *The Nation* (December 1946);
Herbert Garfinkel, *When Negroes March: The March on Washington Movement in the Organizational Politics for FEPC* (1959);
Harvard Sitkoff, "Harry Truman and the Election of 1948: The Coming Age of Civil Rights in American Politics," *Journal of Southern History,* Vol. 37 (1971);
Harvard Sitkoff, "Racial Militancy and the Interracial Violence in the Second World War," *Journal of American History,* Vol. 58 (1971);
A. Russell Buchanan, *Black Americans in World War II* (1977);
Harvard Sitkoff, *A New Deal for Blacks: The Emergence of Civil Rights as a National Issue, The Depression Decade* (1978);
Peter J. Kellogg, "Civil Rights Consciousness in the 1940s," *The Historian,* Vol. 42 (1979);
Jerrell H. Shofner, "The Legacy of Racial Slavery: Free Enterprise and Forced Labor in Florida in the 1940s," *Journal of Southern History,* Vol. 47 (1981);
Lenwood G. Davis and George Hill, *Blacks in The American Armed Forces, 1776-1983: A Bibliography* (1985);
Jack E. Davis, "'Whitewash' in Florida: The Lynching of Jessie James Payne and Its Aftermath," *Florida Historical Quarterly,* Vol. 68 (1990);
Stetson Kennedy, *The Klan Unmasked* (1990);
Merle E. Reed, *Seedtime for the Modern Civil Rights Movement: The President's Committee on Fair Employment Practices, 1941-1946* (1991);
Joseph A. Cernik, "The 1940s: John 'Buck' O'Neil and Black Baseball in Florida," in James J. Horgan and Lewis N. Wynne, eds., *Florida Decades: A Sesquicentennial History, 1845-1995* (1995);
Gary R. Mormino, "World War II," in Michael Gannon, ed., *The New History of Florida* (1996), chapter 18;
Eric Tscheschlok, "'So Goes the Negro': Race and Labor in Miami, 1940-1963," *Florida Historical Quarterly,* Vol. 76 (1997);

Eliot Kleinberg, *War in Paradise: Stories of World War II in Florida* (1999);
Charlton W. Tebeau and William Marina, *A History of Florida* (1999), chapter 26;
Abel A. Bartley, *Keeping the Faith: Race Politics, and Social Development in Jacksonville, Florida*, 1940-1970 (2000);
Jon Evans, "The Origins of Tallahassee's Racial Disturbance Plan: Segregation, Racial Tension, and Violence During World War II," *Florida Historical Quarterly*, Vol. 79 (2001);
Gail Buckley, *American Patriots: The Story of Blacks in the Military from the Revolution to Desert Storm* (2003);
Tameka Bradley Hobbs, "'Hitler is Here': Lynching in Florida During the Era of World War II," Ph.D. diss., Florida State University (2004);
Dennis Halpin, "'Race Riot,' 'Midnight Melee,' and Other 'Crimes' Reconsidered: African American Soldiers' Protests in 1898 Tampa," *Gulf South Historical Review*, Vol. 20 (2005);
Margaret Vandiver, *Lethal Punishment: Lynchings and Legal Executions in the South* (2006);
Thomas P. Honsa, "Doing the Job: The 1964 Desegregation of the Florida Army National Guard," *Florida Historical Quarterly*, Vol. 87 (2008).

GI JOE MEETS JIM CROW:

RACIAL VIOLENCE AND REFORM IN WORLD WAR II FLORIDA

Gary R. Mormino

The Florida Historical Quarterly, Volume 73, issue 1 (1994), 23-42.

Where were you on December 7, 1941, and what did you experience on that memorable day? If you were Master Sergeant Warren Bryant, stationed at Tampa's MacDill Field, you were reminded of your place in American society. Bryant explained the coming of war: "When the Japanese bombed Pearl Harbor . . . all of the whites at MacDill Field were running around with loaded guns. We [blacks] had no guns and no idea of what was going on, so you can imagine what was running through our minds until we learned of the Japanese attack. Even with this knowledge it was of no comfort to be practically penned in our area with armed patty boys allover everywhere. We trusted them just about as much as a coiled rattlesnake."[1] "GI Joe Meets Jim Crow" examines the tensions and violence that erupted on and off military camps in Florida during World War II and their role in the development of the civil rights movement.

In the weeks following Pearl Harbor, African American leaders pledged a fight on two fronts— victory abroad against fascism and victory at home against racism. Articulating the urgency of fighting on two fronts was relatively easy; the reality of confronting segregated armed services and the Jim Crow South proved daunting.[2]

Although the United States fought World War II with images of democracy pressing the fight against tyranny, the U.S. military structure mirrored America's racially segregated society.[3] The *Bradenton Herald* ran a flyer in 1943 announcing, "Negroes 18 to 50 years old may enlist as mess attendants in the U.S. Navy."[4] The navy, however, operated under a racial caste system, and the U.S. Marines excluded African Americans entirely at the start of the war. As the war progressed, the military, pressed for manpower and pressured by group leaders, liberalized recruitment policies. In the summer of 1942 the marines, for the first time in 167 years, created a Marine Corps Negro Battalion. "Negroes having training as barbers, cooks, bakers, clerks, and truck drivers have been urged to enlist immediately," ran a marines advertisement.[5]

As Floridians marched off to basic training, the state's newspapers reported the news in black and white. "Two contingents of colored boys . . . headed for camp," reported the *DeFuniak Herald* in1942. Later it noted, "Here are the names of the young men (white) who will leave."[6] Other notices included: "17 White Men Off to Camp," "37 Negroes Sent to Camp Blanding," and "225 Negros Are Called to Blanding."[7]

Historically, military service has offered minority groups in American society the opportunity to affirm their loyalty to the host society. Thus, immigrants volunteered in numbers out of proportion to their size in order to validate their patriotism. African Americans, however, encountered roadblocks in their path to military respect. "From the beginning of World War II," argues Richard Dalfiume, "the army set out to implement its version of separate but equal."[8] Many black leaders remembered the bitter experiences of World War I when African Americans volunteered for the Great Crusade, only to return home to an America beset by race riots, a revived Ku Klux Klan, and nativist violence. Throughout the Second World War, Florida's American Legion refused First World War African American veterans a charter.[9]

The very presence of black troops in the South sparked controversy in some quarters. Throughout the war, selecting camps for the training of African American soldiers vexed the War Department.[10] In 1944 Florida Congressman Robert Sikes protested to Rear Admiral George D. Murray upon hearing reports that white and black sailors were billeted together at the Pensacola Naval Air Station. The admiral reassured Sikes that "in no cases is indiscriminate mixing of these groups permitted."[11]

While many soldiers who trained in Florida found the weather balmy, others found the racial climate chilling. Between 1941 and1946 racial conflict boiled over on and off Florida military bases. Participants included commissioned and noncommissioned officers, civilians and prisoners of war, military police and county sheriffs, Northerners and Southerners.

Tallahassee was the site of some of Florida's most serious racial disorders during World War II. Beneath the veneer of southern charm stood a city and region fiercely dedicated to preserving a segregated society. In 1940 Tallahassee had a population of 16,240, of which 40 percent were black. Tallahassee's large black neighborhood attracted African American servicemen from the Third Army Air Force stationed at Dale Mabry Field, located three miles west of the capital, and from the Amphibious Training Center at Camp Gordon Johnston sixty miles away in Carrabelle.[12]

Mobilization for war jarred the rhythms of city and campus. The 1942 homecoming game at Florida Agricultural and Mechanical College reflected the changes. In 1941 fans packed Florida Stadium, forcing many white spectators to stand on the sidelines. The state mandated new seating procedures, which segregated black soldiers to the sidelines while white fans received reserved seating. "Two white military policemen who had been stationed there to keep the soldiers in the restricted area were busily engaged in forcing these former Florida students [now soldiers] to leave the regular grandstand," reported the *Atlanta Daily World.* An African American soldier filched a nightstick from an MP, and twenty-five MPs invaded the stadium searching for the offender and putting a "damper on the game."[13]

Tallahassee's Frenchtown became the setting for a series of ugly military riots, which frequently escalated into racial disorders. A familiar scenario emerged: African American troops from rival military bases converged upon Frenchtown. Arguments degenerated into a fracas, almost always made worse by the arrival of white Tallahassee and military police.

In September 1942 Tallahassee police responded to a fight between black soldiers and civilians in Frenchtown. Police shot and killed Private Wilbur Harris, allegedly for resisting arrest. According to the Tallahassee *Daily Democrat,* "Civilian officers and M.P.'s then lined up the negro soldiers and civilians along the streets until an emergency squad from Dale Mabry Field, armed with rifles, arrived."[14] Two months later a black soldier at Dale Mabry Field violated racial decorum when he attempted to purchase a drink from a vending machine reserved for white civilian workers. Scores of black soldiers and whites scuffled, resulting in injuries to eight individuals.[15]

In the spring of 1944 authorities at Dale Mabry Field confronted "mutiny." According to testimony, a group of black soldiers refused to obey orders until granted a forum to air their grievances about racial practices. Five soldiers, all northern blacks, received dishonorable discharges and long prison sentences.[16]

Protests echoed in the black press. A person identified as "A Constant Reader" wrote to the *Pittsburgh Courier* pleading: "Please tell me how the President of the United States knowing that we are at war, allows the Negro soldier to be treated so intolerably? . . Does he condone the treatment of those soldiers in Alabama and those in Tallahassee, Florida?"[17]

Black troops chafed at conditions encountered in north Florida. On one occasion the NAACP received a letter entitled "Mistreatment of Soldiers in Dixie," signed "Members of the 1869th engr avn bn [engineering aviation battalion]." The letter listed a litany of problems faced by "several hundred negro soldiers here at Dale Mabry Field." Writers noted, "Above all we have Southern White Crackers as officers over us who abuse us, and treat us worse than we would treat the lowest of dogs." The complaints pointed out that German prisoners of war received more respect and better food than African American troops. Indeed, "we are treated more like prisoners of war than members of the armed forces."[18] Private E. Bryant claimed the commanding officer thinks, "The Negro's radical." He closed the letter, "I am always in there continuously fighting for the rights of the Negro in the service."[19]

African American soldiers also wrote hometown newspapers. "A Negro Soldier" appealed to the *Baltimore Afro American* to expose conditions at Camp Gordon Johnston. "We cannot go to the church services on the camp," he exclaimed, adding, "The service clubs are off limit for us." The author fumed over a recent episode. Black troops had organized a dance and invited female guests from Tallahassee. "There were about 30 lounging chairs for our guests to relax in but the white M.P. made them get out of them." During the evening the white military police "got a rope and started roping our girls off like sheep. . . . They were herded up like a flock of sheep." "Most of us hail from the North," confessed the soldier.[20]

Letters and protests went unanswered, and in August 1944 another disturbance flared up in Frenchtown. The *Atlanta Daily World* described the tumult: "Armed with revolvers, riot guns and tear gas bombs, a group of Tallahassee civilian policemen, taking part in a disturbance involving only military personnel, placed the lives of hundreds of race citizens in danger." A city official recommended to military authorities that black soldiers from Camp Gordon Johnston be banned from visiting Tallahassee on weekends.[21]

Normally, Sundays in Tallahassee passed quietly with ample portions of old-time religion, fried chicken, and rest. But on one Sunday in October 1944, Tallahassee reverberated with police sirens responding to two separate military riots. In the first imbroglio, black soldiers from Camp Gordon Johnston clashed with civilian and military police. Trouble could have been avoided, argued the *Atlanta Daily World,* "if the local police had allowed the colored MPs from Dale Mabry Field to arrest a soldier in this section. The police took things into their own hands, thereby creating excitement when they approached one of the men with drawn pistols. The soldiers then surrounded the police and would not allow them to take the soldiers." The paper reminded readers that while white MPs carried guns, their black counterparts generally employed nightsticks. Following the second incident involving soldiers and police, Brigadier General Holcombe, commanding officer at Camp Gordon Johnston, announced that "no more Negro soldiers would be conveyed to Tallahassee."[22]

Alarmed by the fractious behavior of African American troops, the intelligence officer at Dale Mabry Field filed a "Weekly Report Concerning the Racial Situation." Major Sakser observed in November1944, "There is of course still an occasional gripe from Negroes who are compelled to occupy rear seats in the city buses."[23]

From the beginning of the war, the military made efforts to boost the flagging morale of African American troops. In 1942 the Army Air Force arranged a visit by the Ninety-ninth Fighter Squadron, the first such outfit manned by blacks. Benjamin O. Davis, Jr., served as commanding officer of the decorated unit. His father, Benjamin O. Davis, was the first African American to hold the rank of general. General Davis visited troops around the world, urging harmony, and preached more understanding between townsfolk and soldiers at home. Panama City, for instance, sponsored a GI Joe Day for Negro Troops. Groups such as Lee Norman and his band came South in an "All-Colored USO Show." Dr. Mary McLeod Bethune, Joe Louis, and Sugar Ray Robinson also toured Florida military camps.[24]

The Negro Athletic Leagues and "all-colored" USO extravaganzas could not assure harmony. In April 1945 Tallahassee experienced its final and most serious military riot. Police battled at least 250 black soldiers from Dale Mabry Field and Camp Gordon

Johnston who descended upon Frenchtown. The troops— many of whom had just received combat orders— had announced their intent to "paint it [Frenchtown] red" and "tear it apart." The neighborhood suffered heavy damage as rioters ransacked stores and establishments. Tallahassee police responded with tear gas, and military police, armed with tommy guns, arrested scores of soldiers. Authorities declared martial law for several hours. According to the *Tampa Bulletin,* a black newspaper, the guilty soldiers disappeared the next morning. The Tallahassee city manager recommended that authorities keep a detachment of MPs in the city.[25]

Warnings had surfaced for some time about the potential explosiveness of conditions in north Florida. In March 1945 the NAACP's Roy Wilkins received a letter from A. Maceo Smith of the Texas NAACP. Smith had just interviewed former Dallas resident Corporal James Otis, who in early 1945 had served at Dale Mabry Field. Otis related "that there are more than 3,000 Negro soldier sat this Florida installation who are being discriminated against to the maximum degree." Moreover, "there is no Negro chaplain assigned to this contingent to whom these men may express their distaste for this treatment in confidence. Of the 3,000, 200 are wounded and sick soldiers needing hospital care."[26]

Letters to the NAACP record an outpouring of frustration and the growing militancy of African American soldiers. Three such 1944 letters pinpointed problems at Tallahassee and Camp Gordon Johnston. Louis Alexander, writing "somewhere in Dutch New Guinea . . . where he read about troubles in Tallahassee," declared, "Being one of the many soldiers that was forced to take training at Camp Gordon Johnston, Fla., I found many things and conditions that were a blow to soldier morale."[27]

In September 1944 William H. Hastie and Thurgood Marshall met to discuss Camp Gordon Johnston. Hastie, then dean at Howard University's law school but earlier a figure instrumental in promoting civil rights for African American soldiers, called for "an investigation of the physical conditions and treatment of Negro troops at the Camp." Several black soldiers had attempted to enlist Hastie's and the NAACP's assistance in exposing racial conditions at Carrabelle. Army officials had assigned blacks exclusively to clean the outhouses, and a group of seventy-five soldiers resisted the order, only to be sent to the stockade.[28] Private John Hammond, director of Negro Activities, contended, "Segregation has reappeared in all its fury."[29] A supporting letter, signed "One who would serve," urged the NAACP's Walter White to investigate Camp Gordon Johnston. "I believe I owe it to my race to report this. May I repeat, destroy this when you're finished."[30]

Disturbed by mounting evidence of racial unrest on and off military bases, the NAACP commissioned a special study of the situation in July 1945. The association selected Jesse O. Dedmon, Jr., to tour fifteen troubled sites, including Camp Gordon Johnston, Dale Mabry Field, and MacDill Air Field. By July 1945, Camp Gordon Johnston contained 7,000 troops, including 1,400 African American soldiers. One hundred white officers commanded the base; two black officers, a captain, and first lieutenant led the "colored troops." The base had no black chaplain. The inspector found the black quarters "excellent" in terms of cleanliness but poor in the quality of recreational opportunities. Army Memorandum No. 97, which prohibited segregation in recreational facilities, was neither posted nor followed. Blacks and whites frequented the same dispensary but at separate posted times. The hospital staffed no black nurses, dentists, or physicians, and hospital lavatory signs indicated "colored" or "negro." African American soldiers complained of no opportunities to pursue advanced technical training and of the disrespect shown by white civilian clerks at the post exchange.[31]

Contemporaries and historians depict Tampa as Florida's most racially troubled city, noteworthy for both the number and intensity of disturbances. Ironically, the coming of the military to Tampa promised optimism, a safeguard against the vicissitudes of economic depression and labor turbulence. On July 14, 1939, the military announced plans for MacDill Army Air Field to be constructed at the southern tip of the uninhabited inter bay peninsula. MacDill became headquarters for the Twelfth Air Force Combat Bomber Command. In mid 1941 the War Department activated Drew Army Air Field, headquarters for the Third Air Force, on the site of today's Tampa International Airport. MacDill and Drew fields helped prepare pilots and training crews for the B-17 and B-29 fleets.[32]

MacDill officials trumpeted the benefits of the base in a steady stream of public relations documents. Beginning in 1943 a lavishly illustrated magazine, *Thunderbird,* was published. African Americans appeared occasionally in it, shown serving food and changing tires, but little else. In fact by 1945 MacDill housed 3,000 black servicemen, comprising a quarter of the base's troop strength. In July1945 a single black chaplain constituted the only officer. In 1945 NAACP officials complained, "The post's policy is complete segregation of the races."[33]

Tampa might have seemed an ideal setting for black troops. In1940 African Americans represented 25 percent of Tampa's population, and a large black commercial district existed along the area known as "the Scrub." Nonetheless, race relations in Tampa foreshadowed trouble. The city boasted not a single African American lawyer in 1940.[34] As events unfolded a black attorney would have been useful.

World War II was not the first encounter between African American soldiers and Tampa. During Reconstruction and again in1898 the presence of black troops sent paroxysms of anger through the white community, contributing to violence and the formation of the Ku Klux Klan. "It is indeed very humiliating to the American citizens and especially to the people of Tampa," argued the *Tribune* in 1898, "to be compelled to submit to the insults and mendacity perpetrated by the colored troops that are now camped in this city."[35]

Relations between the African American community and Tampa police in the decades prior to the 1940s had been at best patronizing and negligent— at worst, racist and brutal. Moreover, corruption infected city and county law enforcement officials, who allowed organized gambling and prostitution to flourish. Recurrent crises involving soldiers and police reinforced Tampa's image as "Hell Hole of the Gulf Coast." In 1942, as a result of repeated episodes of violence and civil rights violations, the American Civil Liberties Union branded Tampa one of eleven centers of repression in the United States.[36]

African American soldiers vividly remembered their introduction to Tampa. One soldier reminisced that upon arriving in Tampa by train a "big red-necked sheriff" met the enlisted men. The deputy pontificated about southern manners and morals and about how social life was limited to one area of town— the black district along Central Avenue. Warren Bryant recalled, "When we got a chance to go to town we had to wait until all of the white soldiers who wished to go had been taken to their destination; then we were crowded like sardines into a couple of buses and driven directly to the colored section. . . . Frankly we [812th Aviation Engineers] were delighted when orders came for us to go. . . . Anything was better than this hell hole."[37]

On July 15, 1941, soldiers and police clashed anew. An argument in the city's black commercial district resulted in the arrest of a black soldier by white MPs. Police sped the arrested man away to the nearby military stockade. While military police milled around the scene of the arrest, a black sergeant verbally harassed an MP. Police began clubbing the sergeant and a Tampa patrolman shot him while he was prostrate. A near riot ensued as black soldiers charged the policemen, resulting in the shooting of a second serviceman.[38]

In June 1943 a racial standoff occurred at MacDill Air Field. The event, never acknowledged in local newspapers, was classified as "a mutiny" by the War Department. According to the investigation, the affair erupted over a trivial incident in the base post exchange for black servicemen. An argument between a black soldier and a "tired, irritable white saleswoman" attracted a crowd, and soon a fight began. Some black soldiers apparently obtained guns, fearful of the consequences of the fracas. Authorities discovered the guns stored in a black barracks and charged Private Frank V. Stovall and eighteen other African American soldiers with conspiracy to riot and mutiny. Julia Padron, Stovall's cousin, asked the NAACP to "make an investigation at once." She added, "Frank thinks they got him and 18 other boys because they are from the North." Alice Baird, Stovall's sister-in-law explained, "We are quite worried about him because he is from the North, and the stories that come in here at the office from the camps in the south are enough to frighten me." On October 16 Stovall and nine fellow soldiers faced a court martial at MacDill Field. All received sentences of ten years (later reduced to five years).[39]

Black soldiers also complained about venereal disease checks— "applied to blacks only"— as they traveled to and from Tampa. Venereal disease would seemingly be a societal problem, but it acquired a racial stigma during the war. The problem was serious. Tampa's Social Protection Division reported in 1945 that venereal disease rates among African Americans stationed locally reached a rate of 415 per 1,000, while the overall incidence was 158 per 1,000 soldiers. Tampa mayor Robert E. Lee Chancey attacked black servicemen rather than the source of the problem. "If we had no Negro soldiers here," he insisted in 1943, "our record for social protection for military personnel would be one of the finest in the United States."[40]

In February 1944 a minor incident between police and black soldiers escalated into a riot. According to newspaper accounts, Tampa police raced en route to a narcotics raid in "the Scrub "when a black serviceman cursed army intelligence captain T. L.Tedford, who was attempting to clear traffic. Captain Tedford ordered military police to arrest the offender. Black soldiers came to the aid of their fellow soldier, thereby preventing his arrest. Soon a crowd of more than 100 angry black residents surrounded the police and servicemen. City and military police reinforcements eventually dispersed the crowd and sped the suspect to the nearby military police substation. There, reported the *Tampa Daily Times,* "a huge mob, estimated at more than 4,000, assembled about the station and demanded that the man be released. Calls for help were broadcast and three armored riot cars . . . all city patrol cars. . . and sheriffs deputies rushed to the battle scene." Altogether more than 100 civilian and military police "armed with machine guns, revolvers and bayonets" confronted the angry crowd. The protestors hurled bottles and flower pots at police. The press described the event's denouement. "Faced by the menacing guns of Army men, the Negroes finally dispersed and police immediately closed every saloon, juke joint, restaurant, theater and store on the street [Central Avenue]. Twenty-four Negroes were taken to the City Jail for trial . . . on charges of creating a disturbance and inciting a riot." The *Tribune* headline pronounced, "Civil and Army Police Quell Rioting Negroes."[41]

A rare wartime news account from a Florida black newspaper adds a fresh dimension to the February 1944 riot. "Innocent Church Leaders Arrested," an indignant *Tampa Bulletin* declared. "Those of us who were beginning to believe we were approaching a day wherein a minority group would be protected instead of being subjected to terrorism, and that racial feelings were ebbing, in an effort to create a united people, were sharply awakened by the men who represent the law in this city." The paper concluded, "How can we expect to even hope for victory with such treatment meted out to innocent Negroes of Tampa Sunday night?" The arrest list, noted the paper, included a deacon and an usher caught outside Beulah Baptist Church.[42]

In February 1945 the *Atlanta Daily World* reported on continuing racial tensions at MacDill Field. "The German prisoners of war," noted the paper, "have started here a system of working hat in hand with the Bourbon South in the matter of giving the Negro soldiers another slap in the face." German POWs assigned as cooks at the MacDill base hospital refused to work if black military patients continued to dine in the same hall as whites, despite the fact that whites and blacks ate in separate sides of the mess hall. Hospital officials stated they were acting on orders from Washington and immediately began a system of feeding the African American personnel in a separate mess hall entirely. Morale, stated the reporter, plummeted "from humiliation to utter disgust."[43]

When evaluating the sheer number of violent racial incidents, which resulted in several deaths and scores of injuries, historians struggle to distinguish between what contemporaries branded as fracases, melees, riots, and mutinies. The difference between an angry crowd and a mob depends upon the perspective of time, distance, and politics. One historian of the South contends that during World War II racial disorders resulted in at least six civilian riots, twenty military riots or mutinies, and forty lynchings.[44] When evaluated individually, no single incident in Florida stands as a defining moment of the war years; when evaluated collectively, however, the violence and racism reveal deep flaws in military policy and civilian attitudes. Moreover, the many individual acts of wartime rebellion and frustration by African Americans had a cumulative effect on civilian and military leaders who in the summer of 1944 expressed growing alarm over the escalation of racial violence throughout the United States. The 1943 riots in Detroit, Los Angeles, Harlem, and Beaumont, combined with their own experiences, made authorities in Florida especially nervous.

In August 1944 the Army Service Forces, headquartered at Camp Blanding, prepared for the worst. In a series of secret documents, the agency anticipated renewed race riots and the imposition of martial law. The Army Service Forces targeted Tallahassee, Jacksonville, Miami, Orlando, Tampa, and St. Petersburg. Reports detail each city. "In the city of Orlando," the report noted, "there is an undercurrent of tension, activated by union organizers and the presence of Northern negro soldiers in the community. Increased earning power caused by war activities. . . result in idleness and disorderly conduct and a resentment on the part of the white population toward negroes['] refusal to perform necessary work." In Miami, it was reported, "There are many negro dives and joints and it is in these areas that negroes of the trouble-maker type reside and congregate." In Tampa, authorities prepared a prospective press release: "Racial disorders, now in progress in Tampa, Florida between members of the Caucasian and negro races, with attendant riots and bloodshed, have progressed beyond the control of civil authorities."[45]

In each targeted city the Army Service Forces identified the location of black-owned newspapers and radio stations. Future emergency orders mandated: "All liquor stores, bars, dance halls, moving picture theaters and public places, where people may congregate have been ordered closed. The streets have been ordered cleared. . . . The congregation of more than three persons at any place is prohibited."[46]

What had war wrought? In particular, what impact did the war have upon African Americans and race relations in Florida? World War II left a lasting military imprint on the state. Installations such as Camp Gordon Johnston, having served its usefulness, quickly returned to nature and developers. Dale Mabry Air Field surrendered its planes and personnel and became Tallahassee Community College.

Violence continued to pockmark MacDill Field, which now served the Cold War. A riot in October 1946 has been called by a leading military historian, "probably the largest riot the Air Force ever experienced."[47] Large numbers of African Americans complained that white troops received preferential discharges.[48] On the evening of October 27, 1946, a fight broke out at the Negro Noncommissioned Officers Club when young black soldiers attempted to enter a dance. White MPs fired into the crowd wounding a soldier. The black troops dispersed, reappearing at the white officers' quarters. Black soldiers chanted, "No more Jim Crow laws." Another crowd of 300 black soldiers marched upon the MacDill Avenue Gate, disarming an MP. The "mob" headed toward a well chosen target: the white-only, Gadsden housing project. Hurling stones and sticks, the black soldiers were repulsed by large numbers of civilian and military police. The chief of staff of the Strategic Air Command ordered an investigation of the "mutiny." The inquiry attributed the unrest to "communist" propaganda, which was brainwashing "the Negro soldiers to demand preference rather than equality." A black counterintelligence agent concluded that the problems stemmed from an appalling lack of opportunities and inferior segregated facilities. Nine GIs received long prison terms for the 1946 MacDill mutiny.[49]

In 1941 accounts of a lynching near Quincy, Florida, created a national uproar. The *New York Times* commented, "Nothing that can happen in this country is better grist for the Nazi propaganda mill than a lynching."[50] Lynchings at Marianna and Live Oak in 1943 and 1944 brought national opprobrium to the Sunshine State, but nothing matched the outrage following the October 1945 lynching of Jesse James Payne in rural Madison County.[51] The Payne tragedy was America's only lynching in 1945, though in many ways it was an anachronism. Lynching as a forum for white supremacy had lost favor since the 1930s. Yet Florida's legal system and political/economic establishment stood uncompromising in its defense of white supremacy in 1945.

Amidst the gloom of racial injustice, faith and optimism abounded. Ocala's the Reverend Edward T. Davis told a story about the war. The government had ordered all eligible men to report to their selective service stations. W. H. Long dutifully appeared at Howard Academy. An imperious white man looked at Long and remarked, "I see you don't love your country." The black man replied, "Oh, but I do love my country, but my country don't love me."[52]

This tale speaks forcefully of signs of optimism for African Americans in the 1940s. Edward Davis epitomized the role of Florida's African American minister. In 1940 the census listed only nine black lawyers but 979 black clergy in Florida.[53] The war accelerated the civil rights movement in Florida, an inner struggle for democracy, in which many of the leaders came from the church. The church took a leading role in accepting visiting black servicemen into the community and spearheaded bond drives, socials, and fund raisers during the war. The Reverend Edward Davis also mediated between Ocala's black and white communities. For example, he reassured whites about "Eleanor clubs," whose members, at a given signal, would allegedly take fatal action against their employers.[54]

Throughout the war, the Reverend Davis headed the Florida State Teachers' Association (FSTA), an organization for African American teachers. Historically, Florida's black teachers and students suffered grievous inequalities. During 1934-1935 Florida's white teachers earned an average salary of $881, whereas black teachers earned only $412. Expenditures reflected even greater racial disparities: in 1934-1935 Florida spent $41 on every white student but only $15 for each black student. In 1944-1945 Florida paid white teachers an average salary of $1,757, while black teachers made $1,174.[55]

Lawyers from the NAACP and FSTA joined with African Americans in the early 1940s in filing lawsuits against Dade, Duval, Escambia, Marion, Lake, Hillsborough, Pinellas, and Palm Beach counties. Thurgood Marshall argued many of these cases. By 1945 Florida's black teachers had triumphed in the courtroom; urban counties now paid teachers' salaries based on training and performance, not race. The price was steep. Almost all of the pioneer litigants—Harry T. Moore (Brevard), Noah W. Griffin (Pinellas), Mary Blocker (Duval), Charles H. Stebbins (Palm Beach), and the Reverend Edward T. Davis (Marion)— lost their teaching jobs because of their principled stands.[56]

Following the teachers' pay cases, the U.S. Supreme Court issued its historic ruling, *Smith v. Allwright,* on April 4, 1944. The decision sounded the death knell for the white primary, which disfranchised African Americans from voting in the all-important primary election. White Floridians reacted hysterically. Governor Millard Caldwell asserted, "This new menace to the independence of the state and party must be resisted with well-directed energy."[57] Senator Claude Pepper intoned, "Southerners will not allow matters peculiar to us to be determined by those who do not know and understand our problem. The South will allow nothing to impair white supremacy."[58] The Smith decision emboldened the wartime crusade for democracy. African Americans prepared to participate in Florida politics on a new level, although the path was paved with more hurdles.[59]

Connecting the bridges of wartime agitation by black soldiers, the battle for the ballot, and civil rights was Harry T. Moore. In1944 Moore and other black leaders formed a new organization, the Progressive Voters' League, designed to mobilize African Americans. Moore served as executive secretary. As head of the Florida NAACP, he also helped double the state's chapters between 1941and 1945. The war also activated the NAACP, as evidenced by the many letters from soldiers who enclosed membership dues. "I love my race and am willing to do anything I am called upon to do, "wrote Sergeant Edward S. Porter, upon receiving his NAACP membership. "It is particularly encouraging to note that the spirit of the NAACP has moved into such places as Perry, Gulf Hammock, Chapley [sic], Dixie County," Moore announced in January 1946. In October 1944 Florida NAACP branches numbered thirty-three with a total of 2,850 members. By September 1945 the organization had grown to forty-eight branches and 7,226 members.[60]

After the war Florida's African Americans pointed with justifiable pride to some tangible, hard-fought victories. For the first time in modern history blacks served on juries in Pinellas and Escambia counties and secured positions as policemen in Daytona, Deland, Miami, Sanford, and Tampa.[61]

World War II had introduced thousands of black soldiers to Florida and in turn dispatched Floridians to the world. Never before had Floridians been exposed to so many new people and ideas. A cross fertilization followed. Black servicemen helped disseminate new ideas and introduced a new militancy at the local and state levels. Black troops, especially individuals reared in the North, railed against Jim Crow. Ironically, the military's failure to provide recreational facilities for blacks forced African Americans to make contacts at churches, fraternal orders, and bars. James McGovern maintained that black servicemen in Pensacola "made a special contribution to the beginnings of significant social and political change among local blacks." The community, for example, organized the Pensacola Improvement Association in 1942, an institution involved in the fight for civil rights.[62]

African Americans emerged from the war with a tempered resolve never again to accept discrimination without protest. Sergeant Willie L. Lawrence, a student from Florida A&M College, wrote an essay, "Will We Still Be Denied," in which he concluded, "Democracy wake up and do not deny me any longer."[63] Spencer Griffin, Jr.'s, 1944 poem, "Our Fortitude," appears in the only extant issue of the *Pinellas Negro Weekly:* "We of the so-called Minority race/ Have often been told to stay in our place/ Our place in the world is wherever we choose/ Be an upright citizen we have nothing to lose."[64] Such individuals formed the new ranks of the civil rights movement nurtured by the war and the local, national, and international forces for change that emanated from the conflict. The Second World War served as a seedbed for the modern civil rights movement.

Gary R. Mormino is professor of history, University of South Florida, Tampa.

1. Quoted in interview of Master Sergeant Warren Bryant, *The Invisible Soldier: The Experience of the Black Soldier, World War II,* comp. and ed. Mary Penick Motley (Detroit, 1975), 250-51.
2. Lee Finkle, *Forum for Protest: The Black Press during World War II* (Rutherford, NJ, 1975).

3. Robert J. Jakeman, *The Divided Skies: Establishing Segregated Flight Training at Tuskegee, Alabama, 1934-1942* (Tuscaloosa, 1992); Finkle, *Forum For Protest,* 156-57; Bernard C. Nalty, *Strength for the Fight: A History of Black Americans in the Military* (New York, 1986), 143-204; Ulysses Grant Lee, *The Employment of Negro Troops* (Washington, DC, 1966); Richard M. Dalfiume, *Desegregation of the United States Armed Forces, 1939-1953* (Columbia, 1969).
4. *Bradenton Herald,* January 5, 1943.
5. Jakeman, *Divided Skies,* vi; *Tampa Morning Tribune,* June 16, 1942.
6. *DeFuniak Herald,* August 6, 30, 1942.
7. *Tallahassee Democrat,* August 21, 1944; *Tampa Morning Tribune,* April 27, 1941, June 4, 1943; *Hendry County News,* April 17, 1941; *Sanford Herald,* July 9, 1945; *Gadsden County News,* January 14, 1943.
8. Richard M. Dalfiume, *A Guide to the Microfilm Edition of the Papers of the NAACP* (Bethesda, MD, 1989), xii.
9. *Pittsburgh Courier,* September 30, 1944.
10. Lee, *Employment of Negro Troops,* 100-07.
11. *Pensacola Journal,* April 19, 1944. See also speech by Alabama Senator John Hollis Bankhead II, in *Atlanta Daily World,* August 4, 1942; *Fort Myers News Press,* August 3, 1942; *Bradenton Herald,* April 21, 1944.
12. Bureau of the Census, *Sixteenth Census of the United States, 1940. Population, Volume II* (Washington, 1943), 124; Tom Wagy, *Governor LeRoy Collins of Florida: Spokesman of the New South* (University, AL, 1985), 11-12, 48-49; Mary Louise Ellis and William Warren Rogers, *Favored Land, Tallahassee: A History of Tallahassee and Leon County* (Norfolk, VA, 1988), 151-52, 157.
13. *Atlanta Daily World,* November 3, 1942.
14. Tallahassee *Daily Democrat,* September 6, 13, 1942.
15. Ibid., November 6, 1942; *Tampa Tribune,* November 7, 1942.
16. *Pittsburgh Courier,* January 8, 1944; Tallahassee *Daily Democrat,* May 4, 1944; *Fort Lauderdale Daily News,* May 4, 1944.
17. *Pittsburgh Courier,* July 29, 1944.
18. Mistreatment of Negro Soldiers in Dixie, *Papers of the NAACP:* pt. 9, ser. B, Discrimination in the U.S. Armed Forces, 1918-1955, Armed Forces Legal Files, 1940-1950, roll 13, 613-14. All subsequent references to this source are taken from pt. 9, ser. B of the collection unless stated otherwise.
19. E. Bryant to NAACP, October 14, 1944, *Papers of the NAACP:* roll 11, 582-83.
20. Philip McGuire, *Taps For a Jim Crow Army: Letters from Black Soldiers in World War II* (Santa Barbara, CA, 1983), 5, 19-20.
21. Tallahassee *Daily Democrat,* August 10, 1944; *Atlanta Daily World,* August 18, 1944. For additional commentary on problems encountered at Camp Gordon Johnston see Lee, *Employment of Negro Troops,* 244, 266.
22. *Atlanta Daily World,* October 8, 1944; *Pittsburgh Courier,* October 14, 1944; Tallahassee *Daily Democrat,* October 2, 1944.

23. Frank J. Sakser, Historical Report of Dale Mabry Field, Tallahassee, Florida, November 1944, quoted in Erica R. Clark, "Tallahassee and Dale Mabry Army Air Base" (unpublished manuscript, Florida Collection, State Library of Florida, Tallahassee), 12.
24. *Tampa Tribune,* March 21, October 16, 1942; Ellis and Rogers, *Favored Land,* 150; *Panama City News Herald,* September 1, 5, December 26, 1944; Orlando Air Field *The AAFSATONION,* April 10, 1943; Camp Blanding *Bayonet,* January 14, 1944; *Atlanta Daily World,* August 15, 1945.
25. Tallahassee *Daily Democrat,* April 2, 4, 1945; *Gadsden County News,* April 5, 1945; *Tampa Bulletin,* April 21, 1945. The Franklin Delano Roosevelt Library, Hyde Park, New York, houses the only extant copy of the April 21, 1945, *Tampa Bulletin*
26. A. Maceo Smith to Roy Wilkins, March 12, 1945, *Papers of the NAACP,* roll 12, 52.
27. Louis Alexander to NAACP, September 7, 1944, *Papers o f the NAACP,* roll 12, 679-81.
28. William H. Hastie to Thurgood Marshall, September 15, 1944, *Papers of the NAACP,* roll 12, 678.
29. John Hammond to Walter White, September 11, 1944, *Papers of the NAACP,* roll 12, 676.
30. "One who would Serve" to White, September 18, 1944, *Papers of the NAACP,* roll 12, 682-86.
31. Data for Camp Investigation, MacDill Field, July 9, 1945, *Papers of the NAACP,* roll 9, 733, 742-45.
32. *Tampa Morning Tribune,* July 14, 1939, May 5, 1947; Karl Grismer, *Tampa* (St. Petersburg, 1950), 279-81.
33. *Thunderbird: MacDill Field Quarterly* 1-2 (1943-1944); Data for Camp Investigation, MacDill Field, July 12, 1945, *Papers of the NAACP,* roll 9,733, 750-93.
34. Bureau of the Census, *Sixteenth Census of the United States, 1940. Population, Volume III* (Washington, 1943), 666. While Tampa supported no African American lawyers, the city did boast fifty-one black clergymen and forty-three black teachers in 1940. The Tampa City Federation of Negro Women's Clubs erected a recreation center for servicemen. See *Tampa Daily Times,* June 26, 1943; *Tampa Morning Tribune,* June 26, 1943.
35. Maria Louisa Daegenhardt Archer Reminiscences, Historical Museum of Southern Florida, Miami, transcription by Patsy West; James McKay, Jr., "History of Tampa of the Olden Days," *Tampa Times,* December 18, 1923; *Tampa Morning Tribune,* May 12, 1898; Willard Gatewood, Jr., "Negro Troops in Florida, 1898," *Florida Historical Quarterly* 49 (July 1970), 1-15.
36. Alan M. Osur, *Blacks in the Army Air Forces during World War II: The Problem of Race Relations* (Washington, 1977; reprint ed., Washington, 1980), 90.
37. Robert P. Ingalls, *Urban Vigilantes in the New South: Tampa, 1882-1934* (Knoxville, 1988); Gary R. Mormino and George E. Pozzetta, *The Immigrant World of Ybor City: Italians and Their Latin Neighbors in Tampa, 1885-1985* (Urbana, 1987), 280-86; Virginius Dabney, *Below the Potomac: A Book About the New South* (New York, 1939; reprint ed., Port Washington, NY, 1942), 128; *Tampa Daily Times,* January 15, 1944; Motley, *Invisible Soldier,* 250-52. Gordon Chambers also served with the 812th Aviation Engineers and recalls today the bitter encounters with civilian and military police. Interviews with Gordon Chambers, April 5, 12, 1994, notes in author's possession.

38. *Tampa Daily Times,* July 16, 1941; *Tampa Morning Tribune,* July 17, 1941; Lee, *Employment of Negro Troops,* 350-51.
39. Stovall Court Martial, *Papers of the NAACP,* roll 5, 725-779; Ibid., pt. 9, ser. C, Discrimination in the U.S. Armed Forces, 1918-1955, The Veterans Affairs Committee, 1940-1950, roll 4, 34456; Osur, *Blacks in the Army Air Forces,* 86, 103, 194.
40. Osur, *Blacks in the Army Air Forces,* 103; *Tampa Morning Tribune,* July 14, August 24, 1945; *Tampa Daily Times,* July 15, September 1, 1943; Dawn Truax, "Victory Girls and Social Protection in World War II Tampa," in *Florida at War,* ed. Lewis N. Wynne (St. Leo, 1993), 29-49.
41. *Tampa Morning Tribune,* February 21, 22, 1944; *Tampa Daily Times,* February 21, 22, 1944; Lee, *Employment of Negro Troops,* 375.
42. *Tampa Bulletin* clipping in *Papers of the NAACP,* roll 12, 181. Sadly, only fragments of the black press have survived. During the war an extensive black press existed in Florida: the *Miami Whip, Pensacola Courier, Jacksonville Sentinel, Tampa Bulletin,* and *Pinellas Negro Weekly.* Only three extant single issues have been found.
43. *Atlanta Daily World,* February 9, 1945. The juxtaposition of German POWs and the Jim Crow South is well documented. For another incident in Florida see the case of Herbert F. Keresky, *Miami Herald,* May 7, 1985.
44. Albert James Burran, "Racial Violence in the South During World War Two" (Ph.D. diss., University of Tennessee, 1977), 2.
45. Racial Disturbance Plan. District No. 5, Fourth Service Command, State Defense Council, box 57, ser. 419, RG 191, Florida State Archives, Tallahassee.
46. Ibid. Authorities declassified the files on January 22,1993.
47. Alan L. Gropman, *The Air Force Integrates, 1945-1964* (Washington, 1978), 32.
48. *Chicago Defender,* April 27, 1946.
49. Gropman, *Air Force Integrates,* 64-70, 277-78; *Tampa Daily Times,* October 28-29, 1946; *Tampa Morning Tribune,* October 29, 1946; *St. Petersburg Times,* October 29, 1946; *Pittsburgh Courier,* January 11, February 8, 1947; Nalty, *Strength for the Fight,* 229-31, 245.
50. *New York Times* quoted in "Wartime Lynchings," *The Crisis* 48 (June 1941), 183.
51. Burran, "Racial Violence in the South During World War Two," 201; Jack E. Davis, "'Whitewash' in Florida: The Lynching of Jesse James Payne and its Aftermath," *Florida Historical Quarterly* 68 (January 1990), 277-98; *Tampa Daily Times,* June 17, 1943; *Pensacola Journal,* June 17, 18, 1943; "Wartime Lynchings"; Tallahassee *Daily Democrat,* August 25, 1944, *Atlanta Daily World,* October 13, 1945.
52. Edward D. Davis, *A Half Century of Struggle for Freedom in Florida* (Orlando, 1981), 163.
53. Bureau of the Census, *Sixteenth Census of the United States, 1940. Population, Volume III,* 648.
54. Davis, *Half Century of Struggle for Freedom in Florida,* i, ii, 36, 133, 162; *Ocala Star-Banner,* September 19, 1943; *Pinellas Negro Weekly,* October 8, 1944.
55. Davis, *Half Century of Struggle for Freedom in Florida,* i, ii; Gilbert L. Porter and Leedell W. Neyland, *History of the Florida State Teachers Association* (Washington, 1977); J. Irving Scott, *The Education of Black People in Florida* (Philadelphia, 1974), 2-

3, 64-80; *Papers of the NAACP,* pt. 3, ser. A, The Campaign for Educational Equality, 1913-1950, 24 rolls, see especially rolls 6 and 22; "Teachers Win Raise," *The Crisis* 50 (November 1942), 360; "Teacher's Salaries," *The Crisis* 49 (March 1942), 100; *Atlanta Daily World,* July 11, 26, 1942; February 3, April 9, May 18, 1943; *Biennial Report of the Superintendent of Public Instruction of the State of Florida, 1944-46* (Tallahassee, 1946), 118; *Biennial Report of the Superintendent of Public Instruction, 1936* (Tallahassee, 1936), 205-06.

56. *Atlanta Daily World,* May 18, 1943; Scott, *Education of Black People in Florida,* 64-80.

57. *Tampa Morning Tribune,* April 4, 1944; *Pensacola Journal,* April 4, 7, 8, 1944; *Bradenton Herald,* April 4, 1944.

58. Jacksonville *Florida Times-Union,* April 5, 1944, *Miami Herald,* April 5, 1944; *Tampa Morning Tribune,* April 5, 1944; "Time Bomb," Time, April 17, 1944, 20.

59. *Papers of the NAACP, pt.* 4, The Voting Rights Campaign, 1916-1950, 13 rolls, see especially rolls 6 and 7 for the torturous fight in which African Americans in Florida engaged to secure the franchise; Charles D. Farris, "Effects of Negro Voting Upon the Politics of the Southern City" (Ph.D. diss., University of Chicago, 1953).

60. Caroline Emmons Poore, "Striking the First Blow: Harry T. Moore and the Fight for Black Equality in Florida" (master's thesis, Florida State University, 1992); Harry T. Moore, "Development and Activities of NAACP in Florida During 1945," Tampa *Florida Sentinel,* January 12, 1946; Edward S. Porter to NAACP, September 29, 1942, *Papers of the NAACP,* roll 13, 670-72.

61. James R. McGovern, *The Emergence of a City in the Modern South: Pensacola, 1900-*1949 (DeLeon Springs, FL, 1976), 167; *Pensacola Journal,* May 15, 1943; *Tampa Daily Times,* December 2, 1941; *St. Petersburg Times,* December 2, 1941, July 21, 1947; *Tampa Morning Tribune,* February 10, 1944; *Pittsburgh Courier;* November 27, 1943, December 9, 1944, May 17, 1945; Council of Social Agencies, *Jacksonville* Looks at its Negro Community: A Survey of Conditions Affecting the Negro *Population in Jacksonville and Duval County, Florida* (Jacksonville, 1946), 84; *Atlanta Daily World,* August 27, 1942.

62. McGovern, *Emergence of a City in the Modern South,* 167. See also *St. Petersburg Times,* September 26, 1943; *Ocala Star-Banner;* September 19, 1943; *Tampa Daily Times,* June 26, 1943; *Cocoa Tribune,* January 21, 1943; *Tampa Morning Tribune,* April 15, 1944.

63. Willie L. Lawrence to White, October 3, 1943, *Papers of the NAACP,* roll 12, 806-07.

64. *Pinellas Negro Weekly,* October 8, 1944. Griffin was incinerator foreman at Mac-Dill Air Field.

African American soldiers during a drill at MacDill Field. Photograph reproduced from *Thunderbird: MacDill Field Quarterly* 1 (April 1943)

11

BEARER OF THE TORCH

As the prior articles in this book demonstrate, the historical freedom struggle in Florida has followed a long and twisting path that is characterized more by consistency of resistance and protest than acquiescence and submission to oppression. Although no single book can review and analyze the full-range of historical permutations comprising this experience, *Florida's Freedom Struggle* is designed to highlight many of the lesser-known and unsung aspects of this historical continuum. James C. Clark's article on the significance of Harry T. Moore and the central role of violence in Florida's subjugation of African-Americans is yet another illustration of reactionary whites' attempts to suppress a black freedom drive. Moreover, when contextualized within the message of the previous article on the burgeoning spirit of protest in the World War II era, Clark's study of the rise and demise of perhaps the nation's first modern civil rights martyr, Harry T. Moore, provides compelling evidence that the modern crusade did not start with the fallout of the *Brown* decision in 1954. Instead, it has deeper roots, most notably in those planted by the African-American GI Joes and the NAACP's legal actions during the war, which, in turn, sprouted numerous individual and collective actions of black protest.

Harry T. Moore grew up near the black Bible-belt town of Live Oak, where he excelled in school. He graduated from Florida Memorial College and later Bethune-Cookman College after which he pursued a career in teaching at communities near Melbourne on the east coast of the state. He eventually settled in Mims with his wife and fellow educator, Harriette, where the two of them became outspoken critics of such racial injustice as lynching, police brutality, denial of voting rights, and disparity in teacher's pay. Clark chronicles Moore's work and achievements, his and Harriette's murders at the hands of white supremacists, and the unsolved FBI investigation that followed. The author's purpose is not to recount the life of Harry Moore but rather to demonstrate that he was every bit as assertive in fighting for equal rights in the post-World War II years as those who followed in the wake of his Klan-orchestrated death in 1951.

Moore and his wife held teaching and administrative positions within the segregated Brevard County school system. Moore, as head of the local NAACP chapter, enlisted the help of NAACP lawyers to work on a suit filed for equal pay in 1937 by teacher John Gilbert, who subsequently lost his job for instituting legal action against racial discrimination. Although Gilbert's suit—possibly the first filed in Florida for equal pay—failed, the author suggests that it did, however, encourage African-American educators to litigate later with successful outcomes, though he doesn't indicate how involved Moore was in them.

Clark finds that Moore thereafter pursued a personal struggle to end racial injustice with "the tenacity of a bull dog." Indeed, from that point forward Moore worked tirelessly to mobilize the efforts and consciousness of the black community for a new and profound attack on Jim Crow racism. To this end, he argued, African-Americans must undertake political action in alliance with individual and local challenges to Florida's caste system. Although at the time somewhat disorganized, Moore soon came to believe that the state NAACP held the key to blacks' mobilizing for statewide attacks on Jim Crow and loss of voting rights. At the outset of World War II, Moore organized the first NAACP state conference, and in 1945 formed the Progressive Voters League (PVL) to encourage black voter registration.

Moore also helped mobilize returning World War II veterans to speak out against Florida's many ruses used to prolong its "lily-white primary" that effectively prevented blacks from participating in the political life of the state. Moore proved successful in this effort. From 1947 to

1950, the number of blacks registered in Florida more than doubled. Moore's own energy and drive and the dedication of Harriette to the cause certainly contributed to this post-war success, but readers should not overlook, as well, the role World War II black veterans played in this event. In retribution for seeking voter gains, the author finds that Harry and Harriette Moore lost their teaching jobs. Not deterred, Harry Moore continued his post-war civil rights crusade and assumed the newly created position of State Executive Director of the Florida NAACP, a position that often failed to pay Moore.

During this period, Moore became perhaps the most outspoken person in the state against what he saw as white Florida's penchant for violence toward African-Americans. In particular, Moore condemned police brutality against blacks in their own communities and the heinous practice of "legal" lynchings by white police officers. It was a crusade against such a "legal" lynching by Central Florida's notoriously racist Sheriff Willis McCall that launched Moore into his most aggressive and tireless campaign—an action that led to his becoming, as author Ben Green determined, "the most hated black man in the State of Florida."

His attacks on "good ol' boy" McCall arose in 1951 from the sheriff's killing of a manacled black man accused of raping a white woman and the shooting of a second black prisoner in custody in the so-called Groveland Case. It was certainly because of Moore that the "Sammy Shepherd shooting" became not only state but national news. Eventually, the national NAACP chief counsel, and future U.S. Supreme Court Justice, Thurgood Marshall took charge of the case in an effort to expose McCall and prevent the execution of the remaining black defendant, Walter Irvin. Moore would not live long enough to witness Marshall's success in preventing Irvin's execution. He and Harriet died as a result of injuries sustained on Christmas night in 1951. A bomb exploded under the bedroom of their family home in Mims. This brutal event in Florida's history sent shock waves around the nation.

The FBI assisted the state in investigating the murders, even though locals raised questions about the FBI's jurisdiction in the case. Through informants, the FBI focused on a Klan group from Orange County with ties to Sheriff Willis McCall. Two now dead suspects were believed to have planted the bomb, so the FBI focused on bringing perjury charges (within FBI jurisdiction) against those remaining Klansmen who had lied under oath. Although no suspects were ever convicted of Moore's murder, Clark concludes that FBI infiltration of the Klan brought about a sharp decline in racial violence in the area. Nevertheless, the record demonstrates that the fatal bombing of the Moores did not deter black protest in the Sunshine State, but rather energized it much as with the military experiences in World War II and the protests that followed it.

POSTSCRIPT:

In 1999, Ben Green published *Before His Time: The Untold Story of Harry T. Moore, America's First Civil Rights Martyr*, an award-winning book based heavily on research in the FBI's files on the Moores' killing. The book, and a following Public Broadcasting Service show on Moore, rekindled public interest in the unsolved case. This flurry of new interest in the dusty case moved Florida Attorney General Charlie Christ to re-open it. He released his findings in 2006, "The investigation, led by the Attorney General's Office of Civil Rights in conjunction with the Florida Department of Law Enforcement (FDLE), points to extensive circumstantial evidence that the Moores were victims of a conspiracy by [at least four] exceedingly violent members of a Central Florida Klavern of the Ku Klux Klan."

FURTHER READING

"Fighting the Klan," *Southern Patriot*, Vol. 4 (1946);

George Breitman, *Jim Crow Murder of Mr. And Mrs. Harry T. Moore* (1952);

"Bigotry and Bombs in Florida" and "Florida: Klan v. Conscience," *Southern Patriot*, Vol. 10 (1952);

"The Bomb Heard around the World," *Ebony* (April 1952);

Joseph North, *Behind the Florida Bombings* (1952);

Florida Legislative Investigative Committee, *Communism and the NAACP* (1958);

William C. Berman, *The Politics of Civil Rights in the Truman Administration* (1970);

Steven F. Lawson, David R. Colburn, and Darryl Paulson, "Groveland: Florida's Little Scotsboro," *Florida Historical Quarterly*, Vol. 65 (1986);

Caroline Emmons Poore, "Striking the First Blow: Harry T. Moore and the Fight for Black Equality in Florida," M.A. thesis, Florida State University (1992);

Tywanna Whorley, "Harry Tyson Moore: A Soldier for Freedom," *Journal of Negro History*, Vol. 79 (1994);

Caroline Emmons, "'Somebody Has Got to Do That Work': Harry T. Moore and the Struggle for African-American Voting in Florida," *Journal of Negro History*, Vol. 82 (1997);

Caroline S. Emmons, "Flame of Resistance: The NAACP in Florida, 1910-1960," Ph.D. diss., Florida State University (1998);

Robert W. Saunders, Jr., *Bridging the Gap: Continuing the Legacy of Harry T. Moore* (2000);

Jake C. Miller, "Harry T. Moore's Campaign for Racial Equality," *Journal of Black Studies,* Vol. 31 (2000);

Michael Newton, *The Invisible Empire: The Ku Klux Klan in Florida* (2001);

Michael R. Gardner, *Harry Truman and Civil Rights: Moral Courage and Political Risks* (2002);

Caroline Emmons, "'Not A Single Battle But Rather A Real War': The Fight To Equalize Teachers' Salaries in Florida In The 1930 and 1940s," *Florida Historical Quarterly*, Vol. 81 (2003);

Glenn Feldman, ed., *Before Brown: Civil Rights and White Backlash in the Modern South* (2004);

Tameka Bradley Hobbs, "'Hitler is Here': Lynching in Florida During the Era of World War II," Ph.D. diss., Florida State University (2004);

Ben Green, *Before His Time: The Untold Story of Harry T. Moore, America's First Civil Rights Martyr* (2005).

Civil Rights Leader Harry T. Moore

And The Ku Klux Klan In Florida

James C. Clark

The Florida Historical Quarterly, Volume 73, issue 2 (1994), 166-183.

Harry T. Moore, shown here in 1945, founded the Brevard County branch of the NAACP and later served as Florida Coordinator for that organization. He co-founded the Progressive Voters League, traveling throughout the state registering African American voters. State Library and Archive of Florida.

On Christmas night 1951 Harry Tyson Moore became the first civil rights leader assassinated in the United States when a bomb placed beneath the bedroom of his small frame home in Mims, Florida, exploded. It killed Moore and his wife Harriette. For many years Moore had been an ambitious fighter for civil rights in Florida. He led the first effort in Florida to achieve equal pay for black teachers, organized the state's first black voter registration drives, established the first state conference of the National Association for the Advancement of Colored People (NAACP), and spoke up when law enforcement officials murdered or assaulted blacks in Florida. He was a quiet man whose calls for blacks to unite to secure their rights began in the 1930s.[1] Even in death, at the age of forty-six, he would have a profound impact on civil rights. His murder touched off a massive investigation by the Federal Bureau of Investigation that led to indictments and spotlighted the influence and activities of the Ku Klux Klan in Florida.

Some studies date the origins of the civil rights movement to1954 when the United States Supreme Court handed down *Brown v. Board of Education* overturning the doctrine of separate but equal, or to 1955 when the Montgomery, Alabama, bus boycott began. More recent studies, however, have identified civil rights activity beginning in the 1920s and the 1930s and still others trace its origins to World War II. Steven F. Lawson wrote that "scholars are beginning to reexamine the ideological roots of the freedom struggle, exploring the legal, theological, and political legacies left by leaders and organizations of the 1930s and 1940s."[2]

Moore's involvement in civil rights paralleled the early growth of the movement. A neighbor, Crandall Warren, gave Moore information about the NAACP in 1934, and, from his home in Mims, Moore organized the Brevard County Branch of the NAACP and was selected its first president.[3] Almost immediately the Brevard chapter drew attention. The NAACP magazine *The Crisis* noted that the chapter "aided its neighboring branches in such cases as need whole-hearted cooperation. In Volusia Co., a colored boy said to have killed a white woman was taken from his county cell to the death cell at Raiford, Florida, and, with aid from the local branches, ours included, the sentence was commuted, for further investigation."[4]

Although Moore had a reputation as a quiet and shy man who seldom laughed, it is said that he possessed "the tenacity of a bulldog."[5] One of Moore's first efforts was to challenge the inequity in pay between white and black teachers. Moore was employed as a teacher and principal at the black elementary school in Mims, and he could see how unfair the system was to black students and teachers. Moore was also active in the Florida State Teacher's Association (FSTA)—the black counterpart to the white Florida

Education Association—and was elected president of District Four. The fact that white teachers in some counties were paid more than twice that of blacks increasingly troubled Moore. "Is it fair for county school officials to pay Negro teachers several hundred dollars less than they pay white teachers with the same training and experience?"[6] Although the state appropriated $800 per year for each teacher, with the county expected to add more, Brevard County did not even pay black teachers the $800. Moore wrote that teachers and principals received less than $100 per month for an eight-month term. It was about half of what white teachers received[7].

Like other southern states, Florida's race relations operated under the doctrine of separate but equal. In theory black students were supposed to receive an equal education, but in practice their buildings, books, and buses were greatly inferior to those of white students. In many rural areas the school calendar was shorter so that blacks could spend time working in the fields during the planting and harvesting seasons. In March 1938 John Gilbert, Moore's fellow principal in Brevard County, brought the first suit in Florida to obtain equal pay for black teachers. Although the suit was filed as *Gilbert v. Board of Public Instruction of Brevard County, Florida,* Moore was equally involved, raising

On Christmas night, 1951, a bomb exploded under the home of Harry T. Moore, killing him. His wife Harriette died nine days later from injuries sustained in the blast. The murders remain unsolved. State Library and Archive of Florida.

money and securing legal advice with the help of the NAACP.[8]

The suit brought Moore into contact with Thurgood Marshall, then a young NAACP attorney. Marshall visited Brevard County at least once to meet with Gilbert and Moore in 1937. But there were problems with the case. S. D. McGill, the Florida attorney hired to help represent Gilbert, wrote Marshall: "I have been in conference several times with a committee of teachers in regards to the case and while they appear to be real anxious to get some court action going, they are unwilling to have their names connected with it in such a way that it will attract the attention of their several school boards. Most of them are afraid of losing their positions in the school system."[9] Their concerns were justified; the Brevard County school board fired Gilbert for bringing the lawsuit.[10] The Florida Supreme Court refused to hear Gilbert's case, holding that he had no standing since he was no longer employed by the school system. Gilbert's and Moore's efforts, however, encouraged other black teachers to sue for equal pay. Vernon McDaniel, a black teacher in Escambia County, filed one such suit in 1941. A federal judge ruled in favor of McDaniel, but before he issued his decree, the school board in Escambia County agreed to equalize salaries in exchange for McDaniel withdrawing his suit.[11] By 1950 black teachers were earning 86 percent of the salaries of white teachers in Florida.[12]

Moore also focused his attention on two other major issues: violence against blacks and voting rights. He wrote that blacks "complain bitterly about the injustices that we suffer in this country. We bemoan the inequalities in educational opportunity, the segregation, police brutality, lynching, and other evils that are heaped upon Negro citizens; but so few of us are willing to take positive action for the alleviation of these conditions. Mere talk will not suffice. If we are to receive the proper respect from those who govern us, we must exercise some voice in their election."[13]

Moore realized that the Brevard County chapter of the NAACP, even with its more than 400 members, could not provide an adequate base to accomplish his goals. He believed the NAACP would be more effective in Florida if it were organized into a single, state-wide unit. The NAACP was loosely organized, consisting of branches operating under the national office in New York. In the late 1930s Moore recommended that the Florida chapters organize into a state conference, but it was not until 1941 that he was allowed to form the first NAACP state conference in the country. Moore was elected the first president.[14]

Three years later, in 1944 the United States Supreme Court ruled in *Smith v. Allwright* that blacks could not be prohibited from participating in Democratic Party primary elections. Southern blacks had been allowed to vote in general elections, but, in an era when the Republican Party was almost nonexistent in the South, that right was nearly worthless. All of the major decisions were made in the Democratic primary— a whites-only election process. During the 1948 campaign, which featured significant elections for governor and president, Moore wrote to NAACP members: "Do not be misled. The Democratic primary is THE ELECTION in Florida."[15] Moore pushed for increased black voter registration, and in 1945 he formed the Progressive Voters League (PVL) in Florida. PVL chapters had been organized in a number of southern states to encourage black voter registration. While the NAACP actively registered voters, it attempted to be nonpartisan. The national organization sought influence through lobbying both parties for civil rights legislation in Washington and through legal action to overturn discriminatory laws. Moore took a more activist view, however, and wanted the PVL not only to register voters, but also to endorse candidates and to take stands on major political issues, primarily related to civil rights.

Moore's campaign coincided with the end of World War II as thousands of black soldiers returned to the South after experiencing greater freedom in the North and overseas. Sociologist E. Franklin Frazier wrote that during and especially after the war, "The Negro was no longer willing to accept discrimination in employment and in housing without protest."[16] Moore mobilized this anger in his crusade for racial equality.

On November 15, 1945, Moore issued a call for action in Florida: "Who are more directly responsible for the inequalities in educational opportunities, the lynchings, the police brutality, and other injustices suffered by Negroes, our state and county officials or the Administration in Washington? All of these evils can be traced directly to the prejudiced attitude of local officials. . . . The fact is that practically every city, county, and state official in Florida is selected in the Democratic Primaries. In order to help select these officials, Negroes must vote in the Democratic Primaries."[17]

Under the slogan "A Voteless Citizen is a Voiceless Citizen," Moore launched one of the most ambitious registration campaigns in the South.[18] In 1944 approximately 20,000 blacks were registered in Florida, about 5.5 percent of those eligible. Two years after the Supreme Court ruling, the number of blacks registered to vote had more than doubled to 48,157. In 1950 there were 116,145 Florida blacks registered to vote, or 31.7 percent of those eligible.[19] The percentage was more than 50 percent higher than other southern states.[20] Not only were the state NAACP and the PVL successful in leading the campaign to register blacks, they were able to register impressive numbers of voters in rural areas where intimidation by whites was greatest. And by 1950 more than 50 percent of the blacks in Moore's largely rural home county had registered.[21]

In a 1946 letter to PVL members, Moore wrote that it was time for black voters "to make their power felt."[22] To Democratic candidate she wrote, "We seek merely the fundamental rights of American citizenship, equality of opportunities, equal protection of the law, justice in the courts, and free participation in the affairs of our government." He asked Florida congressmen for their views on issues such as antilynching legislation.[23] North Florida Congressman Joe Hendricks wrote, "I deeply abhor lynching and will never take part in one regardless of the circumstances" but added that he would not support antilynching legislation.[24] Although the poll tax was a major issue for blacks in other southern states, it had been repealed in Florida in 1937.

The PVL held rallies to support the 1950 reelection campaign of U.S. Senator Claude Pepper. Although Pepper lost, league endorsements were helpful in electing some local white candidates. In most elections the PVL merely endorsed the lesser of two evils, but increasingly politicians agreed to meet with PVL members to discuss their agenda. In Brevard County Moore's efforts led to the appointment of the first black deputy sheriff in 1950 who could arrest both whites and blacks. [25] There were a few black police officers and deputies employed in Florida, but they were assigned only to patrol black neighborhoods and could arrest only blacks.

Moore's involvement in politics once again brought him into contact with Thurgood Marshall, this time in the fight over voter registration. He wrote to Marshall, "I regret to say that we have been blocked in our efforts to register as Democrats for the state and county primaries."[26] Marshall referred the matter to the Department of Justice, but Theron L. Caudle, an assistant attorney general, said that because of a lack of witnesses and other problems— primarily technical— the government would not pursue Moore's complaints.[27] Although Moore was instrumental in increasing black voter registration, election officials refused to allow Moore to register.[28]

Moore's civil rights activity in Florida led to personal retribution. In 1946 Moore and his wife were fired from their teaching positions in Mims because of Moore's active role in the NAACP and PVL.[29] Mrs. Moore had not been active in her husband's civil rights work but was fired in an effort to get the two to leave the county. Because of his leadership role in the NAACP and his work in the movement to secure equal pay for black teachers, it would have been extremely difficult for him to find another teaching position. Instead, Moore was named to the newly created post of state NAACP executive director, a full-time, paid position. As state director he was to establish new chapters, enlist members, and coordinate the activities of the chapters. He was to be paid from dues raised in Florida and report to the state board, not the national NAACP.

The push for equality, led by Moore and the NAACP, brought a violent reaction in Florida. In December 1951 Miami witnessed a series of attacks against a black apartment complex, a synagogue, and a church.[30] But the greatest violence came in central Florida, an area that depended upon the citrus industry and that needed black labor in the groves. The Ku Klux Klan was especially active in the major citrus-producing areas.[31] The Klan operated without the interference of police—and often with their assistance—to carry out violence against blacks. Moore called on Florida governors to remove those officers he believed responsible for crimes against blacks: "It was the sheriff of Madison County who permitted the lynching of Jesse James Payne in 1945. It was a Suwannee County constable who made a Negro prisoner jump into the river at Branford two years ago. It was the sheriff of Gadsden County who carried Leroy Bradwell, Negro veteran of Midway, away from his mother's home one night in January 1946. Bradwell's people have not seen him or heard from him since that night."[32] But Moore's demands for state investigations of the cases were ignored.

With Moore's assistance, one case drew national attention. Moore became active in what was known as the Groveland rape case. Many people, including NAACP Executive Director Walter White, believed Moore's murder was a result of his role in raising money for the defense of the Groveland defendants.[33]

The case began early on the morning of July 16, 1949, when four black men— Samuel Shepherd, Walter Irvin, Charles Greenlee, and Ernest Thomas— were accused of raping Norma Padgett, a white woman, and assaulting her husband in the Lake County community of Groveland.[34] Greenlee, Irvin, and Shepherd were quickly arrested. Thomas fled and after a week of eluding police was shot and killed in a wooded area in north Florida, about 200 miles from where the search began.[35] The rape charge brought hundreds of Klansmen to Groveland demanding that the prisoners be lynched. Lake County Sheriff Willis McCall refused to turn them over, and the mob went on a rampage, setting fire to five black homes and shooting into others. All blacks around Groveland were forced to flee. The National Guard was called in to halt the violence.[36]

Greenlee, Irvin, and Shepherd were convicted despite questionable evidence. Irvin and Shepherd were sentenced to death, Greenlee to life in prison. Moore raised money to hire defense attorneys, wrote letters to public officials, and campaigned throughout the state on behalf of the men. He also pushed the NAACP to provide legal and financial support for the defendants.[37]

In 1951 the United States Supreme Court overturned the Irvin and Shepherd convictions and ordered new trials. The court ruled that the defendants had not received a fair hearing because of extensive pretrial publicity, including the release of their alleged confessions, though none of which were admitted into evidence. Greenlee did not appeal his conviction, fearing he would receive the death penalty in a new trial.[38]

The court ordered a new hearing in Lake County. Moore sent a letter to Florida Governor Fuller Warren urging that the state not turn the men over to Sheriff McCall. In November 1951 McCall drove to the prison and brought the two prisoners back. He claimed that during the return trip the two manacled men tried to overpower him, and he was forced to shoot. He killed Shepherd and seriously wounded Irvin, who later claimed that the men had been shot in cold blood.[39] Moore called on Governor Warren to remove McCall, but his request was ignored.

As Moore became more active in civil rights in Florida, he became increasingly controversial within the NAACP. He was far better at campaigning for causes than directing the organization. His administration of the NAACP was disorganized, and membership

Sheriff Willis McCall stands over Walter Irvin and Samuel Shepherd whom he had just shot during an alleged escape attempt on November 6, 1951. Shepherd was killed, but Irvin lived to dispute McCall's version of events that night. State Library and Archive of Florida.

in Florida declined from 8,872 in 1948 to 2,300 members in 1950.The Florida NAACP was nearly $2,300 in debt, almost exactly the amount owed to Moore in back salary.[40] Moore claimed that it was not his fault that membership had fallen. He believed an increase in annual dues from one dollar to two dollars had discouraged membership.[41] The dues increase did have a negative impact on membership, but the organization was also losing members throughout the South because of increased opposition from whites. Many southern political leaders, in particular, condemned the NAACP as a radical, pro-communist organization. Blacks who joined the NAACP risked violence or loss of their jobs.

In 1950 the national NAACP began a movement to oust Moore as executive director. Gloster Current, national director of branches for the NAACP, led the drive. He wrote, "I am convinced that Mr. Moore, while he is well-intentioned and interested in our work, is not doing as much as could be done to revive the work in that state."[42] Also, Moore's involvement in the PVL bothered Current and Walter White. Moore wrote letters using both his NAACP and PVL titles. As early as 1947 Current wrote: "May I suggest that in the future, you not sign your name as representing both the NAACP and the Progressive Voters' League of Florida, Inc. on the same communication. A separate communication might better be sent from each organization. Otherwise, the impression may get out that the two organizations are interlocking."[43]

During September 1950 the national organization devised a plan to force Moore out. Daniel E. Byrd, the NAACP field secretary, wrote that he was going to Florida to do a "hatchet job" on Moore.[44] In November the national leaders thought they had an agreement for Moore to resign the following March, but in April 1951 Current wrote, "Harry Moore was to have resigned in March but at this late date you can see Moore is still trying to hold on."[45]

Moore knew there was a plan to oust him, but there was little he could do about it.[46] In November 1951, just one month before his murder, Moore was removed as executive director during the state convention at Daytona Beach. Moore wrote: "In some respects this meeting was about the worst we have had. Really it was not a State meeting, because the National officers came in and took over."[47]

As Christmas 1951 approached Moore was out of work, and the state NAACP owed him nearly a year's salary. But he was still a symbol of protest throughout the state. Moore and his family spent Christmas Day at the home of Moore's brother-in-law, Arnold Simms, about 600 yards from the Moores' home. Another brother in-law, George Simms, who had recently returned from military duty in Korea, was also present.[48]

Around 9:00 P.M., Moore, his wife, his daughter Anna, and his mother Rosa returned home. Harriette Moore went to her bedroom in the northeast corner of the house. Anna was in the living room reading and then went to her room. Harry and Rosa talked about the family for awhile, and then around ten o'clock Moore and his mother went to their bedrooms. About 10:15 P.M., Harry Moore got into bed next to his wife. Five minutes later the bomb exploded. Harry died soon after he arrived at the hospital, and Harriette died on January 3, 1952. Rosa and Anna Moore were not injured.[49] The Moore home was nearly demolished.

On the morning of December 26 Brevard County Sheriff H. T. Williams called Federal Bureau of Investigation Special Agent Ed Duff in Daytona Beach and requested FBI assistance.[50] Williams supervised a small department and was not prepared to conduct a major criminal investigation. On December 29, 1951, United States Attorney General Howard McGrath ordered a full investigation, saying that the question of jurisdiction would be determined later.[51]

FBI Director J. Edgar Hoover, later an opponent of the Reverend Martin Luther King, Jr., and the civil rights movement, committed the full resources of the bureau to investigate the killings. On one memo Hoover scrawled, "Give very prompt & thorough attention."[52] At one time as many as twenty agents worked full time on the case. The bureau took over a small motel in Mims as a command headquarters, and Hoover was kept advised of the case almost daily. Hoover's interest may have been a result of pressure from the Truman administration. The case received worldwide attention, and Arthur B. Spingarn, president of the NAACP, asked President Truman to "invoke all the powers of the federal government to the end that Harry T. Moore may vindicate in death those principles and practices he sought in life."[53]

From the beginning there were questions about the FBI's jurisdiction in the Moore killings. Murder was not a federal crime, and in 1951 there was no civil rights violation involved in his death.[54] All the federal government could do was file perjury charges if anyone made false statements under oath during the investigation. For members of the Klan it created an unusual situation. They could admit to crimes covered by state jurisdiction and know that they would not be charged with a federal crime, but if they lied about their activities, they could be charged with perjury.[55]

At first the investigation focused on Brevard County. FBI agents questioned everyone who lived within two miles of Moore's home; they checked local motels, hotels, trailer camps, and a small airport in nearby Titusville. One of the FBI's routine checks led to the Mims Confectionery Store where agents learned that several months earlier two white men had entered the store and asked where the "rich Professor Moore lived." One man said they were looking for the "Professor Moore that doesn't have to work and just travels around and has money." O. K. Washington, who knew Moore, was in the store at the time and gave agents a detailed description of the two men. He claimed one wore a cowboy hat and boots, the other a red baseball cap.[56]

Agents sent the descriptions to informants throughout Florida. In Orange County, located just north of Brevard County, one informant said the descriptions matched two members of the Ku Klux Klan—Earl Brooklyn, who frequently wore a red cap, and Tillman H. Belvin, who often wore cowboy boots and hat.[57] Washington was shown pictures of numerous Klansmen and he identified a photograph of Brooklyn, although he said he could not testify under oath that it was indeed Brooklyn in the photograph. He did not pick out Belvin's picture.[58]

Believing they had a lead in Moore's murder, FBI agents widened their investigation into Orange County, a largely rural area with a population of about 100,000. Its economy was based primarily on citrus and the processing plants that turned the fruit into juice. The county contained active Klan chapters in Orlando, Winter Garden, and Apopka, which FBI informants had infiltrated.[59]

On January 18, 1952, the FBI questioned Brooklyn at its office in Orlando. At first he denied belonging to the Klan, but under intense questioning he admitted membership. He said he had not been active in the Klan in more than a year and denied any involvement in the Moore killings.[60] Brooklyn had lived in Orange County for most of his life and worked as a driver for a cement company. A Klan member told agents that Brooklyn had been active in Klan violence, had a reputation of being difficult to control, and was moody and unpredictable.[61] Belvin was interviewed on March 25,1952, and admitted joining the Klan in the 1930s but denied involvement in the Moore murders. He told agents he was dying of cancer and wanted to tell the truth.[62] The two men gave statements about where they were on Christmas Day, but their stories contained contradictions.

The most significant information came from an informant who told agents that months before the murder Brooklyn had displayed a drawing showing the location of the Moore home. The informant stated that Brooklyn had shown the drawing to other Klansmen after a meeting and had asked for assistance in staking out the Moore home. The agents were skeptical and asked the informant to reconstruct Brooklyn's map from memory. He accurately drew a diagram of the house, including Moore's bedroom, front door, and a railroad track located near the house. A second informant said he also had heard Brooklyn discussing Moore but assumed it was part of a plan to beat the civil rights leader.[63] Agents were convinced that Belvin and Brooklyn had played a role in the bombing, and on January 28, 1952, Hoover ordered Brooklyn, Belvin, and several other Klansmen placed under surveillance.[64]

During the course of the investigation, agents learned the details of dozens of crimes committed by Orange County Klansmen. They uncovered a pattern of Klan violence that included murders, beatings, and terror of both blacks and whites, primarily in the Winter Garden and Apopka areas. Each of the three Klan chapters in the county had a "wrecking crew" made up of members who carried out attacks on Klan targets. The wrecking crew took victims for a "ride," at which time they were warned, beaten, and sometimes murdered.

Within three months FBI agents documented numerous crimes. Although many Klansmen refused to talk, others gave extensive details about the offenses in which they and other Klansmen had been involved. Agents also found citizens who reported crimes that authorities had ignored, and they learned that several ranking government officials were also members of the Klan. William Dunnaway, police chief of Apopka— the Klan center in Orange County— admitted that he was a Klansman. John Talton, an Orange County commissioner; Charles E. Limpus, clerk of the Orange County Criminal Court; Earl Y. Harpole, city manager of Winter Park; and Orange County Sheriff Dave Starr were also identified as Klansmen.[65]

Even though the FBI heard details of other crimes, as a federal agency it had no jurisdiction over these activities. FBI agents believed, however, they were getting close to finding Moore's killers. A telegram from an agent in Orlando to FBI headquarters on January24, 1952, indicates that agents thought they were having success. "Nervousness and dissension created by instant [current] investigation resulted in call of special meeting of select group from Winter Garden and Orlando Klans. . . . Other contacts indicate investigation and interviews now in progress have created dissension among Klans causing members to question loyalty of other members."[66]

Joe N. Cox of Winter Park, an organizer of the Orlando Klan chapter, became anxious when interviewed in his home on March10, 1952, and admitted being a member of the Klan. He said he had not been active for several years and had no knowledge of recent Klan activity. Cox told agents his Klan oath did not allow him to say anything more.[67] Cox was interviewed again on March 29, and agents said he was visibly nervous. He kept asking FBI agents Robert Nischwitz and Robert Sunkel about the evidence they had gathered and wanted to know if it would stand up in court. The following day Cox committed suicide in his backyard.[68]

On August 25, 1952, T. H. Belvin died of cancer, and on December25, exactly one year after Moore's murder, Earl Brooklyn died.[69] With the bureau's leading suspects now dead, agents decided to concentrate on lesser charges against the Klansmen, including perjury and filing false information on government employment applications.[70]

A grand jury in Miami began hearing testimony on October 6,1952, and on June 3, 1953, returned indictments against six members of the Orange County Klan. The six, T. J. McMennamy, William Bogar, Harvey Reisner, Ernest Glen Morton, Robert L. Judah, and Emmet Hart, Sr., were indicted for giving false testimony in connection with the beating of Orange County union organizer Albert Boynkin.

On December 30, 1953, the government's case collapsed when Federal Judge George W. Whitehurst dismissed the perjury indictments. As the government had feared from the beginning, the problem was jurisdiction. Whitehurst ruled that the federal government lacked jurisdiction, and therefore even if Klansmen had lied, they could not be charged with perjury. The government appealed but lost.[71]

In 1978 Ed Spivey of Winter Park called the Brevard County sheriff's office and said he wanted to talk about the murder of Harry T. Moore. Spivey had been a Klansman and was linked to Klan violence, although he was not questioned in the Moore case. Two officers were sent to interview Spivey at his Winter Park home. Spivey had been drinking heavily and his conversation was rambling and difficult to understand. At times he broke down and began to cry.[72] Spivey said Joe Cox, the Klansman who committed suicide, had admitted killing Moore for $5,000. Spivey said he asked Cox who had paid the $5,000, but Cox would not say.[73]

Two things about Moore remain unknown: the names of his killers and what further role he might have played in the civil rights movement if he had not been murdered. Could he have become a national civil rights leader or would his removal from his NAACP post have ended any subsequent involvement in the movement?

No one emerged to take over Moore's leadership role in Florida. With the help of moderate Governor LeRoy Collins, Florida avoided the violence and confrontation that marked attempts at integration in most southern states. FBI infiltration of the Klan brought a sharp decline in Klan violence in central Florida. But Florida lacked the civil rights activity that might have brought about quicker integration. Blacks held a successful bus boycott in Tallahassee in 1956, but an attempt by Dr. Martin Luther King, Jr., to integrate facilities in St. Augustine in 1963-1964, was met with violent opposition.

Moore remained largely forgotten until the 1990s. A new investigation into Moore's death by the Florida Department of Law Enforcement in 1991 failed to turn up new information about the murder, but it did draw attention to Moore's civil rights activities and has gained for him the recognition he deserved. A county office building in Brevard County has been named for Moore, and the county has held ceremonies to honor the fallen civil rights leader.

James C. Clark is a doctoral student in history, University of Florida.

1. Moore was born in Houston, Florida, a small community near Live Oak, in 1905. His father died when he was ten years old, and Moore was raised by his mother, Rosa, and several aunts. He attended schools in Daytona and Jacksonville before graduating from Florida Memorial High School in Live Oak in 1925. He was a bright student-nicknamed "Doc" because of his ability in science and math—and he became a teacher. Moore taught briefly in Houston. He moved to Brevard County in 1925, and, to supplement his income, he sold insurance for Atlanta Life.
2. Steven F. Lawson, "Freedom Then, Freedom Now: The Historiography of the Civil Rights Movement," *American Historical Review* 96 (April 1991), 456-71, quote on 457.
3. Caroline Poore, "Striking the First Blow: Harry T. Moore and the Fight for Black Equality in Florida" (master's thesis, Florida State University, 1992), 22.
4. *The Crisis* 42 (January 1935), 28.
5. Poore, "Striking the First Blow," 24-25.
6. Harry T. Moore, "An Open Letter to Florida Negro Citizens," January 10, 1948, group 2, box 35, NAACP Papers, Library of Congress, Manuscript Division, Washington, DC (hereinafter, NAACP Papers).
7. H. T. Moore to Walter White, August 2, 1937, pt. 3, ser. A, The Campaign for Educational Equality, 1913-1950, *Papers oft he NAACP,* roll 9, 694-96.
8. Gilbert Porter and Leedell Neyland, *History of the Florida State Teachers Association* (Washington, 1977), 66-67.
9. S. D. McGill to Thurgood Marshall, November 5, 1937, pt. 3, ser. A, *Papers of the NAACP,* roll 9, 728-29.
10. Press release from NAACP, nd., pt. 4, The Voting Rights Campaign, 1916-1950, *Papers of the NAACP,* roll 6, 802.
11. Porter and Neyland, *History of the Florida Teachers Association,* 67.
12. Robert A. Margo, *Race and Schooling in the South, 1880-1950: An Economic History* (Chicago, 1990), 54.
13. Moore to Florida State Teacher's Association, n.d., William Gray Papers, Florida A&M University Black Archives, Tallahassee, FL (hereinafter, Gray Papers).
14. *The Crisis* 59 (February 1952), 75.
15. Moore, "Open Letter to Florida Negro Citizens, January 10, 1948."
16. E. Franklin Frazier, *The Negro in the United States,* rev. ed. (New York, 1957), 682.

17. Harry T. Moore to Progressive Voters League members, November 15, 1945, pt. 4, *Papers of the NAACP,* roll 6, 992-93.
18. Report of Agent Tobias E. Matthews, Jr., February 11, 1952, file 44-4118, Records of the Federal Bureau of Investigation, Washington, DC (hereinafter, FBI Records). All subsequent references to the FBI Records are taken from file 44-4118.
19. H. D. Price, *The Negro and Southern Politics: A Chapter of Florida History* (New York, 1957), 33.
20. Numan V. Bartley, *The Rise of Massive Resistance: Race and Politics in the South During the 1950's* (Baton Rouge, 1969), 8.
21. Price, *Negro and Southern Politics,* 45.
22. Moore to Progressive Voters League members, n.d., Gray Papers.
23. The NAACP first proposed federal antilynching legislation in 1919. In 1921 the first bill was introduced in Congress to make lynching a federal crime. The bill passed the House by a wide margin, but in the Senate Southerners were able to block it through a filibuster. There were attempts nearly every year for the next two decades to pass antilynching laws, but they always failed.
24. Moore to candidates, April 12, 1946, Gray Papers.
25. Steven F. Lawson, *Black Ballots: Voting Rights in the South, 1944-1969* (New York, 1976), 132.
26. Moore to Thurgood Marshall, April 23, 1946, group 2, box 35, NAACP Papers.
27. Theron L. Caudle to M. W. Perry, December 5, 1946, pt. 4, *Papers of the NAACP,* roll 6, 919-20.
28. Moore to M. W. Perry, January 21, 1947, pt. 4, *Papers of the NAACP,* roll 6, 925-26.
29. Statement of Damon Huntzler, December 27, 1951, FBI Records.
30. *Pittsburgh Courier,* December 28, 1951.
31. See Jerrell H. Shofner, "Communists, Klansmen, and the CIO in the Florida Citrus Industry," *Florida Historical Quarterly* 71 (January 1993), 300-09.
32. Moore, "An Open Letter to Florida Negro Citizens," January 10, 1948.
33. *Pittsburgh Courier,* January 5, 1952.
34. Steven F. Lawson, David R. Colburn, and Darryl Paulson, "Groveland: Florida's Little Scottsboro," *Florida Historical Quarterly* 65 (July 1986), 1.
35. Ibid., 4.
36. Statement of Ira B. Hall, May 10, 1952, FBI Records.
37. FBI Miami to J. Edgar Hoover, February 28, 1952, FBI Records.
38. Lawson, et. al., "Groveland: Florida's Little Scottsboro," 10.
39. Ibid., 19.
40. Lucille Black to Daniel E. Byrd, November 21, 1950, group 2, box 35, NAACP Papers.
41. Report of Agent Tobias E. Matthews, Jr., February 11, 1952.
42. Gloster B. Current to Lucille Black, May 17, 1950, group 2, box C221, NAACP Papers.
43. Gloster B. Current to Moore, July 3, 1947, 2, box 35, NAACP Papers.
44. Daniel E. Byrd to Lucille Black, September 29, 1950, group 2, box 35, NAACP Papers.
45. Gloster B. Current to Ruby Hurley, April 18, 1951, group 2, box C221, NAACP Papers.
46. FBI interview with the Rev. K. S. Johnson, December 29, 1951, FBI Records.
47. Ibid.

48. Report of Agent Tobias E. Matthews, Jr., February 11, 1952.
49. Ibid.
50. Ibid.
51. Howard McGrath to J. Edgar Hoover, December 29, 1951, FBI Records.
52. Hoover note, January 8, 1952, FBI Records.
53. NAACP news release, January 3, 1952, box 10, file 10, Workers Defense League Papers, Wayne State University, Detroit, MI.
54. William C. Berman, *The Politics of Civil Rights in the Truman Administration* (Columbus, 1970), 448-49. Title 18 of the United States Criminal Code contained three sections that could be used to prosecute civil rights violators. Section 51 was designed to protect individuals against state interference with laws passed by the federal government. Section 52 allowed the federal government to become involved if state officials deprived individuals of their rights through willful misuse of their powers. Section 441 applied only to antipeonage cases.
55. FBI Miami to Hoover, March 22, 1952, FBI Records.
56. Ibid., January 8, 1952, FBI Records.
57. Statement of confidential informant T-4, January 4, 5, 1952, FBI Records.
58. FBI Miami to Hoover, January 8, 1952, FBI Records.
59. Hoover to FBI Miami, March 15, 1952, FBI Records.
60. Statement of Earl Brooklyn, January 18, 1952, FBI Records.
61. Statement of Carl E. Parker, January 15, 1952, FBI Records.
62. FBI Miami to Hoover, March 25, 1952, FBI Records.
63. Statement of confidential informant T-5, January 4, 5, 1952, FBI Records.
64. Hoover to FBI Miami, January 28, 1952, FBI Records.
65. Statement of informant T-l, March 22, 1952, FBI Records.
66. FBI Miami to Hoover, January 24, 1952, FBI Records.
67. Statement of Joe N. Cox, March 10, 1952, FBI Records.
68. Ibid.
69. FBI Miami to Hoover, December 29, 1952, FBI Records.
70. Ibid., February 10, 1952, FBI Records.
71. *Miami News,* December 30, 1953.
72. Statement of Ed Spivey, January 19, 1978, Records of Seminole-Brevard State Attorneys Office, Rockledge, FL.
73. Ibid.

12

SEGREGATION LEFT IN THE WAKE

It is often surmised that *Brown v. Board of Education* in 1954 ushered in the modern period of desegregation in "moderate" Florida. In truth, the state stonewalled enactment of *Brown* and continued its centuries-old practice of white supremacy through most of the modern civil rights era. It would take years of individual and collective protest by leaders, organizations, and "everyday" people of the Sunshine State to finally unravel the ties of racism, or, at least the legal knots of inequality. By the late 1960s, over 90 percent of students in Florida attended segregated schools (although some districts had adopted "plans" for desegregation), and in the Democratic presidential primary of 1972, George "segregation forever" Wallace won every county of the state. Indeed, "moderate" Florida did not adopt true racial progress until the election of the state's first "reform" governor, Rubin Askew, in the 1970s. The final chapter in this book should remind readers that Florida's racial past is filled with repression and resistance that has lasted as a continuum from colonial to present times. The movement for black rights and dignity manifested itself in many periods and in many forms, but it always exhibited a grass-roots determination of, as in the anthem of the modern civil rights movement, "We Shall Overcome."

Patricia Dillon continues the recent trend of civil rights historiography by exploring the grass-roots struggle of one of Florida's many black communities to overcome the state's stonewalling during the years of the modern civil rights movement, notably by using as a case study the school desegregation struggle in the town of Sanford. Her purpose is to understand the daily struggles of one black community as it evolved from a segregated to an integrated setting. The author determines that racial inequity manifested itself most often—and disturbingly for black parents—in the town's public school system. Into the 1950s and 1960s, black teachers earned less pay than their white counterparts, children matriculated in a shorter school year, black schools received less funding, and black students suffered the worst ravages of officially sanctioned or tolerated segregation in sports and recreation. While *Brown* did little more than move the Sunshine State to a policy of delay and subterfuge, Sanford's black community quietly instituted its own daily struggle for desegregation. Indeed, as Dillon notes, Sanford's black community had a deep history of self-improvement and attacks on Central Florida's color line, and World War II, *Brown,* and the ensuing heightened civil rights periods simply accelerated its multi-generational protests.

Dillon cites Jim Crow housing and recreational facilities as areas of conflict, but blacks' major concerns over the decades seemed to lie with segregated and inferior instruction for their children. In the early 1950s, similar to other Florida towns, Sanford attempted to sidestep equal schooling by increasing funding for black schools. The school board boasted that it now invested more funding on black schools than on white ones, but the author points out that the board spent much of this money on bringing black programs and facilities into compliance with modern building codes rather than on desegregation and otherwise elevating black schools to the quality of white schools. Dillon attributes Florida's "calm reaction" to *Brown v. Board* to such factors as the state's diverse population, a burgeoning tourist industry, and Governor LeRoy Collins's moderate stance. However, she also notes that Sanford and probably other districts in Florida simply ignored enforcement of *Brown* or sought to delay it indefinitely through various rouses. In regard to Florida's moderation factor, readers may want to think critically about what led Dr. Martin Luther King, Jr. to claim that his bloody protest in St. Augustine in the early 1960s was one of the worst he could cite for any state of Dixie. How might the black community have interpreted those words in the heat of its desegregation struggles?

The author's strongest point is that the Civil Rights Bill of 1964, passed by Congress a full ten years after *Brown,* and not the Court decision itself evolved as the actual driving force behind desegregating public schools in Florida: the bill authorized governmental agencies to withhold federal money from programs practicing discrimination and authorized the U.S. Attorney General to use the federal courts to force desegregation in non-compliant school districts. Like many systems in Florida, Sanford still resisted meaningful desegregation of its public schools through such tactics as "freedom of choice" and "student assignment" plans, but now the power of the federal government, the federal courts, and the determination of everyday black parents (often supported by NAACP court challenges) finally rang the death knell for segregation in Sanford. Recognizing this reality, and only after recognizing this reality, did white officials adopt sweeping integration policies for its schools.

This was a scenario characterizing many districts across Florida as local schools failed to thoroughly desegregate in the wake of *Brown* until black individuals and organizations like the NAACP forced compliance by using the expanded powers of the federal government and courts. In this regard, the African-American activists of the modern civil rights era followed a long history of black struggle by pursuing redress "at all time through all means possible." This article should be read in conjunction with the recently published book, *Old South, New South, or Down South?: Florida in the Modern Civil Rights Movement.*

FURTHER READING

Charles U. Smith and Lewis M. Killian, *The Tallahassee Bus Protest* (1958);

Joseph A. Tomberlin, "Florida Whites and the Brown Decision of 1954," *Florida Historical Quarterly,* Vol. 51 (1972);

Helen L. Jacobstein, *The Segregation Factor in the Florida Democratic Gubernatorial Primary of 1956* (1972);

J. Irving E. Scott, *The Education of Black People in Florida* (1974);

Joseph A. Tomberline, "Florida and the School Desegregation Issue, 1954-1959:

A Summary View," *Journal of Negro Education*, Vol. 43 (1974);

Richard Kluger, *Simple Justice: The History of Brown v. Board of Education and Black America's Struggle for Equality* (1975);

Patrick S. Washburn, *A Question of Sedition: The Federal Government's Investigation of the Black Press during World War II* (1986);

Charles U. Smith, ed., *The Civil Rights Movement in Florida and the United States* (1989);

Steven F. Lawson, "Freedom Then, Freedom Now: The Historiography of the Civil Rights Movement," *American Historical Review*, Vol. 96 (1991);

Fred Powledge, *Free at Last: The Civil Rights Movement and the People Who Made It* (1992);

Allen Morris, comp., *The Florida Handbook, 1933-1994* (1993);

Maxine D. Jones and Kevin M. McCarthy, *African Americans in Florida* (1993);

Marvin Dunn, *Black Miami in the Twentieth Century* (1997);

Steven F. Lawson and Charles Payne, *Debating the Civil Rights Movement, 1945-1968* (1998);

Kathryn L. Nasstrom, "Beginnings and Endings: Life Stories and the Periodization of the Civil Rights Movement," *Journal of American History*, Vol. 86 (1999);

Glenda Alice Rabby, *The Pain and the Promise: The Struggle for Civil Rights in Tallahassee, Florida* (1999);

Charlton W. Tebeau and William Marina, *A History of Florida* (1999), chapters 27 and 29;

Gary R. Mormino, *Land of Sunshine, Land of Dreams: A Social History of Modern Florida* (2005);

Barbara Shircliffe, "African Americans and the Struggle for Opportunity in Florida Higher Education, 1947-1977," *History of Education Quarterly*, Vol. 47 (2007);

William G. Crawford, Jr., "The Long Hard Fight for Equal Rights: A History of Broward County's Colored Beach and the Fort Lauderdale Beach 'Wade Ins' of the Summer of 1961," *Tequesta*, Vol. 67 (2007);

Dan R. Warren, *If It Takes All Summer: Martin Luther King, the KKK, and States' Rights in St. Augustine*, 1964 (2008);

Irvin D.S. Winsboro, ed., *Old South, New South, or Down South?: Florida and the Modern Civil Right Movement* (2009).

Civil Rights And School Desegregation In Sanford

Patricia Dillon

The Florida Historical Quarterly, Volume 76, issue 3 (1998), 310-325.

The civil rights movement in the United States reached beyond the federal legislation that eradicated legal segregation. The movement also fundamentally transformed how white and black Americans interacted on a daily basis in small communities and large urban centers. Historians such as John Dittmer, William H. Chafe, and David R. Colburn have analyzed how national laws affected racial relations at the community level. While Dittmer and Chafe examined the movement in states traditionally associated with the civil rights movement—Mississippi and North Carolina respectively—Colburn looked at the movement in Florida, a state whose contemporary popular image as a tourist haven dominated by theme parks masks its history of racial tension. Seeking to address Florida's controversial past, Colburn and other historians of the state, such as David Goldfield, Randall Miller, George E. Pozetta, Tom Wagy, and Charles U. Smith, have successfully documented the importance of Florida in the national civil rights movement.[1]

This article continues in the current vein of civil rights historiography by exploring the interaction between the black and white communities within the town of Sanford, Florida. Sanford never made national headlines during the civil rights movement, although the city's blacks did participate in sit-ins, marches, and demonstrations. Nevertheless, an examination of the history of Sanford in the crucial decades of the 1950s and 1960s contributes to an understanding of the daily struggles in one town as it evolved from a legally segregated to a desegregated community.

As the seat of Seminole County, Sanford marched into the twentieth century confident in its ability to ensure sustained economic prosperity and population growth. In reality, however, prosperity was distributed unequally between the white and black communities. This was especially evident in the field of education. In September 1908, the *Sanford Herald* lauded the opening day of Sanford High, which served both white grammar and high school students, by praising its new physical and chemical laboratories and its newly appointed faculty and school board.[2] Two years later, faced with problems of overcrowding in the combined educational facility, the town constructed a new school solely for high school students. The *Sanford Herald* described it as "a splendid brick structure three stories high, handsomely finished and equipped with all modern conveniences."[3] By contrast in 1929, the Sanford School—for black students— consisted of two separate buildings, inadequately insulated, heated by a wood stove, and without electricity.[4]

Despite inequitable educational facilities, Sanford blacks took great pride in their schools and many teachers emerged as prominent community leaders. One of the most renowned was Joseph Nathaniel Crooms. In 1906, the Orange County School Board appointed Crooms principal of Hopper Academy, which served both grammar and high school students. It consisted of ten classrooms and one auditorium and, as was true of Sanford's other schools, was soon overcrowded.[5]

In 1926, Crooms and his wife, Wealthy, donated seven and a half acres for the construction of Crooms Academy.[6] The Academy became the center of the black community, educating its future leaders and providing a stimulating environment in which blacks could question and debate their second-class status within Sanford and the nation. Throughout the 1960s, Crooms Academy graduates emerged as respected civil rights leaders within the black community Inequities within the nation's school systems

Faculty of the Crooms Academy, Sanford, 1943. Photograph courtesy of the Sanford Museum.

constituted one of the main targets of the modern civil rights movement. Teachers' salaries reflected prevalent racial discrimination. Throughout the 1920s salaries for Sanford's white teachers ranged between $100 to $200 per month, while black teachers received $45 to $120. Another contentious issue within Sanford's school system was the different term lengths for black and white students. Until the mid- 1920s, white students in Seminole County attended school for eight months, black pupils for only six. Seminole County School Superintendent T. W. Lawton justified this discrepancy to Florida State School Superintendent William N. Sheats by arguing that "colored children will not attend with any degree of regularity for a longer term than six months."[7] School funding, not student attendance rates, dictated the length of Sanford's school terms.

The advent of World War I encouraged cooperation between the black and white communities— despite profoundly unequal social, economic, and political conditions— in support of the war effort. In October 1918, all branches of the Seminole County American Red Cross, including "4 Colored Auxiliaries," met to coordinate their fund-raising activities.[8] Two months later the *Herald* commended the black community for its contributions to the War Works Fund Drive.[9]

As blacks supported the war effort, they entertained hopes that their contributions would lead eventually to equality at home. Many black servicemen who served overseas encountered for the first time societies unburdened by the racial caste system. They returned to the United States with a renewed desire to fight for equality and respect within their own country. These hopes, however, were quickly dashed. The majority of white Americans, overcome by the technological and cultural changes wrought by the war, sought a return to "normalcy." This desire manifested itself in the growing popularity of the Ku Klux Klan and the formation of other white supremacist groups intent on enforcing traditional race relations.[10]

The early postwar period witnessed the lynching of over seventy African Americans throughout the United States, several of whom were veterans still in uniform. The Ku Klux Klan, reorganized in 1915, boasted a membership of over five million by 1920.[11] No government or newspaper reports exist which indicate the presence of Klan activities in Sanford. The city council, nonetheless, unanimously passed a resolution on September 12, 1921, denouncing any individuals or associations who attempted to take "into their own hands the administration of the law and the regulations of the life and affairs of Sanford's citizens."[12] The councilmen characterized such actions as unconstitutional, unlawful and a bad example to others. They also reasoned that "any act or acts of violence attempted or done by any person or persons, not duly authorized by law to do so is a menace to good government [and] is an evil to others."[13] The councilmen passed their resolution not because they sought racial justice, but rather because they feared that mob action hindered the capability of law officers and posed a potential threat to the well-being of Sanford's citizens.

At the dawn of the Second World War, Sanford's black and white communities again pushed aside racial animosity, at least on the surface, to unite behind the war effort. Sanford's residents contributed to various war fund drives, and both its black and white male citizens volunteered for the draft, although they registered at segregated draft offices.[14]

For African Americans, World War II was a war not only against the Axis powers but also against racism and discrimination. Returning servicemen and women vowed not to abandon their quest for equality as their World War I cohorts had been forced to do, but rather to enlarge its scope and confront all aspects of America's segregated society. African Americans refused to continue to accept their second-class citizenship which entailed all the responsibilities and duties of the ruling class without any of its benefits. The ensuing civil rights movement exposed and attempted to eradicate the historical anomaly of a democratic country discriminating against a significant portion of its people.

Sports emerged as a major arena for civil rights activities. Most white southerners refused to entertain the image of a black man besting a white man, even if only on the baseball field or in the boxing ring.[15] In 1946, Sanford's citizens encountered this scenario when Jackie Robinson, playing for the Montreal Royals, a Brooklyn Dodgers farm team, appeared in town for a "pre spring" training camp.[16]

Until this time, Florida's sporting events were strictly segregated. A few arenas throughout the state provided small Jim Crow sections, but most denied blacks admittance. On March 4, Jackie Robinson and his wife, Rachel, arrived in Sanford for a series of "pre-spring" training exhibition games against the St. Paul Saints. Sanford's Mayflower Hotel refused to allow Jackie and Rachel to remain with the other players. Instead, the Robinsons, along with John Wright, another black team member, stayed at the home of David Brock, a local African American doctor. On the second day of training, Robinson and Wright returned to Brock's home after practice and were informed by Branch Rickey Jr., son of the Brooklyn Dodgers' team president, that they had to leave immediately for Daytona Beach. According to Rickey, a group of Sanford citizens had warned him that they would not tolerate blacks and whites playing on the same field and had ordered the players out of town.[17]

Dodgers officials refused to elaborate on Robinson and White's quick departure from Sanford and reported to the press only that the players wanted to get settled in Daytona before the start of spring training. On April 7, the Royals again returned to Sanford to play a pre-scheduled game against the Saints. Robinson appeared in the starting line-up and made the first run of the game. The first run, however, also proved to be his last. At the end of the second inning, Sanford's chief of police ordered Royals manager Clay Hopper to remove the black players. Hopper felt there was no point in resisting and removed Robinson and Wright from the dugout.[18] Though the *Sanford Herald* later reported that the Saints beat the Royals 8 to 6, the article failed to mention the ejection of Robinson and Wright.[19]

Segregated sporting events filtered down from professional contests to neighborhood baseball diamonds. A month before the confrontation between Robinson, Wright, and the Sanford police chief, a group of black teenagers appeared before the city council requesting funds to construct a baseball park in Goldsboro, the black section of Sanford. The teenagers promised to furnish the labor if the council graded the field and supplied the clay. In this instance the commissioners approved the request. In the following years, however, inequitable recreational facilities emerged as the rallying cry for Sanford's civil rights proponents.[20]

As these sporting events illustrate, Sanford's black and white communities continued to develop as two separate entities. Segregated housing and zoning ordinances contributed to this demarcation. In spite of the fact that the Supreme Court had ruled in *Buchanan v. Warley* in 1917 that racially segregated zoning was unconstitutional, southern officials quickly learned how to disguise even the most blatant discriminatory zoning ordinances. White home owners ensured the "correct" makeup of their neighborhoods by inserting private deed restrictions within their sale contracts. The construction of housing projects also strictly followed racial lines.[21]

On September 3, 1951, the Sanford Housing Authority laid the cornerstone for Castle Brewer Court, the city's first housing project for African Americans.[22] A year later, the city dedicated the cornerstone of another black housing project, William Clark Court. Dr. Mary McLeod Bethune, President Emeritus at Bethune-Cookman College, delivered the main address. Bethune credited the late William Clark, black realtor and builder, for developing the Goldsboro neighborhood of Sanford. Clark had purchased several lots in the area and quickly populated the community by selling them on terms as low as five dollars down and five dollars a month. When Goldsboro had existed as a separate city, Clark had served as one of its mayors. The Housing Authority of Sanford, in recognition of Clark's community service, named the new project in his honor.[23]

Low cost housing programs received support from both Sanford's white and black communities. The location of such projects, however, sparked heated debate. On September 25, 1950, citizens jammed the city council office to protest the re-zoning of a white neighborhood to accommodate black housing. A delegation of white citizens presented the council with a petition containing over two hundred signatures objecting to the proposed zoning program. The Sanford Housing Authority quickly capitulated to the white residents' demands and revoked its zoning recommendation. The committee justified its decision by reasoning that the proposed housing site would be situated across town from the black business district and movement between the two locales would severely increase city traffic.[24]

Throughout its history, Sanford's city council enforced its rules and regulations without representation from the black community. In April 1950, Seminole County Commissioners denied Talvanis Scarbrough, an African American, the right to run for congressional committeeman on the grounds that he had only recently moved to Seminole County (though he had lived in the county for at least nine months). Three years later, Matthew Lee Williams, a prominent leader of the African American community, became the first black to run for the Sanford City Council. Though Williams received 250 votes, he lost the election to Earl Higginbotham, a white employee with Standard Oil.[25]

One of the most important rulings of the civil rights era occurred on May 17, 1954, in *Brown v. Board of Education of Topeka, Kansas.* In this case, the Supreme Court reversed the earlier ruling in *Plessy v. Ferguson* that had upheld the "separate but equal" doctrine. Chief Justice Earl Warren ruled "that in the field of public education the doctrine of separate but equal has no place."[26] Before the *Brown* ruling, many school officials had attempted to placate the courts by increasing funding for black schools. In the early 1950s, southern school board members more than tripled their expenditures on school construction and maintenance.[27] Sanford was no different. In October 1950, in response to the Sanford Negro Welfare League's criticism of the inferiority of the town's black schools, Sanford school board officials reported that, in the past two years, they had spent $44,403 more on black than on white institutions; in particular, they pointed to the construction of a new library and football field at Crooms High School. The board neglected to mention, however, that these increased expenditures were necessary to bring black schools up to current building codes. A sanitation report compiled in the 1940s revealed that Sanford Grammar School lacked adequate lighting, self-closing toilet doors, and enough rooms to accommodate its burgeoning student population. The report also recommended that Hooper Academy's school building, sanitation facilities, and drinking fountains receive extensive repairs.[28]

The *Brown* decision, though, mandated that southern officials end their charade of a "separate but equal" school system. While the decision initiated one of the most fundamental social transformations in American history, few Floridians acknowledged the ruling. The majority of state newspapers, including the *Sanford Herald,* failed to report the Court's decision.

Florida's calm reaction differed from the violent protests erupting in other southern states. Florida's relatively low percentage of blacks, situated within an increasingly diverse population, helped to mute inflammatory rhetoric. After World War II, a large number of military personnel, previously stationed in Florida, returned to live permanently in the state. Retirees from other parts of the country, utilizing Social Security benefits and early retirement options, increasingly chose Florida as their retirement haven. Since the 1920s, immigrants from abroad had moved to the Sunshine State and established their own thriving ethnic communities. In 1930 Tampa's Ybor City boasted the second largest Hispanic community in the South. By the 1950s, Jewish, Canadian, and Greek communities also contributed to the ethnic composition of the state. Along with its increasingly diverse population, Florida's growing dependence on tourism served to inhibit those reactionary demonstrations that would have tarnished the state's "vacation land" image.[29] Florida governor LeRoy Collins emerged as the most important proponent for racial moderation. Though he openly supported segregated schools, he refused to stoop to confrontational tactics or race-baiting rhetoric. In his 1957 inaugural address, he declared integration inevitable and urged Floridians to accept the process gracefully. Most Florida community leaders followed the governor. They opposed desegregation but refused to openly defy the Supreme Court.[30]

Sanford reacted calmly to the *Brown* decision. No mention was made of the ruling in either the school board or city council minutes. City officials also denied a national pro-segregation group the opportunity to speak in their town. In December 1954, Sanford resident L. A. Baker asked the council to permit Bryan Bowles, president of the National Association for the Advancement of White People (NAAWP), to hold a public meeting. Mayor Earl Higgenbotham denied the request saying "he did not feel that any material good could come from such a speech."[31] He cited the cordial relationship between the city's black and white communities stating "that there has been no trespassing from either side . . . no trouble in schools and churches . . . [and] the colored people are cooperating with the whites, the police, the city and county in every possible way."[32]

The most contentious disagreement between the white and black communities continued to revolve around the use of recreational facilities. The minimal funding appropriated for black playgrounds and recreational centers failed to match those that the city allocated to the white football fields, swimming pool, civic center, and baseball diamonds. In the late 1950s, African Americans demanded either the integration of the superior white facilities or the construction of "separate but equal" recreational centers.

In July 1958, between forty and fifty black teenagers marched on the Sanford Civic Center's Youth Wing. Though the Center allowed blacks daytime use of the facilities for recreational activities, officials barred them from entering the building at night for social functions. Within ten minutes after the teenagers reached the Center, Police Chief Roy Williams disbanded the group. He recounted: "There was no disorder. All of the Negro youth left in an orderly manner when told they were approaching the problem in the wrong manner."[33]

However, on the following afternoon, two black youths brandishing pocket knives

In the late 1950s, black teens marched on the Sanford Civic Center (Pictured here, 1960) to protest the facility's discriminatory practices. Photograph courtesy of the Sanford Museum.

allegedly threatened a group of white teenagers, warning, "We'll see you at the Civic Center tonight."[34] Bracing for a possible race riot, Chief Williams stationed six extra policemen at the Center while Sanford's high school students enjoyed their regular Saturday evening dance. The *Sanford Herald* reported "an ominous and tense feeling permeating throughout the evening as police officers checked every area . . . for any groups that might be congregating and attempting to move on the Civic center."[35] Though the newspaper reported that a number of African Americans were seen driving by the Center, no one stopped or attempted to approach the building.[36]

The following week the city council met with the demonstration leaders to discuss constructing their own youth center. No commissioner suggested allowing the black youths to use the Civic Center separately from their white counterparts. The image of black and white teenagers dating and socializing in the same building, even on different nights, appalled the sensibilities of the stately councilmen.[37]

Conflict over the segregated recreational facilities continued into the 1960s. In April 1961, the local chapter of the National Association for the Advancement of Colored People (NAACP) presented the city with a petition calling for the desegregation of all parks, playgrounds, and ball fields. Although the newspaper reported that city officials threatened to close all recreational facilities if blacks attempted to integrate, minutes of the city commissioners' meeting fail to mention any such measure. The final reference to this incident occurred on April 20, when the newspaper listed the names of all African Americans who had signed the desegregation petition.[38]

In other areas around the nation, civil rights advocates increasingly defied segregation ordinances. On December 1, 1955, Rosa Parks boarded a bus in Montgomery, Alabama, and took a seat. When she refused to relinquish her seat to a white passenger she was arrested and imprisoned, but the resulting year-long boycott by Montgomery's black population ended segregation of mass transit in the city.[39]

The boycott in Montgomery touched off similar protests throughout the United States. On May 27, 1956, two Florida Agricultural and Mechanical University (FAMU) students, Wilhelmina Jakes and Carrie Patterson, boarded a Tallahassee city bus and sat in the only vacant seats, located in the front of the bus. The driver ordered the co-eds to stand in the back, but the students resisted. They offered to leave the bus if the driver returned their fare, but he refused. The police arrived on the scene and arrested the women, charging them "with placing themselves in a position to cause a riot."[40]

On the following day, Broadus Hartley, FAMU student government president, urged his fellow students to follow Montgomery's example and boycott the city's buses for the remainder of the semester. Their actions launched the first mass civil rights demonstration on an American campus and the first student-initiated boycott.[41]

Tallahassee's black business and religious leaders supported the students' actions. Reverend C. K. Steele organized the Negro Inter Civic Council (ICC) to represent the black community during the boycott. ICC leaders met with Tallahassee city officials and presented them with a list of demands which included the seating of passengers on a "first-come-first-serve-basis"; the hiring of more black bus drivers; and the extension of courteous treatment to black riders. City leaders refused to meet the demands and the boycott continued. However, on December 21, 1956, the Supreme Court upheld *Browder v. Gayle* which ruled that segregation on public transportation violated the due process and equal protection clauses of the Fourteenth Amendment. Shortly after the ruling, ICC leaders boarded a Tallahassee city bus and rode in the front seats.[42]

In 1957, two African American students traveling by Greyhound bus from Bethune-Cookman College to Orlando sat among white passengers. After the driver made sure no white passengers were standing, "the bus continued with the whites and coloreds mixed without incident."[43] This event exemplified Sanford's white residents' typical reaction to the gradual desegregation of their community. As long as African Americans asserted their rights unobtrusively and did not inconvenience the white community, integration proceeded in a slow but non-confrontational manner.

On July 2, 1964, President Lyndon B. Johnson signed the Civil Rights Act. Its passage redefined social interaction within every American community.[44] Sanford Mayor A. L. Wilson, in an open letter to the *Sanford Herald,* implored all citizens to abide by the Civil Rights Bill. Three days later, the mayor happily reported that "the people of Sanford are taking the provisions of the new civil rights bill in stride and are remaining God-loving and law abiding, peaceful citizens."[45] The newspaper also cited unofficial accounts of food and beverage businesses quietly integrating without incident.[46]

Another component of the Civil Rights Bill, Title VI, empowered the federal government to withhold money from any program that maintained discriminatory practices. Even though federal educational aid was a relatively recent phenomenon, Florida's schools depended heavily on their allocations. The threat of losing such aid prompted Sanford, along with other Florida communities, to finally address school desegregation.[47]

On February 18, 1959, school board members at Orchard Villa Elementary School, in Dade County, unanimously voted to admit four black students for the next semester. On September 8, the four black children attended school with only eight registered white pupils. White students were absent not only because parents insisted that they boycott the integrated school, but also because of the changing racial structure of the surrounding neighborhood. Most white families left when increasing numbers of black residents moved to the area. On October 7, the Orchard Villa School Board registered 379 black students and replaced the white faculty with black teachers. Instead of designing an innovative desegregation program, the board merely created another all black school.[48]

In the following years, however, other Florida schools introduced integration on a more permanent level. In 1961-62, four counties— Volusia, Broward, Palm Beach, and Hillsborough— admitted blacks to formerly all white schools. By the end of the 1963 term, 3,650 African American students, 1.5 percent of the total black school enrollment population, attended integrated schools. Ninety-eight percent of all black pupils, however, remained in segregated institutions.[49]

Sanford eventually enacted a "freedom of choice" plan to initiate school desegregation. This plan allowed parents and students to select the school they wished to attend. The program, however, limited integration by relying on residential segregation. Most parents chose schools within their neighborhoods and, since residential patterns remained segregated, school populations continued to reflect this trend.[50]

On January 28, 1965, the Seminole County School Board presented its desegregation plan to the Department of Health, Education, and Welfare. The plan allowed Seminole County pupils to attend schools closest to their homes and enabled students to transfer to any county school as long as such a "transfer is not based on racial considerations."[51]

Earlier that month the school board approved two out of three applications by black students to attend schools near their homes. Ingrid Burton, "a straight A student at Crooms High School," transferred to Seminole Junior High. Jocelyn Harold, "also an above average student," was reassigned to Southside Elementary School. The board denied Charlotte Ringling's request because she lived closer to Hopper Elementary than Southside.[52]

In July 1965, the school board focused on desegregating school faculty and recreational facilities. The Personnel Assignment Ordinance mandated that black and white faculty and administrators jointly attend all meetings and training programs. The board also demanded that all students be granted equal opportunity to participate in any school activity and utilize the services of any recreational facilities.[53] On August 12, 1965, the *Sanford Herald* reported that "the majority of schools will enroll Negro and white students. . . . Token desegregation was begun last school year and school officials anticipate routine adjustment in a matter of days."[54]

For the next several years, Sanford's black and white communities continued to work toward desegregation. By the 1970s, the federal government ruled that "freedom of choice" plans inherently limited integration and mandated busing of children to previously segregated schools.[55] Though de facto segregated schools still exist in the nation's inner cities and affluent suburbs, most white and black students casually interact on a daily basis.

Historian Glenda Rabby has argued that the civil rights movement occurred not only in the "halls of Congress or the White House," but also, and more dramatically, "in the main streets of communities across the nation."[56] The integration of Sanford's black and white communities transpired in the shadow of the more spectacular civil rights battles. The national media failed to cover Croom's high school students' march on the Civic Center or the quiet integration of Sanford's drinking and eating facilities following the Civil Rights Act of 1964. Major television networks also neglected to report on the peaceful desegregation of Sanford's school system. Lack of media attention, however, does not lessen the significance of the act. Together these incidents, along with the violent and nationally televised confrontations in Little Rock, Selma, Birmingham, Montgomery, St. Augustine, and Tallahassee, eradicated legalized segregation in the United States.

Patricia Dillon is a graduate student in history at Mississippi State University in Starkville, Mississippi.

1. John Dittmer, *Local People: The Struggle for Civil Rights in Mississippi* (Urbana, 1994); William Chafe, *Civilities and Civil Rights: Greensboro, North Carolina, and the Black Struggle for Freedom* (New York, 1980); David R. Colburn, *Racial Change and Community Crisis: St. Augustine, Florida, 1877-1980* (New York, 1985); David R. Goldfield, *Black, White, and Southern: Race Relations and Southern Culture, 1940 to the Present* (Baton Rouge, 1990); Randall M. Miller and George E. Pozzetta, eds., *Shades of the Sunbelt: Essays on Ethnicity, Race, and the Urban South* (Boca Raton, 1989); Tom Wagy, *Governor LeRoy Collins of Florida: A Spokesman of the New South* (Tuscaloosa, 1985); and Charles U. Smith. ed., *The Civil Rights Movement in Florida and the United States: Historical and Contemporary Perspectives* (Tallahassee, 1989).
2. *Sanford Herald,* July 23, 1920.
3. Ibid., November 18, 1910.
4. Proposal for National Register of Historic Places: Georgetown, 1990, p. 8, City Clerk's Office, Sanford.

5. William N. Sheats, *Biennial Report of the Superintendent of Public Instruction of the State of Florida* (Tallahassee, 1918), 729. At this time, Sanford was part of Orange County. Seminole County was established in April 1913.
6. Proposal for National Register of Historic Places: Georgetown, 1990, p.11.
7. William N. Sheats, *Biennial Report of the Superintendent of Public Instruction* (Tallahassee, 1928), 729.
8. *Sanford Herald,* October 4, 1918.
9. Ibid., December 6, 1918.
10. C. Vann Woodward, *The Strange Career of Jim Crow,* 3d rev. ed. (New York, 1974), 114, 116; Roger Biles, *The South and the New Deal* (Lexington, 1994), 10.
11. David Goldfield, *Cotton Fields and Skyscrapers: Southern City and Region, 1607-1980* (Baton Rouge, 1982), 148; Woodward, *Strange Career of Jim Crow,* 115.
12. Minutes, Sanford City Commissioners, September 12, 1921, Vol. 2, 277-78, City Clerk's Office, Sanford.
13. Ibid.
14. *Sanford Herald,* October 15 and 29, 1940, August 13, 1941.
15. Randy Roberts, *Papa Jack: Jack Johnson and the Era of White Hopes* (New York, 1983).
16. Jules Tygiel, *Baseball's Great Experiment: Jackie Robinson and His Legacy* (New York, 1984), 101.
17. Ibid., 103, 106-107.
18. Ibid., 109-110.
19. *Sanford Herald,* April 8, 1946.
20. Minutes, Sanford City Commissioners, March 25, 1946, Vol. 8, 269.
21. Roger L. Rice, "Residential Segregation by Law, 1910-1917," *Journal of Southern History* 34 (May 1968), 189; Goldfield, *Cotton Fields,* 68.
22. *Sanford Herald,* September 3, 1951.
23. *Sanford Herald,* May 30, 1952.
24. Minutes, Sanford City Commissioners, September 25, 1950, Vol. 10, 116; *Sanford Herald,* September 26, 1950.
25. *Sanford Herald,* April 15, 1950, October 13, 1953; Minutes, Sanford City Commissioners, November 4, 1953, Vol. 11, 143.
26. Woodward, *Strange Career of Jim Crow,* 146-47; Tony A. Freyer, "Brown vs. Board of Education," in *Encyclopedia of African-American Civil Rights: From Emancipation to the Present,* eds. Charles D. Lowry and John F. Marszalek (New York, 1992), 71. 73.
27. Woodward, *Strange Career of Jim Crow,* 146.
28. Minutes, Seminole County Board of Public Instruction, October 12, 1950, Book 8, 220-22, Seminole County School Board Building, Sanford.
29. Raymond Arsenault and Gary R. Mormino, "From Dixie to Dreamland: Demographic and Cultural Change in Florida, 1880-1980," in *Shades of the Sunbelt,* 178-79, 185.
30. David Colburn and Richard Scher, "Race Relations and Florida Gubernatorial Politics Since the *Brown* Decision," *Florida Historical Quarterly* 55 (July 1976), 154; Wagy, *Governor LeRoy Collins,* 60; Joseph Aaron Tomberlin, "The Negro and Florida's System of Education: The Aftermath of the *Brown* Case" (Ph.D. diss., Florida State University, 1967), 57, 76.

31. Minutes, Sanford City Commissioners, December 13, 1954, Vol. 11, 328.
32. Ibid.
33. *Sanford Herald,* July 28, 1958.
34. Ibid.
35. Ibid.
36. Ibid.
37. Minutes, Sanford City Commissioners, August 25, 1958, Vol. 12, 408.
38. *Sanford Herald,* April 18-20, 1961.
39. Goldfield, *Black, White, and Southern,* 76, 95-96.
40. Leedell W. Neyland, "The Tallahassee Bus Boycott in Historical Perspective: Changes and Trends," in *The Civil Rights Movement* in *Florida and the United States,* 30-31.
41. Ibid., 31; Glenda Alice Rabby, "Out of the Past: The Civil Rights Movement in Tallahassee, Florida" (Ph.D. diss., Florida State University, 1984), 15-16.
42. Rabby, "Out of the Past," 19; Neyland, "The Tallahassee Bus Boycott," 33, 39; Marshall Hyatt, "Montgomery Bus Boycott," in *Encyclopedia of African-American Civil Rights,* 362.
43. *Sanford Herald,* January 17, 1957.
44. Mark Stern, *Calculating Visions: Kennedy, Johnson, and Civil Rights* (New Brunswick, N.J., 1991), 80, 160.
45. *Sanford Herald,* July 6, 1964.
46. Ibid.
47. Hugh Davis Graham, *The Uncertain Triumph: Federal Education Policy in the Kennedy and Johnson* Years (Chapel Hill, 1984), xviii, 5.
48. Colburn and Scher, "Race Relations and Florida Gubernatorial Politics Since the *Brown* Decision," 160; Wagy, *Governor LeRoy Collins,* 128-30.
49. Tomberlin, "The Negro and Florida's System of Education," 200, 220.
50. Charles Grigg and Charles U. Smith, "School Desegregation in Florida," in *The Civil Rights Movement* in *Florida and the United States,* 206. A number of historians also credit southern business leaders for urging compliance with school desegregation legislation. Their actions did not stem from their belief in black equality, but rather from the fear of losing northern business investment. Though motivated by self interest, businessmen often provided important mediation between the white and black communities. The most violent confrontations occurred in southern cities when business leaders failed to advocate compromise. See David R. Colburn, "The Saint Augustine Business Community: Desegregation, 1963-1964," and Steven F. Lawson, "From Sit-In to Race Riot: Businessmen, Blacks, and the Pursuit of Moderation in Tampa, 1960-1967," in *Southern Businessmen and Desegregation,* eds. David R. Colburn and Elizabeth Jacoway (Baton Rouge, 1982), 211-35, 257-81.
51. Minutes, Seminole County Board of Public Instruction, January 28, 1965, Book 12, 235.
52. *Sanford Herald,* January 25, 1965; Minutes, Seminole County Board of Public Instruction, January 19, 1965, Book 12, 233.
53. Minutes, Seminole County Board of Public Instruction, July 8, 1965, Book 12, 268.
54. *Sanford Herald,* August 12, 1965.

55. Minutes, Seminole County Board of Public Instruction Minutes, March 27, 1969, Book 14, 48.
56. Rabby, "Out of the Past," 4.

Epilogue

FLORIDA'S TROUBLING AND VIOLENT RACIAL PAST

Irvin D. S. Winsboro

"Florida means land of flowers.
It was on a Christmas night
In the state named for the flowers
Men came bearing dynamite . . .
On Christmas night the killers
Hid the bomb for Harry Moore...
As from the grave he cries:
No bomb can kill the dreams I hold
For freedom never dies!"

--Langston Hughes, 1952

With powerful insight and emotion, acclaimed poet and novelist Langston Hughes reminded Americans in "The Ballad of Harry Moore" how dangerous life has been for blacks in a state with a name and reputation based on such tranquility of thought as "flowers." Yet, imbedded in Hughes' ode to civil rights martyr Harry T. Moore is also an attack on injustice in Florida and a reminder of how African-Americans in thought and deeds struggled to ensure that Moore's dream of justice and equality might someday become a reality.

Although basing his symbolism on the tragic murder of Moore in the early 1950s, in reality Hughes' metaphor on racial violence could characterize Florida from the first European contact to the dawn of the new millennium. Often the history books and popular literature portray Florida as an exception to the more radical and violent states of Dixie. Close scrutiny of the Sunshine State's troubling racial past challenges the validity of this assumption. For African-Americans—as the chapters in this book underscore—it was all too often not tranquility but rather whips, nooses, and the letters KKK that circumscribed their lives for roughly five- hundred years in this "land of flowers."

There is, therefore, much more to contemplate in Florida's past. Indeed, this work deconstructs those persistent notions that race relations were tranquil in Florida and more progressive than in other states in the region. From the time of Spanish contact to the post-segregation years, *La Florida* has constructed social and cultural structures at multiple levels to perpetuate racial inequality. Of particular interest to students of Florida history are the ways those with power not only used laws and tradition to oppress blacks, but also exercised violence to keep blacks "in their place." Even though the racial caste system is often submerged or overlooked in the literature, it is, nevertheless, a troubling aspect of the state's past which should not be neglected.

The roots of inequality and violence reach back into the earliest days of the Spanish conquest. Despite Spain's less restrictive policies on race than those in the British colonies of North America, the Spanish created systems of labor and settlement based on racial stereotypes and economic exploitation. Even the qualified freedom the Spanish offered escaped slaves from British Charles Town came at a high price: African-

Americans had to commit to defending and dying for the Spanish Crown's lands. Indeed, they sometimes suffered grievously as a result of British raids on St. Augustine, as was the case when the British destroyed the black community of Fort Mose in 1740. The Spanish occupation is one of the longest eras in Florida's history and its attenuated subjugation of people of African descent cannot be totally mitigated by the suggestion that the Spanish practiced a more humane color line than the British. In fact, it is hard to imagine that Africans in the New World made such distinctions between Spanish and British practices of white supremacy (see chapters 1, 2, and 3).

Like the Spanish, the British did not welcome blacks as equal participants in their colonial experiment (1763-1783/84). Moreover, the British sought to expand the institution of slavery in Florida by transplanting planters along with their valuable "property" to their colonies in East and West Florida. Whereas the Spanish had granted a small space for black agency, the British allowed for few such distinctions in their rigid hierarchy. This had the dual effect of encouraging free blacks to emigrate out and discouraging enslaved blacks in neighboring areas from fleeing into the British enclaves. Another factor in shaping the freedom struggle of the British period arose from attempts by the colonizers, particularly in East Florida, to import large numbers of slaves for the desired plantation economy there. This resulted in a demographic shift in Florida with blacks now accounting for larger numbers in the colony, which precipitated growing inflexibility in the color line. The British continued to impose their brand of racial denigration and oppression on Florida until the beginning of their protracted withdrawal at the conclusion of the American Revolution in 1783. During the turmoil of reversion to Spanish sovereignty, countless numbers of slaves seized upon any opportunity to escape (see, especially, chapters 2 and 3).

Once back in control of *La Florida,* the Spanish government promised to return escaped slaves to their owners but made few efforts to do so. Similarly, in 1802, the Creek, Seminoles, and Miccosukees agreed to comply with the ruling on returning black cohorts, but in reality they often remained hospitable to fleeing blacks. United by a mutual fear of Anglo hegemony and respect for each other's particular skills, both Seminoles and blacks came to fiercely guard their autonomy in the back-country of Florida. To the dismay of many whites, especially Georgia planters, enslaved blacks during the second Spanish period continued to escape (or sought to escape) to the Florida frontier to secure dignity and freedom in conjunction with Native Americans. However, land-hungry white settlers and international affairs cast an ominous cloud over both groups' aspirations by the second decade of the nineteenth century (see chapter 4).

In retrospect, it was the War of 1812 and its conclusion that doomed the colonial era in Florida and its racial status quo. The war not only signaled the demise of Spain's tenuous hold on Florida, it also presaged a new and distinctive era in Florida's racial dynamics. Most troubling for blacks during the war and its aftermath was the new determination by American planters and other whites to wrest Florida away from its Spanish overlords and reshape it into the image of the slave-holding South. As the war ended, numerous escaped slaves populated the colony. The British, in a bid to nettle the United States, continued to assist the former slaves, even going as far as transporting some to British possessions like Bermuda and the Bahamas (see chapter 4).

For freedom-seeking blacks, the final warning signs of Florida being compromised as a place of asylum came in 1816. It was that year that General Andrew Jackson ordered American troops under the command of Colonel Duncan L. Clinch to destroy the so-called Negro Fort, a community of 300 blacks and Seminoles living at Prospect Bluff on the Apalachicola River. In the attack on the fort (a former British installation), the American forces killed over 200 free blacks and dispatched an undisclosed number to slavery. In 1818, slaveholder Andrew Jackson continued his campaign to capture escaped slaves and to neutralize Florida as a haven for them by boldly marching U.S. forces into Spanish Florida. In this affair, the Americans sought to eliminate the black and Native American presence in what would become known as Middle Florida and lay the groundwork for expanding the slaveocracy into Florida. Many historians have labeled this action as the First Seminole War, but the destruction of the fort and Jackson's unsanctioned intrigue in Florida boded even more horrors for the African-American population—that the relatively benign Second Spanish era was about to end and a new American era of chattel slavery was on the horizon (see chapters 3 and 4).

In 1821, the United States took possession of Florida as a new territory and thus ended one of the longest eras of the state's history. This passage marked the beginning of the end for escaped slaves and free blacks controlling their own destiny by forming alliances with the Indians and maintaining autonomous settlements such as the Negro Fort. For African-Americans, the raising of the U.S. flag over Florida in 1821 served as a demarcation point between two epochs. During the territorial days through statehood in 1845, white settlers advanced into Florida, bringing with them their deep-seated beliefs in racial hegemony and slave labor. The cycle of African-American resistance began anew (and that of Native Americans too), but now white visions of cotton culture and chattel labor all but obliterated self-determination for blacks in Florida, except in the southernmost reaches of the peninsula. Blacks continued to search for freedom as "Black Seminoles," but the U.S. determination to remove Native Americans west of the Mississippi River ensured that self-expression for non-whites in the land of flowers would remain a tenuous proposition at best (see chapters 3, 4, and 5).

By the time Florida became the twenty-seventh state in the Union, it had firmly established slavery and supported it with Slave Codes every bit as harsh as those passed by other Southern states. For the most part, Florida's Slave Codes prevented blacks, including the minute numbers of "free Negroes," from exercising even the smallest measure of self-expression. The codes forbade slaves from making seditious statements, bearing firearms, and suggesting or adopting any form of independent, "insurrectionist," or "insolent" behavior. As in all cotton states, whites in Florida always feared slave insurrection and violence if for no other reason than the huge numbers of enslaved. By the 1840s, blacks accounted for 48 per cent of the state's total population, and slaves outnumbered whites in 5 counties and comprised large numbers in ten more of Florida's twenty-six counties. By the eve of the Civil War, the U.S. Census of 1860 enumerated Florida's population as 77,746 whites, 61,746 slaves, and 932 free blacks. Given the black population's propensity to seek freedom at all times through all means possible, it is little wonder that John Brown's attempt to start a widespread slave rebellion at Harper's Ferry, Virginia in 1859 unnerved white Floridians. Even the staunchest supporters of slavery knew in their hearts that the repeated stories of Sambo happily serving "ol' massa" were nothing more than a self-serving myth (see chapter five).

The Civil War proved wrong the myth of loyal slaves, yet the structure of racial oppression and the determination of African-Americans to achieve total freedom did not end with those events. Moreover, the first book in the Gold Seal Series of the Florida Historical Society Press, *Florida's Civil War: Explorations into Conflict, Interpretations, and Memory,* demonstrates that during the conflict large numbers of enslaved African-Americans fled to and often joined the Union forces, despite the risk of enslavement or execution if captured by an enemy who considered them slaves in rebellion. Indeed, an often overlooked aspect of Florida's freedom struggle is the significant role blacks played in the Union victory over Confederate Florida. In the numerous skirmishes, raids, and larger conflicts that extended to every corner of the state, approximately 1,300 black Floridians often fought with bravery and distinction. Even so, their aggregate roles in Union land and sea campaigns and their own "special cause" of destroying slavery in the southernmost Confederate state have often been ignored or underrepresented in the steadily expanding stream of literature on the Sunshine State (see *Florida's Civil War: Explorations into Conflict, Interpretations, and Memory).*

The antebellum era, the Civil War, Reconstruction, and the "Lost Cause of the Confederacy" all bear similar characteristics of the black freedom struggle. Throughout these times, African-Americans resisted oppression both physically and psychologically, and during these years blacks increasingly turned to religious practices to build a sense of community and struggle. As scholar Albert J. Raboteau has noted, this "invisible institution" of black religious practices on the plantation rapidly converted to independent and flourishing black churches during the years of Reconstruction and thereafter.[1] It should be noted, as well,

1 Albert J. Raboteau, *Slave Religion: The "Invisible Institution" in the Antebellum South* (New York: Oxford University Press, 1978).

that after the Civil War the black church became a primary factor in the public life of African-Americans in Florida. By the end of Reconstruction in the 1870s, a small number of African-Americans arose as leaders in the state, including Robert Meacham, a pastor in the A.M.E. Church, and Jonathan C. Gibbs, a minister in the Presbyterian Church. Indeed, black ministers played instrumental roles in the black community in the late-nineteenth century, providing educational opportunities for black youth that included Edward Waters College in Jacksonville (see chapter 7 and *Florida's Civil War: Explorations into Conflict, Interpretations, and Memory*).

During Reconstruction, most white Floridians joined their like-minded brethren in other former Confederate States and staged a counter-revolution, thus recreating the oppressive and elitist practices of the "Old South." These reactionaries turned to all manner of ruses, including violence. In 1867, reactionaries had established the Constitutional League of Florida Southern Society, Florida's version of the Ku Klux Klan. In their attempt to repulse "Negro Supremacy," the League and its successor KKK branches had killed more than twenty "Republicans" by 1868. By the waning years of Reconstruction, the number of deaths had increased to over 150 white and black victims in Jackson County alone. Florida was well on its way to resurrecting the oppressions and values of the antebellum South.[2]

From the end of Reconstruction in the 1870s to the time of *Brown v. Board of Education* in 1954, Florida embarked on an extended era of massive growth in transportation, development, population, and urban centers, but because of the specter of Jim Crow few blacks had cause to celebrate those events. As a result of racial polarization and violence, blacks found themselves generally locked out of the Sunshine State's expanding opportunities. Segregation and white concepts of "proper place" did not allow for either individual or collective African-American success in this "state on the move." Even so, blacks continued their efforts at transformation and community building, and, as underscored in this book, black women played key roles in those generational struggles.

---

2 Seth Weitz, "Defending the Old South: The Myth of the Lost Cause and Political Immorality in Florida, 1865-1968," *The Historian* 71 (Spring 2009), 83.

Post-Reconstruction witnessed a rigid re-segregation once the white autocracy (the so-called Bourbons) consolidated its control over the state. By the 1880s, the Sunshine State had essentially re-codified its Old South concept of racial protocols as evidenced by inferior and under-funded schools, debt peonage (e.g., the sharecropping and crop lien systems), and rigid Jim Crow practices and laws. When blacks could find employment, many men worked as subordinate laborers in shops, saw mills, and factories, and many capable black women could secure jobs only as domestics and nursemaids for white families. To help maintain white supremacy, Florida's ruling class frequently utilized Klan terror. Michael Newton in *The Invisible Empire: The Ku Klux Klan in Florida* identifies the Sunshine State as having a "130-year history as one of the Klan's strongest and most violent realms . . . ."[3] (see chapter 8).

As Florida departed the 19th century, leaders had embraced many new priorities with "for whites only" riders. As authorities in Tallahassee planned for growth in the railroad, cattle, lumber, citrus, and tourist industries, they simultaneously enacted laws to rescind many of the rights blacks had realized during Reconstruction. Not only did the era witness a growth in social discrimination, it also ushered in new Jim Crow laws and practices that effectively segregated and disfranchised African-Americans well into the 20th century and perhaps beyond.

When the Supreme Court decreed its infamous "separate but equal" doctrine in *Plessy v. Ferguson* (1896), Tallahassee had already legislated it. The Florida State Constitution of 1885 provided for strict segregation of the races, and continued to define a subordinate status for African-Americans in the constitutional revisions of 1905, 1913, and 1939. Florida was the first state to adopt the discriminatory poll tax (1898), and the state maintained a race-based penal practice that included a convict lease system and often the execution of twice as many blacks as whites.

When legal sanctions did not work to "keep blacks in their place," Floridians often turned to violence to enforce their code of white

---

3 Michael Newton, *The Invisible Empire: The Ku Klux Klan in Florida* (Gainesville: University Press of Florida, 2001), xv; see Jerrell H. Shofner, "Customs, Law, and History: The Enduring Influence of Florida's 'Black Codes'," *Florida Historical Quarterly* 55 (Winter 1977): 277-98.

supremacy. From the 1880s to the 1930s, Florida frequently led the nation in the annual per capita deaths by lynching. Even into the World War II years, with its extensive black military presence, lynchings continued to plague Florida. As noted in a recent study, "'Hitler is Here': Lynching in Florida During the Era of World War II," wartime Florida exercised its penchant for extra-legal executions four more times.[4] Not content to rely on the hangman's noose, whites carried out pogroms against black communities in Ocoee in 1920 and Rosewood in 1923, a decade during which the Klan claimed almost 400,000 members in the state. The violence and terrorism continued after World War II as racists operating outside the law carried out "legal" lynchings such as those in Groveland by Lake County Sheriff Willis C. McCall. White supremacists also planted the bomb that killed Harry T. and Harriette V. Moore and perpetrated larger-scale bombings in Orlando and Miami. As Florida witnessed this sort of mayhem, and the U.S. Supreme Court deliberated *Brown*, Florida chronicler Stetson Kennedy noted of the Klan, "it was [its] civic duty to lynch."[5]

Throughout it all, as historian Paul Ortiz has noted in his acclaimed book, *Emancipation Betrayed*, "African American resistance . . . was continuous over time, but its effectiveness varied with changes in regional

---

4 Robert L. Zangrando, *The NAACP Crusade Against Lynching, 1909-1950* (Philadelphia: Temple University Press, 1980), 3-21; W. Fitzhugh Brundage, "Introduction," in *Under Sentence of Death: Lynching in the South*, ed. W. Fitzhugh Brundage (Chapel Hill: University of North Carolina Press, 1997), 4; Stewart E. Tolnay and E.M. Beck, *A Festival of Violence: An Analysis of Southern Lynching, 1883-1930* (Urbana: University of Illinois Press, 1995), 37-38; Phillip Dray, *At the Hands of Persons Unknown; The Lynching of Black Americans* (New York: Random House, 2002), 344; Tameka Bradley Hobbs, "'Hitler is Here': Lynching in Florida During the Era of World War II" (PhD. diss., Florida State University, 2004).

5 Molefi K. Asante and Mark T. Mattson, *The Historical and Cultural Atlas of African Americans* (New York: MacMillan, 1992), 95, 101; Arthur F. Raper, *The Tragedy of Lynching* (Chapel Hill: University of North Carolina Press, 1933), 28; Margaret Vandiver, *Lethal Punishment: Lynchings and Legal Executions in the South* (New Brunswick, N.J.: Rutgers University Press, 2006), 22-27; see Gary R. Mormino, "GI Joe Meets Jim Crow: Racial Violence and Reform in World War II Florida," *Florida Historical Quarterly* 73 (July 1994): 230-42; Kennedy quoted in Martin A. Dyckman, *Floridian of His Century: The Courage of Governor LeRoy Collins* (Gainesville: University Press of Florida, 2006), 9.

and national economic, political, and legal structures."[6] Based on their own experiences and reality, black women particularly adopted realistic strategies to secure power and dignity for their communities. In efforts to resist oppression "over time," to borrow Ortiz's words, all people of African descent created self-help societies, along with black newspapers, insurance companies, schools and colleges, towns, music and literary ventures, sports teams, and fraternal and civil rights organizations. The "Great Migration" of Southern blacks to the North in the early twentieth century stirred the hope of thousands of African-Americans in Florida, who abandoned their homes for opportunity elsewhere. As this book discloses, such black agency did not begin in the Jim Crow era but rather originated in the generational movements by people of African decent to create their own vehicles for self-expression and resistance since colonial times. This is, indeed, the lesson of *Florida's Freedom Struggle* (see chapters 9, 10, and 11).

If the end of Reconstruction marked the impending nadir of race relations in the Sunshine State, World War II and the post-*Brown* years of civil rights actions heralded yet another mobilization of the state's freedom struggle. It is often surmised that *Brown* launched the modern civil rights movement in Florida, but recent scholarship argues convincingly that the movement more correctly traces its roots to the World War II era. In those years the impetus for reform sprang from the extensive black military experiences in Florida (more than 50,000 African-Americans served in or passed through the 170 instillations in Florida during the conflict), and from black association with the "Double V" crusade (victory over fascism abroad and bigotry at home), and groundbreaking legal actions. NAACP lawyers filed numerous suites to counter injus-

---

6 Paul Ortiz, *Emancipation Betrayed: The Hidden History of Black Organizing and White Violence in Florida from Reconstruction to the Bloody Election of 1920* (Berkeley: University of California Press, 2005), xix; see Gary R. Mormino, "A History of Florida's White Primary," in *Sunbelt Revolution: The Historical Progression of the Civil Rights Struggle in the Gulf South, 1866-2000*, ed. Samuel C. Hyde, Jr. (Gainesville: University Press of Florida, 2003), 133-50; and Robert Cassanello, "Avoiding 'Jim Crow': Negotiating Separate and Equal on Florida's Railroads and Streetcars and the Progressive Era Origins of the Modern Civil Rights Movement," *Journal of Urban History* 34 (March 2008): 435-57.

tice, including those filed in tandem with the black Florida State Teachers Association against such targets as Dade, Duval, Escambia, Marion, Lake, Hillsborough, Pinellas, and Palm Beach Counties (see chapter 10). In 1944, Florida NAACP leader Harry T. Moore and other black activists created the Florida Progressive Voters League in an effort to energize the freedom struggle. By the war's end, the NAACP numbered over 7,000 members in Florida and not long after registered nearly 100,000 new voters. Progress toward racial breakthroughs was also buttressed by Executive Order 8802, which FDR issued in 1941 after labor leader and Floridian A. Philip Randolph threatened to organize a march of some 50,000 strong on the nation's capital demanding fair hiring in defense industries. Three years later the U.S. Supreme Court's stunning ruling in *Smith v. Allwright* (1944) enabled Southern blacks to register in the Democratic Party, thus enabling them to participate in the all-important heretofore "lily white" Democratic primaries. The *Allwright* decision laid the foundation for subsequent high court rulings that eroded the color line. Like much of black America, black Floridians were poised for a new freedom era during the decade of the 1940s not the 1950s (see chapters 10 and 11).

It is often postulated that Florida accepted the *Brown* decision more readily than the other one-time Confederate states. In reality, the racist contagion that had characterized the state from colonial times did not disappear in the wake of *Brown*. Rather, it resurfaced in the policies of state government, back-room scheming, and in the platform of the "all-American" Klan and White Citizens Councils (often termed the "genteel Klan"). Tallahassee pursued yet other avenues of oppression such as both open and closed investigative bodies and reinforced other of Florida's historical policies of reaction. Despite this continued oppression, the national media promoted an image of a business-friendly and racially progressive Sunshine State. Two years after *Brown*, the *New York Times* reported that Florida's "human and climate temperatures remain mild" in comparison to the rest of Dixie.[7]

At the same time, voter registration as a percentage of the total black

---

7 "Report on the South: The Integration Issue: Florida," *New York Times*, March 13, 1956.

population declined slightly from the early 1950s, as Florida's color line once again signaled struggle for African-Americans. For African-Americans struggling to realize the promises of *Brown*, Florida's stubborn adherence to its color line might have seemed something other than "mild" and progressive. The racial demarcation did not change because the state's power brokers did not want it to change. As the 1960s dawned, only one school district in Florida had moved to desegregate, Dade County (in advance of a Court order), which technically desegregated Orchard Villa Elementary by enrolling four black students. The media framed the event as proof positive of a racially moderate and socially progressive Sunshine State, but within months "white flight" had turned Orchard Villa into virtually a one-race schoolhouse.[8]

While black Floridians struggled to move their state to the vanguard of the civil rights movement, reactionary forces fought to keep the Sunshine State mired in its Jim Crow past. It is true that some of the state's New South leaders avoided the incendiary rhetoric of neighboring states, but in truth Florida delayed substantive change in its racial codes and conduct in much the same fashion as other states in the Deep South. In brief, Florida was less in the vanguard of change than on the ramparts of resistance to it (see chapter 12).

White determination to perpetuate a bifurcated society following *Brown* only steeled the black community's will to resist. Following the decision, blacks quickly broadened their extant freedom struggle and carried out direct-action marches and militant protests, some of which were the earliest actions in the South and many of which met with the white virulence observed in other southern states. While *Brown* transformed the collective consciousness of blacks throughout the nation, in Florida, like much of the South, it also stimulated the latest generation of African-Americans to undertake resistance with a new fervor.

The evidence of black agency and the violent backlash of white reac-

---

8 Southern Education Reporting Service, *A Statistical Summary*, 11; Tomberlin, "The Negro and Florida's System of Education," 196-98; *Tampa Tribune*, September 9, 1959; *Tallahassee Democrat*, September 10, 1959; Registration data compiled from Division of Elections, Bureau of Election Records, R.A. Gray Building, Room 316, Tallahassee, Fla.

tionaries in the Sunshine State are clear and compelling. From the assassination of civil rights activist Harry T. "Doc" Moore (arguably the South's first celebrated martyr of the many blacks who died in the pre-*Brown* decades in the cause of civil rights) to the crosses burned on the lawns of Tallahassee bus boycotters, to the ax-handle assault on blacks in Jacksonville, to the alleged police brutalities and killing of black protesters, white violence in Florida frequently mirrored the actions of the most rabid states of the South. These actions could be found throughout the cities, towns, and counties of the state. As readers of this work will note, actions and counter-actions lasted right through the 1960s. The situational violence included charges of white police killing black youth and the murder of Johnnie Mae Chappell as well as those occurring at beaches and pools in St. Augustine when protesters attempted to desegregate them, even resulting in segregationists calling for "bullet[s] between the eyes" of protest leaders.[9] When 500 whites attacked marchers led by Dr. Martin Luther King, Jr., he compared the assault to the bloody events of Birmingham, Alabama led by Eugene "Bull" Connor.[10]

Nevertheless, the Sunshine State's actions seldom received the media coverage that other states attracted. History books rarely properly address this subject. Indeed, during the movement itself most of the black freedom struggle continued, as in past eras, to be published in the black press and seldom reached white audiences. With Florida's long history of segregation and racial mayhem, it is of little surprise that blacks across the state protested Jim Crow in personal and flexible ways for generations. No matter which repressive tactics surfaced, the determination by everyday blacks to counter oppression paralleled that of their colleagues elsewhere in Dixie.

The fragmentation of the national civil rights movement in the late 1960s did not witness an end to the freedom struggle in the Sunshine State. Just as the struggle had predated for centuries the modern civil rights movement in Florida, resistance to white injustice continued in various ways into the new millennium. However, whereas many of the

---

9 Quoted in Patsy Sims, *The Klan* (New York: Stein and Day, 1978), 154.

10 See David R. Colburn, *Racial Change and Community Crisis: St. Augustine, Florida 1877-1980* (Gainesville: University of Florida Press, 1991).

protests in the post-*Brown* years targeted school and public segregation and the impingements on voting rights, the attenuated struggle zeroed in on the more "everyday" occurrences, such as police brutality, housing discrimination, labor and hiring practices, health care, and competition for jobs. In some cases, black anger over white racial policies and practices erupted into violent riots, such as those occurring in St. Petersburg, Overtown, and Liberty City towards the end of the century.[11] There simply was no quiescent Sunshine State following the decline of the modern civil rights movement.

In a recent article in the *Florida Historical Quarterly*, historian Raymond A. Mohl argues that much of the resistance and rage at the municipal level in Florida derived from black resentment of competition for jobs and housing by new immigrants (especially Hispanics) and the wounding or killing of African-Americans by white police officers. Mohl's thesis deserves further study and analysis. Additionally, in many of Florida's late-20th century boom cities, particularly Miami, the racial paradigm was further complicated by the arrival of many new immigrants of color from homelands such as the Bahamas and Haiti. In Miami, for example, multi-generation blacks and in-migrating people of color discovered that the civil rights movement had not demonstrably opened new life opportunities. Whites and the new Hispanic immigrants—800,000 Cubans alone entered South Florida from 1959 to 1980—dominated the political and economic life of Florida's metropolises. As a result, African-Americans frequently found themselves in losing struggles for representation, jobs, and housing. As Mohl's research about South Florida suggests, "it appears that the Cuban migration into Miami short-circuited the economic and political gains blacks were making elsewhere."[12]

---

11 See Daryl B. Harris, *The Logic of Black Urban Rebellions: Challenging the Dynamics of White Domination in Miami* (Westport, Conn.: Praeger, 1999); Marvin Dunn, *Black Miami in the Twentieth Century* (Gainesville: University Press of Florida, 1997), especially chapters 7 and 8.

12 Raymond A. Mohl, "On the Edge: Blacks and Hispanics in Metropolitan Miami Since 1959," *Florida Historical Quarterly* 69 (July 1990), 40; see Dunn, *Black Miami*, especially chapter 9; and Morton D. Winsberg, *Atlas of Race, Ancestry, and Religion in 21st-Century Florida* (Gainesville: University Press of Florida, 2006).

As the new millennium dawned, the racial tensions in Miami and other areas of Florida merely reflected, albeit in new dimensions, the types of daunting challenges African-Americans had been facing in the "land of flowers" since the time Native Americans witnessed the European "invasion." The struggle has manifested itself in many voices and personal and collective actions, but always it reflected the African-American will to overcome the power paradigms of Florida based on skin color. In this regard, the black community has been proactive rather than reactive and has never accepted the practice of white supremacy. The story of black struggle and white hegemony in the Sunshine State has been inspiring and troubling, but students of history must have a full grasp of this "freedom struggle" to understand and appreciate this complex and diverse land.

CHRONOLOGY

1513	Juan Ponce de León stepped ashore on what is now Florida and called it *La Florida*, or "the Flowery Land."
1528	Panfilo de Narváez led an expedition into Florida with 300 men, including "Estevanico the Black."
1565	Pedro Menéndez de Avilés arrived on the east coast of Florida and established *San Agustín* (St. Augustine), what is now the oldest permanent European settlement in the United States
1565-1763	Generally considered by historians to be the first Spanish colonial period.
1738	Fort Mose established two miles north of St. Augustine, quickly populated by escaped slaves from the British colonies and arguably the first free black town in North America.
1763-1783/84	British controlled East Florida and West Florida until the two-year reconversion of the Floridas to a Spanish colony.
1783/84-1821	Second Spanish colonial period. Spain officially ceded Florida to the United States in 1821.
1821-1845	Florida existed as a territory of the United States.
1835-1842	Second Seminole War during which blacks fought with Seminoles against Indian removal and/or return to slavery. American commander Thomas S. Jesup termed this a "Negro War" rather than an Indian War.

1845 On March 3, Florida became the twenty-seventh state of the United States of America. It existed as a slave state until the conclusion of the Civil War.

1861 On January 10, Florida seceded from the Union, and on February 10 joined the Confederacy, which became the Confederate States of America on April 22.

1863-1865 Twenty-nine regiments of United States Colored Troops served in Florida's Civil War. Over 1,000 blacks in Florida joined the USCT, and another 255 served in the Union Navy, many with distinction.

1865 On October 25, Florida annulled secession and decreed an end to slavery in the state.

1889 Governor Francis P. Fleming, a fierce proponent of Jim Crow, removed African-American Judge James Dean from his position of Monroe County Judge for Dean's performing an interracial marriage. Dean, who had graduated first in his class from Howard University Law School, argued unsuccessfully against his removal before the U.S. Supreme Court 1891 and subsequently died a pauper in Jacksonville in 1914.

1898 Spanish-American War impacted Florida; Tampa served as a major embarkation port for both white and black troops.

1917-1918 Florida hosted World War I segregated training facilities for the U.S. Armed Forces.

1920 On November 2, whites in Ocoee began a mob attack on a black section of town, resulting in an estimated 30 deaths, the public lynching of July Perry, and a general black flight from the area.

1923 On New Year's Day, whites in the Rosewood area undertook a week-long mob action to terrorize the black community. The white mob burned houses, churches, and schools and killed an undetermined number (possibly as high as 30 or 40) of black men and women. Some blacks fought back and those that survived the "Rosewood Massacre" fled their town, never to return.

1941 Floridian and national labor leader A. Philip Randolph created the March On Washington Movement (MOWM) to force President Roosevelt to end racially discriminatory hiring practices in the burgeoning defense industries across the nation.

1941-1945 Florida provided segregated training facilities for tens-of-thousands of men and women preparing for armed service in World War II.

1951 On Christmas night, white terrorists bombed the home of civil rights activists Harry T. and Harriette Moore, resulting in the immediate death of Harry and the subsequent death of Harriette. This event in Mims, Florida sent shockwaves throughout the nation and contributed to the growth of the modern civil rights movement.

1954 *Brown v. Board of Education*, the U.S. Supreme Court decision overturning the "separate but equal" doctrine. The Court based its ruling on the legal principle that racial discrimination in education was inherently unequal.

1956 On May 27, the Tallahassee Bus Boycott began as a protest to the "colored" sections of public buses. The eventual success of the boycott proved to be one of the earliest successful protests of the modern civil rights era.

1963-1964 African-Americans in St. Augustine undertook massive efforts to desegregate schools and public facilities (e.g., public swimming accommodations) and met violent resistance from Klansmen and white supremacists. Dr. King joined the movement in the summer of 1964, and later commented that this Florida city accounted for some of the worst white mob violence he had seen anywhere in the South.

1964 On July 2, President Johnson signed into law the Civil Rights Act of 1964, the most sweeping civil rights measure since the post-Civil War era. Many scholars believe that white mob violence in St. Augustine in that year served as the immediate impetus for Congress to enact the new law.

1965 Enactment of the federal Voting Rights Act of 1965, eliminating poll taxes, literacy tests, and other discriminatory state practices designed to impede African-American suffrage.

1974 Dedication of the Mary McLeod Bethune Memorial in Lincoln Park, the first such monument to a black man or women on public land in the nation's capital. The federal government followed this by issuing a postage stamp in 1985 honoring the famed Florida race leader and national advisor to presidents.

1980-1989 Liberty City Riots erupted in May when courts acquitted 14 white police officers for beating a black motorist to death in Miami. The riot resulted in 18 deaths and over 800 injuries and launched what some scholars termed "Miami's decade of fire," ending with the 1989 riots in Overtown, Liberty City, and Coconut Grove.

INDEX